Malcolm McGregor

The Norwich memorial; the annals of Norwich, New London County, Connecticut, in the great rebellion of 1861-65

Malcolm McGregor

The Norwich memorial; the annals of Norwich, New London County, Connecticut, in the great rebellion of 1861-65

ISBN/EAN: 9783337208202

Printed in Europe, USA, Canada, Australia, Japan

Cover: Foto ©ninafisch / pixelio.de

More available books at **www.hansebooks.com**

The Norwich Memorial

THE

ANNALS OF NORWICH

NEW LONDON COUNTY, CONNECTICUT

IN THE

GREAT REBELLION OF 1861-65

BY

MALCOLM McG. DANA

PASTOR OF THE SECOND CONGREGATIONAL CHURCH, NORWICH, CONN.

NORWICH, CONN.
J. H. JEWETT AND COMPANY
1873

To the

BRAVE MEN OF NORWICH,

WHO, UNDER THE IMPULSE OF A NOBLE PATRIOTISM,

WENT FORTH TO DEFEND THEIR

IMPERILED COUNTRY,

IS THIS

Memorial

OF THEIR SUFFERINGS, ACHIEVEMENTS, AND TRIUMPHANT VALOR,

RESPECTFULLY INSCRIBED BY

THE AUTHOR.

PREFACE.

THE following Memorial history is intended to present the military record of those who went from Norwich to serve in the Union armies or fleets during the war of the rebellion. The writer's design has been to give with this, some account of what was done at home, during the same period, by the citizens, and also by the town in its corporate capacity, for the action of both is entitled to honorable mention in a volume like this. The narrative is surely worth preserving, and is one too, which may interest not only us, but those who shall occupy our places hereafter.

The annals of the town during so exciting a series of years as that covered by the war, the sacrifices made by the people, the heroes furnished for the field of conflict, the martyrs who laid down their lives on the country's altar, — all this is of historic significance, and constitutes a story to which none of us can be indifferent. Such memorial records, not only perpetuate the names of those whose honorable deeds conferred a real glory upon their native towns, but serve to inspire in after generations a reverence for truth and justice, and a desire to emulate the brave actions of those who have preceded them.

So many years have elapsed since the war closed, that the remembrance of many facts and incidents that should have been preserved, has faded away. Had this history been taken in hand earlier, much more could have been gathered up which would without doubt have added to its worth and interest. The narrative has, however, been made as full and varied as under the circumstances was possible. The author from the first was reluctant to undertake the work, but it was urged upon him by the Committee having the matter in charge, with an earnestness and cordial trust, that led him to overlook his own unfitness for the task. Not a resident of Norwich till the closing year of the war, he of course could not write from personal knowledge concerning the events which here transpired. Still the hope is entertained that the history may for this reason be found to be all the more impartial and independent, written, as it is, from the view-point of one who was not himself a party to the events therein related, or affected by the various jealousies which the war gave rise to in different localities. No one can have a higher appreciation of the splendid war record of the town, of the noble achievements and sacrifices of those who have added a new lustre to its name and history than the writer, and his service in preserving these civic annals has been rendered with a willing heart.

While engaged in this work, only words of encouragement have been spoken to the editor by his fellow-citizens, and nothing that they could do to show their interest in the undertaking, or facilitate its accomplishment, has been omitted. His thanks are due to the late publishers of the "Bulletin" for the free use of the bound volumes of their journal, and to Mr. Bolles, the present editor, for many favors. To the Hon. J. T. WAIT, he is indebted not only for suggestions and items of information that have added to the value of the narrative, but also for his encouraging and helpful words. The patriotic fervor which made him so prominent during the years the conflict raged, has been manifested again in urging on the preparation of this memorial volume. To Mr. Campbell, lately of the "Bulletin," the editor is under obligation for personal favors and aid, and also to Mr. J. W. Stedman, of the "Advertiser."

Gratefully would the author make mention of his especial indebtedness to Dr. Louis Mitchell, who from the first announcement of the work has taken a lively interest in it, and cordially rendered every assistance in his power. His own remembrances of war-times, his carefully preserved record of the men who went from Norwich, made him invaluable as a helper, and on all matters concerning which there was doubt, a safe counselor. By Dr. Mitchell the "Three Months' Roster," as well as the "General Muster Roll" of all in the service was prepared, and many an hour of wearying pen-work has he assumed in our behalf, doing with accuracy and readiness what very few would have been willing to undertake, and fewer still able to accomplish.

By L. E. Forrest Spofford, who served with honor in the army, and lost an arm in his country's service, the editor was furnished with duplicate lists of the General Muster Roll, compiled with his characteristic accuracy, and of special value in verifying the names which appear on the "Roll of Honor."

For the exceedingly attractive appearance of this volume, our readers are indebted to Messrs. Jewett & Co., who relieving the Committee of all financial responsibility, secured its publication in the most tasteful typographical manner possible, and then generously offered the book at its actual cost to the Sedgwick Post, G. A. R., of this city. Whatever profits have therefore resulted from the sale of the work, have inured to the benefit of the charity-fund of this Post. In their part of the undertaking the publishers have shown commendable enterprise, and have been actuated by

PREFACE.

a patriotic desire to present the Memorial in the form and dress most calculated to enhance its value in the eyes of every purchaser.

It was our own conviction that a history of this character should be written, perpetuating the story of what was accomplished by our citizens in a great emergency, and a grateful people could but desire some fitting memorial of services such as we here record.

Our contribution to the fair fame of the town we have sought to make in this form. The work, more arduous than at first may be suspected, has been undertaken amidst the unintermitted pressure of professional duties, and for this reason, if for no other, should meet with considerate and kindly judgment. The volume, representing the labor of such hours as in our limited leisure we could devote to it, is now submitted to the public, and while it cannot be supposed to be wholly free from errors and faults, it is hoped that it may prove a worthy addition to our local history. May those into whose hands this Memorial comes, find as much pleasure in reading, as the author did in writing it, and may all hearts be stirred with fresh admiration for the valor and patriotic devotion which made our war-years so signally illustrious. This story of the part Norwich took in the struggle for constitutional government, and the preservation of institutions our fathers gave us, should make every resident and native thereof proud of its past, and devoted in the future to the furtherance of its true honor and prosperity.

M. McG. D.

NORWICH, CONN., *June 1st*, 1873.

CONTENTS.

I. INDEX TO NAMES OF NORWICH CITIZENS . . . . . i.
II. INDEX TO BATTLES AND ENGAGEMENTS . . . . . xvi.

I.

1861. Opening of the War. — Threats of Disunion. — Action of Congress. — Inauguration of Mr. Lincoln. — Impressions produced by the Inaugural Address. — Hopefulness of the North. — Effect of the News of the Bombardment and Surrender of Sumter. — "Battle Sunday." — Proclamation by President Lincoln and Governor Buckingham. — Loyal Manifestation of Feeling in Norwich. — Display of the National Colors . . . 1

II.

1861. Call for Three Months' Troops. — First Great War Meeting. — Subscriptions of Citizens to the "Sinews of War Fund." — First Company organized. Departure of First, Second, and Third Companies. — Muster Roll of Soldiers in the Three Months' Service 18

III.

1861. Call for Three Years' Men. — Our Men in the Fourth Regiment. — Fifth, Sixth, and Seventh. — Officers, and Record of the Eighth Regiment. — Representatives in the Ninth, Eleventh, Twelfth. — Appointments for the Thirteenth Regiment. — Its Record 39

IV.

1862. Third Call for Troops by the President. — The Governor's Proclamation. — War Meeting in Breed Hall. — Recruiting Committee raised. — County Mass Meeting. — Our Men in the Fourteenth Regiment. — Orders for the Eighteenth Regiment to rendezvous at Norwich. — Officers and Men from the Town. — Its Departure. — Subsequent History. — Representatives in the Twenty-First Regiment. — Its Military Record . . 57

V.

1862, *continued*. Call for Nine Months' Men. — Change of Fourth Regiment Infantry to First Regiment Artillery. — Officers from Norwich. — Our Men in the First Connecticut Cavalry. — Great War Meeting. — Offers in Aid of Enlistments. — The Twenty-sixth Regiment ordered to rendezvous at Norwich. — Its Officers and Subsequent Record. — The Emancipation Proclamation. — Tribute to it by the Mayor 75

CONTENTS.

VI.

1863. The Campaign in the West. — Conscription Act of Congress. — Draft ordered. — The Riot in New York. — Loyal League in Norwich. — Another Call for Troops. — All Day War Meeting. — Town Quota raised. — Comments of the Rebel Press on the Situation 93

VII.

1864. Thirtieth Regiment called for. — Town Meeting. — Quota of Town raised. — No Draft necessary. — General Grant commissioned Lieutenant-general. — New Call for Troops. — Town Quota filled. — Retirement of Provost-marshal Bromley. — Constitutional Amendment providing for Soldiers' voting passed by General Assembly and ratified by the People 107

VIII.

1861-65. Whole Number of Men furnished by Connecticut. — Tabular Statement of the several Calls for Troops by the National Executive, and Quotas of Town and State. — Statistics as to the Casualties among our Troops during the War. — Number of Officers from Norwich. — Industries created by the War. — Reception of Veteran Regiments. — Results of the Year. — The Record of the State according to the Adjutant-general's Report   122

IX.

1861-65. Navy. — Effective Service rendered during the War. — Number and Names of the different Squadrons. — Norwich as represented in the Navy. — Officers and Men in this Arm of the Service . . 130

X.

1861-65. Relief of Soldiers and their Families. — Citizens' Service. — Subscribers to "Sinews of War Fund." — General Contributions to Patriotic Agencies. — Special Service of various Norwich Citizens. — General Record of the Town 152

XI.

1861-65. "Soldiers' Aid Society." — Efforts of the Ladies of Norwich in Behalf of the Soldiers. — Number of Packages sent to Hospitals and Camps. — Amount of Money raised and expended. — Responses by Letter to the "Aid." — Auxiliary Societies in other Towns. — Personal Activity and Patriotic Service of the Women of Eastern Connecticut during the War 177

XII.

Losses of Norwich during the War. — Character of those who died in Service. — "The unreturning Brave." — Obituary Notices. — Officers. — Enlisted Men 202

XIII.

In Rebel Prisons. — Experiences of our Men in Libby. — Number confined in Andersonville. — Their Sufferings and Death. — Representatives in other Prisons. — Narratives of Escape. — Changes at Andersonville. — Present Appearance of the Cemetery 297

XIV.

Emancipation Measures in the Confederate Congress. — The "Black Cornerstone." — Signs of Despair. — Mr. Lincoln on the Peace Projects. — Orders to General Grant. — Final Advance of the Union Armies. — End of the Rebellion. — Capture of Richmond. — Effect of the News. — Public Celebrations. — Surrender of Lee. — Death of President Lincoln. — Norwich Pulpit on the Event. — Proclamation of the Mayor. — Funeral Solemnities in the City and Country 311

XV.

Miscellaneous. — Town Action. — Appropriations for Bounties. — Town Committee for securing Enlistments. — Tabular Statement of National, State, and Town Indebtedness. — Charities of the War. — Tables showing the Military Population of United States and its increase ; Number of Men called for by the Government ; Number of Enlistments and Discharges ; Strength of the Army at different Dates ; Deaths 314

XVI.

"Our Roll of Honor." — Complete Roster of Commissioned Officers, Army and Navy. — Alphabetical Roll of Norwich Soldiers, with Rank and Date of Enlistment 325

XVII.

Soldiers' Monument. — Citizens' Meeting with Reference to Raising Funds. — Committee Appointed. — Memorial Volume. — Resolutions Concerning it. — Action of Town in Reference to the Monument. — New Committee Raised. — Appropriation for Same. — Design of the Monument. — Where placed. — General Appearance. — Editor's Last Words 331

LIST OF ENGRAVINGS.

Birge, Brevet Major-General H. W.
Buckingham, The Hon. W. A.
Coit, Brevet Brigadier-General James B.
Coit, Brevet Lieutenant-Colonel Charles M.
Dennis, Brevet Brigadier-General J. B.
Ely, Brevet Brigadier-General W. G.
Farnsworth, Lieutenant-Colonel Charles.
Goddard, Lieutenant Alfred.
Harland, Brigadier-General Edward.
Lanman, Admiral Joseph.
Learned, Brevet Major Bela P.
McCall, Captain John.
Peale, Lieutenant-Colonel Henry.
Rockwell, Brevet Brigadier-General Alfred S.
Rockwell, Captain Joseph P.
Selden, Lieutenant-Colonel Joseph.
Soldiers' Monument.
Wait, Lieutenant Marvin.

THE NORWICH MEMORIAL.

I.

THE OPENING OF THE WAR.

"Thank God! the free North is awake at last!
When burning cannon-shot and bursting shell,
As from the red mouth of some volcan's hell,
Rained on devoted Sumter thick and fast,
The sleep of ages from her eyelids past.
One bound — and lo! she stands erect and tall,
While Freedom's hosts come trooping to her call,
Like eager warriors to the trumpet's blast!
Woe to the traitors and their robber horde!
Woe to the spoilers that pollute the land!
When a roused Nation, terrible and grand,
Grasps in a holy cause the avenging sword,
And swears from Treason's bloody clutch to save
The priceless heritage our Fathers gave."

W. H. BURLEIGH.

ON the twelfth of April, 1861, the army of the Confederate States opened the terrible drama of Rebellion by the bombardment of Fort Sumter in the harbor of Charleston, South Carolina. The air had been thick with threats ever since the election of Mr. Lincoln to the chief magistracy of the government in November, 1860. Months before his inauguration several of the Southern States had, as they termed it, seceded from the Union. Congress, on meeting, promptly raised a large " Committee on the State of the Union," and the whole country was eager for some pacificatory measures. The long, exciting winter passed in hopeless attempts to avert the threatened calamity of disunion.

On the fourth of March, 1861, Mr. Lincoln was inaugurated President of the United States, and in his inaugural address calmly, but firmly, indicated what the policy of the Government would be in the new emergency which it was called to meet. In closing his appeal to those striving to destroy the Federal Union, he used these words: " In your hands, my dissatisfied fellow-countrymen, and not in mine, is the momentous issue of civil war. The Government will not assail you. You can have no conflict without being yourselves the aggressors. You have no oath registered in Heaven to destroy the Government, while I shall have the most solemn one to ' preserve, protect, and defend ' it. We are not enemies, but friends. We must not be enemies. Though passion may have strained, it must not break our bonds of affection." The tone of the address and the positions taken in it, commended themselves to the patriotism of the country, and many felt that even yet civil war might be averted. The North, hopeful to the last, saw the Southern States go through the form of secession, looked on as they instituted a common government, and marshalled an army to carry out their insurrectionary designs, — and still believed war, civil war, could not come. It was hard to make the loyal-hearted believe that our great experiment in a national polity, " which binds a family of free Republics in one united government — the most hopeful plan for combining the home-bred blessings of a small State with the stability and power of a great empire, was to be treacherously and shamefully stricken down in the moment of its most successful operation."

But the telegraphic announcements of the twelfth of April dispelled all illusions, and opened all eyes to the sad conflict which the treason of a portion of the States had precipitated upon a once peaceful country. "The traitors are firing on Sumter," read the first dispatch. "Anderson answers gun for gun." The surprise was intense; men stood stupefied with dismay,—then with quick response gave voice at once to their indignation and their loyalty. The weary six months of parleying at length passed, and the tocsin of war now sounded forth. From the bitterness of humiliation and helpless inactivity, the loyal North awoke to meet, at every hazard, the issue thus relentlessly forced upon it.

In no town in New England was deeper excitement produced by the war news, than in Norwich. Its sympathies, as its popular vote declared, were decidedly with the Administration, so early burdened with the unprecedented duties incident to civil strife. The events of the winter had only intensified the loyalty of its citizens, and prepared them to meet with harmony and promptest energy, the call that it was seen would soon have to be made, for troops and financial help. Intense excitement continued through Saturday, the thirteenth, as successive telegrams reported the stars and stripes still waving over the beleaguered fort. The name of the gallant commandant was on every lip, and the hope expressed that the garrison would hold out until reinforcements, known to be on their way, could reach them. The streets of the city were crowded by anxious citizens awaiting further news, or discussing that already received, while from the adjoining towns and villages, men came riding in to learn the latest tidings from the seat of war. Little else was known for some time, than that Anderson was making a brave resistance.

On Sunday, April fourteenth, came the telegram announcing that Sumter had surrendered. The reception of this news created the profoundest feeling, and stirred every patriot's heart to its inmost recesses. It was the memorable "battle Sunday," when on the streets and in the porches of the churches men spoke to one another with bated breath of this first act of rebellion. In most of the pulpits of the city appropriate reference was made to the event that clearly foreshadowed a bitter and bloody struggle.

On Monday, April fifteenth, appeared the President's proclamation, calling for seventy-five thousand troops to defend the suddenly endangered government. The proclamation of Connecticut's "war governor," Hon. Wm. A. Buckingham, soon followed, urging upon patriotic citizens throughout the State, to volunteer their services and meet the appeal of the National Executive for troops. So war was really begun, and with characteristic promptitude all efforts were now combined to meet the stern duties opening before every loyal heart. The national colors were everywhere displayed throughout the town, testifying to the predominant sentiment of loyalty. They swung in the breeze over Main Street, and waved from the tower of the First Church; the Free Academy, engine halls, factories, school-houses, and numerous private dwellings hung out the symbol of the country's unity. The adjacent villages caught the city's enthusiasm, and threw out where they could the national banner. Citizens laid aside all previous political differences, and under the impulse of a common patriotism, stood together for the support and defense of the Government. "Men have ceased to be Republicans or Democrats," spoke out "The Daily Bulletin"; "they are simply Patriots or Tories; only this line divides us." One purpose seemed to animate all hearts,— a determination to maintain at every sacrifice the national Union. "Heart throbbed to heart, lip spoke to lip with a oneness of feeling that seemed like a divine inspiration." In the spirit of "Our Country's Call," by the poet Bryant, the

loyal masses of the North rose up to face the grave duties of the crisis: —

> "Lay down the axe, fling by the spade;
> Leave in its track the toiling plough;
> The rifle and the bayonet blade
> For arms like yours, were fitter now;
> And let the hands that ply the pen,
> Quit the light task, and learn to wield
> The horseman's crooked brand, and rein
> The charger on the battle-field."

Reluctantly accepted, the struggle forced upon the nation was entered upon, and the contest for the great inheritance of Constitutional Freedom began. The long weary years of varying fortune and costliest sacrifice were not foreseen, though at the very commencement of the conflict lives and property were freely and solemnly laid upon the altar of country. With earnest heart and faith, the war for the Union was waged, none doubting who had a part in the strife, that it would be triumphantly waged, and that as the grand result, would come the reëstablishment for all time of the mild sway of the Constitution and the Laws. The country, springing thus from a positively supine and dismantled condition into an attitude of vigor, owed it all to the manly sincerity which the grave perils of the hour brought out of the bosom of the people. Earnestness of conviction, trust in God, newness of life, — these came as the forerunners of ultimate success.

II.

1861.

THREE MONTHS' MEN.

"In Freedom's name our blades we draw,
  She arms us for the fight,
For country, government and law,
  For liberty and right.
The Union must, — shall be preserved,
  Our flag still o'er us fly !
That cause our hearts and hands has nerved,
  And we will do or die."
                    GEORGE P. MORRIS.

THE first call upon Connecticut for troops was by a telegram from Hon. Simon Cameron, the Secretary of the War Department, dated at Washington, D. C., April eighteenth, 1861, requesting one regiment of militia for immediate service. In Norwich the work of enlisting men was earnestly entered upon, and most heartily responded to on the part of the citizens.

The first "War Meeting" was called for Thursday morning, April eighteenth, in Apollo Hall, for the purpose of adopting measures to fill up at once all military companies about forming, and fit them out for immediate service. In this gathering the ability and patriotism of Norwich were fully represented, and the key-note of popular action during the years of the war was here struck. Hon. H. H. Starkweather was appointed chairman, and several brief and earnest speeches were made in furtherance of the object of the meeting. It was a new rôle in which old and well-known citizens were now to appear. The interests and incidents of the exciting hour seemed to nerve all for high and generous action. There were eloquent words spoken on the occasion, but more eloquent were the deeds done, and those present remember now with feelings of patriotic pride the revelations of that earliest assemblage which ruthless rebellion had made necessary. Hon. John Breed, who was on the platform, surrounded by those of younger years and lustier strength, came forward, and said with his characteristic emphasis and gravity, "I had not intended to speak a word here to-day, but the time has come when our colors have been assailed, and these boys (alluding to those who had volunteered) have got to see to it. I'm an old man, but I've never seen the time when I so wanted to be back again with the boys as during the last two or three days." Governor Buckingham having been called on to say a few words, spoke briefly but with the deepest feeling, affecting many to tears who listened to his weighty words of counsel and of cheer. He read some dispatches just received from men offering to volunteer. "Connecticut moves slowly," said he, "but the good old State is true and sure when once started." He spoke of the honest pride he felt in seeing the spirit manifested in this crisis by the sons of Connecticut.

On motion of David Young, Esq., a subscription paper was ordered to be immediately started in the hall, and a committee of seven was, in connection with this paper, appointed to take charge of the same, and raise such funds as might hereafter be required. Messrs. Amos W. Prentice, F. M. Hale, J. F. Slater, James A. Hovey, David Smith, Henry Bill, and John W. Stedman at once prepared and presented the "Subscription Paper," headed with the following significant words: —

"THE SINEWS OF WAR."

"We the undersigned, citizens of Norwich and vicinity, hereby agree to pay the sums affixed to our respective names, for the purpose of purchasing uniforms, or contributing in any other manner to the successful formation and enlistment of companies in this vicinity."

Amidst the most intense enthusiasm, coupled with feelings of terrible earnestness, which could be read in the very countenances of those present, were the names of the rapidly offering subscribers called out. The first name that went down on the paper was Hon. W. A. Buckingham for one thousand dollars, on the announcement of which the audience rose to their feet, and gave such a response as made the building fairly shake. The next to be signed was the name of Wm. P. Greene, Esq., for a like amount, which was also greeted with shouts of enthusiastic rejoicing. The exciting work went on, as one citizen after another came up to the stand, and wrote their names for varying sums, each signature being cheered with heartiest applause. The men wrote their subscriptions "as though they were in earnest about it, and were doing such work as would make their children proud to remember them."

Meanwhile the speaking was kept up. Senator Foster, pointing out with clear and eloquent words some of the duties of the hour, was received with marked enthusiasm, while Judge Hovey, called out by the audience, responded with loyal expressions, urging united and liberal action in the matter before them. Interspersing the signing of the subscription paper, and the speeches of the occasion, came telegrams and notes proffering contributions from those not present. The meeting at length adjourned with three cheers for the Stars and Stripes, reporting for this eventful day's work an aggregate of twenty thousand dollars. "Thank God and the true hearts of our citizens for so brimming a success," were the closing words of the "Norwich Bulletin's" report of this grand war rally.

The first great mass-meeting of all the citizens, was held two days after the rally just described in Apollo Hall. This was to give expression to the "sense of the city in this awful hour of our country's peril, and to adopt measures to strengthen the hands of the government in upholding the laws, and maintaining the Constitution of the country, and the union of the States." The gathering was called for April twentieth, the Saturday evening preceding "Battle Sunday." Breed Hall was packed to its fullest capacity, the galleries being filled with ladies, who continued their sewing on the outfit of Captain Chester's company, while the offices on the floor below the hall were occupied by yet others, engaged in the same urgent work.* His Honor Mayor Carew presided, sustained by the following representative citizens as Vice-presidents : David Smith, James A. Hovey, Ebenezer Learned, F. M. Hale, John Dunham, John T. Wait, Henry B. Norton, Augustus Brewster, Erastus Williams, Lewis Hyde, Charles Osgood. Secretaries: George Pratt, Hiram B. Crosby, Alfred P. Rockwell, John W. Murphy.

Mayor Carew on taking the chair, said "that this was in no sense a party meeting, but a meeting where every man could act who loved his country, and was willing to aid in its support." After music by the band, there followed a number of speeches, each one of which was listened to with the closest attention, for this was the meeting in which our citizens foreshadowed the courses they would adopt in reference to supporting an administration to which many of them had not lent the support of their votes ; and also what measures they would unite upon in prosecuting the war already begun. Never before had Norwich greater occasion to be proud of the patriotism of its citizens ; while to see them rise above all partisan predilections, and stand together for the public weal, was in itself a sublime sight.

Mr. John T. Adams spoke briefly, " expressing the mingled emotions of sadness and exultation with which he was filled, — sadness that traitors were swarming in the land, and joy that Connecticut was so nobly doing her duty. Our blessings and our prayers will follow those who are going from our firesides."

John T. Wait next addressed the meeting. He said, " Though he did not vote for Mr. Lincoln, his duty as an American citizen was now to give him his cordial and unequivocal support in the great struggle he is making to preserve the government. The President had proved himself an able statesman, a true patriot, and an honest man. He deplored the evils of civil war, but saw no excuse for the seceded States. He bade God-speed to the noble volunteers from Norwich, and did not doubt they would defend their flag to the death." Mr. Wait's decided and patriotic position was most cordially cheered, and the audience applauded him with the most unbounded enthusiasm.

James A. Hovey, who spoke next, said, " He had always been a Democrat, but he loved his country more than party ties. Jeff Davis has declared that he made war upon none but Black Republicans, but he would find that they were not the only men he had to meet. The North is now united in the support of the constitutional authorities of the government, and would sustain them at all hazards, and at any cost of blood or treasure." Hon. L. F. S. Foster followed, saying, " that he considered party platforms of little importance when our country was in peril. All must now unite in defense of the government and flag."

S. H. Grosvenor was called out, and responded, " That he

had feared Connecticut was not going to do her duty fully, but to-night he felt that the fires of the Revolution were rekindled. He assured Captain Chester, who with his brother officers had just taken his seat on the platform, that the ardent sympathies of the people went with him, and their warmest welcome would be his if he returned."

George Pratt being loudly called for, came forward, saying, " He felt sad at beholding the women at work, and the large audience of earnest men, for it made him realize the painful necessity that called them together. The seceding States had rushed madly into war, but they had mistaken the men of the North, and would find them a wall of fire."

Hiram B. Crosby then presented the following resolutions, advocating earnestly a united support of the Government : —

Resolved, — That in view of the great and overwhelming dangers that now threaten the very existence of our nation, it is the duty of all good and loyal citizens, to lay aside, without any exception or reservation whatever, all party ties, party issues, and personal prejudices, and rallying beneath the flag of our country, to pledge our lives, our fortunes, and our sacred honor to the support of the Constitutional Government of these United States.

Resolved, — That we tender to the Governor of this State, and through him, to the President of the United States, our cordial sympathy and coöperation, and as an earnest of our sincerity, we give up to their service the flower of our youth, and the best blood of the good old town, which has never faltered in the perils of our country.

These resolutions spoke the sentiment of Norwich citizens, and subsequent history shows that they lived up to the very letter of them during the years of the rebellion. They were passed amidst profound feeling, and elicited the greatest applause. Every loyal man gave his heartfelt indorsement to them, and registered secretly his vow to stand by them, let come what would.

The speaking still went on,— Mr. Learned giving expression to the fears he entertained that Washington might be taken, but if so, then, he added, "it must be retaken if it costs oceans of blood, and millions of money,"— to which sentiment the House gave its amen, in its outbursting cheers.

Edmund Perkins was next called for, and spoke with great earnestness for a few moments. "He feared, too, the Capitol would be taken. If so, he pledged himself to start for Washington at once. He would assign his property to his family and his creditors, and was ready to offer his life, which belongs to his country." Again the hall shook with applause, for every heart now was wrought up with the most intense feeling.

Jeremiah Halsey said, "Massachusetts would avenge the blood of the nineteenth of April, and the loyal States would join with her. We are fighting to preserve our liberty against despotism."

Short and enthusiastic speeches still followed, by Alfred P. Rockwell, Edward T. Clapp, C. G. Child, H. H. Starkweather, and John W. Murphy.

Three cheers were proposed by L. H. Goddard, and given with a will, for S. T. C. Merwin, and E. Kempton Abbott, the Norwich boys in the "Hartford Rifles."

Dr. Bond concluded the speaking of this memorable evening by a few remarks, showing the necessity of placing our trust in the God of Battles, and offered up a fervent prayer.

Thus ended this significant Union mass-meeting. Everybody felt the stronger for this popular expression of feeling. The patriotism of all the citizens of every party found utterance, and it was discovered that all were agreed upon one course, and that the emergency could be met but in one honorable way. The Democratic paper, "The Aurora," under the editorship of Mr. Stedman, lent its sanction to the position and policy that in this assemblage were advocated with consenting mind, and pronounced the meeting "the largest and most spirited ever held in our town, and an overwhelming evidence of the unity of feeling and patriotic determination of our people. The war," it added in its editorial comments, "is one of the necessary results of the attempt to break up the Union, and so long as it lasts, we believe it to be our duty, as it is the duty of every man who acknowledges allegiance to the Union under which we live, to sustain the constitutional authorities of the Government, in the exercise of all the powers that may be necessary to bring it to a speedy termination."

The sterner work of enlisting meanwhile went on. The earliest to enter the ranks of the country's defenders from this city were Samuel T. C. Merwin, Edward K. Abbott, and George R. Case, who, eager to be off in the first Connecticut regiment, enlisted in the "Hartford Rifles," Capt. Joseph R. Hawley's company. John B. Dennis about the same time enlisted in the "Worcester Light Infantry," which was attached to the famous Sixth Regiment of Massachusetts, his name being the first signature on the company's roll. To the command of the first regiment from this State, one of our most distinguished citizens was appointed, Colonel Daniel Tyler. He was the only professional soldier that went forth in the first three regiments, and to him was largely due the discipline and soldierly bearing that from the beginning of the war characterized the Connecticut troops. Frank S. Chester, book-keeper in the Thames Bank, son of Rev. A. T. Chester of Buffalo, was among the earliest to enlist here, receiving not only the cordial approval of the directors of the bank, but their generous pledge to continue his salary while in service. To him and James B. Coit belongs the credit of raising the first military company in Norwich under the President's call for three months' volunteers. Colonel H. H. Osgood of the Governor's staff, hearing that young Chester had determined to enlist, presented him to Captain Harvey's military company, which had proceeded to their armory in Uncas Hall, to take a vote on the proposition to enlist in a body. The vote being in the negative, Colonel Osgood then stated that Mr. Chester was acquainted with the manual of arms, and would make a fit leader for those of the boys who were willing to volunteer. The enrolment book provided by Mr. Coit was at once opened, when entering promptly his own name, the names of all others who were ready to enlist were rapidly signed. Thus was the nucleus of the first company obtained, and by subsequent enlistments the requisite number of men was secured, when under the name of the " Buckingham Rifles," the organization was completed in the choice of the following officers : —

Captain.
FRANK S. CHESTER.

Lieutenants.
THOMAS SCOTT.   WILLIAM A. BERRY.

Sergeants.
FRANCIS MCKEAG, JAMES L. COBB, ANTHONY STAUBLY, AUSTIN G. MONROE.

Corporals.
JOHN B. JENNINGS, CHESTER W. CONVERSE, GORHAM DENNIS, THOMAS C. LAWLER.

Every effort was now made to fit out with the utmost dispatch these first volunteers, — the whole of Sunday, the twenty-first instant, being spent in Breed Hall by some three hundred and fifty ladies, in making up the needed uniforms. The last Sabbath had been passed in nervous waiting for the news from the scene of the first conflict of the war; this one was spent in working upon the outfits of those who had risen up in their young strength and earnest patriotism to defend the menaced government. While the busy fingers of patriotic women prepared the uniforms for the first soldiers Norwich was to send forth to the battle front, earnest congregations gathered in their accustomed churches to supplicate the favor of Heaven upon these who had offered themselves thus promptly and nobly at the call of the imperilled country. "The beating of drums, the marching and drilling of military companies, the display of flags, and fluttering of bunting, the presence of unusual crowds in the streets, the hum of labor where the uniforms were being made, the earnestness and enthusiasm that seemed to animate the multitude, and the eagerness of the people to learn the latest intelligence by telegraph, — all combined to make such a Sabbath as will long be remembered."

On Monday, the twenty-second instant, came the parting scene with the first company. Marching forth from Uncas Hall amid the enthusiastic cheers and tearful benedictions of an immense crowd, the company, preceded by its youthful captain arm-in-arm with the Governor, made its way to the depot, and thence was borne away in the train for the place of rendezvous. The affecting scenes that transpired at the depot, the intense feeling manifested at parting with the brave boys, made all realize the altered times in which they were living, and the new duties and sacrifices that now were to be met. The work of enlisting did not slacken with the departure of this company. Books for enrolment were opened in different places in the city. A new volunteer company was at once started by Edward

Harland, under the name of the "Norwich City Rifles," and was officered as follows:—

Captain.

Edward Harland.

Lieutenants.

Charles Spalding.   William W. Barnes.

Sergeants.

James R. Moore, John E. Ward, Jasper A. H. Shaw, Joab B. Rogers.

Corporals.

Paris R. Nickerson, Charles W. Carpenter, John T. Fanning.

At the same time another company was organized under the title of "Rifle Company A," and chose as officers:—

Captain.

Henry Peale.

Lieutenants.

George W. Rogers.   James J. McCord.

Sergeants.

John Lilley, E. S. Francis, D. G. Chapman, Charles Young.

Corporals.

George W. Swain, James D. Higgins, Arthur F. Ryder, H. W. Lester.

This company was the next to leave the city, departing Wednesday, April twenty-fourth, to be mustered into service in the Second Regiment at New Haven. The same enthusiasm, the same deep, tender feeling, marked its departure as had that of the first company. Norwich had now sent forth in little over a week's time about two hundred men, and still there was no flagging in the loyalty which had thus promptly made such a creditable exhibit. These two companies were attached to the Second Regiment, to the lieutenant-colonelcy of which another Norwich citizen was appointed, — David Young, Esq., — he being the first of our citizens to make a personal tender of his services to the Governor, writing to that effect when the news of Sumter's surrender reached the city. On Lieutenant-colonel Young fell largely the care and conduct of the regiment, Colonel Terry being absent from the command a portion of the time in consequence of sickness. Captain Harland's company left the city for Hartford April twenty-ninth, where it was received into the Third Regiment. Throngs of citizens, young and old, accompanied the boys to the depot, and gave them on departing their heartfelt benedictions. The three regiments which had been called for to meet the emergencies of the hour, in each of which Norwich was represented, left the State respectively on the tenth, the fourteenth, and the twenty-second of May. At first detained in Washington, and united in one command under General Tyler, they were soon ordered to cross into Virginia, and occupied the advanced post of the Union lines, with General Longstreet in their immediate front. Subsequently they were brigaded with the Second Regiment of Maine, under Colonel E. D. Keyes of the Eleventh Regulars. To this brigade fell the honor of opening the memorable battle of Bull Run, and to the close of that disastrous day on which it was fought, they maintained their ranks, covering the retreat with solid columns. Each of the three regiments was specially commended by Colonel E.

D. Keyes for the gallantry and good order evinced, while Lieutenant-colonel Young of the Second Regiment was, in the official report of his superior in command, mentioned for his "coolness, activity, and discretion." The Connecticut regiments returned to Fort Corcoran, their old camping ground prior to their advance into Virginia. Remaining here a short time, they were ordered home, to be mustered out of service. The Norwich companies from the Second Regiment arrived in the city on the tenth of August, and were received with public honors and a collation in Breed Hall. Captain Harland's company from the Third Regiment returned to Norwich on the fourteenth, and was accorded an equally hearty and generous ovation.

The casualties reported among those who enlisted from Norwich in the three companies, were, —

JOSEPH STOKES, private, Captain Chester's company, died July 25, 1861.
AUSTIN G. MONROE, sergeant, Captain Chester's company, prisoner.
JOHN B. JENNINGS, corporal, Captain Chester's company, prisoner.
CHARLES A. MURRAY, private, Captain Peale's company, prisoner.
JAMES F. WILKINSON, private, Captain Chester's company, prisoner.
DAVID C. CASE, private, Captain Harland's company, killed July 21, 1861.
DAVID ROSENBLATT, private, Captain Chester's company, never heard from.

We subjoin the full list of those who served in the three months' service, affording thus an opportunity of judging how generally these men reënlisted, and how largely they became the officers, through commission and promotion, of the subsequent regiments Connecticut sent into the field.

ROLL OF HONOR.

ROSTER OF OFFICERS AND MEN IN THREE MONTHS' SERVICE.

Also, Showing Rank and Date of Enlistment in Subsequent Service.

FIRST REGIMENT.

FIRST ENLISTMENT.

FIELD AND STAFF.

RE-ENLISTMENT.

Name.	Enlisted. 1861.	Rank.	Discharged. 1861.	Date and Rank	Remarks.
Daniel Tyler	Apr. 23	Col. (B. G. V. May 10; unconfirmed.)	July 31.	March 10, 1862. B. G. V.	Resigned March, 1864.
Morton F. Hale	May 28	Qr. Master	"	June 15, 1862. Lt 14	Capt. and Com. Sub. U. S. V.
Jno. L. Spalding	Apr. 22	Sergt. Maj.	"	Capt. 18 Mass. Adj. 29.	M. O. Oct. 24, 1865.
Wm. G. Ely	Apr. 22	Br. Com. (A. D. C.)	"	Sept. 4, 1861. Lt.-col. 6.	Colonel 18. Res. Sept. 18, 1864. (B. G. V. brevet.)

32 THE NORWICH MEMORIAL.

RIFLE COMPANY A.

Name.	Enlisted. 1861.	Rank.	Discharged. 1861.	Date and Rank.	Remarks.
E. K. Abbott	April 22	Enlisted man	July 31	Nov. 29, 1861. Capt. 12	Resigned August 25, 1862.
Geo. R. Case	"	"	"	Jan. 22, 1862. Corp. 13	Capt. I.a. N. G. M. O. Feb. 11, 1864.
S. T. C. Merwin	"	"	"	Aug. 8, 1862. Lt. 18	Prom. Capt. M. O. June 27, 1865.

INFANTRY COMPANY G.

H. M. Scholfield	April 22	Enlisted man	July 31	Nov. 27, 1861. Priv. 11	Died of wounds, Antietam, September 28, 1862.

SECOND REGIMENT.

FIELD AND STAFF.

David Young	May 7	Lieut.-colonel	August 7		

RIFLE COMPANY A.

F. S. Chester	May 7	Captain	August 7	Capt. 2d N. Y. Art.	M. O. Oct. 1864.
Thomas Scott	"	First Lieut.	"	" " "	Killed in action June, 1864.
Wm. A. Berry	"	Second Lieut.	"	July 14, 1862. Sgt. 18	2 Lt. M. O. June 27, 1865.
Francis McKeag	"	Sergeant	"		
Jas. L. Cobb	"	"	"		
Anthony Staubly	May 7	Sergeant	August 7	July 17, 1862. Sgt. 18	M. O. June 27, 1865.
A. G. Monroe	"	" (Prisoner June 19, 1861.)			
J. B. Jennings	"	Corp'l. (Prisoner at Bull Run.)			[1864.
Ch'y W. Converse	"	Corporal	August 7	Feb. 1, 1862. Sgt. 13	1t. La. N. G. M. O. May 28,
Gorham Dennis	"	"	"	Sept. 5, 1861. 2 Lt. 7	Resigned January 3, 1862.

ROLL OF HONOR. 33

Name.	Enlisted. 1861.	Rank.	Discharged. 1861.	Date and Rank.	Remarks.
Thos. C. Lawler	May 7	Corporal	August 7.	Oct. 30, 1861. Lt. 9	Resigned February 25, 1862.
Barber, Ezra N.	"	Enlisted man	"	Oct. 25, 1861. Sgt. 11	M. O. October 25, 1864
Brogan, Jno.	"	"	"		
Brown, Wm. H.	"	"	"		
Carroll, Wm P.	"	"	"	Sept. 5, 1861. Corp. 7	Reen. Vet. Died Nov. 5, 1864.
Case, Jno. P.	"	"	"	Aug. 26, 1862. Corp. 26	M. O. August 17, 1863.
Coit, James B.	"	"	"	May 26, 1862. Lt. 14	Maj. Resigned Sept. 6, 1864. (B. G. V., brevet.)
Daniels, Jno. L.	"	"	"	Nov. 23, 1861. Sgt. 11	Lt. Resigned August 4, 1862.
Dugan, Thos.	"	"	"	Aug. 1, 1862. Priv. 21	Died (Andersonville) June 4, 1864.
Flannigan, Ed.	"	"	"		
Gilchrist, Jno. W.	"	"	"		
Harvey, Jas.	"	"	"	Jan. 28, 1862. Priv. 12	Disch. dis. July 13, 1862.
Hughes, Asa L.	"	"	"	May 26, 1862. Priv. 26	Disch. dis. December 15, 1862.
Ladd, Amos K.	"	"	"	Jan. 28, 1862. Corp. 13	Adj 73d U. S. C. M. O. June, 1866.
Lathrop, Erast. D.	"	"	"	March 30, 1862. Priv. 1 Art.	Disch. dis. December 24, 1862.
McKee, James	"	"	"	Aug. 5, 1862. Corp. 18	M. O. June 27, 1865.
Miller, Henry C.	"	"	"	May 30, 1862. Sgt. 14	Disch. dis. November 17, 1862.
Minard, Enos G.	"	"	"		
Morrison, Jno. H.	"	"	.		
O'Donnell, Geo.	"	"	Disch. dis. June 6, 1861.	Aug. 21, 1862. Lt. 18	Capt. dismissed Sept. 1, 1864.
Rogers, Eben. H.	"	"	Missing Bull Run.	Aug. 9, 1862. Priv. 15	M. O. June 27, 1865.
Rosenblatt, David.	"	"			
Smiley, Jno. S.	"	"	Enlisted man	August 7.	
Snow, Henry L.	"	"	"		

Name.	Enlisted. 1864.	Rank.	Discharged. 1861.	Date and Rank.	Remarks.
Smith, Edward...	May 7	....Enlisted man.....	August 7.		
Stearns, Chas. J...	"	"	"		
Sietson, Vine.....	"	"	"	Aug. 28, 1862. Sgt. 26.......	M. O. August 17, 1863.
Stokes, Joseph....	"	....(Died July 25, 1861.)			
Tiffany, M. V. B...	"	....Enlisted man......	"	Aug. 21, 1862. 2 Lt. 18......	Capt. M. O. June 27, 1865.
Tingley, Jno. H...	"	"	"	Apr. 21, 1862. 2 Lt. 1 Art...	Resigned December 31, 1862
Toomey, Thos.....	"	"	"	March 20, 1862. Priv. 1 Art...	Disch. dis. March 7, 1863.
Kernlick, Frank...	"	"	"		
Wheatley, Chas....	"	"	"		

RIFLE COMPANY B.

Henry Peale......	May 7	.....Captain.........	....August 7.	July 12, 1862. Capt. 18......	Lt.-col. M. O. June 27, 1865.
Geo. W. Rogers....	"	.....1st Lieut........	"	Aug. 30, 1862. Corp. 26......	M. O. August 17, 1863.
Jas. J. McCord....	"	.....2d Lieut........	"	Feb. 18, 1862. Capt. 13......	M. O. January 6, 1865.
Edwin S. Francis...	"	.....Sergeant........	"		
John Lilley.......	"	.....Sergeant........	"	Aug. 14, 1862. Serg. 18......	Prom. Capt. M. O. June 27, 1865.
Chas. Young......	"	.....Sergeant........	"	March 29, 1862. Sgt. 1 Art...	Vet. M. O. September 25, 1865.
Jas. D. Higgins....	"	.....Corporal........	"	Aug. 2, 1862. 2 Lt. 18......	Hon. disch. October 27, 1864
Henry W. Lester...	"	.....Disch. dis......	June 26.		
Arthur F. Ryder...	"	"	July 3.		
Geo. W. Swain....	"	"	August 7.		
Barlow, Jas. C.....	"	.....Enlisted man.....	"	July 23, 1863. Priv. 1 Art....	Deserted July 31, 1865.
Barlow, Otis W....	"	"	"	Aug. 5, 1862. Corp. 18......	M. O. May 30, 1865.
Beebe, Dan. E.....	"	"	"	July 30, 1862. Priv. 18......	Died December 1, 1862.
Beckwith, Chas. H.	"	"	"		

ROLL OF HONOR.

Name.	Enlisted. 1861.	Rank.	Discharged. 1861.	Date and Rank	Remarks.
Brown, Geo.	May 7	Enlisted man	August 7	Jan. 28, 1862. Corp. 13	Dropped fr. Roll Oct. 31, 1864.
Butler, Jno	"	"	"	Oct. 25, 1861. Priv. 11	Hon. disch. Dec. 6, 1864.
Carkins, Amos B.	"	"	"		
Cragg, Geo. G.	"	"	"		
Dennison, Jno. J.	"	"	"		
Fanning, Wm. D.	"	"	"		
Fletcher, Jos. E.	"	"	"	Sept. 21, 1861. Sgt. 8	Disch. dis. January 9, 1863.
Gould, Aug.	"	"	"		
Hempstead, Hen.	"	"	"		
Jaques, B. F.	"	"	"	July 22, 1862. Corp. 18	M. O. June 27, 1865.
Jewett, Jos. H.	"	"	"	Dec. 1, 1863. Priv. 8	Lt. M. O. as Adj. Dec. 12, 1865.
Johnson, Robert	"	"	"	Oct. 30, 1861. Sgt. 9	Vet. M. O. August 3, 1865.
Kerr, Robert	"	"	"	July 18, 1862. Sgt. 18	2 Lt. M. O. June 27, 1865.
Kingston, Elias, Jr.	"	"	"		
Lillibridge, Clark	"	"	"		
Loomis, Chas. A.	"	"	"	Feb. 1, 1862. Sgt. 13	Vet. Deserted Aug. 30, 1864.
Loomis, Jno. W.	"	"	"		
McGarry, And.	"	"	"	Oct. 30, 1861. Corp. 9	Disch. dis. October 16, 1862.
Maples, James S.	"	(Prisoner Bull Run.)	"	Aug. 25, 1862. 2 Lt. 26	Res. to acc. prom. Aug. 11, 1863.
Murray, Chas. A.	"	"	"	July 12, 1862. Priv. 18	2 Lt. M. O. June 27, 1865.
Nash, Eugene S.	"	Enlisted man	August 7	Feb. 1, 1862. Corp. 13	Vet. Deserted Aug. 30, 1864.
Parker, Jos M	"	"	"	July 15, 1862. Sgt. 18	Capt. 32 U. S. C.
Potter, Jas	"	"	"	Aug. 26, 1862. Priv. 26	M. O. August 17, 1865.
Roath, Warrington D.	"	"	"	1861. A. M. U. S. N. Prom. Lt. July 1863.	Resig. March 7, 1865.

Name	Enlisted 1861	Rank	Discharged 1861	Date and Rank	Remarks
Rogers, E. P.	May 7	Enlisted man	August 7	Aug. 11, 1862. Sgt. 18 ...... Lt. 29.	Resigned Aug. 3, 1865.
Sherman, Wm. M.	"	"	"		
Smith, Geo. F.	"	"	"		
Smith, Thos. H.	"	"	"		
Smith, Wm. K.	"	"	"		
Spencer, Robert R.	"	"	"		
Stark, Henry	"	"	"		
Summers, F. B.	"	"	"		
Town, Geo. S.	"	"	"	July 21, 1862. Sgt. 18	M. O. June 27, 1865.
Walden, Wm. H.	"	"	"		
Warden, Alex	"	"	"		
Warren, Walt P.	"	"	"		
Whitmore, Hor. W.	"	"	"	Aug. 29, 1862. Sgt. 26	M. O. August 17, 1863.
Williams, Geo. E.	"	"	"		

THIRD REGIMENT.

INFANTRY COMPANY B.

Name	Enlisted 1861	Rank	Discharged 1861	Date and Rank	Remarks
Strauss, Jacob	May 11	Enlisted man	Aug. 12		
Schaefder, Jno.	"	"	"		

RIFLE COMPANY B.

Name	Enlisted 1861	Rank	Discharged 1861	Date and Rank	Remarks
Edward Harland	May 11	Captain		Aug. 30, 1861. Lt.-col. 6 ..... Col. 8. B. G. V.	Res. June 20, 1865.
Chas. W. Spalding	"	1 Lieut. (Res. May 20.)			
Wm. W. Barnes	"	2 Lieut.	Aug. 12		

ROLL OF HONOR.

Name.	Enlisted. 1861.	Rank.	Discharged. 1861.	Late and Rank.	Remarks.
Jas. R. Moore	May 11	Serg	Aug. 12	Sept. 21, 1861. Lt. S	Capt. Discharged May 30, 1865.
Jno. E. Ward	"	(Pro. 1 Lt.)	"	Sept. 21, 1861. Capt. S	Col. M. O. March 13, 1865.
Jasper A. H. Shaw	"	"	"		
Joab B. Rogers	"	"	"	Oct. 26, 1861. Sgt. Cav	Capt. Disch. Feb. 2, 1865.
P. R. Nickerson	"	Corporal	"		
Chas. H. Carpenter	"	"	"		
Jno. T. Fanning	"	"	"	Aug. 6, 1862. Sgt. 18	Lt. 29. M. O. Oct. 24, 1865.
Allen, Jas. A.	"	Enlisted man	"		
Armstrong, H. S.	"	"	"	July 30, 1862. Sgt. 18	M. O. June 27, 1865.
Arnold, Ludwig	"	"	"		
Brahman, Hen. T.	"	"	"		
Breed, Jno.	"	"	"	Sept. 5, 1861. Priv. 7	Vet. Discharged July 20, 1865.
Breed, Chas A.	"	"	"		
Brown, Leander	"	"	"	Sept. 24, 1861. 2 Lt. S	Died July 30, 1862.
Burke, Charles F.	"	"	"		
Burke, Hor. E.	"	"	"		
Calhoun, Martin	"	"	"	March 14, 1862. Priv. 1. Art. Vet.	M. O. Sept. 25, 1865.
Carruthers, Wm.	"	"	"	July 14, 1862. Qr.-mr. Sgt. 18	Lt. M. O. June 27, 1865.
Case, David C.	"	(Killed Bull Run, July 21.)			
Faulkner, F. W.	"	Enlisted man	"		
Foster, Joel M.	"	"	"	Aug. 12, 1862. Corp. 15	M. O. June 27, 1865.
Francis, Chas.	"	"	"		
Frazier, Geo. W.	"	"	"	Sept. 5, 1861. Sgt. 7	Hon. disch. Sept. 12, 1864.
Gates, Hor. P.	"	"	"	Sept. 25, 1861. Priv. S	Adj. (A. A. G. U. S. V.) Res. Dec. 19, 1865.
Gavitt, Edwin.	"	"	"		

Name.	Enlisted. 1861.	Rank.	Discharged. 1861	Date and Rank.	Remarks.
Griffin, Thos.	May 11	Enlisted man	Aug. 12		
Gayle, Jno. W.	"	"	"		
Huntington, C. L. F.	"	"	"		
Jillson, G. W.	"	"	"		
Keables, N. A.	"	"	"	Aug. 30, 1862. Priv. 26	M. O. August 17, 1863.
Keeler, Jno. M.	"	"	"		
Leonard, Isaac N.	"	"	"	Aug. 25, 1862. Sgt. 26	2 Lt. M. O. August 17, 1863 U. S. N.
Maples, Wm. L.	"	"	"		
Marshall, Geo. B.	"	"	"	July 29, 1862. Corp. 18	M. O. June 27, 1865.
Metcalf, Jno. G.	"	"	"		
Nickels, Jas. R.	"	"	"	May 29, 1862. Sgt. 14	Capt. Died of w'ds Feb. 20, 1865.
Rogers, Horace	"	"	"	Sept. 5, 1861. Priv. 7	Disch. dis. March 10, 1863.
Ross, Wm. J.	"	"	"	July 23, 1862. Corp. 18	Maj. 29. M. O. Oct. 24, 1865.
Schaik, Fred. E.	"	"	"	June 6, 1862. Sgt. 14	Lt. Died of w'ds May 6, 1864.
Sterry, Tully W.	"	"	"		
Swan, H. W.	"	"	"	Jan. 7, 1862. Priv. 13	Disch. dis. June 5, 1863.
Sweet, Jas. H.	"	"	"	Sept. 8, 1862. Priv. 26	Transferred Signal Corps.
Torrance, Jas.	"	"	"	Jan. 8, 1862. Sgt. 13	Killed Pt. Hud'n, May 24, 1863.
Trimier, Richard.	"	"	"	July 14, 1862. Priv. 18	M. O. June 27, 1865.
Vergason, Jas. H.	"	"	"	Oct. 25, 1861. Priv. 11	Deserted December 17, 1862.
Whittlesey, G. W.	"	"	"	Feb. 18, 1862. Sgt. Maj. 13	Adj. Resigned Oct. 9, 1863.
Williams, G. E.	"	"	"		

III.

1861.

THREE YEARS' MEN.

' Northmen, come out!
Forth unto battle with storm and shout!
Freedom calls you once again,
To flag, and fort, and tented plain;
Then come with drum, and trump, and song,
And raise the war-cry wild and strong.
Northmen, come out!
. . . . . .
" Northmen, come out!
Forth unto battle with storm and shout!
He who lives with victory 's blest,
He who dies gains peaceful rest.
Living or dying, let us oe
Still vowed to God and liberty!
Northmen, come out!" — C. G. LELAND.

ON the third of May, 1861, President Lincoln issued his second call for troops, to serve for a period of three years unless sooner discharged. Recruiting had been vigorously kept up from the first outbreak of hostilities, and the enlistments were still freely tendered. The presence of the Governor, who seemed with wise foresight to anticipate the needs of the General Government, contributed to keep up the public interest in securing volunteers. With tireless devotion he sought to second every appeal of the National Executive, and through him Connecticut, and Norwich too, were kept fully abreast of the calls from time to time made upon them for men. The reverse at Bull Run seemed to rouse anew the patriotic spirit of our citizens, while the zeal of private individuals and the liberal action of the town gave a fresh impetus to recruiting. The Fourth and Fifth Regiments had already been accepted by the War Department for three years, as the condition of receiving from the State the second and third three months' regiments, which were really in excess of Connecticut's quota under the first call for troops. In the Fourth, Norwich was represented by Major Henry W. Birge, Assistant Surgeon Edwin Bentley, with some eighteen or twenty men scattered through the different companies. It was mustered into service at Hartford in June, 1861, and sent to Chambersburg and associated with General Patterson's troops. In November it was stationed at Fort Richardson, near Washington. In January, 1862, the regiment was changed from infantry into artillery; and under the management of Robert O. Tyler, who was appointed Colonel, reorganized as the First Artillery. Major Birge was, meanwhile, transferred to the command of the Thirteenth Regiment Infantry.

For the Fifth Regiment a fine Irish company had been recruited from this city, called the Jackson Guards, under Captain Thomas Maguire. Some disagreement concerning the regiment's arms, and the appointment of subalterns, led to the revoking of Colonel Colt's commission, and the regiment was disbanded. The greater portion of the Norwich Company reorganized, and was accepted into the First Regiment Heavy Artillery of New York. Captain Maguire subsequently became Major in the New York service. William A. Berry, a member of the company, was chosen Captain, and after serving full three years, was killed at the siege of Petersburg. He was succeeded by Captain Thomas Scott, also of the Norwich company.

The Fifth Regiment was then reorganized, and Orris S. Ferry commissioned Colonel. It was mustered into service July, 1861. In this regiment Norwich had no officers, and not over twenty privates. It was first sent to Virginia, where it served creditably in many sharp conflicts with the enemy. At the battle of Cedar Mountain, among those who fell bravely fighting, was Sergeant Alexander S. Avery, of Norwich, August ninth, 1862. At the hard fought battle of Resaca, Ga., May fifteenth, 1864, out of ten men who had reënlisted from Norwich, four were reported wounded, — John G. Blake, Thos. W. Baird, Delano N. Carpenter, Stephen Corcoran.

On the fifteenth of August the Governor issued orders for receiving volunteers for the Sixth, Seventh, Eighth, and Ninth Regiments, a part of Connecticut's quota under the recent call of the President. Recruiting offices were opened by some of those who had served in the three months' campaign, and every effort by citizens and former soldiers was made to have Norwich well represented in the new regiments.

The Sixth Regiment received a company recruited mainly in Windham County, by Captain W. G. Ely of this city, who was appointed Lieutenant-colonel, *vice* Edward Harland, but was soon transferred to the command of the Eighteenth. The Quartermaster, and twelve enlisted Germans, were from Norwich. Alfred P. Rockwell of Norwich was appointed, in June, 1864, to the coloneley vacated by the death of Colonel Chatfield. Mr. Rockwell had previously served as Captain of the First Light Battery, C. V., and had been stationed on James Island, and other parts of the Carolina coast, coöperating in the siege of Charleston.

To the Seventh Regiment Norwich sent one company under Captain John B. Dennis, who had served three months in the Massachusetts Sixth. This was the first regular company of three years' men that had gone forth from the city, proceeding to New Haven as its appointed place of rendezvous. It had become an old story to see men depart for the scene of conflict; the romance of the war had worn off, and it had now become a stern duty, about which men went without useless parade or boasting. The earnest feeling of the public had not changed, but it had sobered, and was less given to those manifestations which had marked the departure of the first troops for the war. Theodore Burdick and Gorham Dennis, lieutenants in this company, were also from Norwich. The former, subsequently promoted to the command of a company, was killed at Fort Wagner, July eleventh, 1863. The regiment was under the command of Colonel Alfred H. Terry of New Haven, and was the first which landed on the soil of South Carolina. It served with distinction in the South, and was afterwards engaged upon the James River, and in the trenches before Petersburg. Captain Dennis and twenty of his company were taken prisoners in June, 1864, while guarding the picket line before that city. He was detained some months a prisoner, and, with others from Norwich, was among the Federal soldiers sent to Charleston to be placed within range of the guns of our batteries, in retaliation for the bombardment of the city by General Gilmore. Transferred, in the course of his captivity, to six different prisons, he, after one ineffectual attempt, finally made his escape with thirteen companions on the twenty-fourth of December.

In the Eighth Regiment Norwich was largely represented, contributing nearly all the line officers, and most of the privates of Company D, with its Captain, John E. Ward. Tuesday, September fourth, this second regular company for three years' service left the city for the rendezvous of the regiment at Hartford, where it was mustered in on the twenty-first of the month.

Norwich had a deeper interest in this regiment than in any that had thus far been raised, as the following partial roster shows: —

Colonel.

EDWARD HARLAND,

Previously Captain Company A, Third Regiment.

Adjutant.

CHARLES M. COIT.

First Assistant-surgeon.

DE WITT C. LATHROP.

COMPANY D.

Captain.

JOHN E. WARD,

Previously First Lieutenant Company D, Third Regiment.

Lieutenants.

JAMES R. MOORE,   CHARLES A. BREED.

Sergeants.

JOHN MCCALL,   CHARLES SHEPARD,   AMOS L. KEABLES,
JOSEPH E. FLETCHER.

The regiment left the State for Jamaica Plain, Long Island, October seventeenth, where it was the first one to be visited by the committee representing the recently formed organization of "the Sons of Connecticut" in New York, by which it was presented with a handsome regimental flag. This regiment was in General Burnside's expedition to North Carolina, and bore with uncomplaining faithfulness the discomforts and perils of the voyage. On the seventh of January the fleet approached Roanoke Island, held by three thousand rebels under General Wise. The troops effected a landing in the night, and the next morning, shivering with cold and drenched with rain, prepared for battle. The Eighth was posted on an old road leading towards the right flank of the main battery, by which the enemy might turn the left of our advancing forces. The position was one of great importance, and was held with steady coolness, eliciting the approval of Generals Burnside and Foster.

On the eleventh of March came orders for an advance on Newbern. In this action the Eighth bore a leading part, moving by the flank, until reaching the open ground in front of the rebel works, where it was admirably formed into line by Colonel Harland, who ordered the men to fix bayonets, and then gave the word to charge. The regiment dashed forward on the double quick, and was the first to enter the enemy's works, and plant within them its own colors. Shortly after, in the siege of Fort Macon, the most arduous service fell upon this regiment, which it most creditably sustained. Two of the Norwich officers, after a few months of effective service, died, — Dr. De Witt C. Lathrop, at Newbern, April, 1862, by illness produced by over exertion in the duties of his position ; and Lieutenant Breed in July, of fever, contracted while engaged in important service on the Signal Corps. Ordered North in July, the regiment joined McClellan, and was in the battle's front at South Mountain and at Antietam, Colonel Harland having now command of a brigade. In the latter conflict, September seventeenth, 1862, the regiment conducted with great steadiness, leading in a charge, which resulted in taking a position of great importance, from which, after stubborn fighting and severe loss, they were forced to retire. Colonel Harland took command of the division during the battle, General Rodman having fallen, and by his admirable handling of its disorganized regiments, reformed it, and put it at once in a posture of defense. The Eighth lost some valuable officers, and by its defiant courage and steadiness saved the fortunes of its army corps. The story of its splendid valor is in these words, which summed up its action in that bloody battle, "We faced the foe until half the regiment were shot down, and retired only when we were ordered." Among the slain was Lieutenant Marvin Wait, of Norwich. He was the first commissioned officer from the town that fell in battle. Enlisting when but nineteen, he left college and home to enter as a private his country's service; he was soon promoted to be Second Lieutenant of Company A, and served as a member of the Signal Corps at the battle of Roanoke Island, on Burnside's flag-ship, and at the reduction of Fort Macon. A writer in one of the Norwich journals, speaking of his conduct at the battle of Antietam, says, "After his sword-arm had been disabled by a shot, he took his weapon in his left hand, and still pressed on, encouraging his men by his heroic fortitude." He was a noble specimen of the young men of culture and lofty patriotism that Norwich sent forth to the war. Brave and manly in his bearing, generous-hearted and beloved, he was one whose name is still fondly cherished, the history of whose self-sacrificing valor reflects a new honor on the town and commonwealth he represented in the Union ranks. Six months after the battle of Antietam, the Connecticut brigade, in which was the Eighth, was ordered to Falmouth, marching one hundred and seventy-five miles in twelve days. Here the regiment encamped, putting "their little dog tents upon the sticky red mud of Virginia, made smoky fires outside of wet wood, half cooked their scanty food, warmed and dried themselves as they could, standing by wretched fires in the rain, then spread their blankets on the soft mud and slept." But such sleep brought only rheumatics and ill-temper, and led the men to vote Virginia mud and weather insufferable.

On December eleventh the preparations were complete for the fatal battle of Fredericksburg under General Burnside. The Eighth volunteered to lay the pontoon bridge, and assisted by others accomplished speedily its task. On the thirteenth Colonel Harland took his position with his brigade below the town, while his own regiment served on the picket line, until the whole force was ordered to recross the Rappahannock. It fortunately sustained but slight loss, Connecticut troops suffering less proportionately, than any other State that had regiments engaged.

In the spring of 1863, the Connecticut brigade embarked for Newport News, and soon after the Eighth in conjunction with it was called to take part in the siege of Suffolk. On the nineteenth of April occurred a brilliant episode, which added to the laurels of this already famous regiment. In company with a detachment of the Eighty-ninth New York, it was ordered to capture Fort Huger. The command devolved on Colonel Ward. The two battallions were ferried in a small boat, with a canvas screen drawn round it to conceal the men, into proximity to the fortifications. As the boat grounded, the men leaped into the water, and making for the shore, paused only to rally about their officers, then charged upon the enemy's works, and without firing a shot captured the battery, planting their bullet-rent colors on the breast-works and marching off the rebel garrison, placed them as prisoners on the gun-boat. The guns just taken, were quickly turned upon the rebel forces, that were seen swarming from the adjacent woods in order to recapture the position. The whole affair was one which showed the dash and cool well poised courage of the regiment, and ranks among the most brilliant of its achievements.

Colonel Harland was promoted Brigadier-general in April, 1863, well deserving the position, and becoming next to General Tyler, the ranking officer from Norwich. On the seventh of May, 1864, the regiment participated in the battle of Walthall Junction, Va., and sustained an aggregate loss of seventy-four officers and men. Colonel Ward, on whom the command of the regiment had devolved, was severely bruised with a shell ; Captain James R. Moore, now in command of Company D, disabled by a serious wound ; and Lieutenant Alfred M. Goddard, of Company B, mortally wounded. Young Goddard had returned from the Sandwich Islands, where he was engaged in business, on purpose to enlist in the defense of his country. His ardent patriotism gave him no rest until he could return to his native land, and share in the honors and perils of her defense against intestine foes. He received a commission as First Lieutenant in Company B, July, 1863, and was assigned to duty on General Harland's staff. Subsequently at his own request, he rejoined his company, and served in the ranks with distinction up to the time of his death. Of his courage on the day of the fatal battle, his Captain wrote, " He was so thoughtful and considerate, not rash or impetuous, but cool and collected, ready for any emergency, willing for every duty." In his grand young strength he fell fighting for his country, and by his death added another name to the list of those of whom Norwich had just reason to be proud. The regiment was complimented by Brigadier-general Burnham, for heroism in this action, and as it returned from the field was cheered by the whole brigade.

From the twelfth to the sixteenth of May the regiment was engaged in battle at Fort Darling, where the Union forces were repulsed ; and the gallant Captain McCall, who had won his promotion from a lieutenancy, for bravery at the capture of Fort Huger, was instantly killed by a shot from the enemy. "This young officer possessed all the prominent characteristics of a good soldier. He was cool, steady, prompt, and skillful." Enlisting as a private, his personal courage and military qualities gained him his position among the commissioned officers. The mortal remains of these two young men were brought to Norwich for interment. The city and military authorities, as well as the citizens generally, vied with personal friends in honors to the patriot dead. They fell in the full vigor of their young manhood, leaving behind them the record of a noble patriotism and brave service in the field.

In the advance upon Petersburg, in June, 1864, the regiment was again conspicuous. In the absence of Colonel Ward and Lieutenant-colonel Smith, the command devolved on Captain Charles M. Coit, of this city, a brave and efficient officer, subsequently made Lieutenant-colonel by brevet. In a charge made on the enemy's works, the regiment won the highest praise for its gallantry from General Smith, who, witnessing its action, said he "felt like giving a commission to the whole regiment that had done that gallant deed." In the assault upon Fort Harrison, in September, 1864, the Eighth, and three companies of the Twenty-first, headed the storming column, and charging across an open field, stopped only to reform, when with a shout they rushed into the ditch over the parapet, capturing the fort, and replacing the Confederate flag with the standard of Connecticut. The regiment lost eight killed and sixty-five wounded; among the latter were Lieutenants Foss and Keables of Norwich. In a further advance made under General Butler, in October, some severe fighting took place, in which Captain Charles M. Coit, serving on the staff of the brigade commander, was severely wounded. The regiment maintained its well-earned reputation for daring and fidelity to the end of the war, and was mustered out in December, 1865, with a proud record for efficient service in the field.

To the Ninth Regiment, composed mostly of Irishmen, Norwich furnished a large part of Company H, called the Sarsfield Guards, recruited in this city. Silas W. Sawyer was chosen Captain, Thomas C. Lawler, First Lieutenant. The regiment was mustered into service at Lowell, Mass., and was thence ordered to New Orleans, performing three years of arduous duty in the regions bordering upon the Mississippi; afterwards it participated with the army under General Sheridan, in the campaign up the Shenandoah Valley.

Norwich had thus contributed to the four regiments called for by the Governor in August of this year. Other companies were still recruiting in the city, but as yet none of them were full. A patriotic meeting of the citizens, pursuant to a call therefor, was held in Apollo Hall on September sixteenth, to consider what measures could be adopted to facilitate the speedy filling up of these companies, or their consolidation and prompt forwarding to the appointed rendezvous. Mr John F. Slater was appointed chairman. Mr. Ebenezer Learned addressed the meeting " upon the importance of immediate action, and moved that the ' Patriotic Fund Committee ' be instructed to appropriate the funds already in their hands in such a manner as they shall deem best calculated to promote the interest of the cause; and when these are exhausted, to call in additional installments, to meet the demands of the occasion." The motion, after brief speeches from Rev. J. P. Gulliver, Messrs. H. H. Starkweather, Henry Bill, and John Breed, was unanimously carried. Under the impulse supplied by this meeting, the work of recruiting was pushed on more vigorously, and the companies, for which a limited number of enlistments had been secured, began to fill up.

The Legislature was convened in October, and the terse and earnest message of the Governor set before the members the necessities of the national situation: —

"Instead of inquiring how much we have done," he said, "shall we not inquire what more can we do? It is a privilege to live in a day like this, to take a bold and energetic part in the conflict which is now raging between law and anarchy; and during this revolution, which, in the onward progress of events is to accomplish the wise designs of an overruling Providence, to exert an influence which shall aid in advancing this nation to such a position of strength and moral power, that every citizen may safely, and fully, and speedily enjoy the blessings of freedom. This is a high honor within our reach, a rich privilege which we may enjoy, and a solemn duty which God calls us now to perform."

A law was passed at this session authorizing his Excellency, Governor Buckingham, to enlist, organize, and equip, according to his discretion, an unlimited number of volunteers; and providing for the expense by ordering an additional issue of bonds of the State to the amount of two millions of dollars; making a grand total for the year of four millions of dollars which had been raised in this way. The intrusting of the disbursement of this large sum to one man, evinced the marked confidence reposed in the judgment and integrity of the Executive. Orders were now issued by the Governor for the acceptance of all full companies offering for the war.

A fine company, called the "Harland Rifles," mainly recruited in Norwich, was mustered into the Eleventh Regiment. John H. Norris, G. W. Keables, and James E. Fuller, were appointed Lieutenants; and Joseph H. Nickerson was subsequently promoted to be Captain in this regiment; all of whom were from this city.

The Eleventh was in Burnside's Expedition to North

Carolina, and a portion of the command with Colonel Kingsbury was on the Voltigeur, when she stranded off Cape Hatteras, twenty-three days of great peril elapsing before the men could be got off.

In the renowned battle of Antietam, so destructive to human life, the Regiment suffered the most severely of any from Connecticut. Besides losing its Colonel, it was nearly halved, reporting out of a muster of four hundred and forty, ninety-seven killed, and one hundred and two wounded. In the battle of Cold Harbor, Va., where the Eleventh joined the army of the Potomac, it fought with signal bravery, losing heavily in officers and men. Before Petersburg it served with great faithfulness, and when mustered out in December, 1865, reported as the whole number of men connected with the regiment two thousand four hundred.

In the Twelfth Regiment Norwich had a few enlisted men and one commissioned officer, — Lieutenant A. Dwight McCall.

The Thirteenth Regiment was largely officered by Norwich men.

Colonel.

HENRY W. BIRGE,
Previously Major of the Fourth Regiment.

Adjutant.
GEORGE W. WHITTLESEY.

Quartermaster.
JOSEPH B. BROMLEY.

Second Assistant-surgeon.
NATHAN A. FISHER.

COMPANY F.

Captain.
JAMES J. McCORD,
Previously Second Lieutenant Company B, Second Regiment.

Second Lieutenant.
JOHN C. ABBOTT.

COMPANY K.

Captain.
ALFRED MITCHELL.

In addition to these, William P. Miner and Robert Ripley were commissioned Lieutenants, and upwards of half a hundred privates were also from this town, most of the latter in Captain McCord's Company.

The Thirteenth was noted for its fine appearance and neat equipments, and was a favorite with General Butler. It had in Colonel Birge an accomplished officer, whose handling of a regiment was considered in the Gulf Department to be unsurpassed. Ordered at first to New Orleans, its entrance into that city May fifteenth, 1862, where it was assigned the post of honor, produced a marked sensation, and it was declared to be " the finest looking regiment that ever entered New Orleans." After performing garrison duty in the city for some time, the regiment was ordered to join the Reserve Brigade under General Weitzel, under whom it had a leading position in the battle of Georgia Landing, and by him was complimented for its bearing in this its maiden fight.

During the winter of 1862-63, it was engaged in the routine life incident to its position. The humorous Quartermaster of the regiment, Joseph B. Bromley, beguiled the tedium of the camp life by his wit, and at the same time

won an enviable reputation for his success in catering to the wants of the men. Colonel Sprague, in his history of the regiment, gives the following, as characteristic of the man: —

"The principal difficulty at this time was in getting wood. Our Quartermaster, never long at a loss for expedients, finally proceeded to the depot of the Carrollton Railroad, and commenced loading his teams. The Superintendent is said to have come up, and to have held the following dialogue with Bromley: —

"'What are you going to do with that wood?'

"'Cook rations. Go on with your loading, Corporal.'

"'Who are you?'

"'Bromley, Quartermaster of the Thirteenth Connecticut Volunteers. Allow me, sir, in turn to inquire whom I have the distinguished honor to address.'

"'I'm Superintendent of this railroad.'

"'All right. Go on with your loading, Corporal.'

"'The wood belongs to the railroad.'

"'So I supposed!'

"'But I forbid you to take it.'

"'Put your protest in writing, in red ink. Tie it with a piece of red tape. I'll approve it and forward it. You see we've got to have wood to cook with. Can't eat beans and pork raw. I'd prefer 'em raw, but the men are so unreasonable they want 'em cooked.'

"'But that wood's necessary for the use of the railroad.'

"'It's necessary for the use of the Thirteenth Connecticut.'

"'I should like to know how a locomotive is going to run without wood.'

"'I've often wondered how a regiment could be run without wood.'

"'General Butler orders me to run this railroad.'

"'Colonel Birge orders me to run the Thirteenth Connecticut.'

"'Who's Colonel Birge?'

"'Who's Colonel Birge? Why, the d—deuse! don't you

know Colonel Birge. If there's one man above another that everybody knows, it's Colonel Birge.'

"'Will Colonel Birge pay for the wood?'

"'Colonel Birge pay for the wood? Why no! It's a reflection on your sagacity to ask such a question.'

"'Who will pay for it?'

"'The Quartermaster's Department. If there's one thing above another that I admire in the Quartermaster's Department, it's because they'll always pay for wood. Now, my friend of the railroad persuasion, if you'll come and see me, I'll give you receipts, and help you fix up the proper papers to present to the Quartermaster's Department.'

"'How long will it be before I get pay?'

"'It will be some future day, — the futurest kind of a day, I'm afraid.'

"The Superintendent posted off to see Colonel Birge. Brómley preceded him however, and cautioned sentinels to admit no citizen without a pass. 'Halt!' said the sentry; and the Superintendent gave up the pursuit in despair.'

"The instructions which Bromley gave to Corporal Strange, a member of his staff, as he termed him, were quite significant. 'Strange, we're going on an expedition. I want my staff to be on the lookout for turkeys, geese, pigs, and sheep. Don't be the aggressor in any contest. Stand strictly on the defensive; but, if you're attacked by any of these animals, show fight, and *don't forget to bring off the enemy's dead.*"

In the following spring the campaign was opened by the battle of Irish Bend, April fourteenth, 1863. In this engagement the regiment won new honors for its admirable discipline and coolness; and among the spoils it bore away from the field was an elaborate and costly silk flag, bearing the inscription, "The Ladies of Franklin to the St. Mary's Cannoniers," a trophy which has found its way to the archives of the State. On the twenty-fourth of May following, and again on the fourteenth of June, the regiment was engaged in battle at Port Hudson; on the latter occasion, though in the reserve, by sheer force of enthusiasm and stress of the emergency, it worked its way to the forefront of the hottest battle. The assault on the Fort proved unsuccessful, and led General Banks, then in command, to call " for a storming column of one thousand men." To the lead of this forlorn hope Colonel Birge was assigned, at his own request, his splendid regiment furnishing one quarter of the desired number of stormers. It was a brave thing to do, and was the fruit of no sudden impulse, no wild thoughtless desperation. The gallant Colonel kept from his men, that he had by choice been appointed to lead the column, not wishing to influence any of them to volunteer, unless self inclined. When, however, it became known that he was to command the 'forlorn hope,' there were many accessions. Two hundred and forty-one of this noble regiment for days and weeks looked death in the face and offered all on their country's altar. They knew well the ground over which they would have to pass, and that the chances were against their ever returning. It was a volunteer service, in a trying hour, and at the risk of life itself. Some of the officers wrote out their wills, transferred money and keep-sakes to comrades who were to remain behind, and wrote their last messages to loved ones at home. It was, as we now contemplate it, one of the most heroic incidents of the war, an imperishable memorial of the self-sacrifice and courage of the men, and their leader, of both of whom the country had every reason to feel proud. By request of the rest of the men, permission was obtained of Colonel Birge that the remainder of the regiment should follow immediately in rear of the stormers, as their first support, a position only less perilous than that assigned to the storming column itself. This virtually brought the whole regiment into the assaulting force. Fortunately the rebels surrendered the post before the final assault was ordered. As a special mark of honor, the storming column was designated to enter Port Hudson to receive the surrender; this it did, the second position being given to the Twenty-sixth Regiment, under Lieutenant-colonel Joseph Selden of Norwich, the colors and band of the Thirteenth being selected from all others to grace the pageant. The regiment, after a return home for a "veteran furlough," took part in the Shenandoah campaign, and was actively engaged in the battles at Winchester, Fisher's Hill, and Cedar Creek.

In the Battle of Winchester, September, 1864, and the actions that followed in quick succession, the Thirteenth had a leading part. General Birge's division was in the advance, he himself directing and joining in the charge, which resulted in the utter route of General Early's army. Having meanwhile been promoted to be a Brigadier-general, during this Shenandoah campaign and subsequently, General Birge commanded a division. For his gallant service at Cedar Creek he was recommended by General Sheridan for a brevet commission of Major-general, which he received while in the field, winning thus the highest brevet rank gained by any army officer from Norwich.

IV.

1862.

Three Year's Men, continued.

" Listen, young heroes ! Your country is calling !
   Time strikes the hour for the brave and the true ;
  Now, while the foremost are fighting and falling,
    Fill up the ranks that have opened for you !

" Stay not for questions while Freedom stands gasping !
   Wait not till Honor lies wrapped in his pall !
  Brief the lips' meeting be, swift the hands' clasping, —
    Off for the war, is enough for them all.

" Never or now ! cries the blood of a nation,
   Poured on the turf where the red rose should bloom ;
  Now is the day and hour of salvation, —
    Never or now ! peals the trumpet of doom."

O. W. Holmes.

DURING the early part of this year the Union forces made steady progress, and it seemed for a while as if the war was to be brought to a speedy close. All loyal hearts were encouraged, and as it was supposed there would be no more calls for troops, enlisting quite generally ceased. The War Department issued orders April third, discontinuing the recruiting service in every State. The requisition upon the Governor in May by the authorities at Washington for six hundred men to fill up the Eighth, Tenth, and Eleventh Regiments, met with feeble response in Norwich and vicinity. This led to the call for another regiment, and a company was begun in the city for the Fourteenth, but enlistments came in slowly.

On July first President Lincoln issued his third proclamation, calling for three hundred thousand volunteers to serve or three years or the war. Governor Buckingham earnestly seconded this call by an appeal to the State on the third of the month, to furnish promptly its quota of men. "Close your manufactories and workshops, turn aside from your farms and your business, leave for a while your families and your homes, and meet face to face the enemies of your liberties! Haste, and you will rescue many noble men, now struggling against superior numbers, and speedily secure the blessings of peace and good government." These were the closing words of the appeal that again helped to arouse the war spirit of the town. The disheartening result of McClellan's campaign before Richmond caused new solicitude, and though the loyal citizens

"Bated no jot of heart or hope,"

it brought them to realize the need of stronger determination and greater sacrifices, if they would do their part in putting down the still regnant rebellion. One of those stirring war meetings, which from time to time had been held for the purpose of helping forward enlistments, was called for Friday, July eleventh. His Excellency, W. A. Buckingham, presided. Breed Hall was tastefully decorated with flags and bunting, and crowded to its utmost; the enthusiasm and intense feeling of the occasion were not in vain. Besides the most earnest protestations on the part of leading citizens to sustain the war till the rebellion was crushed, a number came forward, and amid the cheers of the multitude enrolled their names among the new recruits now imperatively needed. The meeting spoke the sentiment of Norwich in the following spirited resolution, —

Resolved, That in common with the people in other parts of the State, we agree to stand by the flag of the Union, and to put forth all our energies for the suppression of the Rebellion, believing, as we do, that the Constitution is the supreme law of the land, and must be maintained in every State of the Union at all hazards ; and in furtherance of these sentiments the following committee is hereby appointed, — James Lloyd Greene, John T. Wait, Amos W. Prentice, William M. Converse, J. F. Slater, H. B. Norton, J. W. Stedman, Charles Johnson, James S. Carew, Lorenzo Blackstone, Charles A. Converse, N. C. Brakenridge, H. B. Crosby, — whose duty it shall be to take such measures as may be necessary to procure the speedy enlistment of troops."

This Committee decided at once to offer as bounty to those volunteering from Norwich thirteen dollars, making, together with what the State and Government offered, a total amount of one hundred dollars to each recruit. Again, on Thursday, July twenty-fourth, a County mass meeting was held on Franklin Square, presided over by Hon. J. T. Wait, where the enthusiasm of the town and county flamed forth, roused as it was by the speeches of patriotic citizens and soldiers temporarily home. Among the episodes of this monster meeting was the introduction of fourteen members of a Greeneville company now almost full, who sang with thrilling effect a song composed for the occasion. The key-note of the speaking was struck in the repeated and earnestly presented question, " What can I do to aid the Government ? " The kindled excitement and interest of this meeting were carried over into a second gathering in Breed Hall in the evening, where representative gentlemen of the County spoke. The enlistment books were kept open on the platform, and during the continuance of the meeting numbers came forward amidst prolonged and hearty cheering, and enrolled their names. As the result of these popular demonstrations, enlisting, and persuading others to enlist, became the business of the hour. Love of country asserted itself once more above every personal and partisan feeling.

The first regiment to feel the effect of this new awakening of the war spirit was the Fourteenth, to which Norwich contributed as follows : —

COMPANY E.

Captain.
WILLIAM H. TUBBS.

First Lieutenant.
MORTON F. HALE,
Promoted Brigade Commissary of Subsistence, December, 1862.

Sergeants.
JAMES R. NICKELS,
Promoted Captain.

FREDERICK E. SCHALK,
Promoted First Lieutenant.

HENRY C. MILLER.

In Company K, Lieutenant James B. Coit, afterwards promoted Captain and Major; H. P. Goddard, Sergeant-major, afterwards promoted Captain ; and Lieutenant George C. Ripley, together with about forty enlisted men. The regiment left camp in Hartford August twenty-fifth, and without being allowed time for necessary instruction, was ordered at once into the hard-fought battle of Antietam, September, 1862. Here it suffered severely, and though a new regiment, bore itself with great merit. It had been hurried by forced marches to the battle-field, without knapsacks, or regimental baggage, and was thirty-six hours under fire at Antietam, with scarcely anything to eat or drink during all this time. From this time onward it was kept in almost constantly active service, and was emphatically a fighting regiment. At the battle of Fredericksburg it continued in the Second Corps, which, with the Ninth Corps, formed the right grand division under General Sumner. It was the only Connecticut regiment warmly engaged, and was in the division that opened the battle. After making three separate charges under severe artillery fire, it fell back only when the division was retired, bearing with it the body of the brave Lieutenant-colonel Perkins, who had been severely wounded. The aggregate loss of the regiment was one hundred and twenty-two. At the battle of Chancellorsville the Fourteenth was actively engaged, fighting with great coolness, its brief experience having made it among the most reliable of Connecticut regiments; here its losses were again heavy, and the splendid regiment which left the State August, 1862, ten hundred and fifteen strong, was already reduced, by reason of its constant fighting, to two hundred and nineteen men in service. At Gettysburg, July, 1863, the conduct of the regiment is spoken of in the highest terms. It was one of the most trying battles in which it had been engaged, yet one in which it distinguished itself by a number of effective charges, capturing five regimental flags and over forty prisoners, and sustaining a loss in the aggregate of sixty-six. In the Virginia campaign under General Grant it also shared, participating in the terrible battles of the Wilderness, and a Spottsylvania winning new laurels, losing here a brave Norwich officer, Lieutenant Schalk. At the battle of Reams' Station, August, 1864, Captain Nickels was killed. Both these young men were from Norwich, and had served with credit to themselves and the country for which they had cheerfully periled their lives. James B. Coit, who was specially mentioned for his gallantry, was also wounded, and thus forced to resign, having been promoted from a First Lieutenancy to be Major, and afterwards was brevetted Brigadier-general. The regiment was present at the surrender of Lee, and was mustered out May, 1865, with the consciousness of having had a severe service, and of having won its proud title, — the "brave Fourteenth."

In the next three regiments of the six that the Governor had called for under the President's proclamation of July first, Norwich had no official representation, and therefore no special local interest. At the patriotic mass meeting of the county nothing had contributed more to arouse throughout the town an ambition to maintain its eminence for devotion to the National Cause, than the announcement that orders had been issued for a New London County Regiment to rendezvous at the Fair Grounds near the city. It was the first regiment that was mustered into service from Norwich. For this reason the Eighteenth Regiment was regarded by our citizens as peculiarly their own. The five county companies were recruited in town, and the costly colors, National and State, were the gift of the Norwich ladies. The roster of officers of this favorite regiment from the town was as follows, and accounts for the deep interest our community took in it from the beginning of its existence clear through its eventful history : —

Colonel.
WILLIAM G. ELY,
Previously Lieutenant-Colonel of the Sixth Infantry, subsequently brevetted Brigadier-general.

Quartermaster.
DWIGHT W. HAKES,
Afterwards Captain, and Brevet Major.

THREE YEARS' MEN.

Surgeon.
CHARLES M. CARLETON.

Sergeant-major.
JOSEPH P. ROCKWELL,
Promoted Adjutant and Captain.

Quartermaster-sergeant.
WILLIAM CARRUTHERS,
Promoted First Lieutenant.

Commissary-sergeant.
HENRY HOVEY.

COMPANY A.

Captain.
HENRY C. DAVIS.

Lieutenants.
ADAM H. LINDSLEY, JAMES D. HIGGINS.

COMPANY C.

Captain.
ISAAC H. BROMLEY.

First Lieutenant.
SAMUEL T. C. MERWIN,
Promoted Captain.

Second Lieutenant.
HENRY F. COWLES,
Promoted First Lieutenant.

COMPANY E.

Captain.
ISAAC W. HAKES, JR.

First Lieutenant.
FREDERICK A. PALMER.
Promoted Captain.

COMPANY F.

Captain.
HENRY PEALE.
Promoted Major and Lieutenant-colonel.

Second Lieutenant.
JOHN A. FRANCIS.

COMPANY I.

Captain.
SAMUEL R. KNAPP.

First Lieutenant.
JOHN H. MORRISON,
Promoted Captain.

Second Lieutenant.
MARTIN V. B. TIFFANY,
Promoted Captain.

Of the enlisted men, over two hundred and fifty are credited to Norwich on the rolls of the Adjutant-general. The colors were publicly presented to the regiment in the afternoon of the twenty-second of August, by Governor Buckingham in behalf of the ladies, and received by Colonel Ely with fitting words of acknowledgment. Then forming into line, the regiment marched to the city to embark for its destination. Norwich had previous to this time sent forth single companies amid inspiriting cheers and tender farewells, but this was the first regiment it had seen depart for the seat of war. It was not strange, therefore, that the city put on its holiday attire, that ladies filled the windows and balconies along the line of march to wave their adieus, and that the streets were thronged with those anxious to have a last look at the brave men who were justly the pride of the district, and bid them as they went forth a hearty God-speed. Public and private buildings were gay with flags, and the national colors floated from the shipping in the river; the whole city was in a tumult of excitement as it parted from the regiment in which it had so large an interest, and for which it had done so much.

Stationed at first near Baltimore, it was ordered, in May, 1863, to Western Virginia. On the thirteenth to the fifteenth of June it took a prominent part in the battle of Winchester, where a large proportion of men and officers were taken prisoners. During the night of the fifteenth the order for the silent evacuation of Winchester was given. The First and Second Brigades were intercepted in this retreat by a superior force of the enemy, and after two gallant charges the Eighteenth became separated from the main body, and in a final charge alone was repulsed by the enemy now greatly outnumbering it, a part of the regiment being captured, including Colonel Ely. This was the first battle in which the Eighteenth had been engaged, and its behavior reflected credit on both officers and men. The total loss of the regiment was five hundred and sixty-seven, thirty-one being killed, forty-four wounded, including five commanders of companies, which witnesses to the severity of the fighting, and the desperateness of these successive charges. The "Richmond Whig," commenting on the latter, says, "the Yankees charged our battery three times, and got within a few yards of it, but were driven off. So many were killed at gun Number One, that it had to be abandoned, and we had fired every round of ammunition from gun Number Two. Then they made a final charge and got nearer than before, and we thought we were about to be captured, ... but finding a few rounds of ammunition in the caisson of Number One, and putting them in gun Number Two, we drove them back for the last time." Most of the privates captured in this engagement were subsequently paroled, but the officers were confined for nine months in Libby and Belle Island prisons. Colonel Ely was one of a party that escaped from Libby in February, 1864, by tunneling, but was recaptured, and carried back into close confinement. The handsome regimental colors presented by the ladies of Norwich were preserved, being carried for two days wound round the body of the color-sergeant, George Torrey of Woodstock, who escaped capture. While the arrangements for the surrender made by Colonel Ely were pending, Major Peale, with upwards of thirty men, got away; and Company D, which had been detailed for provost-guard duty, escaped intact. About two hundred of the regiment finally were gathered together at Maryland Heights, where Major Peale took the command, setting himself earnestly at work to reorganize the regiment, and put it immediately into fighting trim. Ordered to join General French of the Third Army Corps, the regiment, now led by Major Peale, had severe fighting and marching, in connection with the Army of the Potomac, which was then following up General Lee. The regiment was soon ordered to Martinsburg, Va., where it received back the imprisoned men, captured in the battle of Winchester, who arrived from Camp Parole October third, 1863, and here it remained all winter, performing picket and other duty, until the opening of the Spring campaign in the Shenandoah Valley under General Sigel (who was soon succeeded by General Hunter).

Again it was put in motion, marching southward, over the ground where so many were captured a year before, to Winchester, and thence pushed forward towards New Market. Here it went into action, numbering about ten officers and some three hundred and fifty men, after marching fifteen miles in a drenching storm, and fought with unquestioned gallantry nearly five hours, standing in mud knee-deep. General Sigel was forced to retreat, being overmatched by superior numbers. Major Peale's report credits the regiment with effective and courageous conduct, while his own handling of it in this engagement brought out his admirable qualities as a commander. The Eighteenth was in the extreme advance, and suffered severely, while the exhausting demands of their forced march before the battle, and their retreat after it, harassed by a pursuing enemy, told upon the men. At Cedar Creek General Hunter relieved General Sigel, and after a brief respite, the regiment, together with the army, moved forward by rapid marches towards Piedmont. Colonel Ely, who had been exchanged, now rejoined the regiment, and took the command in the battle of Piedmont, Va. In his report, he says, "Our troops fought with undaunted bravery, and at five, P. M. routed the rebels, captured two thousand prisoners and five thousand stand of arms. The Eighteenth was on the right of General Hunter's line of battle; its colors took the lead in the first charge, and floated defiant till we triumphed. All of the color-guard were wounded except one. Our banner riddled by minie balls and cannon-shot, and a loss of one hundred and twenty-seven in killed and wounded, tell our story." Among the killed was Adjutant E. B. Culver, an officer of great merit, an earnest patriot, and widely beloved here by friends and citizens, who lamented his early death. Corporal J. F. Bradley and William H. Hamilton, who had left good situations in our city to enter their country's service, were also among the slain. The regiment, greatly reduced in numbers and much exhausted, made its bivouac in the rear of the rebel position, and on the following morning, saddened by its losses, but rejoicing over its victory, pushed on with the army to Staunton. General Hunter in reviewing the regiments prior to the battle of Piedmont, had said to the Eighteenth, " he expected them to sustain the honor of Connecticut, and wipe out New Market." He was more than satisfied with the bearing of the regiment, and took occasion publicly to acknowledge its splendid conduct.

On the tenth of June, reinforced by the commands of Generals Crook and Averill, Hunter continued on his course southward, passing through Lexington, and destroying in his march considerable public property. Rations however began to grow scarce, and the army, two hundred miles from its base, began to experience the hardships incident to such an ill-planned state of things. On June fifteenth, the Blue Ridge was reached, and ascended near its highest point, — the peaks of the Otter. The weary march was still kept up, the men suffering for food, and obliged to be in readiness to encounter the rebels, who now began to show signs of an intention to oppose the advance on Lynchburg. All that night, the regiment lay on its arms, while its advance engaged the rebels within four miles of the city. On the eighteenth, an artillery duel continued through the day, and two unsuccessful charges were made on its line. The Eighteenth bore the brunt of this engagement, in which

Yours truly
John B. Dennis

Colonel Ely was wounded in the throat, and temporarily disabled, and eight others suffered from the enemy's fire.

General Early had now reinforced the rebels, and they in turn prepared to make one of their forward movements, through what in waggish dialect had been christened "the back doah" of the Union. The regiment in consequence had before it ten days of incessant fatiguing retreat. Hunter had made what was called a "bold dash" at Lynchburg, had brought on an indecisive battle, and then was forced to hurry back across the mountains, his command arriving at Martinsburg jaded, ragged, and dispirited. The Chaplain of the Eighteenth wrote concerning these severest days in the regiment's history, "the scenes of that terrible march will never be recalled by any survivor without a shudder, the sufferings of the men were severe, yet they conducted themselves with soldierly manliness and propriety."

Soon after the regiment in Crook's column passed down the left bank of the Potomac, reaching Snicker's Ford July eighteenth. "The command forded the Shenandoah river on the same day, and participated in an engagement with the rebel army, which invaded Maryland and Pennsylvania during the early part of July, in which engagement the regiment acted well its part, and suffered severely." Thus ran the report of Lieutenant-colonel Peale, subsequently in charge, Colonel Ely having been assigned to the command of the Second Brigade. The regiment in falling back had a spirited engagement at Winchester, Va., but was forced to continue retreating as far as Martinsburg, Va.

It was not understood by the public generally, why the Eighteenth, and the Shenandoah Valley Army with which it was associated, were so often found contending against superior numbers, and obliged so repeatedly to fall back or retreat. The explanation is in the fact that they were set to watch this back way of getting into Pennsylvania and

Maryland, through which the rebel General Early about twice a year attempted to penetrate with a force far exceeding ours. As a consequence the fighting necessary to be done by our troops was exceedingly hard, and always against great odds. When General Sheridan came into the valley he admitted that his men had no such unequal-matched battles to fight, as in the previous years had made those in the Shenandoah, in which the Eighteenth participated, so sanguinary and disastrous. No regiment fought more bravely, but it uniformly had before it every time it went into action a force outnumbering its own. The Eighteenth was, soon after this, ordered to join the forces under General Sheridan, and under him took part in an engagement with the enemy at Berryville, Va., September third, 1864, Captain Tiffany commanding in the absence of Lieutenant-colonel Peale. Colonel W. G. Ely, who of late had been in command of the Second Brigade, First Division, Army of Western Virginia, at this time resigned, and received the appointment subsequently of Brevet Brigadier-general. He had served with courage and ability for more than three years, retiring with honor from the position his soldierly qualities had won him. The regiment had now become much reduced in numbers, owing to its constant fighting, and was sent to Charlestown, Va., to act as garrison for that place, — thence it went to Martinsburg, Va., performing picket and provost duty. At its subsequent head-quarters, in Hall-town, it remained, doing valuable service until ordered to Martinsburg to be mustered out, June, 1865. Under command of Lieutenant-colonel Peale, who had been in constant service since the war broke out, it returned to Hartford, where it was awarded a public reception, bringing back from an arduous service a well-earned name for courage and fidelity.

In the next two regiments Norwich had no local interest.

Charles J. Arms, Adjutant of the Twentieth Regiment, is the only name on the original muster roll, and he was transferred to the staff of Brigadier-general Harland.

The Twenty-first was the last of the seventeen regiments raised on the several calls of the President for three years' service or the war, and was the second regiment ordered to rendezvous at Norwich. Among the officers from the town was Hiram B. Crosby, appointed Major, who on the death of Colonel Dutton and Lieutenant-colonel Burpee, succeeded to the regimental command. J. Hamilton Lee was made Assistant Surgeon, Christopher A. Brand Sergeant-major, being promoted subsequently First Lieutenant. J. D. Plunkett, at first Sergeant, rose to be Second Lieutenant; with these were about thirty privates.

On Wednesday, September seventeenth, when the State and Regimental Flags from the ladies of Norwich and Stonington were presented to the Twenty-first, an immense crowd of visitors thronged the Camp. His Honor, Mayor Greene, made the presentation speech in behalf of the donors, from which we extract the closing passages:—

"Colonel Dutton, the ladies of Norwich and Stonington place this flag in your hands, and in those of the brave men under your command, fully persuaded you will never disgrace it, but will add new lustre to the brilliancy of its fame. Take it, and guard it as the most priceless treasure ever committed to mortal hands. With it they also give you the State Flag of the State of Connecticut, confident that your valor and skill will add yet more brightness to the star which represents her in the national flag.

"'Take your flags, and, trusting in the holiness of your cause, and in your own strong arms, march on to victory and renown; and when the conflict is over, and the victory won, — when freedom's flag floats high and wide over all the land, — the ladies who present you to-day with these colors will welcome home with all honor the saviors of their beloved land."

Colonel Dutton, receiving the flags, responded in words whose emphasis, his position, and the gleaming line of bayonets borne by his men, drawn up behind where he stood, made memorably impressive : " Representing this regiment as its chief officer, I desire to thank the ladies of Eastern Connecticut for their magnificent present. At some future day — many months hence, perhaps — we hope to bring these colors back to you, time-worn, dust-covered, perhaps bullet-torn they may be, but polluted by the touch of a rebel — *never !* "

The regiment had a good record for bravery and soldierly bearing, taking part in the battles of Fredericksburg, Suffolk, Drury's Bluff, Cold Harbor, before Petersburg and Fort Harrison. Of the conduct of the regiment in the severe battle of Drury's Bluff, a New York officer, who was an eye-witness of the scene, wrote : —

" Never shall I forget its splendid behavior on that terrible sixteenth of May, 1864, when the field at Drury's Bluff was covered with from eight to ten thousand men, killed and wounded from both sides. The Twenty-first, firm and fearless, stood the horrible charge, and repulsed it on their front. Many times, in the heat of that conflict, I looked towards the regiment, fearful that I should see it overwhelmed. It did its noble State immortal honor on that day, as it has in every battle in which engaged."

The regiment remained in front of Petersburg until the third of September, performing picket duty, and engaged in skirmishes with the enemy. It was then ordered within the line of defenses at Bermuda Hundred, and remained in that position until September twenty-eighth, when it was ordered to join the general advance of the Union army. It took up its march across the James river, and with its division shared in the assault on Fort Harrison. In this action the regiment fought with conspicuous valor.

With the First Connecticut Battery, and the Eighth Regiment Infantry, it held a position in the advance into Richmond, on its evacuation by General Lee; and when mustered out in June, 1865, brought home the following high testimonial from General Charles Devens, in whose division it served : " It is fully entitled to the honor of having served most faithfully, and as long as its services were needed ; and having done its duty most nobly under many most trying and dangerous circumstances. It has worthily maintained the honor of the State of Connecticut, her loyalty to the Union of our Fathers, her deep and stern attachment to the principles of popular government and of civil liberty." Such were the words of commendation that were addressed to the Governor. Colonel Crosby, while Major, was specially mentioned for his service at the battle of Fredericksburg, where, by his discretion and courage, he facilitated the retreat of a portion of the army. He proved himself a good officer, as capable as from the outbreak of the war he had been patriotic, resigning because of sickness, September, 1864.

Connecticut was the first State to fill her quota under the call of the President for three years' men. Within forty-five days, eight thousand and thirty-six men had volunteered, and were organized into eight full regiments, and one light battery.

General Daniel Tyler rendered great assistance in equipping these regiments, and preparing them for the field. The State was indebted to him for invaluable service, which only so accomplished a soldier as he was, could have rendered.

He had been, in March, 1862, re-commissioned Brigadier-general, and assigned to the command of a brigade, afterwards of a division, in the army of the Mississippi. While kept from that active service and promotion for which his military knowledge and experience fitted him, he was the true friend of his State and town, and to his personal supervision and instruction was owing the high military character which distinguished our soldiers. General Hawley expressed the feeling of not a few Connecticut officers, when he said, " General Tyler is the father of us all."

The record of the State had thus far been remarkably creditable, while the popular enthusiasm manifested itself in local war-meetings, in generous pledges of assistance to volunteers and their families. The recruiting machinery was in the hands of men of energy and patriotic impulses, and the several towns and counties sought to emulate each other in the promptitude with which they raised their assigned quotas.

V.

1862.

NINE MONTHS' MEN.

"'Qui transtulit sustinet?' motto of light!
'Neath the folds of that banner we strike for the right;
Connecticut's watchword, o'er hill and o'er plain,
'The Hand that transplanted, that Hand will sustain.'

"And now in the darkness of Treason's black night,
'Neath the folds of that banner we strike for the right!
For the Right? 'tis our country we're marching to save, —
The dear flag of the Union in triumph shall wave!
Faith swells in each heart; Hope fires every vein!
'And Thou who transplanted, Oh! always sustain.'"

S. S. WELD.

ON the fourth of August, 1862, appeared President Lincoln's proclamation for three hundred thousand troops to serve nine months, — with orders for a draft to be made, if the quotas of the different States were not filled with volunteers, by the fifteenth of the month. In Norwich it only served to intensify the war spirit, and made all citizens feel that it was no time to despond or slacken in efforts that hitherto had reflected such honor upon the town. The "Daily Bulletin," from the first, pronounced in its patriotic utterances, and eager to second every movement for the raising of the called for troops, — spoke out in bold and earnest tones, — "There is not a loyal heart in these United States who will not rejoice on seeing the President's proclamation. . . . It is an indication of earnest work. It proves that the administration will not suffer this Republic to perish because it hesitates to put forth its full strength. We cannot doubt of the hearty approval and willing response of the people to this new call upon their patriotism. There are many among us who could hardly determine their duty. On the one hand, were the sweet endearments of home, — the wife and children to be provided for, the anxious care for them, which pleads strongly ; and on the other hand, the call for soldiers, which comes home to every man's heart who loves his native land. To them the draft will be welcome."

It was a dark hour in the history of the war, perhaps the darkest that was known at any time during our long struggle. The Peninsular campaign had resulted most disastrously to our arms, though never did troops fight more bravely. The stubborn heroism of our splendid Potomac army, led by such war-worn veterans as Sumner, Kearney, Heintzelman, Hooker, and others, had made its retreat a costly one to the rebel forces, and might even have turned its sad retirement from the advance on Richmond into victory, if there had been the requisite courage and skill on the part of the then commanding general. Following this great failure came the short and unfortunate campaign of General Pope, and the triumphant advance of General Lee into Maryland. The need of more men by the government was urgent in the extreme, and the President's call appeared just at the time when national reverses had produced widespread discouragement and solicitude, and yet, as we shall see, the people met the crisis with undaunted faith, and responded with reasonable promptness to the appeal made to them for more troops.

Going back a little in our regimental history, we find that in January of this year, the Fourth Regiment of Infantry was by order of the War Department converted into the First Artillery. It received two additional companies, and was recruited to eighteen hundred men, and placed under command of Colonel Robert O. Tyler. In a few months, it attained a remarkable degree of efficiency, and was soon after " ranked by military judges as the best Volunteer Regiment of Artillery in the field, and considered equal in all respects to any regiment of the same arm in the regular service."

On the promotion of Colonel Tyler, Henry L. Abbott was appointed to the command, and under him the regiment served until the close of the war. It constituted, during a portion of this period, the basis of an Artillery Brigade, which sometimes exceeded an aggregate of thirty-five hundred men, and had in charge the entire siege train in use in the final siege of Petersburg and Richmond.

From this regiment, after the transference of Major H. W. Birge to the colonelcy of the Thirteenth Infantry, Norwich was represented by Dr. Edwin Bentley, Assistant Surgeon, promoted to the position of Brigade Surgeon ; John H. Tingley, Second Lieutenant, Company A, who had with a noble patriotism served in the ranks as a private during the three months' campaign ; Bela P. Learned, Second Lieutenant, Company D, who also served two years with honor as a field-officer on the staff of General Abbott, transacting with rare efficiency the complicated office duties of the command. Subsequently promoted Captain, he received the appointment of Brevet Major before he was mustered out with the regiment ; Edwin L. Tyler, Second Lieutenant, Company G ; Frank J. Jones, Second Lieutenant, Company L.

On the regimental rolls appear the names of about sixty privates, some of whom were non-residents, and are credited to the town as substitutes. The regiment served through the Peninsular campaign under General McClellan, where its discipline and splendid equipment were severely tested. At the battle of Malvern Hill its guns were served with great rapidity and accuracy, and for its efficient services the names of "Siege of Yorktown," "Hanover Court House," "Chickahominy," "Gaines' Mills," and "Malvern," were ordered to be emblazoned on its colors. When garrisoning Washington, subsequent to this, it was awarded a position of supreme importance, and in the advance under General Grant, the regiment again had a distinguished part, the gallantry of its officers and men attracting attention. Throughout the final campaign against Richmond, it continued to hold the high reputation it had gained, in the earlier one during this year, under McClellan. In the siege of Yorktown in 1862, when the Regiment had been but few months in service, and had received comparatively little exact training, the report of the ordnance officer of its siege-train, Major Doull of the Second New York Artillery, said, "Its labors will compare favorably with anything of the kind that has been done before." It manned the long line of guns in front of Petersburg in 1864 and '65, while eight companies served on the lines in front of Richmond.

When not serving their guns, the greater part of the regiment would act as guards for the reserve artillery, or would be ready to accompany assaulting columns, in order to use without delay any captured artillery upon the retreating enemy. In the assault of the lines of Petersburg, April second, 1865, by the Ninth Corps, a detachment of the regiment joined the assaulting column, and entered among the first the enemy's works, serving instantly four captured light twelve-pounder guns upon the retreating masses of the enemy. Two more were afterwards taken, when the six guns were served gallantly all day and during the night, contributing greatly to the success of the charge, and repulsing the rebels in their desperate efforts to retake the works.

Always to be relied on, its superb discipline jealously maintained by Colonel Abbott, and kept in the best fighting trim, it was a regiment that commanders came to be proud of, the achievements of which brought honor to the State, that through it won a good name for what it furnished in this arm.

On reading over the exact orders issued by Lieutenant Learned, when serving as Acting Assistant Adjutant-general, in which the number of shots fired by each gun, the kind of ammunition used, kind of projectile preferred, and other similar details were required to be reported by the battery commanders to him, the secret of its efficiency is in part disclosed.

When scattered over a front extending many miles, frequently subdivided into smaller companies, the regiment on coming together again exhibits the cleanliness and soldierly appearance, which gave it such brilliant presence when on garrison duty. When it was mustered out, September twenty-fifth, 1865, Major-general Barry, one of the ablest artillery officers in the country, bore this testimony to the character of the regiment : "As chief of Artillery successively of the two principal armies of the United States, during the four years of war, now happily ended, I have enjoyed unusual opportunities for observation. You will on this account value my opinion when I assure you that the First Connecticut Artillery, in intelligence, and the acquirements and services of its special arm, stands unrivaled in the armies of the United States."

We have thus far noted the representatives of our town, in the infantry regiments formed, and in the other arm, of heavy artillery. We come, now, to the cavalry. Into the First Regiment, there went from Norwich Charles Farnsworth, Captain of Company B, who was subsequently promoted Lieutenant-colonel; Henry T. Phillips, Second Lieutenant, afterward First Lieutenant; Joab B. Rogers, Sergeant, promoted to Captain Company A; and seventy-nine privates. Originally a battalion, it left the State in January, 1862, performing arduous service during the first year in the mountain department of Virginia, under Generals Schenck, Fremont, and Milroy.

In April, 1862, Captain Farnsworth was attacked, while on a scouting expedition with only twelve men, and severely wounded. He was passing at the base of a hill so thickly overgrown with brush and small trees that it was impossible to distinguish a man two rods distant. At this point two volleys were fired at him from behind, from the brow of this hill, by concealed rebels. One ball passed through his arm, another through his side. He promptly halted his men, formed them into line, so as to be prepared to receive the rebels if disposed to come to close quarters, when fainting from the loss of blood, he was safely brought into camp. Recovering from the illness this occasioned, he soon rejoined his command, and took part with the regiment in the service demanded of it during the rest of the campaign.

In July, 1863, Captain (at this date Major) Farnsworth, with a command of fifty men, was ordered out by General Naglee to reconnoitre the enemy's position beyond Bolivar Heights, and to ascertain his strength. Coming upon a strong cavalry picket, they charged on them and drove them back on their reserve, two hundred strong. Not halting at this, the gallant Major charged on the whole body of the enemy, and at first with success, capturing many prisoners, but the rebels, seeing the disparity of the attacking force, rallied, and a hand to hand fight occurred, in which Major Farnsworth's horse was shot, and he, with twenty-six of his men were compelled to surrender. Taken at once to Libby Prison, he endured there a weary confinement for some eight months. Soon after his return to his regiment, in May, 1864, having meanwhile been promoted Lieutenant-colonel, he resigned his commission, and was honorably discharged, with the record of a brave and spirited officer, admirably adapted to this arm of the service.

In the spring of 1864 the regiment was attached to the Army of the Potomac, and assigned to the cavalry brigade of General Davies, under Kilpatrick. It now entered upon arduous duty, opening the battle of Spottsylvania, and fighting with marked courage, part of the time dismounted, and then again in the saddle.

In August of this year it was transferred to the army of the Shenandoah, and won, while with General Sheridan, the reputation of being "second to no other cavalry regiment." In the vicinity of Winchester, while with General Wilson's cavalry division, a squadron under Captain Rogers, assisted by detachments from the Third New York and Second Ohio, surrounded and captured an entire regiment of South Carolina infantry, with their colors. Lieutenant Henry T. Phillips, just prior to the battle of Ashland Station, May, 1864, was of marked service in securing ammunition for the regiment, boldly accomplishing that which had twice been ineffectually attempted by other officers. The regiment had a most laborious service during the last two years of the war, fighting now on the skirmish line, dismounted, then leading in the charge upon the advanced forces of the enemy, and at all times recognized as reliable and brave. The varied experiences of the regiment, its losses and desperate encounters, its long raids and dashing charges, make up a story such as only a cavalry regiment of trusty mettle could furnish. It had a very prominent part in the final advance on Richmond, and led in the pursuit and capture of Lee's army. It was the last regiment to leave the renowned cavalry corps of General Sheridan, being detained in Washington on account of its high repute and soldierly appearance. Its muster-rolls bore the names of two thousand six hundred and eleven men. On August fifth, 1865, it returned to New Haven and was there mustered out.

On the rolls of the First Light Battery appears the name of Alfred P. Rockwell, as Captain, the only Norwich officer. In the battle of James Island his command responded to the enemy's fire with great effect, pouring percussion shells into the rebels with telling rapidity and accuracy of aim. In the second engagement on this island, in 1863, the battery again took a prominent part. At the battle of Walthall Junction the rebels charged upon the battery and were handsomely repulsed. At Fort Darling, May 1864, Captain Rockwell had a position on the left of the line, where again the guns of his battery were admirably served and made the enemy respect them. Subsequently promoted Colonel of the Sixth Regiment, he led the latter in the engagements at Bermuda Hundred, Deep Run, Va., and Fort Fisher, N. C., proving himself a skillful officer, and receiving the appointment of brevet Brigadier-general, for his gallantry in the campaign of 1864.

Seven additional regiments of nine months' men were now called for from Connecticut, and Norwich took vigorous measures to furnish promptly its quota. Another great war meeting was held in Breed Hall, Wednesday evening, August twenty-seventh, presided over by his honor Mayor Greene, where again the spirit and enthusiasm of the people were aroused. The war committee announced that the town bounty would be increased to one hundred dollars.

On Saturday, August thirtieth, the citizens were warned to assemble in Town Hall. The highest pitch of popular feeling during the war was on this occasion reached in a meeting of thrilling interest. After ratifying the action of the war committee, raising the bounty of the nine months' men to the amount above named, the assemblage, now overwhelmingly thronged, and wrought up with intense excitement, resolved itself into a committee of the whole, to obtain volunteers. Hon. John T. Wait was conducted to the chair, when individual offers to those who would enlist followed, marked by unprecedented liberality, and awakening the greatest enthusiasm. Hon. H. H. Starkweather, whose practical wisdom and earnest, devoted patriotism had placed him foremost among the more serviceable of our citizens, led off in a tender of one hundred dollars to the first ten men that volunteered. Lewis Edwards promptly made a like offer. Fifty dollars was next proffered by D. A. Delanoy for the third ten that would enlist. H. L. Maples responded with a pledge of twenty-five dollars for the next five recruits. Spear & Brothers joined the bidders, with a promise of fifty dollars for the next five enlisting. J. M. Huntington then added an offer of ten dollars apiece for the first sixty volunteers, Hon. L. Blackstone continued the same generous pledge for the next twenty, and L. H. Chester offered fifty dollars for ten more. A spirit of noble emulation seemed to animate all present, while those who were unable to join in these money proffers came forward, and did what was better, offered themselves.

William P. Greene, Esq., ever mindful of the families to be left by those volunteering, with his accustomed considerateness and liberality, amid the heartiest applause, made his tender of one thousand dollars for their benefit. This turned the current of citizen benevolence only in another direction, and at once Hon. James Lloyd Greene followed with his offer of five hundred dollars, while next to him came Henry Bill, with a promise of one hundred dollars. Dr. R. Tracy joined the new advance with fifty dollars, Jedediah Leavens with fifty dollars, and A. P. Sturtevant brought up the rear with a round one hundred dollar subscription. These offers followed each other rapidly, while equally generous private pledges to the committee, were made after the eventful meeting adjourned, Governor Buckingham adding five hundred dollars to the fund for soldiers' families.

The kindled enthusiasm of this gathering seemed to demand, after a short nooning, a second session, which was held in Franklin Square, where telling speeches were made, interspersed with yet further proffers of pecuniary aid or of personal service. Altogether it was a most memorable meeting, and brought out into sublimest expression the liberality and patriotism of the citizens of Norwich. This splendid action of the town averted the necessity of a draft, and placed at the service of the government more than its assigned quota.

The impetus given to recruiting by these recent war-meetings, contributed to the rapid filling up of the Twenty-sixth Regiment, which was a New London County organization. It was ordered to rendezvous at Norwich, and had a large representation from the town, both as officers and men. Among the former, Norwich furnished, –

Lieutenant-colonel.
JOSEPH SELDEN.

Adjutant.
STEPHEN B. MEECH.

Quartermaster.
BENJAMIN F. TRACY.

Assistant Surgeon.
ELISHA PHINNEY.

COMPANY B.

Captain.
CLARKE HARRINGTON.

Second Lieutenant.
JAMES S. MAPLES.

COMPANY D.

Captain.
SAMUEL T. HUNTOON.

First Lieutenant.
TIMOTHY W. TRACY.

COMPANY F.

Captain.
LOREN A. GALLUP.

First Lieutenant.
EDWARD W. EELS.

Second Lieutenant.
HERVEY F. JACOBS.

COMPANY G.

Captain.
JOHN L. STANTON.

Second Lieutenant.
PLINY BREWER.

On the regimental rolls appear the names of one hundred and twenty-five privates hailing from this town. On the fourteenth of November, the regiment broke camp, and marching through the city, where it was greeted by every demonstration of good-will, it embarked on the steamer, *en route* for New York, amidst the farewells of those who crowded the wharf to look their last look, and speak their last adieus.

The band struck up the conventional "good-by" air, "The Girl I left behind me," as the boat moved off, which carried away the last regiment Norwich and the adjoining towns were called on to raise. The Twenty-sixth was ordered first to New Orleans, and remained for a while at Camp Parapet, drilling, doing guard duty, and on detached service. Soon after General Banks' arrival, it was put in motion to join his command in the projected assault upon Port Hudson. Here, after the investment of this stronghold was completed, the regiment participated in the three several attacks made upon it, serving in General Neal Dow's Brigade. In the first of these, on May twenty-seventh, its position was on the extreme left wing, the advance of which immediately exposed it to a concentrated fire from the enemy. Colonel Kingsley was wounded in the early part of the action, when Lieutenant-colonel Selden took the command, leading the regiment in person, and handling it with courage and skill. Its bearing in this first engagement in which it came under fire, was highly creditable, the men and officers conducting with decided gallantry and coolness, proving that nine months' regiments were equal to any emergency. Captain John L. Stanton, a brave officer, esteemed by his comrades, and tenderly loved by his friends, was shot dead in this assault. The total loss of the regiment was reported as one hundred and seven.

On the long-to-be-remembered fourteenth of June, the

regiment led the advance, pushing its way under the lead of the Lieutenant-colonel to within three hundred yards of the enemy's works, under a raking fire. Here, in a ravine obstructing its further movement, it held its own, under a broiling sun, until night-fall, suffering terribly from the rebel guns. For its courageous and veteran-like conduct on this occasion, the regiment was complimented by a special order from General Dwight. In this action, Lieutenant Hervey F. Jacobs was fatally wounded, and by his subsequent death added another to the swelling list of those who had gone forth from Norwich and sacrificed life to the cause they had with noble patriotism espoused. The regiment was again honored by being selected as one of the ten to enter and receive the formal surrender of Port Hudson, July ninth, 1863, occupying, in the performance of this duty, the second post of honor. The history of the Twenty-sixth was in every respect a noble one.

Its active service in the siege of Port Hudson covered about forty-five days, — days they were in which its courage and military prowess won their meed of well-deserved renown. Returning with depleted ranks, with torn and blackened colors, it received a public welcome such as testified to the appreciation of those who had fondly watched its service in the field.

On the entrance to the Little Plain where a bountiful collation had been prepared, was hung the motto, "Welcome! Twenty-sixth," while the words "Port Hudson," appropriately decorated the stand occupied by the Governor, Mayor, City Council, Colonel Kingsley, and others. After the regiment and its escort had taken their places at the tables, bountifully supplied, and beautifully decorated, Mayor Greene greeted them in these words : —

"Colonel Kingsley, officers and privates of the Twenty-sixth Regiment, it is my pleasure, as it is my duty on this occasion, in the name and by the order of the city of Norwich, to welcome you home to old Connecticut. Some who left in your ranks have not returned; they will return no more; their dust mingles with Southern soil, but their lives were not given in vain; and if it is most noble to live for others, and not for ourselves, then certainly no death can be more noble than that which is in defense of the liberties of our country, and for the protection and preservation of the best interests and hopes of all men. . . . Soldiers, during your nine months of service, you have endured the privations and hardship of the camp and the march, you have faced the perils of sickness, and have braved wounds, mutilation, and death, on the field of battle you have nobly upheld the honor of the State, and have proved, in common with all Connecticut regiments, that though our State is small in size, she is preëminent in the valor and manhood of her sons." . . . .

Colonel Kingsley briefly responded, alluding to the sufferings and achievements of the regiment, to the praise it had won for its brief but valuable service from its commanding Generals. The regiment mustered about five hundred and fifty, seven of their number having been buried along the banks of the Mississippi, a few, unable to be moved, were left in Western hospitals, one died within sight of home, and seven were too feeble to be present and participate in the festivities of the occasion. One hundred and sixty-seven are its reported losses in total. This tells substantially the story of the regiment, whose annals are hereafter part of the history of our town.

The city authorities, as well as the military and fire department, shared in this cordial home-reception, and acted as escort to these young heroes of siege and battle.

On the twenty-second of September, 1862, appeared the great proclamation of President Lincoln, declaring, "That on the first day of January, in the year of our Lord one thousand eight hundred and sixty-three, all persons held as slaves within any State, or any designated part of a State, the people whereof shall then be in rebellion against the United States, shall be thenceforward and forever free, and the government of the United States, including the military and naval authorities, will recognize and maintain the freedom of such persons, and will do no act or acts to repress such persons, or any of them, in any efforts they may make for their actual freedom."

The wisdom of this great act was by the loyal masses of the North deemed unquestionable, while its necessity had long been held to be imperative by leading men throughout the country. Almost unheralded, its appearance debarred that angry discussion which might have followed the announcement of its forthcoming.

At a meeting, September twenty-ninth, in Washington, D. C., composed of the governors of loyal States, an address to Mr. Lincoln was drawn up and presented, which, after pledging to the President their most loyal support, added, in reference to his great act : " We hail with heartfelt gratitude, and encouraged hope, the proclamation, issued on the twenty-second instant, declaring emancipated from their bondage all persons held to service or labor as slaves in the rebel States whose rebellion shall last until the first day of January next ensuing. . . . To have continued indefinitely the most efficient cause, the support and stay of the rebellion, would have been in our opinion unjust to the loyal people whose treasures and lives are made a willing sacrifice on the altar of patriotism, would have discriminated against the wife, who is compelled to surrender her husband, against the parent who is to surrender his child to the hardships of camp, and the perils of battle, and in favor of rebel-masters permitted to retain their slaves. It would have been a final decision alike against humanity, justice, the rights and dignity of the government, and against a wise national policy. The decision of the President to strike at the root of the rebellion, will lend new vigor to the efforts, and new life and hope to the hearts of the people.

"Cordially tendering to the President our respectful assurances of personal and official confidence, we trust and believe that the policy now inaugurated will be crowned with success, will give speedy and triumphant victories over our enemies, and secure to this nation and to this people the blessings and favor of Almighty God."

The address was the work of Massachusetts' distinguished "war-governor," — the eloquent and patriotic John A. Andrew. The general verdict of the press of the country was in favor of the grand edict, with which Abraham Lincoln's name will be forever associated. He himself realized the magnitude of the deed, when in proclaiming the act in force on the first of January, 1863, he with that reverent divine faith which so often lifted him far above the mere petty feelings of political expediency, solemnly concluded with these words: "*And upon this act, sincerely believed to be an act of justice, warranted by the Constitution upon military necessity, I invoke the considerate judgment of mankind, and the gracious favor of Almighty God.*"

Governor Andrew, in his annual Message to the Massachusetts Legislature, bore this graceful and earnest tribute to the great act of the age: "Supporting always the Government without conditions as to its policy, we rejoice with unutterable joy, that its policy is that of human nature, and not that of human sophistry; and we hail the returning day of civic virtues which our national departure from the practice of justice and the principles of our fathers have discouraged in the North, and have overthrown in the South."

Before sunset on that memorable twenty-second of September, the proclamation had been telegraphed to every portion of the Republic. It was hailed by a large majority of the loyal men of the nation with unfeigned joy and gratitude. Bells rang out their joyous peals not only throughout New England, and the teeming cities of the Empire State, but over the broader States of the West, and clear on to those that skirt the base of the Rocky Mountains. Ten States were enumerated as in rebellion, and three million of slaves were set free. After the issue of the proclamation, Mr. Lincoln said, " Now that we have got the harpoon fairly into the monster slavery, we must take care that in his extremity he does not shipwreck the country."

In the House of Representatives, on motion of Mr. Fessenden, of Maine, the following vote was passed by a large majority : " *Resolved*, That the proclamation of the President of the United States of the date of September twenty-second, 1862, is warranted by the Constitution ; that the policy of emancipation, as indicated in that proclamation, is well adapted to hasten the restoration of peace, was well chosen as a war-measure, and is an exercise of power with proper regard for the rights of the States, and the prosperity of free government."

The citizens of Norwich were not indifferent to this edict of liberty, emancipating an enslaved race, and they gave to it at once their heartfelt approval, and outspoken support. Accordingly, on the day when the proclamation went into effect, January first, 1863, Hon. James Lloyd Greene, the patriotic mayor of the city, whose sympathy with the cause of human freedom, and earnest support of the war from its very beginning had won him a high regard amongst our citizens, ordered a salute to be fired, the city flags to be displayed, and the church bells rung.

In thus doing public honor to the act which made the

year forever memorable, he "had the advice and consent of all the members of the common council whom he could find, being a majority of the whole number." It was fit thus to notice this signal event, and every gun fired gave expression to the feelings that thrilled with joy the hearts of all loyal people. When the bill was presented to the city treasurer for payment, after an appropriation therefor had been unanimously made by the common council, he was restrained by an injunction issued by the Superior court, from paying the same. The honorable tribute to the edict in question was, however, shorn of none of its significance, when the undaunted mayor promptly relieved the city of all expense, or litigation, and in outspoken words given to the public, in which the facts of the case were plainly stated, and the items of the bill presented, he with genuine quaintness of expression, thus concluded: "And now, upon my soul, I do exult and rejoice that I, James Lloyd Greene, am the man who ordered and paid for the first emancipation salute ever fired in the State of Connecticut."

Concerning this same event, thus wrote the sweet Quaker poet, J. G. Whittier:—

> "O dark sad millions, patiently and dumb
> Waiting for God, your hour at last has come,
> And freedom's song
> Breaks the long silence of your night of wrong!
>
> "Arise and flee! Shake off the vile restraint
> Of ages! but like Ballymena's saint
> The oppressor spare;
> Heap only on his head the coals of prayer.
>
> "Go forth, like him, like him return again,
> To bless the land whereon in bitter pain
> Ye toiled at first,
> And heal with freedom, what your slavery cursed!"

VI.
1863.

" All hail the land where Freedom dwells, and lifts her starry shield !
Here gaze all nations, bond and free — this is their battle-field !
Humanity and Liberty throughout the struggling world,
Proclaim her cause their own, and cry, Our Flag shall stay unfurled !
       Our Flag shall stay unfurled !
       Our Flag shall stay unfurled !
    Though Freedom's foes may plot her death,
    Yet while a patriot holds his breath,
       Our Flag shall stay unfurled ! "
                         WEISHAMPEL.

UP to this time there had been but slow progress made by our armies, though the expenditure, both of blood and treasure, had been very great. The hopes of the insurgents were still confident, and our forces had sustained enough repulses to seriously discourage the people. Now opened the year, which was the test one of the conflict. It opened well, for it chronicled the fact, that liberty to all was now for the first time inscribed upon our national banners.

The campaign commenced with great vigor in the West, under General Grant, and by the middle of summer Vicksburg had fallen before his persevering skill and valor, and soon after, Port Hudson surrendered to General Banks, thus securing for our possession the great river of the continent, and thereby severing in twain the territory of the Confederacy. About the same time in the East, the gallant Potomac Army endured another defeat under Hooker at Chancellorsville, which led to the bold advance of Lee into Pennsylvania, he venturing to assume again the offensive. The command of our troops was transferred to General Meade, who met the enemy at Gettysburg, and fought him, in a most obstinate and bloody battle, lasting three days, at the end of which our army remained in possession of the field, having inflicted so damaging a defeat on the rebels, that they were compelled to retreat. The tidings of this victory were announced to the country July fourth, which, with the brilliant triumphs of our arms in the West, added new fervor to the popular celebration peculiar to that day. Modestly and reverently Mr. Lincoln anticipated the fuller telegraphic news, which was published on the morning of our national holiday by issuing the following bulletin: " The President of the United States announces to the country, that the news from the army of the Potomac, up to ten P. M. of the third, is such as to cover the army with the highest honor, — to promise great success to the cause of the Union, — and to claim the condolence of all for the many gallant fallen ; and that for this, he especially desires that on this day, ' He whose will, not ours, should be done,' be everywhere remembered, and reverenced with the profoundest gratitude."

A few weeks had effected a complete change in the condition of affairs. In a little more than a month's time, through the numbers killed, wounded, or taken prisoners, over eighty thousand men were lost to the rebel armies. Our losses had been heavy, but the substantial victories gained, inspirited the whole nation, and revived public confidence at home and abroad in the ultimate success of the Union cause. President Lincoln, in view of the recent events, which reflected such lustre upon our arms, appointed August sixth as a day for national thanksgiving, praise, and prayer, inviting "the people of the United States to assemble on that occasion in their customary places of worship, and in the forms approved by their own conscience, render the homage due to the Divine Majesty for the wonderful things He has done in the nation's behalf, and invoke the influence of his Holy Spirit to subdue the anger which has produced, and so long sustained a needless and cruel rebellion ; and to change the hearts of the insurgents, to guide the counsels of the government with wisdom adequate to so great a national emergency, and to visit with tender care and consolation throughout the length and breadth of our land, all those who, through the vicissitudes of marches, voyages, battles, and sieges, have been brought to suffer in mind, body, or estate, and family ; to lead the whole nation, through paths of repentance, and submission to the Divine Will, back to the perfect enjoyment of Union and fraternal peace."

About the same time appeared the following, from the rebel authorities, which shows how the recent successes by our armies affected them : " Now, therefore, I, Jefferson Davis, President of the Confederate States of America, do by virtue of the powers vested in me as aforesaid, call out and place in the military service of the Confederate States, all *white men*, residents of said States, between the ages of eighteen and forty-five years, and not legally exempted from military service ; and I do hereby order and direct that all persons subject to this call, and not now in the military service, do upon being enrolled, forthwith repair to the conscript camp established in the respective States of which they may be residents, under pain of being held and punished as deserters, in the event of their failure to obey this call, as provided in said laws."

This was decidedly a short metre process, as compared with our enrollment system, of which we have yet to speak.

It was coercive to an extent, that only the desperate straits to which the rebels were reduced, can explain. Little else was left a white citizen in the South to do, but to consult the family register, ascertain whether he was of the unfortunate age, if so, to kiss his wife, and, with a supply of corncake sufficient to last him on his compulsory journey, "repair to the conscript camp."

This conscription bill of the Confederate Congress was passed in March, 1862. Nearly a year later, Senator Wilson, Chairman of the Military Committee in the United States, reported a bill for the enrollment of all able-bodied citizens, between the ages of eighteen and forty-five years, black or white, making them liable to military duty at the call of the President. All drafted persons were allowed to furnish an acceptable substitute, or on payment of three hundred dollars be discharged from liability to military service.

Upon the passage by Congress of this every-way reasonable act, in which provision was made for exempting those whom it would be unjust or needlessly severe to subject to military duty, the President appointed Acting Assistant Provost-marshals-general for each State, and Provost-marshals for each Congressional District.

The bill divided the national forces into two general classes. The first comprised all persons subject to do military duty, between the ages of twenty and thirty five; all unmarried persons above the age of thirty-five, and under the age of forty-five. These classes, by the enrolling officers were kept separate, and in the Adjutants' reports are divided, as if distinct. The second general class comprised all other persons liable to do military duty; and these last were not to be called out until those first subject to duty had been called into service.

On July first, 1863, it was ordered by the War Department, that draft should be made from the enrolled militia of the first class, and fifty per centum in addition to the quota called for should be drafted to cover exemptions. The enrollment for this (the Third) District, showed that there were in First Class, 7,848; Second Class, 4,052; Third Class, 3,763; total, 15,663. Captain I. H. Bromley was appointed Provost-marshal. The enrolling officers under him, for Norwich, were Benjamin M. Leavens and Joseph T. Thurston. The quota of the State was fixed at seven thousand six hundred and ninety-two (7,692), the total number to be drafted (being the quota and an additional fifty per centum), eleven thousand five hundred and thirty-nine (11,539). The quota of the District was fifteen hundred and sixty-nine, which, with addition prescribed, amounted to two thousand three hundred and fifty-four. There was great opposition to the draft in many parts of the country, culminating in terrible mobs in New York, Boston, and other cities.

 The riot in New York was one of unprecedented boldness and barbarity, and raged from July thirteenth through the three succeeding days. The most revolting feature was the uniform maltreatment to which the harmless, affrighted colored people of the city were subjected. This outburst of ruffianism, thoroughly wicked and unjustifiable, originated in the sympathy there was with the rebels, and was aided by the public utterances of men of doubtful loyalty, "who detested every form of coercion, save the coercion of the Republic by the rebels." The rioters were effectually put down, when the absent troops could be called in, and the blandly saluted "friends" of Governor Seymour were taught, to their bitter cost, that the government was not to be obstructed in the measures it legally adopted for the suppression of the rebellion. There were threats of similar violence in Connecticut, and secret meetings of the so-called "peace men" were held in various parts of the State. It was widely declared that they were organizing to resist what they called "conscription," and that an assault would be made upon the Provost-marshals' offices for the purpose of destroying the boxes, and preventing the draft. Governor Buckingham, however, showed no disposition to deal leniently with these domestic traitors, and promptly called for two battalions of volunteer infantry. The immediate appearance of these, with a determination to put down any form of opposition to the measures of the National Executive, had a wholesome effect, and the rampant peace men became quiescent. Norwich maintained its loyalty by manifesting a desire to help on rather than retard the execution of the law. And yet there were signs of opposition, and secret threats of violence, that led many of our citizens to apprehend trouble. On the day fixed for the drafting to take place, a vague undefined fear seemed to pervade the community, without any very clear grounds for it. Some of our people went to the meeting prepared for an outbreak; but fortunately for the good name of the town, and to the honor of the citizens, there was not the slightest indication of disorder, nor any appearance of violent opposition to those who had the matter of drafting in charge. The utmost goodnature prevailed, and the factiously disposed, if there were any, submitted with excellent grace, and belied not the name of "peace-men," by which they were generally called. The drafted took their lot with cheerfulness, and those who escaped were congratulated on the propitious fate which spared them the hardships of compulsory soldiering, or its expensive equivalents. Undoubtedly there was in our town, as more or less throughout the State, a bitter feeling of opposition to the "Conscription Act;" but with us it had little influence or character.

Here, as elsewhere, this latent hostility to the means

necessarily resorted to in order to put down the rebellion, led the most earnest and patriotic of our citizens to form a branch " Loyal League." A meeting was held in Treadway Hall, March twenty-seventh, to organize, and there it was voted to accept the pledge which had been adopted in the " League " at New York. The primary object of this association was to " bind together all loyal men of all trades and professions, in common union, to maintain the power, glory, and integrity of the nation." P. St. M. Andrews was chosen president, with a long list of vice-presidents, comprising most of our leading men ; corresponding secretary, H. H. Starkweather ; recording secretaries, John A. Sterry, Geo. H. Rogers, Chas. E. Dyer ; executive committee, J. Lloyd Greene, John L. Devotion, Benj. B. Whittemore, Amos W. Prentice, John W. Allen, H. H. Osgood, John A. Sterry. The meeting then listened to addresses, by which the flow of patriotic sentiment was kept up till a late hour, General Nye, of Nevada, being the chief speaker. Thus was started in Norwich the " League," which throughout the country held in unswerving alliance the loyal masses, and assured the government of the reliable support of the ablest of its citizens. It only imparted a new flavor to the interest and enthusiasm of this meeting, that another of a totally opposite character was in session at the same time in Breed Hall, where the advocates of a treacherous and dishonorable peace held forth, and boldly proclaimed that " it was time to sheathe the sword." The contrast, now that the two gatherings stand side by side in history, is one which has lost none of its suggestiveness ; the latter remains rather as one of those war pictures, in which men are presented in an attitude that now appears far from creditable to their good judgment or their patriotism. The figure such make in the history of our commonwealth is one that posterity, grateful to those who were loyal from the beginning to the end of our conflict, might for their sakes wish altered. The Benedict Arnold school of men failed not during our war to make almost as unfortunate exhibit, as did their more noted progenitors in our earlier struggle for national independence.

The result of the draft in this District was as follows:—

Drafted men accepted	46
Substitutes accepted	346
Paid commutation	232
Exempted for various reasons	1,463
Failed to report	267
Total,	2,354

In Norwich, four hundred and thirty-five were drafted, including a fair proportion of our most prominent and patriotic citizens. On Laurel Hill, fifteen were drafted out of an enrollment of but twenty-one. Most of those drafted, however, either were exempted, or else paid commutation, or provided substitutes, so that very few of them were personally held to service.

On October seventeenth, the President called for an additional force of three hundred thousand men, to serve for three years, or the war. The Legislature had just added three hundred dollars to the large bounty offered by the National Government, making such inducements for volunteering as were never held out by any nation before. The State was called on to furnish five thousand four hundred and thirty-two volunteers before the fifth day of January, or else be subjected to a draft for nearly twice that number. The quota of Norwich was two hundred and six. Our citizens now roused themselves to secure the requisite number of recruits, and going to work with a will, they soon found that their efforts could be made successful. In spite of a driving rain-storm, a war-meeting was held in Breed Hall,

Tuesday morning, November seventeenth, which was fully attended. Hon. David Gallup, of Plainfield, was chosen chairman, who made a brief statement of the objects of the meeting, and urged the prompt and wise devising of measures likely to insure the filling up of the quota of the district, which was eleven hundred and three. Hon. J. T. Wait then addressed the assembly with much earnestness, alluding to the fact, that " the exigencies of the case admitted of but two alternatives. Men must either come forward and enlist, or we must inevitably submit to a draft for double the number asked for by volunteering. When we consider our wealth and our teeming millions of population in comparison with the resources of our fathers, we ought to humble ourselves in the dust, if we cannot come forward and fully respond to the demands of the country." H. H. Starkweather favored a plan by which a uniform system of recruiting might be established in all the towns of the district. Hon. Augustus Brandagee spoke with great warmth, enumerating what Connecticut had done hitherto, and urging increased energy and sacrifice, now that the power of the rebellion was evidently waning.

Governor Buckingham spoke of the industry and diligence that would be necessary in all parts of the State if we wished to raise the requisite number of men, and stated that on the previous day he had received authority from the War Department to organize a regiment of colored infantry. The meeting adjourned for an afternoon session in the Town Hall, where, after stirring addresses, a county committee was appointed, with Hon. J. T. Wait at its head, " whose duty it should be to call one or more district mass meetings, and to take such other means, as a district committee, as may raise volunteers to be credited to the district." Every inducement in the way of bounties by the general government, State, and town was offered to secure enlistments.

The United States bounty amounted to three hundred and two dollars, that of the State was three hundred, while a veteran recruit received an additional offer of one hundred dollars from the general government. This made the soldiers' wages under this last call, equal to the best received in any branch of mechanical industry.

A second war-meeting for the county was held December ninth, in Breed Hall, and continued through the afternoon and evening — Governor Buckingham presiding. Thus far recruiting had met with indifferent success. There seemed to be no lack of determination as to vigorously prosecuting the war, but the men needed for military service could not now be so easily found. Norwich was beginning to experience the effect of her prompt contributions of volunteers hitherto made, while those who had not as yet offered their services, could with difficulty be spared from the positions they occupied. The war spirit of the town, however, was only the more thoroughly awakened, when confronted with this state of things. The enthusiasm produced by the turning victories of the war which had occurred in mid-summer, had not spent itself. All deemed it unwise to falter, now that the army of the Potomac had defeated Lee, and on the bloody field of Gettysburg proved its patient, indomitable prowess. General Grant's victory at Vicksburg, and the surrender of Port Hudson to General Banks' command, had put new heart and hope into the people, and made the prospects of final triumph sure. And yet, it will be recalled by many, how the work of recruiting dragged in the autumn days of this year of great Union victories. The novelty and romance of the war had disappeared. The people were impatient to have it ended, and in New England towns the best and most available material was already in the service.

There was a commendable zeal displayed to avoid another

draft, and to raise the town's quota in the more honorable and satisfactory way.

The selectmen and recruiting committees were cordially supported by the citizens in their efforts to raise the required enlistments. The result was in the end most creditable to the patriotism of Norwich, for not only was its quota of two hundred and six men filled up, but fifty-four additional recruits were secured, to apply on any subsequent call which the necessities of the military service might make imperative. The cost to the town of these recruits was twenty-three thousand one hundred dollars ($23,100). At the town meeting, January twenty-sixth, 1864, to which this report was rendered, provision was made for the enlistment of yet additional men, the feeling being wellnigh unanimous that Norwich must be kept in advance of her assigned quotas, and be thus prepared for any further demand for troops the authorities at Washington might make. At the close of the year 1863, Connecticut had furnished for the army in the field twenty-six thousand and twenty-eight (26,028) men. Of these, twenty thousand four hundred and twenty-six were for three years' service, or the war; five thousand six hundred and two for nine months' service, and twenty-three hundred and forty for three months' service. Every demand on the State for troops had been responded to with alacrity, and there was a surplus to its credit over all calls thus far made. In this particular, Norwich maintained her leading position, and her war-record up to this time reflected the highest honor upon those who had gone forth in her name.

The Governor, in his message to the legislature at its special session in the fall of this year, thus summed up the situation of public affairs: "There are reasons why we should entertain high hope for the future. The proof of the diminished resources and power of our enemies; the reasonable success which has followed the advance of our armies ; the highly prosperous condition of our national finances, hitherto unparalleled in the history of any people engaged in a protracted war ; the more just appreciation of our struggle by enlightened foreign powers, and their greater readiness to acquiesce in our right to settle internal differences without their intervention ; the recent clear manifestations of public sentiment against a peace, which shall recognize rights forfeited by perfidy and rebellion ; the conviction deepening in the minds of all classes of intelligent, philanthropic, and religious men, that we are not only gaining strength and permanency to our government, but that the treachery of its professed friends has become the divinely-appointed means of promoting the cause of humanity, and the universal triumph of right and justice ; — all these indications unite in urging us to renewed exertions to sustain the government, and inspire us with universal hope and confidence that we shall yet witness the execution of righteous laws over a united people throughout our undivided territory." On the whole there had been a steady gain made through this year. The Union armies, in the East and West, had achieved some signal victories ; the popular elections during the fall were an overwhelming rebuke to the disloyal factions in the North, that had sought to embarrass the government. In our own State, Governor Buckingham had been reëlected by a vote decisive enough to silence the peace-party, which made the rallying cry of their campaign, " No more war." The soldiers in the field sent in their earnest and emphatic protests against yielding the State to the control of those " for whom they could have only unmitigated scorn and contempt." It was apparent that public opinion had grown to the full stature of the proclamation of freedom, and had accepted the fact that slavery must die, and the Union be maintained by the stern overthrow of all the forcible resistance which had organized itself into this obstinate rebellion.

The "Richmond Examiner," of the date of December thirty-first, 1863, furnishes us the out-look presented to the rebels at this period. "To-day closes the gloomiest year of our struggle. No sanguine hope of intervention buoys up the spirit of the Confederate public as at the end of 1861. No brilliant victory like that of Fredericksburg encourages us to look forward to a speedy and successful termination of the war, as in the last weeks of 1862. . . . . The Confederacy has been cut in twain along the line of the Mississippi, and our enemies are steadily pushing forward their plans for bisecting the eastern moiety. No wonder, then, that the annual advent of the reign of mud is hailed by all classes with a sense of relief, — by those who think and feel aright, as a precious season to prepare for trying another fall with our potent adversary." While the rebels were thus quietly established in the welcome mud-state, the ever-memorable year departed, carrying with it, for us, the record, not only of splendid victories, but of the grand ratification, and support by the people, of the edict of emancipation. While our foes bewailed their condition, and sought to be penitent "for sins which had occasioned their disasters," the North stood erect, hopeful, the banners of its advancing armies carrying, not only the supremacy of law, but liberty to the bondsmen. With the suppression of rebellion, now felt by all to be a certain thing, was to disappear the last vestige of our national disgrace — American slavery. For us the year left only noblest memories, and "the advent of the reign of mud" was turned to good account by our forces, as they awaited the opening of the next campaign, flushed with victory, and full of confidence.

The enrollment act, which had aroused so much opposition, and furnished the grand theme for all disloyal orators throughout the North, was not unproductive of good results. According to the report of the Secretary of War, rendered to Congress in December, "the law has been enforced in twelve States, yielding fifty thousand soldiers, and ten millions of dollars for procuring substitutes." As the result of the President's emancipation edict, "over fifty thousand colored men (in the Gulf Department), are now organized, and the number will rapidly increase as our armies advance. The freed slaves make good soldiers, are excellently disciplined, and full of courage."

The President concluded his annual message to Congress in December, with these words: "Our chiefest care must still be directed to the army and navy, who have thus far borne their hard parts so nobly and so well. And it may be esteemed fortunate that in giving the greatest efficiency to these indispensable arms, we do also honorably recognize the gallant men, from commander to sentinel, who compose them, and to whom, more than to others, the world must be indebted for the home of freedom disenthralled, regenerated, enlarged, and perpetuated."

The nation joined with him in this deserved tribute to the men, whose courageous achievements had made the year one of progress, and had gathered about its close omens that put all in good heart, as they faced the duties and campaigns of the next (the fourth) year of the war.

VII.

1864.

" Work, patriots, for the Union,
   Till the hour of triumph comes !
  When the lusty shouts of victory
   Mingle with rolls of drums ;
  Till the shadowy clouds of Treason
   Have floated fore'er away,
  And the sunrise beams of hope and peace
   Tell of a brighter day."
                HOWELLS.

THE year 1864 opened full of promise. Every indication from the South pointed to a vigorous, desperate effort on the part of the rebel leaders to make amends for their recent disasters. The latter sought to bolster up their courage by anticipating the reduction of our armies, through the departure of veteran troops, whose term of service would soon expire. This idea was sedulously spread abroad by the rebel press, and it operated for a while as a stimulant of hope, and was one of the means employed to keep up the courage and confidence of the Southern people. The "Wilmington Journal" expressed the belief of the Confederate generals, when saying, "there is a feeling abroad in the land, that the great crisis of the war, the turning point in our fate, is fast approaching." The measures introduced and the laws passed by the Confederate Congress indicated the extremity to which they were reduced.

In January of this year the Congress at Richmond

enacted a law, that each person exempted from the draft should devote himself, and the labor he controlled, to the production of provisions and supplies. These last it required to be contributed for the use of the army, and besides the tithes called for by law, an additional tenth of all the bacon and pork produced was demanded. The sale of all these supplies for the army and families of soldiers, was provided for at designated prices by their Congress.

Up to about this period, no attempt had been made to organize colored persons in regiments for military service. The conscription act had done much to abolish those barriers of caste which had hitherto stood in the way of the government's calling on this loyal element of our population to serve in the army. Yet, in May, 1863, when application was made to the Chief of Police in New York for escort and protection for the Fifty-fourth Regiment colored volunteers of Massachusetts, in marching through Broadway, he responded, that they could not be protected from insult and probable assault. In less, however, than a year afterward, two New York Regiments of colored men, raised mainly through the efforts of the Loyal League, marched proudly down this same street amid the cheers of thousands of applauding citizens, and of all who witnessed their departure, not one ventured the insult of even a hiss.

At the special session of the Connecticut Legislature in November, 1863, a bill was passed for the enlistment and organization of colored volunteers. Massachusetts and Rhode Island had already led off in this direction, and now our own somewhat cautious, conservative State followed. The bill was bitterly denounced " as the greatest monstrosity ever introduced into Connecticut ; " as a provision " to let loose upon the helpless South a horde of African barbarians." The adjectives, however, of these excited opponents made little impression, and the bill passed in the lower House by a vote of one hundred and twenty to seventy-one; in the Senate, by a vote of fifteen to five.

This all showed the advance of public opinion, and relief was experienced, doubtless, by many nervous persons, when it was found that the world stood firm, even after these unprecedented and radical measures had been resorted to in this State, which rather bore the palm of being the steadiest in the "land of steady habits."

Governor Buckingham at once issued his call for colored volunteers for the Twenty-ninth Regiment, to serve for two years, or less. The bounty offered was six hundred dollars, and the pay and uniform the same as that of other soldiers. Each one of these items had been fought over in Congress, and our own General Assembly, and it was only after long and earnest discussion, to which the logic of events supplied some very convincing points, that a colored soldier was put on a par with any other, and treated as a citizen, and respected for his patriotism — a patriotism which in the service he was now invited to enter, exposed him to far greater risks and sufferings than it did his more favored brothers in arms. Candidates for commissions in this regiment were required to pass a severe examination before a board appointed by the War Department.

Norwich was represented in this regiment by David Torrance, Captain Company A, afterwards Lieutenant-colonel, and M. L. Leonard, First Lieutenant; E. P. Rogers, First Lieutenant Company F; C. H. Carpenter, First Lieutenant Company K, and not far from twenty privates. The regiment first joined the Ninth Army Corps, proceeding to Hilton Head and Beaufort, S. C.; thence was ordered North into the Tenth Corps.

The regiment was put into the trenches in front of Petersburg, where it continued for a month, doing hard service, when ordered to the rear only for rest, and the replenishing of its wardrobe. After a few days' quiet, it was again in motion, and was engaged in reconnoisances and skirmishes until November nineteenth, when it was stationed for garrison duty in certain detached forts on the New Market road, which were considered of great importance. In March, 1865, the Twenty-ninth was ordered to Fort Harrison, and appointed to watch the enemy's movements in its immediate front. On Saturday, April second, it witnessed the last rebel parade, and early the next day led in the advance on Richmond, Companies G and C, without doubt, entering the city before any other Union troops. The service it was from the first called to render was a tribute to its valor and efficiency.

Lieutenant-colonel Torrance, who was himself a capable and bold officer, has set forth in his report some of the trials of the regiment, wherein he claims for it the highest merit. "The poor rights of a soldier were denied to its members. Their actions were narrowly watched, and the slightest faults severely commented upon. In spite of all this, the negro soldier fought willingly and bravely; and with his rifle alone he has vindicated his manhood, and stands to-day as second in bravery to none." Such were the words in which Colonel Torrance bore his testimony to what he knew from his own experience.

In the Thirtieth Regiment, also colored volunteers, Norwich had as officers, First Lieutenants, Albert Latham, George Greenman (afterwards promoted Captain), De Laroo Wilson, Quartermaster, and about thirty privates. It was never filled to its maximum, four companies only being completed and organized. These were finally consolidated into the Thirty-first U. S. C. T. The regiment had a good record, and served with credit in many a hard engagement.

General Banks had, prior to this time, directed the recruitment of a Corps d'Afrique in his department, which was the earliest successful effort of the kind. In the First Regiment of this corps, Norwich had George R. Case, who was commissioned as Lieutenant, and rose to be Captain. He is said to have been the first Northern man to accept position as a line officer in a colored regiment. C. W. Converse was commissioned as Lieutenant in the Third Regiment of the same corps, and B. B. Blackman and Jesse Wilkinson were appointed to a Captaincy in the Forty-third Regiment U. S. C. T.

On the first of February of this year, the President modified his call of October, 1863, increasing the number of men asked for from three hundred thousand to five hundred thousand. The quota of the district was eighteen hundred and forty-three men; that of the town three hundred and twenty-nine. The latter, through surplus enlistments already credited, had but comparatively few more to furnish, and promptly met this apportionment.

On March ninth, President Lincoln presented to General Grant his commission as Lieutenant-general. The ceremony took place in the Cabinet Chamber, in the presence of many distinguished personages. On General Grant's entrance into the room, Mr. Lincoln rose and addressed him thus: —

"GENERAL GRANT: The nation's appreciation of what you have done, and its reliance upon you for what there remains to do in the existing great struggle, are now presented with this commission of a Lieutenant-general in the Army of the United States. With this high honor devolves upon you also a corresponding responsibility. As the country herein trusts you, so under God it will sustain you. I scarcely need to add, that with what I have spoken for the nation goes my own hearty personal concurrence."

To which General Grant responded : —

"Mr. President : I accept this high commission with gratitude for the high honor conferred. With the aid of the noble armies that have fought on so many fields for our common country, it will be my earnest endeavor not to disappoint your expectations. I feel the full weight of the responsibilities now devolving on me, and I know that if they are met, it will be due to those armies, and above all, to the favor of that Providence which leads both nations and men."

This appointment was made in accordance with an act of Congress creating the office of Lieutenant-general, and cordially approved by President Lincoln, he nominating General Grant for the position, and the Senate promptly confirming the nomination. On March seventeenth, General Grant assumed command of the Armies of the United States, and after a brief time spent in massing his troops, appointing new army corps commanders, the long-anticipated spring campaign opened. Henceforth there was unity of purpose, each army coöperating and acting under one supreme far-seeing leader, and among the tried and devoted generals under Grant, there were no rivalries or mean jealousies. "Where the first blow will fall," said the "Richmond Examiner," "when the two armies of Northern Virginia will meet each other face to face ; how Grant will try to hold his own against the master-spirit Lee, we cannot even surmise." The fighting was of unparalleled severity, and our advance was against great odds, but resistless.

On July eighteenth, Mr. Lincoln issued his proclamation for five hundred thousand more troops. The general advance of all our armies, and the sanguinary campaign which General Grant had opened, and was pushing with such a steady resistless determination, made it imperative on the government to keep the ranks full. The last grapple with the forces of rebellion had begun, and on the part of the new Commanding General there was an inflexible purpose to fight it through on the line on which he had begun. The call for troops was felt by all to be warranted by the military situation, and the public mind shared in the excitement which the splendid fighting along our eastern battle front had occasioned. Those wilderness engagements, among the most terrific and deadly struggles in the history of warfare, had stirred the whole nation. The stubborn strength of the Confederacy never showed itself so impressively as when it slowly gave way before the persistent onset of the reënforced Potomac Army hurled with crushing power upon the rebel force under Lee.

The quota of the district under this last call was sixteen hundred and one, and that of the town two hundred and seventy-three. At a town meeting held August twenty-third, it was unanimously voted —

"That the Selectmen of this town be and they are hereby authorized and instructed to employ persons to aid them in filling the quota of this town, under the last call of the President for volunteers, and to draw orders on the town treasurer for the payment of expenses."

The resurrection of the peace-men, and the discussions their plans gave rise to, had affected Norwich but little. Our citizens were never to any large extent equivocal in their support of the government, and now that the sternest fighting of the war was going on, they took hold heartily to see that the demands upon the town, in the way of recruits for the advancing armies, were complied with.

Norwich again succeeded in raising the quota, and the draft, which was to be the alternative, was made unnecessary. The assignment to the entire State was more than met, so that there was a credit to the latter large enough to release from any apportionment under the final call for three hundred thousand troops. It is but just to say that a large number of the substitutes furnished by those liable to be drafted, were not Connecticut residents, so that the disgrace attaching to the conduct of many of them does not belong to citizens of the State. The inducements held out for substitutes created a professional class under that name ; who, attracted by the bounties, found their way into Connecticut, and were mustered into service from the State, reflecting, in many instances, by their cowardice and unmilitary bearing, anything but honor on the Commonwealth.

How far Norwich was open to the impeachment of being affected by "the reckless quota-filling madness" that had become so rife, can hardly be determined. Her Selectmen and War Committee sought to secure only worthy men, and few, if any, conspicuous instances of their furnishing any others are now on record. The Provost-marshal, Captain I. H. Bromley, and his successor, Captain Theodore C. Kibbe, both did what they could to keep up the *morale* of the latest recruits provided by the town. The former, on resigning his office, hinted, in his characteristic vein, at some of the perplexities of the position, in the following pithy lines : " The retiring officer has had the satisfaction of knowing, that in the discharge of duties eminently calculated to 'make everybody hate you,' he has met with the most cheering success. Without a pang of regret, he bids an official but affectionate adieu to the gentlemanly substitute-brokers, who have always 'two or three first-rate men, of good moral character,' they want to get in ; to the patriotic selectmen and town agents, who would 'like to look over the lists, to see if James Henry Alexander's name is down ;' to the short-haired substitutes with a complication of diseases, 'who swear they are tough enough to stand marching and fighting;' to the timid young gentlemen from the rural districts, who have 'the rheumatism very bad in wet weather,' and have never been well since the war broke out; to the anxious parties who have for the past three or four weeks waylaid him in the streets, and opened their attack with a dreadful series of 'sposens;' to the aliens from Ireland, and the aliens from Germany, and the aliens who would be willing to swear they were aliens; to the mild-mannered men who 'couldn't understand it;' and those rough-spoken people 'who knew all about it;' to those, and to all of them, he bids a fond and affectionate farewell. He presumes they are all pleased with the change. He certainly is."

In the spring session of the General Assembly, the constitutional amendment providing for the extension of the elective franchise to the soldiers was passed. The amendment was in August following submitted to popular vote, and ratified by a large majority. New London County endorsed the measure by the emphatic vote of twenty-eight hundred and eight, to eleven hundred and eight, and the town vote of Norwich was equally pronounced in favor of this just and patriotic measure, standing seven hundred and fifty-three, to one hundred and fifty-six. Governor Buckingham had tersely presented the subject in his message, declaring, " that freemen who sustain and protect a government, by baring their bosoms to the deadly shafts of its enemies, should have an opportunity to express an opinion in respect to its policy, and the character and qualifications of its officers." Of course, a bitter opposition was made to the project, and all sorts of direful calamities prophesied in consequence of allowing the soldiers the right of suffrage. It was well added by one of the newspapers of the State, " Perhaps we are prejudiced, but it seems to us that a man who does nothing worse than shed his blood for the old flag, ought not, for so small an offense as that, to be disfranchised like a common thief."

To the excitement which had been produced by the unparalleled fighting kept up with a coolness and nerve which showed that a man of iron will was in command, was now superadded that occasioned by a vigorous and unusually bitter election campaign. Americans seem unable to live without the spice and venom of an occasional political contest, in which men turn into pepper-cruets, and the whole country becomes involved in a sort of domestic wrangle. To have one precipitated on the country at this juncture of affairs, was extremely unfortunate. There was little time or strength that could be spared for the ordinary tactics of such an important political election, as this one approaching undoubtedly was. Still the gravity of the interests involved made it necessary to act with wisdom and firmness, and the re-appearance of the, to loyal citizens, ever-provoking "peace-men," put a new earnestness into those who had at heart the success of the government in its yet pending conflict.

Fortunately all the attempted peace projects proved abortive, and the battle at the polls was decisively fought out in November of this year, resulting in the overwhelming re-election of Mr. Lincoln. Norwich stood true to the Union cause, giving a majority of nearly three hundred.

The President, in his message to the thirty-eighth Congress, alluded in these words to the issues thus settled by the suffrages of the people: " Judging by the recent canvass and its result, the purpose of the people within the loyal States to maintain the integrity of the Union, was never more firm, nor more nearly unanimous than now. The extraordinary calmness and good order with which the millions of voters met, and mingled at the polls, give strong assurance of this. Not only all those who supported the

Union ticket, so called, but a great majority of the opposing party also, may be fairly claimed to entertain, and to be actuated by, the same purpose. It is an unanswerable argument to this effect, that no candidate for any office whatever, high or low, has ventured to seek votes on the avowal that he was for giving up the Union. There have been much impugning of motives, and much heated controversy as to the proper means and best mode of advancing the Union cause ; but, on the distinct issue of Union or no Union, the politicians have shown their instinctive knowledge that there is no diversity among the people. In affording the people the fair opportunity of showing to one another, and to the world, this firmness, and unanimity of purpose, the election has been of vast value to the national cause."

Throughout the canvass Mr. Lincoln had sought to disguise not the fact that the war was for *Liberty and Union*. At this time he stated there were nearly two hundred thousand colored men under arms. " There are men base enough to propose to me to return to slavery our black warriors of Port Hudson and Olustee. Should I do so," said he, with indignation glowing in every feature of his sad resolute face, " I should deserve to be damned in time and eternity. Come what may, I will keep faith with the black man."

We have spoken of the encouragement the rebels took in looking forward to this year's campaign, founded on the anticipated depletion of our armies through the expiration of the term of service for which large numbers were enlisted. This was holding Northern patriotism at a low rate, and miscalculated the purpose of these very soldiers to "see the war through." Provost-marshal-general Fry returned figures that must have surprised those who had thus predicted a thinning out of our ranks. From May first, 1863, to January first, 1864, according to his report, our army was reënforced with forty thousand men from the draft. Up to

February of this year, two hundred and sixty-eight thousand volunteers were enlisted, one hundred thousand veterans reënlisted, and twenty-five thousand men organized into an invalid corps, releasing that number of able-bodied men from camp and garrison duty, for the more important service in the field.

The veteran reënlistments, which kept up the strength and character of the Connecticut Regiments in the field, amounted during the year to three thousand six hundred and forty-seven. These were secured through recruiting agents sent to the various organizations, with authority to offer the veteran's bounty of seven hundred and two dollars, and a furlough. The continuance in the ranks of those who had come to understand somewhat of the art of war, was a proof of their patriotism, adding immensely to the effectiveness of the forces in the service of the government. The regiments in this way kept up the high repute which had gained for them a particular celebrity, and made them justly proud of the position they had attained. Colonel Selden and Captain Gallup were detailed by the Governor to visit the Connecticut Regiments in and about New Orleans for this purpose, where they succeeded in reënlisting a large proportion of those hitherto connected with them.

On the return of these veteran regiments to the State for their promised furlough, they were received with overwhelming demonstrations of rejoicing and affection. Public receptions were awarded them, and welcoming addresses from prominent citizens, only voiced the popular admiration for these heroes of many a hard fought fight. They were greeted with an enthusiasm, which the fact that they were home for a brief respite, only served to deepen. Our people had become accustomed to exhibitions of popular feeling on witnessing departing regiments; but it was a new experience this of welcoming home those whose tattered banners and bronzed faces told the pathetic story of their sufferings and achievements.

> "I saw the soldiers come to-day
> From battle-fields afar;
> No conqueror rode before their way
> On his triumphal car;
> But captains like themselves on foot,
> And banners sadly torn;
> All grandly eloquent, though mute,
> In pride and glory borne."

The Governor, in paying a well-deserved tribute to the veterans of the renowned Thirteenth, gave expression to the feelings of all patriot hearts, when he said, "Let me tell you that so long as this heart beats, it will beat with love and gratitude for the men who have offered themselves as a bulwark to the nation. We know the dangers which you have braved have not dampened your ardor, nor quenched your patriotism. . . . . Those at home appreciate your services and your devotion." There was something truly grand in the popular enthusiasm these regiments awakened in the people, and on returning to take part in what was felt to be the death-grapple with the rebellion, they were strengthened anew for their sacrificial service by the benediction of their fellow-citizens, and the grasp of loving hands.

Norwich had a share in the welcome extended to these furloughed regiments. On March twenty-ninth, the Eighteenth, mustering about six hundred strong, under Major Peale, came home for a short visit. In consequence of delay at New York, it did not reach the city till near midnight, but even at that unseasonable hour was warmly received by the waiting crowd, and having been escorted to the hall, where a bountiful collation had been provided, was formally welcomed by Mayor Greene. The regiment had seen hard service, and borne with steadfast courage the reverses that had attended our arms in the Shenandoah Valley. The casualties of battle had thinned its ranks, and many of its members were still in prison; but this only added to the interest with which our citizens regarded the splendid regiment they had sent out amid such proud rejoicings, two years before. The city had watched with deepest solicitude its varying fortunes, and when it took its departure for the field again, it was greeted with every expression of the people's good-will. Halting before the residence of the Governor, the latter made a short address, congratulating Major Peale on the good service which the regiment had rendered while under his command, and expressing the hope that the imprisoned officers might soon rejoin their comrades, and share in the conflicts that awaited them.

Norwich had given to the war its best blood, and while many a brave citizen was brought back for the last rites of sepulture, this was the only returning regiment it had been permitted publicly to welcome. It was with special gratitude too, and joy, that it greeted the return of many officers and privates, who held honored positions in the veteran regiments Hartford and New Haven had publicly received. All our citizens could join in the words addressed by one of the speakers to these furloughed veterans: "We hoped for great things from you, and I proclaim before you, that our hopes have not been disappointed. We are proud of you."

The year closed with a most decided gain on the part of the Union Armies. Grant's campaign had been the most sanguinary of any thus far, but it had accomplished in the main his end. He aimed to overpower and crush by sheer force the rebel army, and he had effectually done it. He had forced it back, at great cost of life 'tis true, and made it take the position of an army defending the rebel capital. The power of the Confederates never received such damaging blows, as in this campaign, which began on the Rapidan, and ended in front of Petersburg, and across the Weldon Railroad.

Some idea of what our armies accomplished in the last ten months of the campaign, will throw some light on the losses of the rebels : —

Guns captured, three hundred and fifty-four.

Total number of prisoners taken, forty-four thousand nine hundred and seventy-three.

Rebel generals put *hors du combat*, twenty-five, not including those wounded in connection with Lee's army.

"Our late reverses have done much towards preparing our people for extreme sacrifices," said the "Richmond Sentinel," indicating the despair that had settled upon the Confederate leaders. At the close of 1864, there was no longer any doubt of the speedy and successful issue of the war. The year had been one of hard fighting, but of great material successes. Norwich had lost some brave officers in the Virginia campaign, and the regiments of the State had held advanced positions in the Potomac Army, suffering in consequence quite severely. The year, however, departed, leaving all full of hope, and the signs of the long prayed for termination seemed at hand.

VIII.

1861–1865.

THE whole number of men furnished by Connecticut during the war, for the service of the United States, for the several terms of service, of all arms, and inclusive of army and navy, was fifty-four thousand eight hundred and eighty-two. The following is the summary, according to careful count of the rosters of the various regiments and organizations, and represents the actual number of men in service from the State.

Three Months' Service.

Three Regiments, Infantry,	2,402

Nine Months' Service.

One (Third) Independent Battery, Light Artillery,	137
Six Regiments Infantry (22d, 23d, 25th, 26th, 27th, 28th),	5,602

Three Years' Service.

One (1st) Squadron of Cavalry,	166
One (1st) Regiment of Cavalry,	2,611
Two (1st and 2d) Regiments Heavy Artillery,	6,086
Two (1st and 2d) Batteries, Light Artillery,	516
Seventeen Regiments Infantry (5th, 6th, 7th, 8th, 9th, 10th, 11th, 12th, 13th, 14th, 15th, 16th, 17th, 18th, 19th, 20th, 21st),	23,727

CONNECTICUT'S CONTRIBUTION TO UNION ARMIES. 123

Two Years' Service, or less.

Two Regiments Infantry, C. T. (29th and 30th),	1,690
Veterans. Reënlistment in the field, . . .	3,647
Volunteer enlistments in the United States Navy, .	2,135
Enlistments in United States Army and Veteran Reserve Corps, ...	1,044
Recruits obtained in Rebel States, . .	1,156
Substitutes, for enrolled men, not drafted, .	3,849
Substitutes, for drafted men (of draft of 1864),	89
Drafted men (by draft of 1864), . .	15
Total,	54,872

Reducing the above credits to the standard of three years, the account of the State stands (taking Adjutant-general Morse's figures) thus, not including the three months' men.

Nine Months' Men,	5,602	Equal to	1,400
One Year Men,	529	" "	176
Two Years' Men,	25	" "	16
Three Years' Men,	44,142	" "	44,142
Four Years' Men,	26	" "	34
Not known,	1,804	" "	1,804
Total,			47,572

Of the enlisted men connected with the various regiments and organizations, one thousand and eighty-four (1,084) were killed. Six hundred and eighty-three (683) died from wounds. Three thousand and eighty-nine (3,089) died from disease. Three hundred and eighty-nine (389) were reported as missing. Five thousand four hundred and fifty-one (5,451) were honorably discharged prior to the mustering of the regiments with which connected. Four thousand three hundred and sixty-one (4,361) were discharged for disability. Forty-nine were dishonorably discharged. Fourteen hundred and eighty-eight (1,488) were transferred to Veteran Reserve Corps. Twenty-seven (27) were executed. Six thousand two hundred and eighty-one (6,281) deserted. Thirty-five (35) were drowned. Nineteen (19) were taken out of their regiments by civil authority. Fifty-six (56) were dropped from the rolls. From these statistics, it appears that one thousand three hundred and twenty-three (1,323) more men died of disease, than were killed or died from effects of wounds received. The whole number of commissioned officers furnished by Connecticut during the war was nineteen hundred and sixty-two (1,962), of whom, eighty-four (84) were killed, forty-two (42) died in consequence of wounds received while in the service, and seventy-nine (79) died from disease.

TABULAR EXHIBIT

OF THE LOSSES SUSTAINED BY EACH REGIMENT AND MILITARY ORGANIZATION IN SERVICE

	Cav.	1 Art.	2 Art.	1 Bat.	2 Bat.	5	6	7	8	9	10	11	12	13	14	15	16	17	18	20	21	22	23	24	25	26	27	28	Total
Killed in Action	24	26	143	–	1	73	43	90	72	5	57	35	50	37	132	15	40	29	52	90	29	–	3	11	14	15	28	9	1084
Died of Wounds	8	25	80	1	–	24	46	44	40	1	54	41	16	13	65	15	24	15	14	37	32	–	4	4	13	30	17	9	682
Died of Disease	125	164	186	21	18	82	104	179	132	240	152	165	188	129	169	143	224	24	72	77	108	20	44	47	56	72	22	65	3082
Total of Casualties	157	219	409	22	20	183	208	313	244	246	268	241	254	174	366	173	294	128	138	204	169	20	51	63	83	117	67	83	4855
Aggregate of Regt.	2611	3367	7740	272	220	1782	1605	1057	2000	1285	1844	2127	1408	1492	2712	1642	1693	1175	1258	1281	1045	928	848	658	841	810	829	625	38540
PERCENT of LOSS*	.000	.007	.053	.081	–	.041	.126	.085	.058	.001	.031	.016	.035	.021	.077	–	.042	.025	.043	.058	.023	–	–	.021	.014	.018	.034	.014	.025
Killed Died of Wounds	.003	.006	.031	–	–	.016	.027	.042	.022	–	.032	.019	.011	.008	.038	–	.027	.012	.012	.029	.033	–	–	–	.016	.037	.021	.014	.017
Died of Disease	.047	.047	.068	.007	.083	.045	.071	.110	.066	.189	.082	.078	.133	.086	.098	.088	.201	.069	.066	.061	.103	.022	.053	.068	.066	.088	.027	.097	.08
Total	.060	.066	.153	.075	.091	.10	.12	.296	.122	.192	.145	.113	.138	.116	.215	.105	.277	.10	.115	.128	.161	.022	.066	.093	.102	.144	.08	.132	.126
BATTLES†	27	13	5	10	4	11	7	89	11	4	23	10	7	9	25	4	5	4	7	10	7	–	1	3	3	2	3	1	–

This percentage is based on the time each Regiment was in service, and not on their several times reduced to a three years' basis.

* Percentage of Loss per Regiment, based on the actual time each was in service.   † Number of Battles, according to Regimental Reports.

Among the general officers furnished by Connecticut, numbering in all thirty, Lyon, Mansfield, and Sedgwick were killed on the field of battle. The aggregate loss to the State of commissioned officers is reckoned at two hundred and twenty-nine.

The total number of men inclusive of unassigned recruits and substitutes, furnished by Norwich for the war, for the several lesser terms of service, of all arms, not counting those in the Navy or those enlisting in other States, was over thirteen hundred ; of these, one hundred and fifty-five (155) lost their lives, thirty-six (36) being killed in battle, one (1) was accidentally shot, thirty-one (31) died of wounds, and eighty-seven (87) of disease contracted while in service, of whom twenty-two (22) met death in rebel prisons.

The whole number of commissioned officers furnished by Norwich was one hundred and fifty-five (155). This includes several who were natives of the town, but who, having removed to other parts of the country, received their appointments from other States, and also several officers in colored regiments, or in other general service, who were commissioned by the United States. The number credited to Norwich, and commissioned by the State, was about one hundred and sixteen (116), of whom thirteen (13) lost their lives, five (5) on the battle-field, five (5) died of wounds, and three (3) of disease.

The whole number of men apportioned to Connecticut under the different quotas, reduced to the three years' standard, was forty-one thousand four hundred and eighty-three (41,483). The number furnished by the State, reducing all the different terms of service to the three years' standard, was forty-eight thousand one hundred and eighty-one (48,181), which shows a surplus of six thousand six hundred and ninety-eight (6,698) in three years' men, without reference to the quota under the call of December.

1864. Under this last call no troops were required to be furnished by the State, as no quota was assigned by the government.

It is a satisfaction to be able to record the fact that Norwich raised its quota under the several apportionments made by the Adjutant-general, and when the war closed, she had a surplus in her favor above the different calls made upon her, to furnish her proportion of the troops required by the General Government. In the early part of the war the town contributed from the resident population to the service of the country. The raising of volunteers was under its own management until July, 1863, up to which time through liberal bounties and the popular maintenance of the war-spirit, there was no lack of enlistments. After the above date the recruiting business was conducted by the provost-marshal of the district, and substitutes and hired recruits were largely procured to meet the call upon the town for men. Notwithstanding the largely increased expenses of the town, necessitated by the war, there was no curtailment in the usual appropriations for schools, for the poor, for general public and civic improvements. There was never a more generous spirit displayed in providing for all that related to the town and city's needs, than during the years of this gigantic civil strife. The war, in fact, created for Norwich, as it did for other places, new business enterprises, and there was even an augmented industry which gave to these trying years the appearance of outward thrift and prosperity. City improvements were projected as in ordinary times, and the citizens, while constantly called upon to give, were able to meet, in the spirit of unquestioned liberality, all the appeals which came to them. Private and public charity received a new impulse, and all classes learned the great lesson of self-sacrificing benevolence. One of the brightest chapters of the war, is the one which contains the history of the

Nation's offerings to general benevolent purposes. In no other way was so strikingly displayed the earnestness and ability of the people, not only to meet the military necessities of the conflict itself, immense as they were, but to provide as they did, with marvelous and unstinted liberality, for the usual and exceptional charities of those crucial years.

The city, during the war, became quite noted for its armories. These were very extensive, and for the time added largely to the industrial enterprise and growth of the town.

A writer in "Harpers' Magazine" in 1864, describing the activity displayed in this line, thus wrote concerning what was doing in this branch of labor: —

"We bid the reader to Norwich, rather than to some other of the many similar enterprises which have grown up in various parts of the land, because the works there, are of all others, the first in the magnitude of their operation, and in the assurance of perpetuity, when minor establishments may, and no doubt will, pass with the passing of the necessity which has called them into existence.

"The ease and celerity with which the capitalists and artisans of Norwich, and of so many other places, have at a moment's call, turned from their looms and their spindles of a life-time, to so untried, so intricate, and so difficult a lot as that of the manufacture of arms, is scarcely less astonishing, than is the wonderful success which has followed their efforts.

"That the national works, as those at Springfield, should be, as they have been, trebled even in extent, as soon as the enlargement was required, is highly creditable to the public capacity and energy; but how much more commendable and gratifying is it, that such an enterprise — guaranteed in its result and reward by the treasury of a great nation — has been in a degree more than rivaled by individual effort, and that effort made boldly in the dark, almost without precedent, and in a new and most difficult labor.

"The capacity of the Norwich Arms Company is greater than was that of the government foundries at Springfield, before their extensive enlargement at the commencement of the war, and is nearly half as great as is that of these works, now in their increased extent. With their present machinery and accommodations, the Company are able to produce about four hundred finished muskets per day, or two hundred of the Springfield arm, and as many more of the new and beautiful breach-loading rifle. Just now, as we write, the works are producing about twelve hundred muskets, three thousand bayonets, and two thousand locks, per week, besides rifles and carbines. The product of the works in their present capacity would reach a value of nearly a quarter of a million of dollars annually, in their yield of four hundred muskets or other arms daily, at the government price of twenty dollars each."

In addition to this large armory, there was an equally enterprising establishment for making pistols, under the charge of Smith & Wesson, and another quite as prosperous, run by Allen, Thurber, & Co., besides the Bacon Arms Company, which is the only one that has continued its manufacturing in Norwich. In fact, during the war Norwich showed more thrift than ever before or since. Of course much of the business was such as the military necessities of the times had created, and could hardly be expected to be permanent, or always as remunerative. Still it is a matter of regret that some branches of industry were permitted to be removed hence, to places which they have helped to build up, and where they have proved of permanent and pecuniary advantage.

Norwich, as it appeared in war-years, was indeed "a wide-awake little town, as vociferous in sounds of busy and thriving industry as any place of its size in the good old State of steady habits, or in all the thronged length and breadth of Yankeedom." Its brilliant war record, the public gifts of its citizens for patriotic and charitable purposes, the deep interest felt in the success of the war itself, and the readiness to contribute in any way to that grand result, all stand as memorials of the energy and loyal zeal of the town.

IX

1861–1865.

NAVY.

> "And is the old flag flying still,
>   That o'er your Fathers flew,
> With bands of white and rosy light,
>   And fields of starry blue ?
> Aye ! look aloft ! its folds full oft
>   Have braved the roaring blast,
> And still shall fly when from the sky
>   This black typhoon has past ! "
>
> O. W. HOLMES.

THE records of the Navy during the war will constitute one of the proudest chapters in its history. At the breaking out of the rebellion it had only ninety-four war vessels of all classes, designed to carry two thousand four hundred and fifteen (2,415) guns. Only forty-three of these ships were in commission. The deep-seated patriotism and

generously proffered resources of the loyal masses of the country, provided in the speediest possible time a volunteer army equal to the demands of the unprecedented emergency.

The Navy, however, had practically to be created, and this could not be done with the same rapidity. And yet in a very brief period of time, the deficiency in this arm of the service was supplied, and six hundred vessels were provided, which maintained not only an unrelaxed blockade from the Chesapeake to the Rio-Grande, but penetrated and patrolled our rivers with a flotilla of gun-boats, and captured blockade-runners, chiefly with British owners, to the value of thirty millions of dollars ($30,000,000). Over two hundred warships were constructed, and four hundred and eighteen merchant vessels (of which three hundred and thirteen were steamers), were converted into ships of war. There were fifty-one thousand five hundred men in the naval service at the close of the rebellion, as contrasted with seven thousand six hundred at the beginning.

The ordnance of the department was by mechanical and inventive skill greatly improved, and the "Monitor," which rendered such timely and unexpected service, was among the products of this awakened attention to the navy. By the latter our armies were nobly supported in the engagements on the coast, and the Mississippi River, as well as at Forts Henry, Donelson, and Shiloh. There were no braver deeds performed than by officers and men in the naval service, and to them was largely due the successful termination of the war itself. The loyalty of those in the navy was of the noblest type, and though there were defections on the part of officers at the beginning of the rebellion, numerous enough to occasion embarrassment and dishonor, yet the subsequent service rendered by those who remained true to the flag, reinforced by volunteer recruits, made ample atonement. It is but justice to these gallant men, and those associated with and under them, to make in every possible way this public acknowledgment.

Less has been written concerning the exploits of the Navy and Marine Corps, than of the volunteer armies, resulting from the fact, that the several States have not shown that interest in the former that they had in the regiments composing the latter, the roster of whose officers and men they were careful to preserve.

We know not the names of those who served in the navy, but the soldiers who enlisted, the officers commissioned in the army, had their respective military records kept for them, through the Adjutant-generals of the several States, and perpetuated by means of the carefully compiled and published registers of the volunteer forces raised.

When the proclamation announcing the blockade of the Southern ports was issued, the Navy Department was compelled to prepare for service all the public vessels which were lying dismantled at the various yards. Vessels of every kind that could be purchased, or chartered, were hurriedly collected, divided into two squadrons, and placed along the coast. One of these two, denominated the Atlantic Blockading Squadron, under command of Flag-officer Charles Stringham, had for its field of operations, the entire coast, from the eastern line of Virginia to Cape Florida. The other, the Gulf Squadron, under Flag-officer William Mervine operated from Cape Florida westward to the Rio Grande.

The task of blockading the coast was unattractive, and required the most unceasing vigilance, and yet was carried out with remarkable strictness, and maintained to the close of the war with increasing efficiency. The expedition to Hatteras Inlet in August, 1861, was the first of a series of naval engagements, which resulted in the reoccupation of important points along the seaboard. The Atlantic Blockading Squadron was subsequently divided into two: the North Atlantic Blockading Squadron, to guard the coast of Virginia and North Carolina, under Captain Louis M. Goldsborough ; and the South Atlantic Blockading Squadron, under Captain S. F. Dupont, to watch the coast from the northern boundary of South Carolina to Cape Florida. The Gulf Squadron was likewise divided into the Eastern and Western Blockading Squadrons ; the latter was assigned to duty on the coast, from and including Pensacola to the Rio Grande, and was intrusted to Captain D. G. Farragut.

In addition to these four large squadrons, it was found necessary for the navy to place a flotilla on the lower Potomac, and also one on the Mississippi and its tributaries.

By all of these squadrons was conspicuous service rendered, and some of their exploits will rank among the most brilliant in the annals of naval warfare. The North Atlantic Blockading Squadron captured Hatteras Inlet, August twenty-eighth, 1861, General Butler commanding the co-operating military force. Roanoke Island was taken on February eighth, 1862, Goldsborough commanding the fleet, and General Burnside the army. Fort Fisher fell before the combined attack of this squadron under Rear-admiral Porter, January fifteenth, 1865, one of Connecticut's most brilliant soldiers, General Terry, leading the auxiliary land forces.

By the South Atlantic Blockading Squadron, Port Royal was captured, November seventh, 1861, Captain Dupont in charge of the fleet, and General T. W. Sherman of the army. The West Gulf Blockading Squadron, under Farragut, bombarded successfully in April, 1862, the forts guarding New Orleans, which led to the surrender of the city to the troops under General Butler. The defenses of Mobile Bay were captured August fifth, 1864, General Gordon Granger directing the military force.

The Mississippi Squadron, under Connecticut's gallant Admiral A. H. Foot, took part in the capture of Fort Henry, February sixth, 1862 ; under C. H. Davis, secured possession of Memphis, June sixth, 1862 ; under Porter, made the famous passage of the Vicksburg batteries, April sixth, 1863. These by no means exhaust the achievements of the navy, for our ships of war were everywhere managed with great skill and courage, and the squadrons, whether engaged in cruising, or in such naval battles like those named, did honor to the nation's flag. The service rendered was of a most varied character, and so effective too, as to entitle this arm to the praise and gratitude of the whole country. Had it not been for the friendly help, and unlawful coöperation Great Britain afforded to rebel privateers and blockade runners, as well as its peculiar affection for Confederate pirates who preyed upon our commerce in ships built in English ship-yards, and fitted out in violation of all existing international law, the Confederacy would not have lasted as long as it did, nor won such infamy for its piratical deeds on the high seas. Of this England is probably now convinced, and the recent Geneva award is but a mild assessment of the damage occasioned us, for which she was proved before the world to be culpably responsible.

The Confederate Navy was made up at first of officers formerly in the United States service, who at the breaking out of the rebellion resigned, thus hoping to escape the charge, which was none the less deserved, of being traitors. At that early period, our government had not gotten over its fatal tendency to deal leniently, so that the resignations of these runaways were accepted, instead of having their names stricken in ignominy from the naval rolls they had disgraced. These were the first to offer themselves to the

Confederate Navy, and though educated, honored, and cared for by our government, in the hour of its peril, they renounced its service, its flag, and their fealty, to tender their service to those plotting its overthrow. To the honor of the North, it may be said, that by far the greater proportion of traitors were from border States, or else from the "sunny South." And the moiety of Northern officers that became turncoats, had lived just long enough in Dixie to have their loyalty endangered.

So far as Norwich was concerned, comparatively few entered the navy. Though near the sea-board, and with more or less interest in this arm of the service, our volunteers preferred enlisting in the army. The State, however, had a distinguished representation in the navy, as the names of Foote, Lanman, Gregory, Rodgers, and others, abundantly show. The number of her citizens holding commissions during the war is estimated as high as three hundred.

Our town stands credited with eighty-nine men, who enlisted at various times, and were mustered into the naval service of the country. Several of these received honorable appointments as commanders, paymasters, and masters of vessels. They maintained the reputation for courage and serviceableness, which those who had entered the army had won.

The names of many of the naval recruits cannot now be obtained, so that the roster of those in this department must necessarily be somewhat incomplete. We are able to present only brief accounts of most of those who enlisted in the navy, and regret exceedingly that we cannot furnish a full list of all who served on any of our ships of war, and who counted on the quota of volunteers raised by the town for the national service. Once or twice during the war, efforts were made by the town officers to secure, through inquiry and advertisement, the names of those who entered the navy, but they were unavailing. We subjoin as perfect a list as it was possible to make out, believing that it is complete, so far, at least, as containing the names of those who held naval commissions.

JOSEPH LANMAN was the ranking officer in the service of the country from this town. He was born in Norwich July eighteenth, 1811, and from personal predilections entered the navy at an early age. He received the appointment of midshipman, January first, 1825, and was ordered to join the frigate " Macedonian," of the Brazil Squadron, in 1827. In 1830, he was attached to the sloop " Peacock," of the West India Squadron. Promoted to Passed-midshipman June fourth, 1831, he next joined the schooner " Dolphin," Pacific Squadron. Serving in these early years with great fidelity and skill, he rose steadily by promotion through the various grades, until attaining his present well-earned rank of Rear-admiral.

His distinguished service extends over a period of forty-eight years, and is one in which the town takes a just pride. One of its own boys, he has now for nearly a half century been in the government's service, filling every position he won, with stainless honor, and has come back now to his native place because reaching the age with which, according to naval rules, active service ends. An officer of wide experience, acknowledged courage, and devoted patriotism, he served through the years of the late war, without having a choice as to place or duty, cheerfully obeying orders, and flying from his vessel's mast-head the flag that he helped to make respected at home and abroad.

In 1848, Admiral (then Lieutenant) Lanman was complimented by being made the bearer of dispatches from the commanding officer of the Pacific Squadron to the authorities at Washington. He was assigned to special duty in 1849-51, and in 1864-65, commanded the frigate "Minnesota," of the North Blockading Squadron. The last years of his active service were spent in command of the South Atlantic Squadron, cruising off the coast of Brazil.

Some of our citizens who have watched with admiring interest his long and honorable career, remember him when as midshipman he began his naval service. Among the episodes of this early period of his life was the following. He had been promised by one, who from the first took no ordinary interest in his course, a sword, whenever he received his first commission. The latter came to him in 1835, when he was commissioned lieutenant. His friend, not forgetful of the promise made to the youth when beginning his public life, immediately took measures to make it good, and finding what the "Regulations of the Navy" permitted, procured an officer's sword and belt, and dispatched them to him with the accompanying note:—

NORWICH, *June* 12, 1837.

MY DEAR SIR,— Not having forgotten the pleasure I promised myself some years since, on your entering the United States Navy (January first, 1825), of presenting to you a sword on your receiving a commission, I seized the earliest convenient opportunity after learning the fact, to procure one, which I should have presented ere this, had not my frequent absence from home, and your infrequent visits to your friends prevented. I learnt on inquiry that I was not at liberty to indulge my taste, but must be governed by the rules and regulations of the Navy Department in the selection.

Will you please accept the accompanying sword and belt, which I trust will *only be used in self-defense, and in the defense of your country*, and receive assurances of regard, with which I have the pleasure to be,

Your friend and obedient servant,
G. L. PERKINS.

Lieutenant JOSEPH LANMAN, *U. S. Navy.*

To this note the youthful Lieutenant replied with that courteousness of speech and manner which through all these years of service have characterized his intercourse with his fellow officers and men, as well as with those whom he met at home and abroad:—

NORWICH, CONN., 13 *June*, 1837.

DEAR SIR, — Your very friendly note of yesterday, together with the sword and belt, I have duly received. For these valued testimonials of your esteem be pleased to receive my unfeigned thanks. Should our common country call me to duty in its defense, be assured, my dear sir, that the recollection of the terms of your very flattering note will inspire a confidence and zeal in the service of no ordinary cast. I need not assure you that a sword presented by a friend and fellow townsman will not be suffered to tarnish while in the possession of your

Obedient servant,
JOSEPH LANMAN, *U. S. Navy*.

COL. G. L. PERKINS, *Norwich*.

That sword is still a valued memento of a friendship yet green, and has not been more sacredly kept, than the honor and loyalty, which so long ago plighted, have now been tested by almost fifty years' service to the country. We have here the promise of the young officer, with life and its experiences before him, and its fulfillment, as seen in the completed record of the Rear-admiral, and both are matters in which Norwich has no ordinary interest.

Naval officers have not a choice of where, or how they shall serve, and to some, even in time of war, it falls to do duty where it is not publicly noticed, and where there is opportunity for little more than fidelity, and the patient accomplishment of what is ordered.

The second attack on Fort Fisher afforded a signal proof that the man who would do his duty well, whether it was of a conspicuous nature or not, could bear himself with distinction, where the service brought him under the more immediate notice of the people.

In this great naval engagement, the most brilliant one of the whole war, Admiral (then Commodore) Lanman was selected to lead the second line in his flag-ship, "Minnesota."

The fleet and land forces on transports arrived off the fort, January thirteenth, 1865, and the next day, under cover of the guns of the former, the troops effected a landing. On the fifteenth the combined attack by land and sea was made. At nine A. M., the squadron was signaled to attack in three lines, and by eleven all the vessels were in position. Each had opened fire as it took its place in line, and the bombardment was kept up furiously all day. By three o'clock the troops were in readiness, and the signal to change the direction of the firing was given, when the guns were turned on the upper batteries away from the point where the assault was to be made.

All the steam whistles were blown, when the troops and sailors and marines dashed ahead, nobly vying with each other to reach the parapet. The sailors were armed with cutlasses and pistols, and were expected to treat the fort as a vessel, and board it. They went forward promptly on the sea-side, pushing boldly up to the fort, until checked by a murderous fire of grape and canister. Notwithstanding this hot fire, officers and men in the lead rushed on; some even reached the parapet, a larger number got as far as the ditch. While the assault on this side was stayed, Terry with his troops came up on the other side, and as the attention of the rebels was diverted, effected a lodgment in the fort, gaining two traverses. The latter are immense bomb-proofs, about sixty feet long, fifty feet wide, and twenty feet high, numbering seventeen in all. Here our men, as Porter in his official report says, "fought like lions," fighting their way inch by inch, chasing the rebels from traverse to traverse, and continuing this hand-to-hand conflict till far into the night. When the capture was signaled to the fleet, the men on the various vessels joined in making the welkin ring with their repeated and hearty cheers. Thus ended one of the most remarkable battles on record, resulting in the capture of Fort Fisher, pronounced stronger than the Malakoff tower, which defied so long the combined power of England and France. Seventy-five guns, some of them superb rifle pieces of very heavy calibre, fell into our hands, with twenty-five hundred prisoners, including two rebel generals.

It was on the whole the most decisive *coup-de-main* of the war, brilliantly executed, and of immense practical advantage. In no other engagement did the army and navy coöperate so harmoniously, while the fourteen hundred sailors and marines bore themselves with dauntless courage, losing three hundred and nine, in killed, wounded, and missing. The forty-four vessels poured an incessant fire on the fort, delivering hot shot and shell at the rate of four a minute for eight hours, expending in the entire bombardment fifty thousand shell.

Taking into account the character and number of the vessels, the size and calibre of their guns, and number of men, it was the greatest naval armament ever brought together, and the result was the grandest ever achieved by the combined forces of army and navy.

In this action Commodore Lanman detailed from his vessel two hundred and forty officers and men to join the assaulting column; and reported, concerning those remaining, "every one performed his duty to the utmost of his ability; the working and practice of the guns could not have been better, and many excellent shots were made." He also superintended the firing of his vessels, witnessing how they were managed during the engagement, and personally directed the force under him. It was a most fearful bombardment, and at its close Commodore Lanman's beard, hair and clothes were completely covered over with saltpetre.

Admiral Porter, in his official report, thus speaks of Commodore Lanman: "Commodore Joseph Lanman was selected to lead the line, consequently he led into action. I was much pleased with the way in which he handled his ship, and fired throughout the action; the whole affair on his part being conducted with admirable judgment and coolness. I recommend him to the consideration of the Department, as one on whom they can place the utmost reliance, place him in any position." In addition to this public notice of his bearing in this battle, Admiral Porter addressed to him the following private letter, expressing his personal appreciation of his gallant conduct in this engagement, and acknowledging his indebtedness to him for so efficiently seconding him in the arduous service assigned to him, the successful issue of which reflected such glory on the whole fleet.

The letter is published here, after special application to Admiral Porter had been made for this liberty. He cordially assented to the request of the committee soliciting the favor, stating in his reply to the latter, "The compliments I paid Admiral Lanman were very sincere on my part, and well deserved on his. It affords me great satisfaction to know that his fellow citizens take an interest in his reputation. I think the navy generally has received very little credit for the part it took in the events which have such a bearing on our present and future happiness."

ADMIRAL PORTER'S LETTER TO COMMODORE LANMAN.

NORTH ATLANTIC SQUADRON, U. S. FLAG-SHIP "MALVERN,"
OFF FORT FISHER, *January* 17, 1865.

COMMODORE: You will proceed to Hampton Roads with your ship, and assume charge of the vessels stationed at that point, regulating the guard vessels according to the orders heretofore issued.

Your authority will extend no further than to the Magazine near Norfolk; that, the Receiving, Ordnance, and School vessels being within the Navy Yard jurisdiction. You will also take charge of the vessels in York River, and inquire into their efficiency, and how they have conducted matters in my absence.

Permit me to express to you on this occasion the high appreciation I feel for your services in reducing this formidable work, and the gallant manner in which you with your ship have on several occasions led the fleet into action.

I well appreciate all such matters. I am not one to forget them, or to lose an opportunity of bringing them before the notice of the government.

I thank you at the same time for the kind personal feeling you have always displayed towards myself, and the readiness in which your ship has always been kept for any service required of you.

I hope soon to see you in Hampton Roads, — from whence you will report your arrival to the Honorable the Secretary of the Navy.

It may be thought desirable to keep your ship in thorough repair, and I think she ought to go into dock as soon as possible.

Very respectfully yours,
DAVID D. PORTER,
Rear-admiral.

To Commodore JOSEPH LANMAN,
 Comd'g U. S. S. "Minnesota."

CHARLES C. ADAMS. Appointed Acting Assistant Paymaster, May 6, 1861, and ordered to the U. S. Steamer "Dawn," Commander William Chandler. She was stationed on York River, Va., for blockade duty. While here, Mr. Adams had his suspicions roused concerning the loyalty of the commander. The evidence of this fact increasing, he at once preferred charges against Commander Chandler, which were sustained before a Court of Inquiry, and the officer "disgracefully dismissed from the United States Service, October 26, 1861." Mr. Adams was soon after detached from the "Dawn" and ordered to join the "De Soto," commanded by W. W. Walker, and doing blockade service in the West Gulf Squadron, from the S. W. Pass of the Mississippi River to the Rio Grande.

The following extract from a letter written while on the "De Soto," will give an idea of the nature of the blockading service. The writer, after detailing some of the hardships of the latter, gives the following interesting narrative:

"On the morning of the eleventh (January, 1863), a large lugger was discovered inside of Vine Island, but soon disappeared. At ten A. M. she was again seen moving slowly to the eastward. At eleven A. M., Acting Master G. W. Ward, of New Haven, volunteered to catch her. Our commander told him to take his boat and do as he pleased. At 12.30 P. M. Ward was in full chase. At 4 P. M. the lugger hove in sight, and at 6 P. M. was anchored as a prize near our ship, and the prisoners brought on board. She has certainly proved to be a very valuable prize, as she has been the means of making valuable captures since. The day after her capture, she was fitted out and manned with a crew of twelve men, under the command of Acting Master Martin, and Master's Mate Portinger, both active and enterprising young officers. They returned in eight days, having captured four boats and eight prisoners, with small arms, having also gained very valuable information in regard to vessels expected from

Havana bound to Grand Caillou Bayou, with contraband goods. On the 19th two vessels were fitted out for an expedition to capture vessels from Havana, trying to run cargoes under English colors, to the most convenient port in Louisiana,— the "Phenix" commanded by Captain Ward, the "St. Joseph" by Mr. Martin. During the 24th, Mr. Ward captured three boats and ten prisoners ; Mr. Martin four boats and one prisoner, all armed with double guns, pistols, bowie knives, etc. ; all of which, of course. were confiscated. Nothing of material importance occurred, if we might except the taking of a few boats, and boarding one of our own men-of-war, supposing her to be an enemy, till the 27th, when a schooner was discovered to the eastward of Grand Caillou Bayou. We waited till she was in the position we wanted her, and at 3 P. M. gave chase. At 5 P. M. we ran alongside the schooner, making her a prize. It was a daring act, and well performed, for the vessel was expected by the troops stationed there, and a small gunboat was cruising in the neighborhood to protect her. You must bear in mind, they were close under the land, and in very shallow water. They must have been seen by the troops, and had they possessed a particle of pluck, would have annihilated our boats. She proved to be the notorious schooner "Major Barbour," from Havana, trying to get to New Orleans with a cargo of coffee, powder, salt, sulphur, leather, acids, quinine, and seventy thousand cigars, first quality.

We took a number of prisoners, among them one who claims to be a Mexican vice-consul at Charleston, who has been engaged in the laudable business of shipping cargoes of coffee from Rio de Janeiro to Savannah, being on his return from the former place when captured. The cigars are good. I smoke several for you every day.

Our prize leaves for the North to-day, under charge of Acting Master Ward, with her officers and prisoners. Her passengers we send by the steamer " Connecticut," now in sight."

In 1863 he was ordered to join the "Conemaugh" at Wingaw Bay, S. C., under Commander Real Worden. The latter being relieved on account of ill health, by Commander Shufeldt of Connecticut, the vessel participated in the attack on Wagner and other forts. Shufeldt and his officers and crew were complimented for their gallantry by Admiral Dahlgren, in presence of the commanding officers of the fleet. In December, 1863, he was transferred to the "Proteus" of the East Gulf Squadron, which had orders to cruise about the Bahamas and coast of Cuba, in search of the rebel privateer "Florida." After four years of active duty, Mr. Adams was detached May 5, 1865, and on October 1, 1865, resigned.

"When I entered the service, I fully and uncompromisingly determined, let the result be what it might, to do all in my power to destroy the institution of slavery, and bring before the proper authority, any persons giving aid, comfort, or sympathy to the enemy. I succeeded in leading many slaves to liberty, but happily for the service, there were few rebel sympathizers in the navy."

WM. A. AIKEN. Commissioned Acting Assistant Paymaster, U. S. N., August 10, 1861, and shortly after ordered to the steam gunboat "Curlew," at Charlestown Navy Yard. Resigned to accept the appointment of Quartermaster-general of Connecticut (with rank of Brigadier-general), July 10, 1862. The following is his account of the first naval expedition of the government, in which he, together with Commander J. W. Bentley, and other Norwich men participated.

"Our first port of destination was New York. Soon after arrival there the vessel was ordered in pursuit of the steamer which had just previously started for Europe, with the rebel commissioners, Mason and Slidel on board.

"The cruise was ineffectual. We next put into Hampton Roads, and for some days awaited the arrival, one by one, of the fleet of war vessels and transports, intended for an expedition against the Southern Coast, at some point then unknown.

"The mystery of our destination added spice to the excitement of preparation.

"The daily arrival of frigates, sloops of war, gunboats and steam transports filled with troops, made our season of delay one of cumulative interest. The desire to get right down to the business of real war, however, made all impatient of detention.

"On Tuesday, October 29th, 1861, at 5.30 A. M., the signal gun was fired from the flag ship "Wabash," and the fleet got under way, bound no one knew where, except the powers in command, until revealed by the opening of the sealed orders given to every commander of a vessel. These orders indicated Port Royal, S. C., as the objective point.

"The fleet encountered a severe gale a little south of Hatteras, which scattered the vessels and caused much solicitude on the part of the officers for the safety of the smaller vessels of the squadron.

"On Monday, November 4th, six days out, Port Royal was sighted. During the day most of the fleet arrived; the effects of the gale being quite perceptible on several of them.

"At 3.35 P. M., the advance shoreward commenced. Some of the vessels of heavy draft struck upon the bar at the harbor entrance and remained fast for some time; none, however, receiving serious damage.

"About 5 o'clock P. M., four rebel steamers hove in sight from the arm of the sea behind the island bordering the coast. They advanced within long range of our gunboats, which now occupied positions a mile nearer shore than the transports. For half an hour shots were actively exchanged without serious effect, when the rebel gunboats retired.

"The night was quiet. At sunrise next morning the rebel gunboats put in a second appearance. The gunboats "Ottawa," "Seneca," and "Curlew," advanced to meet them. About two hours were passed in active practice at long range. Before the skirmish was concluded we got within range of the heavy guns of the forts on Hilton Head and Bay Point, the former commanding the entrance to the port from the south, the latter from the north. As nothing was to be gained by a further advance until preparations were completed for the general attack, our gunboats returned to the squadron.

"Wednesday, November 6th, was passed in active preparations for the event which all were awaiting with impatience. On the following morning about nine o'clock the signal 'up anchor' was hoisted, and all were soon under way to take position in line of battle. The squadron was divided into two parallel sections in the advance. To the Paymaster was assigned the duties of signal officer, together with that of noting the current incidents of the action as a basis for the official report. At 10 A. M. the engagement was opened from the guns of Fort Walker, Hilton Head, followed instantly by the fort on Bay Point opposite. The flagship promptly responded, and each vessel as it moved within range took up the strain. As we advanced, the rebel steamers, now increased in number to eight, retired.

"For about an hour and a half, during which time the squadron was slowly moving towards the forts, an incessant fire was kept up on both sides, the ponderous missiles filling the air with that direful screech which tries the nerves more than the deafening roar of the heaviest ordnance.

"From eleven A. M. to about one P. M. the squadron moved in a circle or ellipse, alternately engaging at close range Bay Point, then Hilton Head.

"Notwithstanding the effect of the tremendous hail of iron descending upon the devoted forts, they replied with wonderful activity. At half past one their fire began to slacken. The gunboats then took position very close to Fort Walker, pouring into it a hot flanking fire. At about two o'clock the batteries ceased firing and the occupying troops could be seen moving in disorderly retreat into the country on the 'double quick.'

"At about three o'clock the line of battle which had been broken up during the engagement, was again formed above the forts, and the squadron moved slowly down abreast of them.

"When opposite, 'All hands on deck!' was called, and officers and men sent up ringing cheers for the victory.

"Within fifteen minutes the Stars and Stripes replaced the stars and bars on the flagstaff of Fort Walker.

"Letters, captured in the forts, indicated that the intended destination of the expedition had been fully known by the rebels and that they felt confident of their ability to repel any attack.

"The great fleet of transports, containing the army of occupation, being signaled to advance, now came up, and the spectacle became exciting beyond description as the thousands of men covering their decks rent the air with their enthusiastic cheers.

"Thus ended the first naval engagement of magnitude during the war."

JOHN W. BENTLEY, was commissioned May 24, 1861, as First Acting Master in the volunteer navy, and ordered to join the U. S. S. "Wabash." In October following he was transferred to the steam sloop "Pawnee," which was one of the vessels in Admiral Dupont's Squadron, engaged in the cayture of Port Royal, S. C. In August 1862 he joined the steamer "Connecticut," on which he served, until ordered to the steamer "Shenandoah," June, 1863. Promoted Commander, March, 1864, he was assigned to the steamer "Banshee," and was preparing to put to sea when he was taken sick and died at his residence in this city, May 27, 1864.

WARRINGTON D. ROATH, was appointed Acting Master in the navy, 1861, serving on the gunboat "New London," under Commander Read. Promoted Acting Volunteer Lieutenant. July, 1863, he was assigned to the command of the U. S. brig "Bohio," afterward to the "Brignonia," of the North Atlantic Squadron, Rear-admiral Porter commanding. Resigned March 7, 1865.

LEWIS G. COOK. Commissioned Acting Master, December 19, 1861, and assigned to steamer "Virginia," of West Gulf Squadron, under command of Admiral Farragut. Subsequently transferred to the Potomac flotilla, he was honorably discharged — 1865.

GEORGE E. MARTIN. Appointed Paymaster's Clerk December 30, 1861, and served on U. S. steamers "Norwich" and "Mendota." Commissioned Acting Assistant Paymaster, November, 1864, and ordered to steamer "Adela." Honorably discharged August, 1865. Reappointed Paymaster's Clerk, August, 1865, and joined U. S. ship "Supply," sailing for Hong Kong, where he died of cholera, August 6, 1867.

GEORGE W. HUNTINGTON, was commissioned Acting Assistant Paymaster, U. S. N., October, 1863. Assigned to duty in the South Atlantic Squadron, and joined the steam gunboat "Ottawa." Engaged mostly in blockade duty, he was present with his vessel in attacks on various rebel fortifications along Southern rivers, and was the first to open communication with Gen. Sherman on his great march to the sea. The vessel participated in the recapture of Fort Sumter, in February, 1865, and also in a combined military and naval attack on some important batteries, twenty miles north of Charleston, S. C. While the "Ottawa" engaged the batteries in front, the soldiers landed below, and prepared to advance on the rebels. The troops hardly landed, when it was known in Charleston, and they hastened to escape from the latter, before General Gilmore should surround them. "It is a great satisfaction to us, that we have had a part in one of the great achievements of the war, but it is a greater satisfaction to know that, whatever may be its immediate cause, the thing is a fact, Charleston is ours. But a few more such facts are needed to solve the peace problem, and we can afford to wait for them." Honorably discharged November, 1865.

AMOS D. ALLEN. Appointed Paymaster's Clerk, November 9, 1863, commissioned Acting Assistant Paymaster, October 21, 1864, and ordered to join steamer "Western

World," of North Atlantic Squadron. Honorably discharged, September 5, 1865.

CHARLES H. COLE, Jr. Appointed Paymaster's Clerk October 31, 1864, and attached to U. S. steamer "Western World." Honorably discharged, June, 1865.

FRANK H. ARMS. Commissioned Acting Assistant Paymaster, April 14, 1864, and ordered to join U. S. steamer "Memphis." Still in service.

FRANCIS S. WELLS. Commissioned Acting Volunteer Lieutenant, May 7, 1863, assigned to command of U. S. steamer "Daylight," North Atlantic Squadron. Transferred subsequently to command of U. S. steamer "Aries." Honorably discharged, 1865.

JAMES H. NASH. Commissioned Acting Ensign, January 20, 1863, and ordered to join store-ship "Brandywine" at Norfolk Navy Yard; afterwards attached to the North Atlantic Blockading Squadron. Honorably discharged, 1865.

ROBERT B. SMITH, Commissioned Acting Volunteer Lieutenant, December 3, 1863, was assigned to the command of the steamer "Nita," East Gulf Squadron, Acting Rear-admiral Theodore Bailey, commanding. Honorably discharged, 1865.

JOHN T. PERKINS, entered the navy, September 4, 1861, as landsman. Promoted to Paymaster's Steward, he served in the "Stars and Stripes" the first year in the North Atlantic Blockading Squadron, and took part in the engagements at Roanoke Island and Newbern. The next two years were spent in the East Gulf Squadron. He was honorably discharged, November 4, 1864.

WILLIAM M. PERKINS, enlisted in the navy, September 17, 1861, as first class boy; joined the steamship "Florida." Sailed in the Port Royal expedition under Dupont. In November, 1862, joined the frigate "Colorado" at Portsmouth. Was transferred to Cairo, Ill., and ordered to the ram "Lafayette." Served on the Yazoo River, and in the passage of the Vicksburg batteries ; also in the first and second Red River expeditions. Honorably discharged, September 17, 1864.

J. H. JEWETT, enlisted as seaman, August 28, 1861. Served on gunboat " Rhode Island" and frigate " Santee."

EDWARD FRANCIS, served as ordinary seaman in the navy.

CHARLES TISDALE, enlisted in May, serving as first class boy.

EDWARD TISDALE, entered the navy and served as first class boy.

GEORGE CLARKE, served in the navy as Paymaster's clerk.

ALBERT SMITH, entered the navy, and served as Paymaster's clerk.

WILLIAM FANNING, enlisted and served in the navy as ordinary seaman.

A. E. FULLER, served in the navy in the capacity of clerk.

HENRY HEMPSTEAD, enlisted in the navy and served as landsman.

CHARLES E. BREED, enlisted in the navy, April, 1864, as Assistant Engineer, died April, 1865.

JOHN P. KEHR, served in the navy, and died July 30, 1862.

X.

SOLDIERS' RELIEF. — CITIZEN-SERVICE.

1861-65.

> "Work, Patriots, for the Union
>   Till the hour of triumph comes!
> When the lusty shouts of victory
>   Mingle with rolls of drums;
> Till the shadowy clouds of treason
>   Have floated fore'er away,
> And the sunrise beams of hope and peace
>   Tell of a brighter day."
>
> C. B. HOWELL.

AT the very commencement of the war the citizens of Norwich turned their attention to making provision for the relief of soldiers' families. The first grand rally of the people on Wednesday, April eighteenth, had this object in view, no less than the encouragement of enlistments,

and with generous promptitude they commenced subscriptions to a fund, which to the end of the war was more than adequate to meet every call upon it. This action on the part of the citizens was in advance of the measures adopted subsequently by the town for the systematic relief of the families of soldiers, by bounties and otherwise, and as an instance of the spontaneous liberality of the people in providing for the immediate needs of the first volunteers, it is deserving of special mention.

The patriotism of the men and women of Norwich, of every grade of means, was from the first pronounced and unwavering, as this splendid record abundantly shows. Mr. Amos W. Prentice stood at the head of this "Patriotic Fund Committee," rendering in this, as in other responsible positions he was called to fill during the eventful years of the war, most efficient and untiring service. Mr. Charles Johnson was appointed treasurer, and with a loyalty as decided as it was uncompromising, received the subscriptions to this fund, and aided in administering the same. His personal correspondence with the soldiers was very extensive, and his generous admiration of their patriotism made him a ready helper of all whom he could befriend, and the best almoner of the public bounty that could have been selected.

The subscription list was the grandest one which ever received the signatures of our citizens, both when we consider its object and the unprecedented liberality to which it showed the people could rise in a trying hour. The original roll on which the names of the subscribers were signed, is carefully preserved by the treasurer of the fund, as a proud memento of the patriotism of our citizens, as well as an historic relic which the passage of the years will convert into a precious heirloom for other days and generations.

The following are the names, and in the order in which

they were signed, on this paper, to whose suggestive title we have already alluded : —

"THE SINEWS OF WAR."

Wm. A. Buckingham	$1,000	B. W. Tompkins	$100
David Smith	500	George Perkins	50
Wm. P. Greene	1,000	Joel W. White	100
J. Lloyd Greene	500	A. F. Gilman	25
John F. Slater	500	E. P. Slocum	25
L. F. S. Foster	300	S. B. Meech	25
I. M. Buckingham	300	Samuel C. Morgan	200
Leonard Ballou	300	E. O. Abbot	100
Ebenezer Learned	300	Pierce & Robertson	50
Chas. Johnson & Son	300	F. Y. Winship	25
C. B. Rogers	300	William Prentice	50
Breed, Prentice, & Co.	500	Gurdon P. Cottrell	25
Henry Bill	300	Gurdon Chapman	25
George L. Perkins	200	L. W. Carroll	300
E. R. Thompson	200	Charles Spalding	100
Joseph Selden	100	I. Johnson	50
James D. Mowry	100	W. T. Almy	50
Frank Johnson	100	H. K. Hammond	50
F. M. Hale	50	Charles N. Farnam	300
Clarke, Harrington, & Co	50	A. H. Hubbard	500
E. Winslow Williams	100	William C. Osgood	50
S. H. Grosvenor	100	Norton Brothers	500
John T. Adams	100	Erastus Williams	100
N. C. Brakenridge	100	W. L. Nichols	25
James A. Hovey	100	Franklin Nichols	50
William Kelley	50	E. Edwards	25
James S. Carew	100	Gurdon Jones & Co.	25
A. Brewster	100	Lewis Edwards	50
Julius Webb	100	M. Safford	25
C. B. Webster	100	R. Farnsworth	100
Enoch F. Chapman	50	A. J. Currier	100
George G. Bottom	50	R. B. Mowry	100
A. Y. Hebard	30	J. M. Huntington and W. H. Huntington	1,000
Gardner Greene	100	John P. Gulliver	100
William Noyes	50	John G. Huntington & Co.	100
Sidney Turner	50	William P. Nash	50
J. Leavens & Son	50	S. K. Parlin	50
Wm. R. Hitchcock	50	Barstow & Palmer	100
James N. Perry	25	Andrew & Nash	100
O. P. Rice	50		

SOLDIERS' RELIEF. — CITIZEN-SERVICE.

R. M. Haven	$25	Louis Mitchell	$25
S. H. Osgood	100	W. R. Wood	50
George W. Smith	100	Charles A. Rallion	50
S. & S. B. Case	100	William P. Greene, Jr.	50
Z. R. Robbins	50	Benjamin D. Greene	50
P. St. M. Andrews	25	Joseph H. Holm	25
Avery Smith	50	James L. Hubbard	100
E. G. Bidwell	50	Charles Lee	100
H. H. Starkweather	50	Russell Rix	50
Joseph A. Starkweather	50	E. P. Partridge	50
Lorenzo Blackstone	300	Nathan Sears	25
H. B. Cruttenden	25	Chauncey Palmer	50
John W. Allen	500	Samuel Mowry	100
Frederick Prentice	100	Chester Clark	50
E. F. Hovey	25	Samuel Prentice	25
Robert Revelle	25	Owen Stead	25
Theodore F. McCurdy	100	Nathan P. Avery	25
Wilson Potter	50	T. C. Gordon	25
Gardner Thurston	25	Charles Browning	25
Willoughby & Co.	100	Charles C. Fuller	25
Edward Chappell	100	C. C. Thompson	25
Alvan Bond	50	Parley Philipps	25
Alfred P. Rockwell	50	Norris G. Lippitt	25
Daniel W. Coit	200	Willard Bliss	50
Joseph T. Thurston	50	John T. Wait	50
A. H. Vaughn	50	Daniel F. Gulliver	100
A. S. Robbins	50	L. H. Smith	25
Mrs. Russell Hubbard	50	William W. Coit	100
Wareham Williams	100	J. Treadwell Walden	50
J. H. Almy	50	Joseph Williams	50
A. Clark	50	George Loomis	100
Hiram B. Crosby	50	Henry Ruggles	50
J. Halsey	50	Mrs. Benjamin Lee	50
Jedediah Huntington	300	A native-born non-resident	50
William H. Law	100	Lewis A. Hyde	25
Augustus Bowen	25	John Dunham	100
Augustus Bowen, Att'y for Wm. R. Potter	50	Richard Colburn	25
		J. G. Hinckley	25
Charles E. Dyer	25	Horace Colton	75
Lewis E. Stanton	25	William McCune	25
George Coit	50	Jesse Caulkins	10
L. H. Maples	25	William W. Avery	50
Benjamin Durfey	50	Pliny Brewer	25
Richard P. Tracy	10	Oliver P. Avery	25
Asa Fitch	500	Miss E. A. Dwight	40

Mrs. B. Lee (additional)	$50	J. B. Shaw	$25
G. A. Jones & Co. (additional)	75	Edward Coit	30
Charles B. Platt	25	A. B. Haile	25
Othniel Gager	50	C. G. Child	25
Richard P. Tracy (additional)	15	Thomas Byrnes	25
Peter Nelson	10	A. H. Emmons	25
Mrs. John A. Rockwell	100	John Eggleston	25
R. P. Stanton	10	John Eggleston (Trustee)	25
Isaac H. Bromley	25	J. W. Hooker	50
Lewis Hyde	50	George W. Kies	25
Wm. Elting & Co.	50	E. A. Huntington	25
James M. Peckham	50	H. G. Ransom	25
Mrs. N. C. Reynold	50	F. S. B.	100
William B. Wilcox	25	C. Starr Brewster	100
J. N. Perkins	50	William Bond	100
B. Boardman	25	John F. Arnott	50
J. L. W. Huntington	50	S. A. Whitney	25
Amos E. Cobb	50	Mary W. Goddard	20
Hakes Brothers	50	William Williams	400
Thomas J. Ridgway	50	Alfred Mitchell	100
William Jennings	25		
Palmer Smith	25	Grand total	$21,395

One of the subscribers to the above fund drew his check payable to " The Stars and Stripes," while one of the lady contributors sent in a silver cup, made in 1811, and held in the family as a valued heirloom, accompanied by the following note : —

"MR. JOHNSON, *Treasurer*, —

" DEAR SIR : I have no money to give you, but this old cup has been in my family through five generations. It is small, but true. May it not have passed through one revolution to help some brave boy now. I have given my younger son to his country, with regret that his older brother [1] cannot be with him.

" Yours. * * * *."

Another lady contributor wrote thus : —

" MR. CHAS. JOHNSON, *Treasurer*, —

" DEAR SIR : At a time when the women of our country with

---

[1] This elder son here referred to returned from business pursuits in another part of the world to enlist, and lost his life on the field of battle.

willing hands to work, and warm hearts to feel, are naturally anxious to do all in their power to help and to cheer the brave men who go forth to battle for the glorious flag which from our childhood we have been taught to hold sacred, — may I, who can do little else than bid them 'God-speed,' be permitted to add my mite to the fund for the benefit of the families of the noble band in whose hearts is enshrined the honor of their country, which, with God's blessing, they will ever defend. It is not in my power to send ready money, but I beg your acceptance of the inclosed coupon — forty dollars.

"Very truly yours,

"E. A. D.

"Norwich, *April* 22, 1861."

It should be stated in this connection, that in consequence of the generous provision of the town for the relief of soldiers' families, and for the promotion of enlistments, elsewhere spoken of at length, the contributors to this fund were not called upon to pay in but fifty per cent. of the amount they severally subscribed. Some, however, had promptly paid their entire subscriptions at the time they made them, and declined to receive back the portion to which in equity, and by vote of the committee, they were entitled. The fund was wisely administered, and brought timely relief and cheer to many a brave soldier, or needy family. There are letters held by the treasurer which attest the heartfelt gratitude of those who by it were assisted, while to the very close of the war, and even longer, did this fund hold out, proving a source of supply, until all immediate war needs had ceased. This was not the only fund raised by public contribution for the relief of soldiers, and those dependent on them. On the thirtieth of August, 1862, in the great war meeting, the doings of which we have already described, our citizens raised considerably over twenty thousand dollars. This was paid over directly to those to whom the moneys were personally promised on condition of enlisting, or to the families of those who by these pledges were induced to volunteer.

Nor does this end the tale of citizen benevolence. The aggregate of these free-will offerings would mount up to a greatly augmented sum, if all that was given for objects connected with the war had been recorded. But many were the individual gifts that escaped public notice, and never were reported. The costly and elaborate swords presented to various officers by individual citizens, represent only one item of expense in which not a few were very lavish, while at different times most generous subscriptions were made for the comfort of those of our soldiers confined in Southern prisons. In addition to a Union thanksgiving collection in November, 1863, and a contribution made at the same time by the Second Congregational Sabbath-school for this object, there was a fund of four hundred and twenty-three dollars raised in the beginning of 1864, three hundred and fifty-eight dollars of which were the result of the "Soldiers' Relief Ball." In April, 1864, at the Union headquarters in this city, where numbers of our citizens had gathered to rejoice over the election news, a sum of two hundred dollars was contributed "to be applied especially for the benefit of the privates confined in Richmond, who suffer most."

There certainly never was a time in which private benevolence had so many calls upon it, as during the war, and in no equal period in our national history was so much given by individual citizens. A new era of liberality and of charitable enterprise seemed to be opened by the war, and the people responded to every appeal for help with unprecedented generosity.

While we cannot specify how much our citizens did individually or in the aggregate, it is enough to know that they became ready contributors to all the great charities which the sufferings incident to our struggle had created,

Governor Buckingham stood at the head of "the Connecticut Chaplains' Aid Commission," and in support of the work of this organization, our people, either singly, or as gathered in the different churches, gave liberally. The objects it had in view, were to supply all Connecticut Regiments with chapel tents, to provide camp libraries and newspapers, and in every practicable way to coöperate with chaplains in their labors for the mental and moral welfare of the soldiers.

To those grand organizations, which did so much to mitigate the hardships of the soldiers, and to rob the battlefield of its horrors, — the Sanitary and Christian Commissions, our citizens were interested and regular donors. They never failed to meet generously the repeated calls the "Soldiers Aid Society" of this city made upon them for pecuniary assistance, and it is to the credit of their benevolence, that all classes shared in it. The giving was not done by the rich alone, but those of humbler means were proportionately as benevolent, while many a donation came from those who were in really straightened circumstances. It would make a memorial of lasting interest to this community could the full list of all that was given during the war by the people, be here presented item by item, but in the absence of this, we have reported enough to show that never before were all animated to such an extent by the impulse of a genuine benevolence.

The war was emphatically an epoch of deeds; words went little ways unless coupled with brave actions, or generous gifts. Philanthropic sentiments were reckoned of little account, unless converted into such personal labors or benefactions, as they naturally prompt to, if sincere.

Our soldiers in the field were made the recipients of private beneficence to an extent that made them feel that those at home counted it a privilege as well as a duty to minister in any way to their comfort. Following with a fond pride the course of those who went out from the town, to fight for all that was dearest, the community felt, and by their actions showed, that the soldiers were entitled to all they could do for them and theirs.

Nor was our citizen patriotism all of one type, — for though it prompted some to give in the manner already described, it led yet others to such personal service and sacrifices as in many cases were never publicly known. One of our citizens, who gave of his own time and effort to aid the government, too infirm to become a soldier, besides being exempt by age from military service, secured for himself a "representative recruit," at an expense of nine hundred dollars, and kept him in the Union army.

Jared Dennis, living at Norwich Falls, contributed five able-bodied sons to the army. Another citizen sent one son into Captain Chester's company, giving him a Spartan father's good-by, in these words, — "Do your duty, my son; if you fall, your brother shall take your place, and after him I shall go myself."

Nor was it by *giving only*, all important as that was, that our citizens at home showed their devotion to the National cause. There were voluntary services rendered to the Governor, which converted not a few into "temporary aids" to him, amid the duties and anxieties which at the commencement of the war pressed heavily upon him. Col. George L. Perkins volunteered to bear dispatches from Governor Buckingham to the Secretary of War at Washington, and on Tuesday the twenty-third of April, was dispatched by his Excellency, being the second "envoy extraordinary," sent from Norwich to our then beleaguered Capital. He had a memorable experience, going "cross-lots," as he termed it, in order to reach that city. Communications were known to be severed, and to get through

Maryland was no easy task, for secessionists and traitors were thicker than hornets. However, all went well as far as Philadelphia, where according to the narrative of Colonel Perkins, " I determined to take the cars to Perrysville, and from thence to Annapolis by boat, accompanied by Major Ames, Quartermaster of the Massachusetts troops. Mr. Felton, President of the Philadelphia and Baltimore R. R. gave us a letter to Colonel Dare, commanding at Perrysville, requesting him to place one of the company's boats at our service, and put on board a military escort of twenty-five men. We left in the latter without delay, though not without some apprehension, as it was reported that two steam-tugs were in the bay to attack any boats conveying troops to Annapolis."

Arriving safely, and reporting to General Butler, they were forwarded by him on a military train to the Junction, and thence by cars, in company with the New York Seventh, and the Rhode Island Regiments under Governor Sprague, reached Washington at noon, Friday, April twenty-sixth.

During his necessary detention at Annapolis, Colonel Perkins had a chance to observe General Butler, who had opened this new route to Washington, by which Baltimore was temporarily avoided. While at his head-quarters, an officer, somewhat new to his duties, reported to him, and meekly waiting to be assigned somewhere, for it was very late, ventured to ask, " Where am I to sleep, General?" The latter turning upon him a look never pleasant to contemplate, replied with considerable emphasis, " Young man, do you take me to be chamber-maid to this military post?" This extinguished the youthful soldier's desire for sleep, and the sleepless Colonel, who might have enjoyed the poor boon thus unsuccessfully solicited by his junior, kept an upright position till his train left at midnight.

On reaching the Capital he reported at once to Secretary Cameron, whose porter, taking in his full commanding figure, and supposing him to be some distinguished magnate, bore his card up in advance of a number of other less fortunate messengers from Northern States. Here his errand was soon made known, and answering dispatches placed in his hands for Governor Buckingham. Colonel Perkins brought back the first reliable report as to the number of troops in and about Washington, and other facts, which showed in what imminent peril the Capital had been up to this date. He met on his return the Sixty-ninth Regiment of New York, fourteen hundred strong, guarding the railroad from Annapolis to the Junction, with orders from General Butler, " to shoot every one seen meddling with the track, as you would a dog, and tumble his body down the embankment." He also passed, en route for Washington, Major Sherman, afterwards the distinguished General, with a United States Battery of four guns.

He reported, as doing guard-duty at the White House, Hon. Cassius M. Clay, commanding one hundred and twenty-one volunteers armed with rifle, revolver, and knife. Hon. Abraham Wakeman of New York, was patrolling as sentinel before the Presidential mansion, when he went to call on Mr. Lincoln. An alarm was given a night or two previous to his arrival, on which occasion this unique company of " Honorables," was formed in five minutes, several in stocking feet, with orders from Clay, " to fire deliberately and fire low, and at the proper time use the knife ; " adding, as only a Kentuckian of his stamp could, " I am fond of chopped meat."

These are facts I glean from the very interesting letter, which conveyed in full to Governor Buckingham, the report of the journey and the discharge of the commission with which intrusted; and with Colonel Perkins' own summary, I give this as one chapter in the varied services in which many afterwards bore an equally important part: —

"I passed through Egypt (*i. e.*, Maryland) without being shot, though in perils of robbers, in perils of mine own countrymen, in perils by plug-uglies, in perils in the city, and in perils among false brethren. In weariness and painfulness, in watchings, in hunger and thirst, in fastings often, and in the night-dampness."

On the eighteenth of June, 1861, Mr. E. P. Slocum, agent of Adams' Express, who always took a lively interest in the well-being of our soldiers, advertised that he would take packages to them free of charge. He supposed many in the community, who had friends and kindred in the three companies Norwich had now in the advance of the Union army, would be glad to avail themselves of this opportunity to have conveyed to such anything that would add to their comfort, and be pleasant reminders of those they had left behind them. The advertisement hardly appeared, before bundles and boxes and packages of all sizes and descriptions began to be delivered, and it seemed as if all the people were actuated by one common impulse.

However, Mr. Slocum bravely stood to his generous offer, and complacently looked on the accumulating pile of good things, of which he was to be the gratuitous almoner, and giving full time for all who felt disposed to get their contributions to his office, crowded now to the full with donations, he started with the proposed free load. Three large express wagons were required to convey the goods to the Depot. Arriving in due time in Washington, he sought most diligently for the means of transporting his precious freight to the expectant boys, who were now encamped on Virginia's sacred soil.

After only such vexatious delays, and magnificent rambles from one end of the city's expanse to the other in search of a vehicle and driver, he succeeded in chartering two ancient steeds, a couple of adolescent darkies, and the waited-for-wagon. He loaded up and started for the Old Dominion. Getting by the inquisitive pickets, numerous enough to prevent any over-long trot with the fiery coursers, he neared the camp.

Discovered while yet a great way distant, the narrator, Mr. Bromley, thus presents the scene: "Mr. Slocum was greeted by the familiar voice of Joab Rogers, who had lifted up his eyes, and discerned him afar off. The alarm once given, the progress of our missionary was a continued ovation. The boys rushed out bare-headed, bare-footed, or in any costume that came handy, and cheered, and shouted 'Hi,' and cheered, and when they got tired of that, gave several rounds of cheers.

"Once in the camp, the boxes were unloaded, and opened in a twinkling. Then the boys stopped shouting, for they found this a difficult matter while doing picket duty on the good things, and crowding cartridges of pies and cakes, and other sundries down their throats, which seemed to have become double-barreled for the occasion. Everybody came out strong in that sudden exigency, and Mr. Slocum thought the spectacle was worth travelling a great way to behold.

"The boys appeared well, brown, and hearty, having experienced a considerable average addition to their bulk and weight. As a sporting item, it is well enough to mention that his ebony jockeys achieved the entire distance from Camp Tyler to Washington, not over ten miles, in five hours."

This may serve to show how soon these "first things," which the necessities incident to war set our people to doing, lost the charm of novelty, and became matters of only ordinary significance, though none the less important and helpful. This is the story of the first boxes sent to the soldiers, but as already stated, such gifts soon became very frequent, and were sent regularly, with a liberality and thoughtfulness that made them of invaluable service to our boys, when in camp, hospital, or prison.

Among other objects for which the Governor dispatched Special Agents, and which showed his thoughtful, wide reaching care, was to look after Connecticut soldiers in the hospitals of the West and Southwest. Capt. L. A. Gallup, formerly of the Twenty-sixth Regiment, was in August, 1863, entrusted with this duty, and reported as follows, on his return from this mission of mercy : —

NORWICH, CONN., *September* 10, 1863.

To his Excellency, WM. A. BUCKINGHAM.

SIR: Agreeable to your instructions issued to me, August 25, 1863, directing me to visit those hospitals in which were left sick and disabled soldiers by Connecticut regiments, while en route from the Department of the Gulf to Connecticut, and ascertain their condition, I have the honor to report that I left Norwich on the evening of August 25th, and proceeded directly to Memphis, Tenn., at which place the first soldiers were sent to hospitals after leaving Port Hudson, La. The medical director at Memphis informed me that the Connecticut soldiers left at that place were in Adams and Union Hospitals. Visiting these, I ascertained that the Twenty-sixth Regiment sent to Adams Hospital, August 1st, twelve enlisted men, and that the Twenty-eighth Regiment sent to Union Hospital, August 14th, nineteen enlisted men. Of this number, twelve have died, twelve had been sent to Connecticut, and seven, all members of the Twenty-eighth, were then in Union Hospital.

Leaving Memphis, August 31st, I returned to Cairo, Ill., where I ascertained that two members of the Twenty-eighth Regiment had been admitted into the Post Hospital at that place, August 17th. Both had recovered, and been sent to Connecticut. From Cairo I proceeded to Mound City, Ill., where I ascertained that twelve enlisted men of the Twenty-sixth Regiment were admitted into the United States General Hospital at that place, August 3d, and that eleven enlisted men were admitted from the Twenty-eighth Regiment, August 17th. Of the number, nine had died, two had been sent to Connecticut, three were then in hospital, and one could not be accounted for.

From Mound City I proceeded to Chicago, Ill. There two commissioned officers and one enlisted man were admitted into the Soldiers' Home, August 4th, and nine enlisted men were admitted into the military department of the Marine Hospital, and one enlisted man into the Post Hospital.

These were all members of the Twenty-sixth Regiment. Of this number six enlisted men had died, and the other seven had been forwarded to Connecticut. Leaving Chicago, I arrived at Toledo, Ohio, September 5th, and there learned that five enlisted men, members of the Twenty-sixth, were admitted into the Infirmary in that city, August 5th. This entire number had died.

I am not aware that Connecticut soldiers were left at places other than those mentioned, while en route to Connecticut from the Department of the Gulf.

As to the condition of the men left at Memphis, I would say, that six of the seven were reported as "doing well," and would be strong enough to proceed in a short time to Connecticut. The other one "was failing," and would not survive many days. Two of the three in Mound Hospital were recovering fast, and one was in a dying condition.

I was assured by the surgeon in charge of those hospitals, that those from Connecticut who were remaining, would be provided with transportation and rations, and forwarded to Connecticut as soon as it was thought advisable to do so.

Although it is painful to know that so many of our number have died, when within a few days of their homes, I am happy to say that the hospitals of which they were inmates, are commodious and well regulated. Those who survived, admitted that they received every care and attention. I would state that the graves of those who have died, have been properly marked.

SUMMARY.

Total number admitted into hospitals,	74
Total number who have died,	32
Total number sent to Connecticut,	31
Total number remaining in hospitals,	10
Total number not accounted for,	1
	—
	74

Very respectfully,
Your obedient servant,
L. A. GALLUP.

Hon. W. A. BUCKINGHAM,
Governor of Connecticut.

Where all were so patriotic, it is not possible to individualize the labors of many, for like the men of whom Macaulay speaks in his "Lays of Ancient Rome,"

> "Then none was for a party ;
> Then all were for the State,
> Then the great man helped the poor,
> And the poor man loved the great."

And yet for memorial purposes, we may justly venture to make special mention of those, who because of their position or means were enabled to render service, which all now remember with gratitude, and speak of with pride.

W. A. BUCKINGHAM, who was the chief executive of the State from 1859 to 1866, was foremost in all patriotic work, not less in his private than in his public and official capacity. He has left a proud record of noble, earnest service in a critical period of the Nation's history. To his keen appreciation of State and National affairs, his promptness of action, Connecticut was indebted for the leading position which she held during the war. Commanding the confidence of his fellow citizens to an unwonted extent, he was trusted as few men have been before or since in similar official stations, and he maintained to the last the respect and gratitude of the Commonwealth. His best and highest title will ever be the one he gained for his signally devoted and able administration of affairs, in a time of unprecedented excitement and peril. — " Connecticut's War Governor."

Early foreseeing in the agitation of the South which followed the election of Mr. Lincoln, the beginning of a fearful conflict, he began to prepare for it. In January, 1861, he had wisely ordered the purchase, on his own responsibility, of knapsacks, cartridge-boxes, bayonets, and everything belonging to the full equipment of at least five thousand men. In April, when the war broke out, he at once resolved to discard all smooth-bore weapons, and arm Connecticut troops with the best rifles. The money necessary to do this, he decided to raise by loans, pledging for security his own private fortune, but this the immediate proffers of loyal men, and the tenders of the banks, made unnecessary.

The State, through his promptitude, aided as he was by able and energetic coadjutors, put her troops into the field in advance of others, better armed and equipped at the first, than those from other States, and this too, without a dollar's expense to the Federal Government. The latter made requisitions upon the Governor, which were promptly filled, such as a Light Battery for Rhode Island, and a second one for the authorities at Washington. On request of the Governor of Ohio, he was able to furnish him four thousand sets of equipments for the soldiers of his State.

When the second call was issued by Mr. Lincoln for troops, and only a limited supply of clothing and camp equipments were in the government store-houses, Governor Buckingham was the first to apply in behalf of the quota of Connecticut, through a special agent, Mr. E. H. Owen, of Hartford, and on the principle " of first come, first served," the orders were issued to make over the supplies on hand to this State. The result was that our troops were the earliest equipped and escaped the sufferings that were experienced by those of other States, who on arriving at the appointed places of rendezvous were kept waiting for their necessary blankets, clothing, and tents.

The General Assembly of 1861, appropriated three thousand dollars for the payment of personal expenses incurred while in the discharge of official duties, but this gratuity he generously declined in 1866, adding as his reason, "that public burdens have rested so heavily upon the people during the past five years, that I do not feel willing to draw from the Treasury money thus appropriated."

During part of the time of his long career as Chief Executive of the State, he turned his salary over to some patriotic object, devoting, in one instance, more than the year's income, to the relief of the families of volunteers.

To have been Governor of Connecticut for the most momentous years since the Revolution, called to the position by the voice of the people, and continued by repeated re-elections, is enough for the patriotic ambition of any man; to have served with zeal, unsullied integrity, and an unfaltering faith in the Nation's cause, is more honor than often falls to mortals in this world, and such honor, as alas, can be trusted to but few.

Connecticut will ever remember with pride, and Norwich hold in grateful recollection — the unwearied services of him who was able to grasp the various interests of the public good, and accomplish well the enormous work thrown upon him, who was capable of being the exponent and also the leader of public sentiment, who could steady the heart of his State, and yet stimulate the Central Government in the path of justice.

HON. WM. P. GREENE, whose name will ever remain with us as a synonym of the purest patriotism and benevolence, was especially active in all movements in aid of the war.

Unobtrusive in whatever he did, few knew how generous and extensive were the gifts he made to the soldiers, or those dependent upon them. Many an incident, illustrative of his loyalty and liberality, lingers in the memory of not a few in this community, who never refer to him but with feelings of admiration and real affection. When called on by Colonel Young and Mr. James D. Mowry, for his contribution to the " Sinews of War " Fund, he replied with that courtesy and deliberate utterance which characterized him, " Put me down, gentlemen, for whatever I ought to give," and dismissing them with this, for his final answer, they departed, and put him down for what alone all knew would satisfy him ; for his name never stood against any subscription, second in amount to that of any other citizen. On learning that Capt. J. B. Dennis of the Seventh Regiment had borne the expenses incident to the recruiting of his company, he and his noble daughter, Miss Lizzie Greene, reimbursed him for all his outlay. The latter, assisted by her brother, the Hon. J. Lloyd Greene, then added the very acceptable gift of blankets for each member of the company. As the Eighteenth Regiment was drawn up in line, to receive the regimental colors, on the afternoon of their departure from Camp Aiken, Mr. William P. Greene advanced to the front of the company raised in the village which bears his name, bade the boys an affectionate good-by, and presented them with a beautiful inlaid box containing one hundred and one two dollar and a half gold pieces. Capt Davis, acknowledging the gift, wrote back from Fort Henry, Baltimore, the following note : —

WM. P. GREENE, —

Kind Sir : I desire in behalf of the company which I have the honor to command, to express to you our sincere thanks for the munificent gift to us on Friday last. . . . Each member of the company will value his gift, not so much as a matter of increase to the liberal bounties of the government and town, but as a token of remembrance from a warm and liberal friend. Not less do we prize those words of counsel and advice, as you bade the Greenville boys an affectionate good-by. They will not be forgotten. We will return with the good reputation with which you complimented us.

Respectfully yours,
HENRY C. DAVIS.

HENRY B. NORTON was another of our citizens whose services, ever generous and unceasing, endeared him to all Norwich soldiers. His name is one which they speak to this day with the warmest feelings. Quick to perceive what should be done, and eager to help wheresoever he could, he rendered the most timely assistance to the Governor. Superintending the transportation of troops, the chartering of vessels, the purchasing of army supplies in the early period of the war, and thereafter attending personally to the wants and comforts of our men in the field, his labors were invaluable. Soldiers came to feel that if he was on the look-out for them, they would not suffer for the lack of anything his thoughtful care and means could provide. Members of the Fourteenth and Eighteenth Regiments write him down as their friend; one whose presence and aid tided them over many a day of pressing need. His services, from first to last, were the free-will offering his patriotism alone inspired him to render, for he declined all commissions, and refused every tender in the way of compensation.

Hon. LAFAYETTE S. FOSTER, who ably represented Connecticut in the United States Senate for twelve years, including those of the war, was also among our most active and patriotic citizens. Rendering distinguished service in Congress, and attaining an eminent position in that body, he was, when in Norwich, an earnest supporter of the war measures of his town. In his place in the Senate he gave his advocacy to all that could help our armies, and sustain the integrity of the government. Inflexibly independent, with honor and honesty untemptable, he spoke and voted only and always according to his own convictions. With nothing of the politician about him, holding fealty of conscience above allegiance to mere party, his course was all the more noble and patriotic, because at times it compelled him to differ from measures that were deemed popular, and imperiously pushed by the political leaders, by whom dissent is not infrequently stigmatized as disloyalty. His voice was heard in most of our war-meetings, and no one sought with greater earnestness than he, to encourage enlistments, and sustain the hopefulness of the people.

Dr. C. B. WEBSTER deserves to be ranked as one of the most patriotic and useful of our citizens during the rebellion. In December, 1862, he made a tender of his services to the government, and was appointed Assistant Surgeon, and ordered for duty to Camp Barker, which was then the temporary home of the thousands of fugitives from slavery. These ex-slaves flocked to Washington in great numbers, and in all conceivable conditions of destitution. Dr. Webster was soon put in charge of what was called "Contraband Camp Hospital," where the medical care of these fugitives fell upon him; and some idea of the nature of the arduous work he performed while here, can be obtained from the fact that during the winter of 1862 there were thirteen hundred cases of small pox.

In the autumn of 1863, the freedmen were removed across the Potomac to the Arlington Estate. Here Dr. Webster continued in service till the spring of 1864, doing for the physical comfort, as well as moral and mental improvement of the contrabands all that a thorough devotion to their every interest could suggest. In this work the anti-slavery

principles of a life-time found opportunity to incarnate themselves in untiring and noble labors. Believing in the manhood of these enfranchised bondsmen, he sought to instruct them in all that related to their daily living, and to the duties incident to their state of freedom. This sort of work greatly interested our own people, and they made Dr. Webster the distributor of boxes of supplies and clothing which they sent to him at different times.

In the spring of 1864, owing to prostration induced by malarial fever, Dr. Webster was forced to resign. After a short rest, he accepted an appointment from the Sanitary Commission, and went to Huntsville, Ala., as medical inspector of troops. About this time the "Hospital Train Service," for the transport of sick and wounded soldiers to the North was extended, and he again accepted the appointment from government of Assistant Surgeon, and was ordered to the charge of a hospital train running from Nashville and Louisville. In this service he continued till near the close of the war, having under his care other hospital trains, clearing out the hospitals at Chattanooga and Nashville, to make room for the new arrivals from Sherman's army on its march to the sea, and for those brought in from the battle near Nashville. It was while here that Governor Buckingham, ever mindful of the comfort of Connecticut troops, appointed Dr. Webster agent to look out for any of the latter who might be in the various hospitals under his charge. The Fifth and Twentieth Regiments, which were in this Department, shared thus in his faithful ministries. For this extra service, he declined compensation, and though in the employ of the State, labored as a volunteer, his name never appearing on the pay-roll of the Commonwealth.

The Sanitary and Christian Commissions furnished him liberally with all needful supplies for sick and wounded soldiers, thus enabling him to provide with generous hand for their physical and spiritual wants. Few men labored with more self sacrificing devotion ; a true friend of the soldier, an ardent advocate of the rights of those whom "military necessity" obliged us to liberate, he was emphatically the man of all others to do the work he did.

Quartermaster-general AIKEN rendered also efficient aid in his position, coöperating with the Governor amid the press of his duties, the successful performance of which was not a little due to the cordial assistance of official associates. General Aiken bore the first dispatches, which the authorities at Washington received after the outbreak of hostilities, assuring them of speedy assistance, on the part of a loyal governor of a loyal State. He reached Washington at ten P. M., Wednesday, April 24th, and, reporting immediately to General Scott, found him at his headquarters, attended only by two members of his staff. After he had read the paper from Governor Buckingham, which General Aiken presented, he said, excitedly, "Sir, you are the first man I have seen with a written dispatch for three days. I have sent out men every day to get intelligence of the Northern troops ; not one of them has returned. Where are the troops?" At ten o'clock the next day General Aiken calling on President Lincoln, found him alone in his business room up-stairs, looking towards Arlington Heights, through a wide open window, near which stood a spy-glass, or telescope, which he had just been using. After reading the dispatches directed to him, with measured emphasis, and amid evident depression of spirits, he asked, "What is the North about? Do they know our condition?" Before General Aiken left Washington that day he saw the white flag run up over the Capitol, which was the signal that the first Northern troops had arrived, and soon the famous Seventh Regiment of New York entered

the city, bringing hope and assurance of safety at a most
critical moment.

Col. J. H. ALMY is another of our citizens whose labors
were of a nature entitling him to special mention and regard. Commissioned as Assistant Quartermaster-general,
he established himself in New York, devoting his whole
time to facilitating the transit of our troops, to ministering to the wants of the sick, and looking out for the general welfare of Connecticut soldiers. With noble efficiency
throughout the war he discharged the duties of his responsible post, and with admirable executive ability saw that
the sick and wounded were cared for, and that his office
should afford such help and information as the throngs
that visited it sought. His disbursements for the needy
and sick were very large, and met by the expenditure
in part of his own salary, and in part by the generous
contributions of the sons of Connecticut. The daily general business of his agency showed the versatile service
and earnest devotion of the man. Among its duties were,
the collection of back-pay and bounties; correcting errors
in passes and descriptive lists; obtaining of furloughs; reception of boxes of sanitary goods and the prompt shipment of the same to their several destinations; care of baggage; procuration of regimental flags, guidons, together
with musical instruments for various bands, and small arms
for officers; discharges for sick and disabled soldiers, and
responses to letters inquiring for the missing, sick, or
dead. At the end of four years his record showed that
more than two hundred thousand soldiers of Connecticut
and other States, sixty thousand of them sick and
wounded, had passed through his hands, all receiving
transportation, many being otherwise assisted. His office
was like unto "Interpreter's House," in Bunyan's story.
He himself was a universal good Samaritan, as the num-

bers of those he cared for with a brother's sympathy and liberality can attest. Connecticut had no more useful servant than he was, and his best eulogy is in the gratitude of soldiers, who never think of him without invoking blessings on him for his kindly work.

The following testimony by Adjutant-general Williams was borne to the efficient and varied efforts put forth by Colonel Almy, during the war:—

"The services of Colonel John H. Almy, of New York City, who was appointed by your Excellency as Assistant Quartermaster-general for the purpose of extending aid to our volunteers passing through the city, and to assist and advise the friends of sick or deceased soldiers, have been of the most extended and beneficial character. His whole time has been devoted to this noble object, and the zeal and efficiency of his labors can be attested by thousands of grateful hearts. The sick and wounded soldier returning to his home has always found in him a friend whose sympathies were wrought into practical form, and many an anxious wife, mother, or sister has received valuable advice and directions in their efforts for the relief of a suffering husband, son, or brother in the field or hospital."

It is to the credit of our town, that so universally our citizens were eager to render any and every assistance to the cause, and to those who went forth to do battle in its behalf, of none could it be said "facile princeps," for the motto of the royal crest seemed to have been adopted by all, "Ich dien,"—I serve. In this home-service all classes of our people were zealous to share, and they brought to it a self-sacrificing, generous spirit, that makes it worthy of honorable record.

XI.

"THE SOLDIERS' AID SOCIETY." — WOMAN'S WORK.

1861-65.

> "No sword have I, no battle-blade,
> Nor shining spear; how shall I aid
> My country in her great crusade?
>
> "I am a woman weak and slight.
> No voice to plead, no arm to fight,
> Yet burning to support the Right."
>   CAROLINE A. MASON.

THE story of our war will never be fully or fairly written, if the achievements of woman in connection with it are untold. And yet their names are not to be found in official reports, nor gazetted for brilliant deeds, such as made many a soldier a hero in the country's sight. It was in hospitals, in Relief Associations in their native towns, in private ministries to the comfort of those they had sent forth with their benedictions, that the patriotism of American women was seen and felt.

The record of Norwich in this respect is one which is deserving of lasting remembrance and honor. All that could be done by our ladies to provide for and encourage our soldiers, was done, with a rare persistency and devotion. From the memorable Sabbath, which followed the President's first call for troops, when they sewed all day on the outfit of the first Norwich company that went forth to the strife, clear through the long years of the war, they were unwearied in their zeal to do for the comfort and cheer of those in the army.

Beginning, as was just stated, their public labors in behalf of the soldiers, on Sabbath, April twenty-first, they continued these noble efforts, which the stern necessities of the crisis made for a while so urgent, for a number of days. As the result of their associated work in this form they made up nineteen hundred shirts of flannel, and checked cotton, besides other articles of apparel required by the soldiers for their outfit, which were never reported. It was owing to their timely services, so cordially and unfalteringly rendered, that the first companies from Norwich were put in readiness for their prompt departure.

During these busy, exciting days, when the Norwich ladies met daily in Breed Hall to sew, the following was the favorite song, which ofttimes relieved the tedium of their work, and gave expression to the feelings, which at this early stage of the war were well-nigh universally shared. The song was written by one of their number, who subsequently became a leading spirit in connection with the "Soldier's Aid," and was first sung by a choir of young ladies on the balcony of the "Wauregan House," on the occasion of the departure of Captain Chester's company.

"THE SOLDIERS' AID SOCIETY." — WOMAN'S WORK.

> "What means this wild rush and commotion,
>   In our homes once so peaceful and free?
> Why burns every patriot's devotion,
>   For his country to die, if need be?
> 'Tis that traitors heap insult upon her,
>   Now they boldly come forward to view,
> And our flag trails in dust and dishonor,
>   The flag of the red, white, and blue.
>
> "Our flag to our eyes is the emblem
>   Of all that the soul holds most dear!
> To defend it, we'll show the proud boaster,
>   Northern men neither tremble nor fear!
> In such danger 'tis no time to dally,
>   We'll swear to be faithful anew;
> Party names all forgetting, we'll rally
>   Round the flag of the red, white, and blue.
>
> "O my country! to-day on thy altar
>   Our best treasures most freely we lay;
> In thy honor no true man will falter,
>   But boldly stand up, come what may!
> While we breathe, we'll desert her cause never,
>   We'll all to our colors prove true,
> The Flag of our Union forever —
>   Three cheers for the red, white, and blue."
>
> E. P.

The "Soldier's Aid Society" was soon after organized, and was the chief organization which the patriotism of Norwich ladies made so serviceable to the soldiers in the field. Its history, from the commencement to the close of its existence, forms a splendid memorial of their earnest efforts in ministering to the comfort of Connecticut troops. The Society was organized in September, 1861, under a call to furnish woolen stockings for the soldiers. Donations of yarn were received, and quickly by willing fingers transformed into warm socks. Considerable finished work was also contributed. At Governor Buckingham's suggestion, an arrangement was soon made for supplying regimental hospitals; and the ladies of Norwich assumed the especial care of the Sixth, Eighth, Eleventh, and Thirteenth Regiments. They called upon the ladies of New London and Windham Counties to coöperate, who generously responded with the proffer of their services. The Society found an increasing field of usefulness opened before it, and sought, with the necessities engendered by the long continuance of the war, to enlarge its operations. This of course added to the labor of those connected with the organization and made the tax upon time and personal service by no means small. At the head of this Aid Society, stood Miss Elizabeth Greene, whose untiring zeal and personal superintendence secured for it that efficiency and widening scope, which made it second to no other kindred association in the State. With time and means at her own command, her work in connection with the Society was one prompted by the purest patriotism, while her executive skill and womanly tact kept up the interest in it, and rallied to its enthusiastic support all classes in the community. Long will she be remembered, by those whom she befriended; and among the many titles she won, for her rare graces of character, and her devotion to other's good, none will place her higher, or be cherished longer, than the one-her war labors especially gained her,—"The soldier's friend." She put her whole heart into her sacrificial serving during the years of the rebellion, and made the sympathy and help of Norwich women felt by Connecticut troops wherever they were to be found, in camp, hospital, or prison. With Miss Greene were associated two other ladies, who shared with her the management and personal direction of the Society's labors—Miss Carrie L. Thomas, and Miss Eliza P. Perkins. With a fidelity and ardor that was steadfastly maintained, they stood to their posts of laborious service, ably systematizing and seconding the

"THE SOLDIERS' AID SOCIETY." — WOMAN'S WORK. 181

great work the Society had in hand. Miss Emeline Norton, towards the latter part of the war, held a responsible position in the Society's management, and gave of her time and strength to keep up its efforts.

In the first year of its existence the Society received: —

1861. October.	By thirty-three subscriptions from Norwich Ladies	$139 65
October 26.	By the Nightingales	29 33
November.	By the Norwich Patriotic Fund	200 00
December.	By Personal subscriptions . .	57 94
	Total for 1861	$426 92

For the second year (1862) the receipts were: —

1862. By Norwich Ladies .	$291 43
Norwich Gentlemen .	250 54
The Nightingales .	43 50
Christ Church	67 00
East Main Street Methodist Church	38 58
Greeneville Congregational Church .	90 00
Sachem Street Methodist Church	49 50
Central Methodist Free Church	63 00
St. Mary's (R. C.) Church .	52 54
First Congregational Church .	101 00
Broadway Congregational Church	192 19
Central Baptist Church . .	53 86
Second Congregational Church .	497 65
Universalist Church . . .	40 00
Grace Church . . .	25 00
Trinity Church . .	71 00
First Baptist Church	18 20
Christ Church Fair .	710 00
Music Vale Seminary . .	15 00
Three Concerts, 152, 48, and 144	344 00
Soldier in Potomac Army .	50 00
Soldier in Eighteenth Regiment	1 00
Miscellaneous . . .	5 05
Subscribers	37 00
Lisbon Lady	5 00
Ladies' Association, Old Saybrook	2 00

182   THE NORWICH MEMORIAL.

Patriotic Fund	$200 00
Lyceum Lecture Committee	55 00
Total for 1862	$3,369 04

The receipts for the third year (1863) were as follows:—

1863. By Norwich Ladies	$468 67
Norwich Gentlemen	1,211 70
Nightingales	130 90
Wendell Phillips	50 00
Miscellaneous	21 27
Patriotic Fund	100 00
Christ Church Collection	75 75
Montville Congregational Church	8 80
Thompson Soldiers' Aid	22 95
Mystic Island	16 00
Hopeville Young People's Soldier's Aid	10 00
"Up Street"	20 00
Contributors	6 50
Total for 1863	$2,142 54

So far as the accounts of the "Aid" can be made out, from the monthly reports published in the daily paper, the receipts for the fourth year (1865) were as follows:—

1864, Nov. to	
1865, Sept. By Christ Church Collection	$25 00
First Congregational Church	96 53
Collections	143 28
Hume's Reading	147 25
Contributors	674 36
Miscellaneous	9 43
Sale of Photographs	40 50
Soldiers	25 00
Sale of sundries	14 90
Juvenile Society	15 00
Total from Nov. 1864, to Sept. 1865	$1,191 25

This hardly represents the exact receipts of the "Aid for the years 1864–65," but owing to the loss of the Society's

"THE SOLDIERS' AID SOCIETY." — WOMAN'S WORK. 183

account-book, it is given as the nearest approximate returns possible under the circumstances.

The number of articles sent off by the "Soldiers' Aid," so far as they can be itemized, are as follows: —

	Total.		Total.
Bed-sacks	460	Slippers	623
Quilts	1,213	Towels	3,122
Sheets	2,021	Handkerchiefs	1,773
Blankets	290	Mittens	1,264
Pillow-sacks	392	Pincushions	613
Pillow-cases	2,018	Thread-bags	441
Pillows	1,139	Coats	79
Flannel Shirts	1,993	Vests	84
Cotton Shirts	2,359	Pants	65
Second-hand Shirts	793	Bound Books	438
Drawers	1,519	Wine — Bottles	284
Wrappers	403	Vegetables — Boxes	2
Socks	6,587	Pickles — Boxes	30
Bandages		Dried Fruit and Jellies.	
Lint and Old Linen.			

These various articles were distributed thus: —

THE ORGANIZATIONS SUPPLIED BY THE AID SOCIETY.

Forwarded To The	Quilts	Pillows	Bed Sacks	Blankets	Pillow Cases	Wrappers	Drawers	Flannel Shirts	Socks	Sheets	Towels	Slippers	Mittens	Handkerchiefs	Cotton Shirts	Packages of Sundries
Woman's Central Relief Association	279	243	74	—	305	73	471	1,265	1,048	463	319	204	—	—	512	352 and 1 barrel jellies, dried apples, etc.
Sixth Regiment	85	—	—	—	—	—	—	—	—	—	—	—	74	—	157	60
Eighth Regiment	—	62	—	64	100	42	248	337	286	84	240	—	146	45	—	50
Eleventh Regiment	30	—	40	8	33	—	24	40	70	74	38	—	—	—	—	140 and 1 hhd. London porter.
Thirteenth Regiment	115	—	102	75	100	—	122	56	70	144	75	105	—	—	—	5
Fourteenth Regiment	—	12	12	—	—	18	18	158	24	26	64	—	—	—	—	71
Eighteenth Regiment	—	21	21	—	15	18	48	48	154	55	52	—	—	—	—	—
Twentieth Regiment	—	—	18	—	—	18	—	—	42	22	60	—	—	—	—	—
New England Woman's Aid Association	186	105	—	—	50	—	22	132	—	48	26	12	—	25	—	258 and 8 vests.
Fairfax Hospital, Alexandria, Va.	—	—	—	—	—	—	8	—	42	—	18	4	—	36	39	—
David's Island Hospital	—	—	—	—	—	—	—	132	73	—	12	—	—	—	4	Dried apples and wine and 24 thread and needle bags.
First Conn. Cavalry	—	—	—	—	—	—	—	—	—	—	—	—	30	—	—	1 box turkeys and 27 thread and needle bags.
Sanitary Commission	—	—	—	—	—	—	—	100	50	—	—	—	—	—	—	Old linen, blackberry syrup, and wine.
Christian Commission	—	—	—	—	—	—	—	39	29	—	—	—	—	—	—	Books and papers.
Connecticut State Agent	—	—	—	—	—	—	—	54	42	—	—	—	—	—	—	1 box wine

Forwarded to the Freedmen : 3 quilts, 103 dresses, 24 aprons, 1 shawl, 19 under-garments, 9 coats, 11 vests, 8 pants, 2 hats, 1 pair boots, 16 shirts, 7 barrels clothing, books and papers.

Besides the supplies forwarded to these enumerated regiments and associations, the "Aid" was solicited to contribute to the following, and did so with a generous hand. Hospital at Fort Schuyler; National Freedmen's Society, Washington; First Regiment S. C. Volunteers; New Haven General Hospital; Freedmen at Port Royal, Dr. Peck; Freedmen at Washington, Dr. Webster; Chesapeake Hospital; Fortress Monroe, Miss Ramsey; Mrs. J. G. Piatt, Washington; Mrs. Tyler, Philadelphia; Freedmen at Newbern.

MONEYS EXPENDED BY THE "AID."

For Flannel	$3,181 57	Yarn		$1,143 48
For Ticking	267 17	Mittens		72 23
Sheeting, Shirting, Calico	1,348 55	David's Island Hospital		65 00
Toweling	16 00	Connecticut State Agent		25 00
Medicines	133 40	Needy Soldiers and families		128 00
Transportation, Carpentry, Sundries	1,529 34	Total from 1861–65,		$7,909 74

All the clothing and surplus funds remaining on hand at the close of the war were distributed, through the "Aid," for the benefit of soldiers and their families.

These statistics give but little idea of the personal labor of the ladies. For the articles they sent away had for the most part to be made up, and represent an amount of work which only the industrious hands of women could perform, and which was a serious tax upon their time and strength. Then, in addition to this simple plying of the needle, on them fell largely the work of collecting the funds they received, representing an amount of solicitation which cost many weary walks, and the most diligent persistency in presenting the claims of the Society to individual contributors.

In the fall of 1862, when all the churches in Norwich took up in behalf of the "Aid" a collection, this generous action on their part was secured through the efforts of a special committee, consisting of Mrs. Charles Johnson and Mrs. John B. Young, who took great pains in bringing the matter before all the several church committees. The result was, that all the congregations, including St. Mary's (R. C.), responded. To the faithful and cheerfully rendered service of these two ladies was the exchequer of the Society indebted for the handsome sums it received from the churches.

In September, 1862, the ladies of Christ Church held a fair, for which they worked with the utmost enthusiasm, and from which they netted for benefit of the " Aid " seven hundred and ten dollars. In April, 1864, after the most painstaking preparation, an elaborate exhibition was given in Breed Hall, for the " Soldiers' Aid," lasting through the greater part of a week. The programme, which was changed each evening, embraced tableaux, charades, statuary, of the most finished description. Amateur vocalists of the city, together with White's Band, contributed their services for the occasion. Many of the costumes were procured from out of town, and every possible effort was made to render the entertainment of unequaled variety and completeness. Between fifty and sixty ladies and gentlemen took part, and their representations were with every advantage that appropriate costume, and study of the characters personated, could secure. The exhibition was the most artistic and successful ever witnessed in this city, and reflected the greatest credit upon the committee, who spent most of their time for three weeks in arranging for it.

To Miss Gertrude May, Mrs. David Young, Miss Emeline Norton, Miss Hannah Ripley, Miss Elizabeth Greene, Mrs. Gardiner Greene, and Mrs. John B. Young, who, with rare taste, and patient labor, projected and superintended this unique entertainment, was the " Soldiers' Aid " indebted for the handsome resultant of nearly nine hundred dollars. The public appreciated their patriotic services, and the exhibition was attended throughout by large crowds, eliciting the heartiest applause. Some of the charades were composed for the occasion, while many of the tableaux were original. Not a few of our citizens well remember the intense enjoyment these entertainments afforded, and recall even now with just pride the industry and zeal of those who wrought their patriotism into so delightsome and useful a form.

Aside from its regular work of preparing and forwarding supplies to the sick and wounded of our soldiers, the "Aid" not infrequently sought to diversify and add to its usual labors.

In November, 1862, in response to an appeal of Colonel J. H. Almy to furnish pies for the Thanksgiving dinner of the Connecticut soldiers encamped on Long Island, the "Aid" received one hundred and sixty pies of various kinds, which were carefully packed in boxes and promptly forwarded. These indispensables of the Yankee's Thanksgiving feast were keenly appreciated by the soldiers, and brought back some feeling acknowledgments.

Again, in November, 1864, the "Aid" issued an appeal to the public for contributions toward furnishing a "Thanksgiving" to Connecticut Regiments. Somehow there was a sort of secret power to these appeals of the Society which made them always effective. The ladies of the "Aid" had the art of putting, as well as doing things, that made them successful in all their patriotic undertakings. So it proved in this instance, for their report runs thus: —

"Received five hundred and seventy-four dollars, two hundred and fifteen turkeys, one hundred and ninety-nine pies, thirty-three chickens, ninety-six cans of tomatoes, four and three-quarters barrels of apples, twelve tongues, forty-five bottles of pickles. Also, divers roast geese, spare-ribs, beef *a la mode*, corned beef, roast veal, brown bread, sugar, cheese, oranges, crackers, gingerbread, cake, crullers, doughnuts, cookies, ginger-snaps, nuts, raisins, plum-puddings, tobacco. From out of town, — two boxes of turkeys, etc., North Stonington; two barrels turkeys, chickens, etc., and one box of apple-sauce, Dayville; one large box roast turkeys, Windham; three smaller boxes roast turkeys, chickens, etc., Danielsonville."

All told, these contributions filled twenty-one barrels and seven boxes, and were forwarded to the Eighth, Ninth, Tenth, Eleventh, Thirteenth, Twenty-first, and Twenty-ninth Regiments. Three hundred dollars were spent for turkeys, chickens, etc., for Connecticut soldiers on the James River, and in the Shenandoah Valley. One hundred dollars were appropriated for purchasing supplies for sick and wounded soldiers of the State in Washington hospitals. One hundred and seventy-four dollars were applied to the Thanksgiving pleasures of sick and wounded soldiers and returned prisoners at David's Island. The stores were generously conveyed free of charge by Adams' Express to New York. Such remembrances as the ladies of the "Aid" received from the happy soldiers, can be better imagined than described. One of the turkeys forwarded had a note attached, addressed "to any soldier or sailor who may receive this Thanksgiving gift," and brought back promptly this feeling acknowledgment:—

CAMP OF MOUNTED RIFLES,
KAUTZ'S CAVALRY, *November* 25, 1864.

Mr. ———, DEAR SIR: I have just risen from eating a good dinner off your turkey, — a jolly good soldier's dinner; and with it was received your kind and sympathising letter, which added good sauce, making a kind gift the better from feeling how truly you felt for us who are in the field, facing the common foe. It is not in the power of my pen to describe the feeling of satisfaction and pleasure, and of gratitude, we all feel that those at

Edward Harland

home could think of the poor soldier. Accept the thanks of one who really enjoyed your bounty. May the good God spare you to eat many Thanksgiving dinners, restore yours in safety to you, and prosper you in all the pursuits of life. Accept, again, the grateful thanks of one who enjoyed your kind gifts, with this acknowledgment of its safe arrival and proper disposition.

Your grateful and obliged friend,

A MOUNTED RIFLE.

Lieutenant-colonel Peale wrote back a warm letter of thanks in behalf of the regiment, whose Thanksgiving bounties made them feel peculiarly loving towards the "Soldiers' Aid." No more welcome "birds" could have been sent to the brave men who were still roughing it amid war's duties and hardships, than these savory turkeys and chickens, and to a New England soldier it was next to being at home, to have one of these pleasant reminders of the great family feast of the year, well supplemented with a genuine Yankee pie.

The following letter from Dr. C. B. Webster, to the "Aid," will show the nature of his labors, and the assistance which was cheerfully accorded him: —

WASHINGTON, *February* 7, 1863.

I learn that the "Soldiers' Aid" in Norwich will coöperate with friends of the contrabands in providing clothing for these destitute people. You may have learned already that I am stationed at the Contraband Camp Hospital in this city. Seeing every day the pressing wants of the sick at this camp, my thoughts turn at once to benevolent friends in Norwich, whose hearts and hands have ever been ready for every good work.

We have here about eleven hundred refugees from slavery. More than three hundred are sick and under medical treatment. Government furnishes to them army rations and medicines. For many supplies almost indispensable to the sick, and for clothing of all kinds these people must still look to the liberality of benevolent friends.

This demand is met to some extent by the Quakers of Philadelphia and New York, but with the numbers to be supplied here, at Alexandria, at Fortress Monroe and the great Southwest, and these numbers likely to increase, it will be seen that the call is urgent. These people come with their little all, contained in most cases in a bundle or box, which a woman can "tote" upon her head. Their great possession they consider their freedom.

The camp is constantly changing, and this is the reason of the continual demand for clothing. The able-bodied find employment soon after arrival, and go out, leaving their places to be supplied by new comers, who sometimes arrive to the number of one hundred and fifty a day. Many of these, however, become sick from exposure on their journey, and are obliged to remain. They need stout clothing, of the coarsest material, large, thick shoes for both men and women, and socks are greatly in demand. Anything, literally anything, in the shape of a garment of any kind can be put to immediate and good service. Nothing can come amiss.

We have two hundred patients in the Small-pox Hospital. We greatly need clothing wherewith to furnish them when they are able to go out, after recovery, or for decent burial. Many thousand must die in the transition from bondage to freedom, and it is sad in the extreme to see the sufferings of great numbers of these poor people, alleviated only by the thought that they die free, and do not leave their children slaves.

May I not appeal through you to many kind friends of the poor in Norwich for the ability to supply a portion of the pressing want?

The "Aid" at once issued their call for contributions, and with the usual success. Many a box went to this camp from this Society which attested the wide sympathy of the ladies, and the promptitude with which they responded to every new appeal for help.

The "Soldiers' Aid," as will be seen from the facts already

given, sent their supplies wherever needed, and did not confine their ministries to Connecticut regiments exclusively. They were as impartial in their serving as such patriotic ardor as they manifested could alone have made them.

Among the many fortunate recipients of their favors was the First Regiment South Carolina Volunteers, under command of that brave soldier Colonel Higginson. He was among the first to advocate the emancipation of the slaves, and the enlistment of the most capable into the military service of the United States. And ever ready to do what he so eloquently urged as an act of justice and a measure fraught with incalculable benefit to the Union cause, he accepted the colonelcy of the first regiment of blacks organized in South Carolina.

Our "Aid" had the honor of contributing the first box of supplies to these swarthy soldiers, and their noble Colonel sent the ladies the following acknowledgment:—

HEADQUARTERS FIRST REGIMENT S. C. V.,
CAMP SAXTON, *February* 13, 1863.

———: Your inestimable box arrived here yesterday in perfect order, the packing being worthy of the contents. It was received with delight by Dr. Rogers and myself, and all the greater from the fact that since our last successful expedition our thoughts have been much occupied with sickness, and we have been compelled to enlarge our hospital accommodation. This is, I find, the sickly period of the year for the negroes — February and March, — while the summer is such for the whites. The physique of these people is peculiar. They have not the toughness of the whites, but instead of this have greater susceptibility, both of disease and cure.

They have a great tendency to pneumonia and pleurisy, and the only way is to take each case very promptly, when they can be cured with the facility of children, while twenty-four hours delay may prove fatal. You will see how directly this bears on the importance of hospital conveniences, and this gives a peculiar value to your donation.

It is the only donation we have received from the North, except a box of mittens just received from Worcester, for the use of our guard at night. The nights here are often uncomfortably cold, ice forming in the tents, though the days are warm. Just now, however, we are having weather like our Northern May.

It is impossible to command this people and not become attached to them. Under military organization they are so prompt and ready in service, so cheerful and patient in action, so free from inconvenient vices, and in general so confiding and so little troublesome.

On the other hand, in battle they show a fiery energy which must give them an important part in the history of the war. I feel sure that no one who aids their usefulness will have reason to repent it.

With sincere thanks, in behalf of the regiment, to the "Soldiers' Aid Society," I am most cordially yours.

THOMAS W. HIGGINSON,
Colonel Commanding First Regiment S. C. V.

Aside from those ladies we have already had occasion to name, there were others whose fervid loyalty prompted them to services deserving special mention.

The "Soldiers' Aid" received an invitation to be represented in the great Northwestern Fair, held in Chicago, in October, 1863, under the auspices of the Sanitary Commission. The response was prompt and hearty, and resulted in the preparation and shipment of a large box filled with articles and gifts from the ladies of this city and vicinity. These donations were exhibited first in the large windows of the "Soldiers' Aid" room, making a display which was creditable to the taste and industry of the contributors.

A letter from one who visited the Fair makes the following reference to this handsome donation from the "Aid":—

"As a Norwich boy, I am proud of the part that was taken by its citizens in not only sending some beautiful articles to the Fair, but also sending a delegation to see them. And here let me say that 'Old Connecticut' was represented by one of the handsomest booths, and some of the finest articles on exhibition. God bless her; she has done her part towards giving our brave soldiers over sixty-five thousand dollars. Who says we of the Northwest can 'leave New England out in the cold' after this."

The "Aid Society" acquired a wide reputation for its efficiency, and calls were made upon it from various parts of the country. It kept such a steady stream of supply flowing toward the needy in our army, that abroad the impression prevailed that it must be a much larger organization than it really was. It had indeed a wider constituency than that represented by Norwich ladies, indefatigable in good works as they were. For, to the honor of the ladies of New London and Windham Counties, it should be recorded, that they generously contributed of their money and effort to it, and the Relief Associations formed in the adjoining towns wisely and cordially became auxiliaries to it. So that it was the grand "Soldiers' Aid Society" for Eastern Connecticut, with its headquarters here, and the leading spirits to whose direction and peerless devotion it owed its name and usefulness, were residents of Norwich. Now that we can look back and review its history, a juster estimate than ever before can be formed as to that unwearied labor and sacrifice, which through all the years of our war made this agency so widely beneficent in its influence. Hereafter the "Soldiers' Aid Society" of Norwich will become the historic witness to the earnest patriotism of the ladies of this town, and of those who in New London and Windham Counties contributed to its treasury and stores of supplies.

We presume very few of our citizens had at the time any very just idea of the amount and extent of the work done by the ladies connected with the "Soldiers' Aid." Their rooms in the Rockwell Building were always the scene of the utmost activity. Here were delivered boxes and packages from auxiliary societies scattered throughout the adjoining counties, where they were carefully repacked and forwarded to their destinations.

All the boxes they sent off, were with but few, if any exceptions, safely received; a fact quite creditable to the business tact and care of the managers at the rooms. Had it been possible to find the letters received by the "Aid," acknowledging the supplies sent forth by it, they would have best revealed how widely distributed were its stores, how keenly appreciated by the recipients, and how prompt and generous were the responses to those who appealed to this Society for help.

Among the knitters of stockings, was a Mrs. Prudence Stoddard, of Noank, aged ninety-four, who sent in with a pair of her own knitting, a note, stating that she had had the privilege of knitting stockings for our soldiers during three wars, beginning with the Revolution. Another lady in Lisbon, aged ninety-one, sent in to the "Aid" one pair of stockings, and one pair of mittens, her own handiwork. Mrs. Cady, of Norwich Falls, and Mrs. Thomas Lathrop, of Norwich Town, aged ninety-two, contributed stockings knit by their yet nimble hands.

Among the most efficient of the societies, auxiliary to "The Soldiers' Aid," was the one supported by Norwich town ladies, whose activity in every good cause entitles them to the highest praise. The name adopted for this sister "Aid Society" was, "The Nightingales," and with most commendable zeal and generous emulation did they labor through the years of our conflict, contributing to the

"Norwich Aid" a steady stream of the choicest stores, and articles for the comfort of our troops.

It originated about the same time that the "Aid" did, under Mrs. Henry Thomas and Mrs. Daniel W. Coit. These two ladies were ably assisted by others, until for constancy and effectiveness in their beneficent giving and working, the Nightingales were unsurpassed.

This Society kept no books of its own, and only a part of what it accomplished appears in the incomplete reports we have given of the "Soldiers' Aid." Everything contributed to the latter by it, was carefully recorded, and no auxilliary was more regular or generous in the offerings it made to the cause.

The Nightingales had a quiet method of working, rather characteristic of all their charitable undertakings; but it was exceedingly productive, and the soldiers in the field or hospital soon came to recognize what came from them. They coöperated so continuously with the larger Society, that the two seemed more like one organization divided into branches for convenience in laboring.

Miss Carrie L. Thomas was among the most active in keeping the Nightingales to their devoted work, and served as a sort of secretary, reporting to the "Aid" their contributions in money and supplies.

The Greeneville ladies acquired a high name for their patriotic devotion to the soldiers. They were steady contributors to the "Soldiers' Aid," and were unflagging in their zeal to do whatever would prove helpful to those who were sick or in want. In 1863, they forwarded two boxes of supplies to the Union prisoners in Richmond; one box was sent to Libby, and the other directed to Belle Isle.

By the colored ladies in Norwich was organized, February tenth, 1864, the first "Aid Society," to render assistance to the sick and needy in the two colored regiments sent forth by the State. Mrs. Walter Burr stood at the head of this association, and with the circle specially interested in its operations did much for the welfare of the members of the Twenty-ninth and Thirtieth Regiments. The record of the doings of this agency has unfortunately been lost, which prevents our giving a summary of what was accomplished.

The following interesting incident, memorializing the patriotism of one of our Norwich ladies, now gone to her exceeding great reward, is worthy of record here. She was among the most active in doing aught that was possible for the comfort of the soldiers, though her labors were so unobtrusive, that not all knew of their extent. Among her papers the following memorandum was found, which will recall her to those who shared with her in the works to which she and others gave themselves during our exciting war years : —

"*July* 4, 1864.

"To day, the anniversary of our glorious independence, I have completed the *one hundredth* pair of socks that I have knitted for the brave soldiers, who are nobly sustaining the honor of our country on many a hard fought battle-field. God grant them success. Theirs will be the glory when the Stars and Stripes wave over a united nation. For them are our prayers, and to them we look with hopeful hearts for the restoration of peace and prosperity in all our borders. The soldier who receives this pair of socks will gratify me by advising me of the same."

The answer came back after her death, and was a response that showed a brave and thoughtful soldier had been the recipient of her humble gift.

On the completion of her fiftieth pair, a similar note had accompanied it, to which there was returned the following grateful acknowledgment : —

STEAM TRANSPORT "ATLANTIC,"
MISSISSIPPI RIVER, *September* 30, 1863.

DEAR MADAM, — I received a pair of stockings, just before leaving Vicksburg, in which was a note stating that they were the fiftieth pair you had knitted, and donated to the soldiers. You say your prayer is always "for those who are battling for right and their country." Would that the same was felt and uttered by all we leave behind us in the North. I much regret that we have foes both North and South to contend with, but we must trust in "Him who rules all things," and feel that right and justice will in the end triumph.

We are enduring hardships and privations that but a few months since seemed almost impossibilities; are doing it to protect our once glorious and yet much-loved country. We have left those behind who are dearer than life itself, and have rallied for the protection of the "old flag." We must, we shall succeed. Many have already fallen, and many more will doubtless meet a soldier's fate before the rebels are conquered; and if it is decreed we shall no more in this life meet our dear ones at home, may God in mercy grant that we may meet where parting is no more.

Allow me to thank you for these stockings; thank you for the kind interest you manifest in the welfare of the soldiers, and may I think that I have an interest in the prayers of the donor, though a stranger.

We have now started on an expedition to the relief of General Rosecrans, and expect to have to march some three hundred miles.

Excuse, and believe me very respectfully
Yours,
W. H. KEELING,
Co. H, First Battalion 13*th U. S. Infantry (General Sherman's Army Corps), Cairo, Illinois.*

Among the most patriotic and devoted of our ladies during the rebellion, was Mrs. Dr. Webster. She shared in the toils of her husband among the Freedmen, and subsequently served with him in his hospital work, becoming a valuable assistant through her own tender ministries to their comfort and relief.

When in Washington, while Dr. Webster had charge of the Freedmen's Camp, she commenced the first school ever taught among them.

At Springdale Camp at Arlington, she opened a day school, attended by from fifty to sixty pupils. While at four other contiguous camps, she had schools every other day. At first she taught these neglected ones, just out of slavery, and in utter ignorance, from cards hung upon the camp buildings or upon trees. As they advanced, she had a supply of suitable books procured for them. In this way she had, in all, the supervision of between five and six hundred scholars. Writing concerning them at one time, she said: " Twelve or fifteen out of this school of fifty are making rapid progress, learning as fast as any children, and all are well. Some are learning arithmetic remarkably fast."

Again, when at Huntsville, she had charge of the school for the freed children. At this early date it was far from popular to have anything to do with these unfortunate people. She had the honor of being a pioneer in what has since become an extensive and confessedly noble work. Many were the ludicrous as well as painful scenes she witnessed, while laboring in behalf of the Freedmen.

The following extract is from a letter of another of our Norwich ladies, who labored with signal zeal and devotion among the Freedmen of Newbern, showing to what works of beneficence an earnest patriotism prompted some of them.

"LIFE AMONG THE FREEDMEN AT NEWBERN."

"We live in an apostolic manner, as far as a community of goods is concerned. Everybody borrows and begs of his neighbor. You cannot buy or hire anything in a respectable and civilized way. If we wish to ride, Lieutenant F. is head of the Ambulance corps, and furnishes as many ambulances as we wish.

"The chief quartermaster is an intimate friend of the family, and we have many favors through him. Lieutenant K. is head of the engineer department, and when we wanted a bell hung, he detailed a man to do it. The bell was found in one house, the wire in another, and after some days work, we can at last get a servant into the house without going out into the rain and cold to call him. To-night, as it looked like clearing, we went out in an ambulance to Howell's Camp, to the entertainment given to the school, but Mrs. Hawley supposing we would not come in the storm, put it off till to-morrow night. We went into the schoolhouse and saw the tree, which looked beautifully. It was an odd ride ; the night was very dark, and the driver missed the road and came near overturning amidst the stumps outside the camp. Returning we rode through the streets, and the camp looked very bright and cheerful. There are no windows to the houses, but you could see the red firelight shining through the cracks between the logs. Many of the doors were open, showing the bright wood fire, and the families sitting round. All was quiet ; we did not see a person outside, except the guards at the church door, but there was singing everywhere.

"We heard 'Rally round the Flag, boys,' 'Shout the Battle-cry of Freedom,' 'John Brown's body,' and as we rode farther on, the voice of prayer from a little gathering, and one of their old wild hymns, 'Jesus died on the cross, on the cross for me.' I never shall forget this last evening of the year.

"New-year's Day in Newbern. I have had many a happy New-year's Day as you well know, but none so truly happy as this one. Last night I could not sleep, and really watched for the morning. At ten, we went to the Methodist church to attend Miss Canady's Christmas tree. She has shown a great deal of taste in making wreaths and adornments for the church, which has been newly white-washed for the occasion, and with the beautiful tree laden with presents (mostly from the Norwich box), presented a charming sight. The flag of the school hung from the singing gallery and a large cross of box was placed in front of the tree. The scholars sang a New-year's greeting, then Mr. James made an address in his happiest manner, followed by the song. There were one hundred and eighty-eight scholars present, from grown up women to little five year olds. A great bag was arranged on a table in front of the tree for the youngest children, who all passed by in order, each one putting in a little black hand, and it was as good as a play to see their faces as they examined the gift, and then held it up for their mothers and fathers to see, who lined the galleries on either side, looking down upon them with eager eyes. The presents of the tree were marked with the names of the scholars. When we had seen them given out we left, the children rising respectfully when we passed down the aisle. Everything passed off with the greatest order and propriety, far more so than many of our Christmas celebrations at home.

"In the afternoon there was a union meeting of all the schools, at the church, when the banners, which had been made by the teachers, were presented to the respective schools, by an appropriate speech. Three of these addresses were by colored men. They all sang and cheered, and had a glorious time generally. They then marched in procession to the 'teachers' house,' where they formed in a hollow square, sang 'Rally Round the Flag,' and cheered President Lincoln, General Butler, and the teachers. Then they called in front of our house, sang 'America,' cheered Mr. James, General Peck, and General Palmer, and separated, each school marching off to its own camp, in military order.

"At sundown Mr. Johnson and I had an ambulance, and taking two of the teachers, started for Howell's Camp. It had cleared off cold, and by the time we arrived we felt as though we must be at home in the North, we were so freezing cold. Mrs. Hawley's tree was splendid. The log schoolhouse and church was full to overflowing, and the lights being all on the tree, behind it, gave a charming effect, much like a bit of fairy land springing out of darkness. Some young soldiers who came with the teachers, made short speeches, helped the children sing, and we had a free and easy time. We had 'Rally Round the Flag,' 'Old John Brown,' 'Happy Land,' and other cheery songs, and left at eight o'clock, only because we could not get back to Newbern unless we came away then. The camp is without the lines, and the bridge over the creek is taken up by the picket guard every night at eight o'clock."

Thus earnestly, through associated effort, did our ladies seek to do what they could for the comfort and cheer of the soldiers. This, however, did not exhaust their patriotic zeal, for some were desirous of performing military duty in the only way allowed them by law. Accordingly, at their own expense, they procured acceptable *representative recruits*, and presented them for enlistment in the service, and in this way had a personal representation in the ranks of the Union Armies. The government, to meet such instances of noble patriotism, had certificates engraved, and issued by the War Department to the persons furnishing such recruits, as an official acknowledgment of their public spirit, and devotion to the weal of the country. The first of these ever issued to a Connecticut lady, was received by Mrs. Augusta E. Ely; her sister, Miss Elizabeth Green, being the honored possessor of a similar one. The example of these two patriotic ladies was followed by others here and throughout the State.

XII.

"*Dulce et decorum est pro patria mori.*"

"THE UNRETURNING BRAVE."

"We think with imperious questionings,
   Of the brothers we have lost,
And we strive to track in death's mystery,
   The flight of each valiant ghost."

. . . .

"No fear for them! In our lower field
   Let us toil with arms unstained,
Till at last we be worthy to stand with them
   On the shining heights they've gained.
We shall meet and greet in closing ranks,
   In Time's declining sun;
When the bugles of God shall sound recall,
   And the battle of Life be won."
                    JOHN HAY.

IT is with a peculiar tenderness we gather up for memorial purposes the many names which make our lengthy "roll of the dead." Here come back to us the remembrances of brothers, and sons, and citizens; — those who might have looked forward to contented and busy lives in the various pursuits they left, but who went forth at the sacred call of patriotism, and fell in the cause they risked all they held dear to maintain. Here we behold in impressive form what our war tax was. These names represent the real sacrifices of families and the community. From the fields where they fought, the smoke of battle has long since rolled away, and great Nature has mantled with her verdure each mound and bastion, but the work they wrought, the end for which they yielded up their lives abides secure. "Other men labored, and ye are entered into their labors," so we solemnly confess it to be true with us. It is fitting, therefore, that we enshrine in memorial phrase these names, which will ever live as symbols of nobleness and signs of endearment. Wiser laws, humaner institutions, liberties enlarged, and faith exalted, — these are the crimsoned trophies their blood, with that of others, secured us. These shall proclaim in language more expressive than human lips can utter, in forms more significant than sculptured marble can exhibit, the work and memory of our lamented dead.

Of the more than twelve hundred Norwich citizens (including representative recruits) who served in the ranks of our armies during the rebellion, and helped on the high seas to maintain the honor of the old flag, who followed through temporary defeat to ultimate victory the national standard, and at last saw the rebel colors go down upon the Appomattox, and shared in the rejoicings with which a grateful nation celebrated its final triumph, one hundred and sixty-seven lost their lives. Forty were killed by the bullet on the field, and the rest died in camp, hospital, prison, or after returning to their homes. These, embracing sixteen commissioned officers, and one hundred and fifty-one enlisted men, constitute the oblation made by Norwich to rebellion.

Our list of the "unreturning brave" presents the names, so far as it has been possible to ascertain them, of all who went from this town, whether serving on its quota or not, and nobly proffered their own lives to secure the country from the perils that threatened its certain destruction. Our limited space and knowledge prevent us from speaking with equal fullness of detail of all these fallen heroes, whose simple military records are here given. We do not claim for them any superior merit of devotion or courage over those who went from other towns and States, and met a like fate.

We are justified in praising our own, for we knew their worth, and when they went forth to do battle in behalf of the cause their patriotism led them to espouse, they went in our names, and were followed by our prayers. It is meet therefore that we speak well of them, for we believe them to have been on the whole good soldiers and true men. They claim from us all a grateful remembrance. We cannot forget that those whom we here commemorate died in our places, and by their cheerful endurance of the hardships of their service, of death itself, saved the State.

> "Four hundred thousand men,
> The young, the brave, the true,
> In tangled wood, and mountain glen,
> On battle plain, in prison pen,
> Lie dead for me and you.
> For me and you —
> Four hundred thousand of the brave,
> Have made our ransomed soil their grave
> For me and you,
> Good friend, for me and you."

To be a good soldier, to maintain an unblemished record, and command the respect of comrades and officers in all the trying scenes of war, is no easy task.

Allusion just here may not be inappropriate to that which we shall have no opportunity of referring to later in our narrative. Against some of the names on our "Roll of Honor," will be found recorded that which carries the impeachment of disgrace, and it is a cause of sincere regret, at this late date, when the issues of the conflict have largely disappeared, to find our representatives in the Union armies branded with the word "deserter," or with what is indicative of ignominious punishment.

We have preferred not to enter into any discussion as to the cases of such, but rather leave them to appear as they do, exceptional; and from the fact that but few names are thus shaded over with aught dishonorable, to claim with greater confidence for our soldiers in general, a more than average record for courage and fidelity.

We know but very little of the circumstances of those whose military history, according to the Adjutant's rolls, was not above reproach. And we are apt now to forget what some high-spirited and true men had to suffer from incompetent or severe officers; what disappointments in the way of promotions, earned or promised, embittered them, and tempted them to unsoldierly conduct. There were well established instances where those who had offended, through thoughtlessness of consequences, or through unusual temptations, were treated with a military rigor which gave some army officers the reputation of arbitrary and needless severity. There were yet other instances where the accused were technically guilty, but the mitigating circumstances so numerous, as to make the execution of the sentence impolitic, if not unjust. We do not claim that all our representatives proved in the army all that we fondly hoped they would. We simply bespeak a charitable judgment upon every soldier, whose record is not altogether stainless. Thankful ought we rather to be, that our boys bore themselves so well, and with such uniform honor For they were away from home restraints, and exposed to the demoralizing influences inseparable from war; they were often brought into contact with bad men, who had entered the army with unworthy motives; many of them were in what they regarded as the enemy's country, and were tempted to chafe under that military surveillance which kept them from indulging in private forays upon what the rules of war obliged them to leave intact.

There were, however, many instances of private daring, and self-sacrificing service, which more than counterbalanced whatever brings discredit upon any on our "roll of honor." There were brave deeds performed by privates which never caught the eye of reporters, and so never found their way into the public papers.

Of J. Dickinson Ripley, Hospital Steward of the Eighteenth, who lost his life soon after the war closed, in the burning of the steamer "Commonwealth," at Groton, it is said, that after the battle of Winchester, in which he was severely wounded, he devoted himself first to dressing the wounds of his regimental comrades, leaving attention to his own sufferings till he had done all he could to mitigate the pain of those whom rebel shots had injured.

Such instances of unselfish devotion to the comfort and help of others, we believe, were not infrequent; and they redeem the common soldiers, those upon whom fell the burdens and few of the honors of the struggle, from the charge of being mere hirelings, indifferent to the high duties which, we claim, must have been inspired by patriotic feeling. In the pocket of a Union soldier, far gone with fever, was found a red morocco Testament, and a poor little note-book half soaked through with rain or swamp-damp, in which a few wandering pencil-notes were still legible, and this little couplet altered from an old song:—

> "Not a sigh shall tell my story,
> Silent death shall be my glory."

I will match that last line, has one well said, against the lines on whose simple feeling great poets have been floated into fame.

In fact, it may be claimed that "it was the distinction of all the better class of volunteers that they bore, not only the brunt of fighting and the lassitude of defeat, but all the infirmity and skepticism of their comrades. And their moral power alone made them equal to it. The best men were centres of conscience, planted like flags that have received oaths that they shall never touch the ground. In other lands the nerve of standing armies, that which alone makes them trustworthy in war, and harmless in peace, is an immovably true and valorous body of officers. But the trustworthiness which volunteered for us was not designated alone by shoulder-straps; it was a conspicuous distinction of the private. The instinct of the soldier filled the gaps where incompetency fell and disappeared. He stepped into the place, and showed his commission till a better one appeared. He secured to nature time enough to grow her General, and fought it out on that line three years before he came."

"The first campaign went on with treason and ravin fastened to the throat of the country, incompetency and inexperience hugging every limb, unguarded expenditure and waste the impudent camp-followers of every regiment, and indefinite policy damping every cartridge. Into this border-land the common soldier built his road; at one end of it a hearth-stone that flickered more tremulously than ever with endeared life-breaths; at the other he could not see the head-board at Andersonville and Salisbury; nor the road thither blazed by the sharp edge of war. We have forgotten the weeks and months of popular depression, when our fate lay in the hands of these men at the front, who rallied instantly at the approach of genuine danger, and were disinfected of their doubts by the prospect of death."

The doing one's duty with an army in the field, bravely and faithfully, is to exhibit a high order of manhood. It was the steady performance of the ordinary service, incident to the camp, the march, the battle, that entitles our citizen-soldiers to the gratitude and praise of the country. We cannot but speak in highest terms of those to whom we owe so much, nor can we help believing that war's trials and responsibilities brought to most, if not to all our soldiers, an exaltation of character. Many a thoughtless, idle boy in our army rose, under the heroic excitement of our war of liberty, to a splendid and resolute manhood.

Many were the deeds of sacrifice and devotion performed by rough, untaught men, while those little known before, awakened the admiration of beholders by their fortitude and patient faith.

Here we have presented to us the names of those who looked death calmly in the face, and when life was sweetest, resigned it without a murmur. Putting a charitable construction on the faults of such as these, for they were not perfect, our object has been to render them the homage of our gratitude and praise ; and by such tributes as their memories still call for from us, to preserve in brief their histories. We point with tender hearts to these chaptered names, for they represent those who sacrificed their young lives that their fellow-men might live in safety and honor.

> " Lord of the ages, thanks
> For every pure career
> Of champions, in a hundred ranks,
> Who girt their armor here ;
> Then bore the day's long toil,
> Or laid a young life down,
> For duty, the dear natal soil,
> And the celestial crown."

THE "UNRETURNING BRAVE."

OFFICERS.

De Witt C. Lathrop, Assistant Surgeon in the Eighth Regiment Connecticut Volunteers, died at Newbern, April 18, 1862, of illness caused by over exertion in the duties of his office. Dr. Lathrop was born in Franklin, New London County, Connecticut, June 20, 1819. He graduated at the Yale Medical School, in 1845, and received his commission in his regiment September 21, 1861. His untiring devotion to the wounded and sick in Craven Street Hospital, following so closely upon the labor and exhaustion of the battle-field of Newbern, taxed his strength beyond his powers of endurance, and brought on typhoid fever. With little thought as to his own condition, he confined his attention to his patients, watching over them with the most solicitous care. He was at once prostrated by the fever, and after some two weeks' illness died. He was an earnest-hearted patriot, and consecrated his whole energies to the duties of his position, and has nobly fallen in the service of humanity and his country. His funeral, which took place on the nineteenth of April, from the headquarters of the Sanitary Commission, was attended by the whole medical staff of his corps d'armee and by many of his friends. The usual military escort of his rank was detailed by General Foster, Military Governor of Newbern, and the funeral services were most impressive and solemn.

He was a noble instance of disinterested devotion to those under his charge, while in his profession he had the reputation of skill and faithfulness. He had endeared himself to the soldiers to a marked extent, for he looked upon each one of them as his brother, and when any fell sick he was unremitting in his attention.

On the first attack of his disease, he was taken to the headquarters of the Sanitary Commission by Dr. Page, and there furnished with every convenience and comfort. The best nursing and medical attendance were provided for him, and everything done that friendly and sympathizing comrades could suggest, and it was while surrounded by these that he breathed his last. His remains were brought to Norwich, and public funeral services held in the First Congregational Church, Dr. Arms, Dr. Bond, and Rev. Mr. Gulliver participating, the interment took place at Windham, the place of his early practice. He left a wife and three sons.

CHARLES A. BREED. First Lieutenant Company D, Eighth Regiment. He had been in the war from the first summons, volunteering in Captain Harland's company of the Third Regiment. With true patriotism he entered the ranks, serving as a private in the three months' campaign. On his return with the company he reënlisted for three years, and was commissioned as Second Lieutenant in Captain Ward's company of the Eighth. He remained in the line until the twenty-fifth of December, 1861, when he was detached for duty on the Signal Corps, in which service he was engaged at the time of his death. He was in the battles of Roanoke and Newbern, and distinguished himself for gallantry at the battle of Camden, and was commended in the official reports. While the regiment was encamped at Newport News, Lieutenant Breed was taken sick with an attack of typhoid fever, and after a short illness died, July 30, 1862.

He was greatly beloved by all his comrades in the field, and all who knew him gave him their hearty praise as a brave, kind, and efficient officer. His character was of that open, genial, friendly nature that won for him the hearts of all with whom he was associated. His body was brought to this city in charge of Lieutenant Marvin Wait and private Michael Keagan, who had devotedly attended and nursed him in his last illness. His funeral took place at the residence of his mother, on Church Street, and further services were held in Christ Church, whither the remains were carried. Rev. Mr. Walden, the rector, performed the impressive burial service, when the solemn cortege, composed of the Norwich Light Infantry under Captain Tubbs, the Norwich brass band, members of the Common Council, and friends, passed to Yantic Cemetery, where all that was mortal of the young soldier was laid in the grave. During the passage of the procession the bells of the city tolled, and the flags were displayed at half-mast. At the cemetery the customary military salute was fired over the young hero's grave, and there consigned to mother-earth they left his precious dust.

MARVIN WAIT was born at Norwich, Connecticut, on the twenty-first day of January, 1843. He was the son of John T. and Elizabeth Wait. His paternal grandfather, whose name he bore, occupied a prominent position as a public man and as a lawyer in New London County, from the beginning of the Revolution until the early part of the present century. His father, also well known as a prominent lawyer, was ardently desirous that the son should follow the profession of his ancestors. Accordingly the studies of young Wait were shaped with a view to this result. He gave early tokens that he was possessed of an active, keen, and inquiring mind. He had a ready and retentive memory, a fondness for books, and an aptness for quotations and application of what he had read, that showed great intellectual ability and appreciation. This fondness for reading did not, however, divert him from the usual pursuits and recreations of boyhood. No one entered with more hearty zest into all the sports and pastimes of youth.

Gifted with a ready wit, unusual conversational powers, and a keen perception of the humorous, he was always prepared with a playful answer or sparkling repartee. It is not easy to communicate to those who did not know him intimately, an idea of the traits which, in his early boyhood, made him such an idol of the home circle. It is sufficient to say that no one was ever more tenderly loved, or more fondly cared for than he, the only son of his parents.

In 1858 he entered the Free Academy in Norwich, and there manifested the same ability which had marked his early studies. He showed a peculiar taste for all studies involving literary aptness, and in them he took a high rank. Here, also, was developed a fondness for declamation, in which, owing to his quick and thorough perception of the meaning of an author, he always excelled.

This taste for, and appreciation of literature, was one of the most marked traits of his mind at this time, and attracted the attention of many of his older friends. The principal of the Academy, after Marvin's death, addressed a long letter to his parents, which speaks of his literary ability as indicating mental powers of a very high order. "In the department of the classics," writes Professor Smith, "I have rarely seen his equal, perhaps never his superior, in ability. In elocution he had no superior, and his command of language was also quite remarkable. His deportment at the Academy was without fault, and I do not remember that he ever received even an admonition."

After he had remained at the Academy somewhat over a year, his parents sent him to Williston Seminary, at Easthampton, Massachusetts. While there he endeared himself, by his generous and lovable traits of character and disposition, to all his acquaintances, as was evinced by letters received by his parents after his death, speaking in the most affectionate and tender manner of "our Marvin."

After remaining two terms at Easthampton he entered the Freshman Class at Union College in the fall of 1860. While in college he showed the same mental and social characteristics which had distinguished his prior student life. He made warm and earnest friends, and took a high rank in all classical and literary studies. Professor Hickok, in writing to his parents, condoling with them upon the loss of their son, pays a merited compliment to his character and ability, as manifested in his college life. After remaining at Union until the spring of 1861, it was deemed advisable by his parents, on account of his health, which at that time seemed feeble, that he should leave college and endeavor to regain his full physical vigor. Accordingly, in March, 1861, he set sail for Europe and spent some months in foreign travel.

During his absence the War of the Rebellion was commenced, and the rebel privateers commenced to prey on the commerce of the United States. His journal of the voyage shows that those on board the ship on the return voyage had serious apprehensions of falling into the hands of those whom he calls "the pirates."

On his return, he again entered college, and for a few months pursued his studies with great zeal and earnestness. But all around him was the fever of military excitement, and it seemed to him that it was his duty to volunteer for the defense of the Union. He left college, came to his home in Norwich, and begged permission of his parents to enlist. With great reluctance, yet unable to withstand his earnest desire, his parents consented that their only son, their pride, to whom they looked for a stay in their after years, should try the uncertain chances of war.

General Harland had at that time just received the appointment of Colonel of the Eighth Connecticut Volunteers, and young Wait, with several of his associates and schoolmates, were enrolled as privates in Company D. Soon after the regiment left the State on its way to the seat of war, Marvin was detailed by the Colonel, who had known him from boyhood, to act as his Orderly. In the intervals of leisure consequent upon the routine of camp life, he made military tactics his constant study and practice, and soon became proficient in all the various duties of officer and soldier.

Letters received from him at this time show how thoroughly he enjoyed camp life, and how he saw the ludicrous side of its discomforts and privations.

When the regiment reached Annapolis, it became necessary to organize a Signal Corps to accompany the "Burnside Expedition," then fitting out, and two lieutenants were to be detailed from each regiment for that purpose. Marvin was promoted to a Second Lieutenancy in Company H, and with his intimate friend, Lieutenant Breed, was examined, accepted, and transferred to the Signal Corps.

This recognition of his merits was very gratifying to his parents and to himself. His letters at this time are full of brief and playful allusions to his promotion, coupled with anxiety that he may not fail in the discharge of his duties.

The Signal Corps embarked on the schooner "Col. Satterlee," January 11, 1862. The vessel was old and ill fitted for the voyage, and in the storm which overtook the expedition, was delayed so that she arrived last of all the vessels at the rendezvous, and after great fears had been entertained for her safety.

Lieutenant Wait entered on his duties as an officer of the Signal Corps, and the carefulness and accuracy of his observations and reports were soon noted by his superior officers. On the ninth of February, the battle of Roanoke Island was fought. Lieutenant Wait was on board the steamer "S. R. Spaulding," and was constantly employed sending and receiving messages. Space forbids giving quotations from his letters, which are full of graphic and interesting accounts of this new life. He was soon transferred to the "Phœnix," and there remained until he went on board the "Virginia." The monotony of the life on board these vessels he found somewhat irksome, and longed for something more active. He regretted that he could not be present at the capture of Newbern, but soon after he went there, remaining, however, but a few days. His anxiety for active service was soon gratified, by his being detailed for signal duty at the reduction of Fort Macon, Beaufort, N. C. The accounts of the battle, from official and private sources, all give great praise to the Signal Corps for the part they took in the bombardment, and Lieutenant Wait, in the letter written to his mother the day of the surrender of the fort, modestly speaks of the compliments bestowed upon him by the commanding officer for his excellent work during the fight. For his gallantry in this action, Lieutenant Wait was awarded a signal battle flag, and was commended in the official reports. After the reduction of Fort Macon, Lieutenant Wait returned to Newbern, and on the eighteenth of May was detailed to take charge of a station at Batchelder's Creek. From there he returned to Newbern, discharging the routine duties of his office. He was promoted to be First Lieutenant in June, and on the second day of July, having rejoined his regiment, came with it to Newport News. In July, Lieutenant Breed, who had been his constant friend and companion, died. His body was sent home, and Lieutenant Wait was granted leave of absence to convey the remains to Norwich. This was the last time that his home-friends and relatives saw him. On the second of August, 1862, a little over a month before his death, he followed the remains of his friend to their last resting-place. At the funeral service, which was numerously attended, there were none who knew Lieutenant Wait, but noticed his noble and manly bearing at that time. He seemed to have grown into manhood since he entered the army, though he was not yet twenty years old.

And now came the last month of his life. He left home, and on the nineteenth of August finally rejoined his regiment, after many wanderings, which he describes vividly in his letters. His last letter was to his mother, and is dated September sixth, 1862. Still with his regiment, the youngest officer there, he went through the battles preceding the fatal one at Antietam. How bravely he bore himself that day, all accounts agree. He was wounded twice, but did not leave the field. To quote from the brief memoir published by Lieutenant Eaton, —

"The unflinching hero was first wounded in the right arm, which was shattered. He then dropped his sword to his left hand; he was afterwards wounded in the left arm, in the leg, and in the abdomen. He was then assisted to leave the line by private King, who soon met Mr. Morris, the brave, indefatigable Chaplain of the Eighth Regiment. The Chaplain then conducted Lieutenant Wait to the fence before alluded to, and private King returned to his company. Lieutenant Wait's last words to private King were, 'Are we whipping them?'[1] A braver man than Marvin Wait never confronted a foe; a more generous heart never beat; a more unselfish patriot never fell. Connecticut may well cherish and honor the memory of such sons."

When the news of his death reached his native town the expression of sorrow and of sympathy with his parents was universal. Resolutions were passed by the municipal au-

[1] As the enemy advanced on the left flank of our regiment, they delivered an enfilading fire. It was under this fire that Lieutenant Wait was pierced by a minnie ball (while laying wounded behind a low wall), which passed through his lungs from side to side.

thorities expressive of the public regret, while letters from many who knew him, testified to the parents of the private grief. He was the first commissioned officer from Norwich killed in battle.

The body was brought home, and the funeral, at the First Congregational Church, was very largely attended. The Rev. Dr. Arms, his former pastor, conducted the services.

The conclusion of the eulogy delivered by George Pratt, at the church, sums up the estimate of his character and achievements : —

"What words can add beauty to such a life, or what praise ennoble such a death? When we think of those who fell on that field, we count them all heroes — we name them all among the brave.

> "'They died like heroes, for no recreant step
> Had e'er dishonored them, no stain of fear,
> No base despair, no cowardly recoil :
> They had the hearts of freemen to the last,
> And the free blood that bounded in their veins
> Was shed for freedom with a liberal joy.'

"Yes, the names of those who fell will be handed down with imperishable glory and lasting fame. Our children's children shall rise up and call them blessed, for they died fighting on the side of the Right, in a contest between Right and Wrong.

"Who would not be proud to be one of such a brave and immortal band? Who would not be prouder still that where all were so brave, the one they loved became conspicuous for bravery? Such honor, rarely achieved, this young hero won. All alike, officers and soldiers, speak of his dauntless and conspicuous courage. All tell of the way his brave and animating voice rang through the ranks of the men, urging them on to victory. A century, had he lived so long, would have brought him no prouder moment in which to die. Dying, as he did, on the banks of that little creek, then unknown, now immortal, he became for us and ours, forever a name and a memory.

"True, he lies here, unheeding all our praise, silent and cold in death. But what a sweet and inexpressible consolation it is to the living, that the one whom they mourn died honorably and gloriously. A long life, uneventful and insignificant, is for the many, — a glorious death, a lasting and honorable memory, is the boon of but a few.

"To-day his native town writes him among her list of heroes; his native State does him honor in the person of her Chief Magistrate; the nation thanks his memory as one among those who saved her in the hour of peril. Such honor as we can pay is now his. We bury him here, far away from the field of his fame, in the midst of the scenes he loved so well; knowing this, that although we may die and be forgotten, his name shall be honored and remembered, and as we lay him to rest, our hearts, one and all, say, " Brave spirit, noble young heart, farewell!"

COMMUNICATED.

JOHN L. STANTON, Captain Company G, Twenty-isxth Regiment. Up to the time of the assault on Port Hudson, little had occurred to break the monotony of camp life. In May, 1864, the active service of the regiment began, and though of brief continuance, was severe. Stanton proved himself a good officer in the care he bestowed on his command, and on the eventful day of its first engagement, showed himself possessed of the best soldierly qualities. In the regiment's charge upon the rebel batteries on the twenty-seventh of May, he led his men, cheering them onward, and when the fatal bullet struck him he was in advance of his company, swinging his sword, and urging it to follow him. He died instantly, and made one of the number of noble officers that fell that day, all of whom, by their personal prowess, reflected honor on the several regiments with which connected. Stanton's loss was deeply felt, and by his own men he was especially lamented. His courageous bearing on the field of conflict, all remembered with pride, and falling as a brave soldier should, with his face towards the foe, they paid him the tribute which his gallant bearing before them well deserved. A faithful officer, a brave soldier, a true patriot, such will he continue to be in the memory of friend and comrade.

HERVY FITZ JACOBS was born in Thompson, Connecticut, on the third day of August, 1838. His parents were Joseph D. and Sarah C. Jacobs. On the twenty-ninth of September, 1856, he was enrolled as a member of the Norwich Free Academy.

July 8, 1859, young Jacobs was admitted to the coming Freshman Class of Brown University. Those who knew him there will recall his mild blue eyes, his ruddy face, and his compact frame. As a scholar, his rank was above the average. During his first term in college he received the appointment of Class President.

Early in 1861 Jacobs left college and entered the store, in Norwich, of his uncle, L. W. Carroll, Esq. Here the Rebellion found him. At the very outset of the struggle the question of enlistment presented itself to his mind, but the oft-repeated predictions of many over-sanguine prophets that sixty or ninety days would see the end of the war, together with his new formed business relations, sufficed to keep him at home.

The year 1861 wore away, and then the early months of 1862, and still the rebellion existed with scarcely diminished proportions. When the July call of the President for three hundred thousand men to serve nine months came, the question of duty became still more urgent. Accordingly as soon as the papers for a company of infantry were received in Norwich he was ready. His name was among the first upon the roll. This was August 28, 1862, and on September fifth the company was organized, at which time Jacobs was chosen Second Lieutenant. At once the young officer commenced the work of preparing himself and his men for active service.

After two months' preparation in camp, the Twenty-sixth received orders to embark for New York, where it remained till December fourth. The regiment then embarked for the South, landing, after a long and rough voyage, at Carrollton, Louisiana. It was here attached to the First Brigade, under command of General Neal Dow.

On the 20th of May, 1863, the regiment was ordered to join General Banks' command in the vicinity of Port Hudson, where it took its position in the rear of the batteries of that fortress. Lieutenant Jacobs was gratified at the prospect. He had often said that he would rather take the chances of battle than to return home without once having met the rebels face to face. At five o'clock on the same day of their arrival upon the field, they were ordered to "fall in" and charge the enemy's rifle-pits. The charge disclosed the fact that the pits were deserted, and also exposed the regiment for the first time to artillery fire. The division of General Sherman, to which the Twenty-sixth belonged, had moved up from the south of Port Hudson to meet General Banks' army which was descending from above. At the close of this day the two bodies of troops were not far apart, and Lieutenant Jacobs, with his company, was ordered to open communication with General Augur's pickets on the right. This movement was executed promptly in the face of the enemy. On the morning of the 27th of May, the troops were early in motion. The light artillery responded sharply to the rebel's fire, and there was every indication that serious work was at hand. After marching and countermarching, and advancing through thick woods until about two and a half o'clock, P. M., the Twenty-sixth with the other regiments of its brigade, was ordered to charge the rebel works. Out of about two thousand men in the brigade, one-fifth, or four hundred, were killed or wounded. The Twenty-sixth lost one hundred and seven killed and wounded. Of this number nine were in Company F (of which young Jacobs was an officer). After the repulse, Lieutenant Jacobs, regardless of the rain of rebel bullets, remained on the field, and rendered all the assistance in his power to his wounded comrades, till the company was ordered to reform with its regiment. It is the testimony of those who were with him in this his first engagement, that he showed coolness and bravery unsurpassed by any.

Saturday, the 13th of June, was marked by skirmishing and heavy artillery fire all along the line. Every one was satisfied that this presaged a more general and determined strife on the morrow. The men of the Twenty-sixth were in fine spirits, and confident of success in the coming charge. The expected orders came, and before day-break, Sunday morning, the 14th of June, the regiment was called out. After marching several miles to the extreme left of the line, it was massed with the division, preparatory to the advance.

The following extract from a letter written on the field by Captain L. A. Gallup will give an idea of the charge, and the circumstances in which Lieutenant Jacobs received his wound.

"It is said that our brigade advanced splendidly, deploying under a galling fire of shell and shrapnel. The rebels handled their artillery admirably. Lieutenant H. F. Jacobs had been detached from my company, to command Company A, which is next on the right of Company F. As we were advancing up the main road in column by divisions, in easy range of the enemy, we were ordered to deploy the column. Soon after the line had been established and Lieutenant Jacobs had assumed command of his own company (A) a twelve pound shell exploded between the two companies, killing four and wounding sixteen men. Lieutenant Jacobs was among the latter. He was wounded by a ball from the shell, in the thigh, the bone of which was injured. I assisted him as well as I could to shelter, finding that he was not bleeding, ordered two men to take him from the field, when I bade him good-by, and advanced up the road."

The sad story of Lieutenant Jacobs' sufferings we may best gather from his own record. The following extracts are from his diary: —

"The morning I was shot, the regiment deployed from column by division into a line of battle. We were advancing steadily in front of the works, the rebels firing all the time. I called out to Company A, as I commanded it, 'Come on boys, we are going over the parapet,' and I thought so, when a ball brought me to the ground. I was wounded about six o'clock A. M. (14th June), and was carried from the field. I had to ride to the old cotton press, where my wound was dressed at seven P. M. I remained there till nine A. M., 15th, when I was carried to Springfield Landing, then by steamer to Baton Rouge. Was carried to Church Hospital; wound very painful all night."

June 16, he writes: "Out of my head half of the time."

June 18. "Oh how I suffered last night. The pain from my head — my wound was almost more than I could bear."

June 19. "It seems to me this morning as though I could not survive but a few days; strength all gone. Was fighting and building fortifications all night under heavy fire. Have suffered much to-day."

June 21. "In great pain all day."

June 22. "Woke up this morning feeling quite smart, but have since been quite sick."

June 24. "Kept quiet as possible all day. Pain unceasing. Cannot sleep. Head hot almost all the time."

June 25. "Moved this morning from Church hospital to the Officers' Hospital. Was carried in my bunk. Got along well till I was taken out and put upon an iron bedstead, when the pain was excruciating."

June 26. "Am fast losing strength. Am conscious I must die. I wanted to live to get home, but it is all right. I have tried to do my duty here. I shall make arrangements to have my body embalmed when I am dead, and sent home, as I think it will be a consolation to all my friends to have it there. I have suffered much since I was wounded, as I have lain on my back all the time. I had as great prospects to live for, and as bright, as almost any one. I should like to live, but if it is designed to be otherwise I am reconciled."

June 27. "Feel quite smart this morning. Wound quite comfortable."

June 28. "Took some morphine last night, and slept till this morning. This is the best sleep I have had since I was wounded. Feel quite like myself."

June 29. "Slept till ten o'clock last night. Feel better now I can sleep. Head continues to feel heavy and dull. Think wound is doing well."

June 30. "Get along very well."

[It is evident from the hand-writing, that he is fast declining, and *is not* getting along well.]

July 2. "Learned brother Wyman is sick with measles. Says will now go "——(unintelligible). "I expect to be on my way very soon."

This is the last date against which the dying soldier wrote. Poor fellow, he *was* on his way soon, yet not to the home, visions of which doubtless filled his troubled brain, but to another and better home, where is neither sorrow, nor crying, nor pain, nor death. Three days and his spirit returned to God who gave it.

It was not till the middle of October that the remains of Lieutenant Jacobs arrived in Connecticut, when funeral services were held in the church near his father's residence, on the 20th of that month.

"A large congregation evinced their deep sympathy with a most interesting family, in the great loss which they were called to deplore. The coffin and hearse were draped with *war-worn* flags of the Forty-seventh Massachusetts Volunteers, which were sent from Boston for the occasion, as a token of respect for a brave companion-in-arms. The pall was borne by the former commanders, teacher, and class-mates of the deceased. The services were conducted by the Rev. Messrs. Hawley and Dunning. The feeling incident to the occasion was greatly deepened by the fact that the same mail that brought the intelligence of the death of Lieutenant Jacobs, also brought the tidings of the death of a younger brother in the same department. Thus were the obsequies of two brothers of hope and promise observed the same day. Lieutenant Jacobs left his home in the freshness and innocence of boyhood, and was carried back to it in early manhood, a voluntary offering to the welfare of his country."

At his grave, Eldridge Smith, his former teacher in the Norwich Free Academy, and Lieutenant-colonel Selden, of the Twenty-sixth Connecticut, bore their loving testimony to the worth of the departed.

A beautiful monument of Italian marble marks the spot where sleep the two patriot brothers. Military emblems — shield, sword, and musket — adorn two of its sides, while the remaining two are occupied with tablets, giving a short account of the departed. Beneath the record of the life of Lieutenant Jacobs are inscribed his last words: —

"*I die at the post of duty.*"   COMMUNICATED.

THEODORE BURDICK, Captain Company B, Seventh Regiment. He went out in Captain J. B. Dennis' Company, which was the first one recruited in Norwich for the war, holding the commission of First Lieutenant. He served with the regiment in the campaign in North Carolina, where it participated in the capture of Port Royal. Through the battles of 1862, he fought, receiving no injuries, and winning his promotion to the captaincy.

In July, 1863, the regiment took part in the attack on Fort Wagner, and in the charge made, which, for lack of support, was finally unsuccessful, Captain Burdick was killed, July 10, 1863. When last seen, he, with his gallant comrades, was bravely fighting on the edge of the parapet. Of the one hundred and ninety-one officers and men of the Seventh, only eighty-seven lived to return from this fatal charge. The regiment was commended for its courage, and Burdick personally did his part to sustain its honor in that terrible assault. While boldly leading his men, he met a soldier's death, and was among the numerous slain in that desperate encounter. He died in the very pride of his manhood, doing his duty; and, like so many others, fell, with only a soldier's epitaph, — " Killed on the field of battle."

EDWARD PAYSON MANNING, Second Lieutenant Co. F, Twenty-sixth Regiment. Lieutenant Manning was born in Pomfret, Windham County, Conn., July 18, 1834. He was the youngest son of Deacon William H. and Lois P. Manning. His early life was not marked by any extraordinary experiences. The influences about him were calculated to develop the manly Christian character for which he was noted in after life. His education, though not collegiate, was liberal, and his natural abilities far more than mediocre. After finishing his studies, his inclination led him to mercantile pursuits, and for about three years he was associated with his brother, the Hon. James W. Manning, of Putnam, the present Comptroller of the State. In the Spring of 1859, he came to Norwich, and became connected with the well-known paper house of A. H. Hubbard & Co., in which he was engaged when the war broke out. His daily life and exemplary deportment, his integrity and business ability, his fine musical talents, and earnest labor in the church and Sunday-school, all served to gain for him many and valuable acquaintances in Norwich.

By nature, Manning was not inclined to military pursuits; nevertheless, from the commencement of the war he was earnest in its support, and contributed to its progress.

He was restless under promptings of duty, while so many of his associates were giving themselves to their country. His affection for, and duty to, his aged and widowed mother, who clung to him, her youngest boy, like the ivy to the rock, influenced him to defer his enlistment. But the pure and patriotic spirit that animated him would not be hushed to silence, and on the 30th of August, 1862, he enlisted in the company recruited by Joseph, afterwards Lieutenant-colonel Selden.

He immediately gave all his influence and time to recruiting, and secured several enlistments from adjoining towns. The company was rapidly filled to the maximum, and on its organization, Manning was appointed Second Sergeant The regiment proceeded to the Department of the Gulf, and joined the Banks' expedition against Port Hudson. At various times he was detailed as Acting Quartermaster and Adjutant, both of which positions he filled with honor to himself, and to the satisfaction of the regiment. On the death of Lieutenant H. F. Jacobs, of Company F, who was mortally wounded in the charge upon Port Hudson, June 14, 1863, Governor Buckingham appointed Manning to fill the vacancy. Wherever duty called him, he was faithful and cheerful. In all the engagements in which the Twenty-sixth participated, while he was Commissary sergeant, he was conspicuous for his bravery in caring for the wounded and dying upon the field. Whether on the march or in camp, whether on garrison duty or in the trenches, the commissariat of the Twenty-sixth was well and punctually supplied, which contributed to the efficiency of the regiment.

After the surrender of Port Hudson, the regiment was ordered home, by way of the Mississippi River, to be mustered out, by reason of expiration of term of service. On his arrival in Norwich, Manning received the congratulations of his friends on his safe return, and apparently perfect health.

But he was almost immediately prostrated by malarious fever, which proved fatal to so many who had bravely faced bayonet and cannon on the bloody plains of Port Hudson. During his brief illness he was surrounded by the kindest friends, while for him the best medical attendance was secured. In his delirium his mind was with the Twenty-sixth in its journeyings, and with his friends who could not arrive in time to be present when the Master called him home.

When told that death was approaching, his delirium gave way to reason, and with a cheerfulness that could only spring from Christian faith, he said, "*It is well; all is bright before me. Do all you can to comfort my mother.*" These were his last sane words. He sank rapidly, and on the morning of the 17th of August, 1863, the very day the muster-out papers were dated, he was summoned to the Army of Heaven, to answer the roll-call in the presence of the King of kings.

He was deeply lamented by all who knew him, and those unused to weep gathered to do the last honors to the dead, and shed tears of grief over the departed. The place made vacant in society, church, and Sunday-school, and in many hearts, is vacant still, and his fragrant memory will ever be fondly cherished. L. A. G.

FREDERICK E. SCHALK, First Lieutenant Fourteenth Regiment, was born January 6, 1838, at Monsheim, Hesse Darmstadt, Germany. The date of his removal with his parents to America we do not learn, but only know that it was at an early age ; that prior to his residence in Norwich he lived for a time at Uncasville, in the same county. For some years before the war he resided in Norwich, as a clerk in a grocery store. At the beginning of the war he enlisted with young Nickels, of whom he was ever a close friend, in Captain (now General) Harland's company of the Third Connecticut. He served very creditably in the three months' campaign, and then returned to his old employer in Norwich. Soon after his return he joined the Broadway Congregational Church in Norwich. He was one of the first to enlist in the Fourteenth, — May 27, 1862, — still accompanying Nickels, who came into the same company — E. Just before the regiment marched he was married to a lady in Lebanon, Connecticut. He was made a Sergeant before the company left the State, promoted to be Second Lieutenant May 16, 1863, and to a First Lieutenancy November fifth.

In all the battles, skirmishes, and marches of the regiment, he bore his part honorably and well, never flinching from any post of honor or danger. Of vigorous constitution and energetic yet cheerful disposition, he was ever ready for duty, for danger, or for fun and frolic. These qualities made him a great favorite, and somehow it seemed as if harm could never come to him. Yet in the terrific carnage of Spottsylvania, where the dear old Second Corps, to which the Fourteenth was attached, covered itself with glory by its brilliant charges, Schalk was stricken down by a bullet. He was removed to the Second Corps Hospital, at Fredericksburg, where, in plain view of the old battlefield of December 13, 1862, he ebbed away his life-blood and died, May 21, 1864 ; dying cheerfully and calmly, despite the absence of the dear ones at home for whom he longed. Perhaps, as he heard the little birds singing in the beautiful May morning, and looked out upon that bloody battle-field of six months before, where the rapidly springing up green grass showed that Nature speedily repaired man's devastations, the roll of the guns of the contending armies a few miles away ceased to echo in his ears, and with the recollection of those divine words, "Not even a sparrow falleth to the ground without his knowledge," fears for the future of his dear wife passed away, and his spirit fled to the land "where the wicked cease from troubling, and the weary are at rest."

The remains were taken home and the funeral held from the Baptist Church in Lebanon, on Sunday, June fifth. There was a very large attendance from the town, the surrounding country, and from Norwich, including some of the officers of his regiment. The funeral sermon was delivered by Rev. Mr. Cunningham, from Genesis v. 24, and was pertinent and applicable. The remains having been embalmed, his friends were enabled to gaze upon the face of the young hero ere his coffin was closed. His sword rested upon the coffin, surmounted by wreaths of flowers. The body was escorted to the grave by the Norwich Light Infantry, his fellow-officers acting as bearers. The farewell volleys having been fired over the grave of him who had given his life so cheerfully for the cause of freedom in an adopted country, we left him "with his young fame about him for a shroud." H. P. G.

ALFRED M. GODDARD, First Lieutenant Eighth Regiment, was born in Marietta, Ohio, June 19, 1836. His parents removed to Norwich when he was quite young, and here he grew up, developing a character of rare beauty and force. Leaving his home at an early age to commence life for himself, he for that reason was less generally known than otherwise he would have been. Yet in the home where a peerless devotion to those he most deeply loved distinguished him, and by friends who were aware of his noble nature, he was held in reverent and affectionate esteem. None knew him but to admire his earnestness of spirit, his commanding self-reliance, his determined energy; and all this tempered by a refinement and gentleness, which gave to his character unusual completeness.

He was one of those choice spirits whose career is invested with all that can stimulate and instruct. Immersed, when quite young, in the cares and duties of a responsible business, he yet displayed a culture ordinarily looked for only in the man of letters. His criticisms on books that chanced to pass under his notice, betray a fine taste, united with unusual analytic power. His journal while in the Pacific abounds in the most graphic portrayal of life on ship-board, and on the Islands. Susceptible to all that was grand and beautiful in Nature, his descriptions of scenery in the Tropics and of the changeful ocean, near and upon which so much of his life was spent, can hardly be surpassed.

Entering, when still under age, the employ of Williams & Haven, of New London, Connecticut, he was by them sent out to the Sandwich Islands, and in connection with a branch house, resided about five years at Honolulu. During that period he made several voyages to the Arctic Ocean, passing two years on McKean's Island, in the Southern Pacific. At the breaking out of the war, he was about leaving Honolulu for Mauritius. When the news reached him that hostilities had actually commenced, he was eager to leave at once for home, that he might enroll himself among those hurrying to the government's defense, but such were his business engagements, that fidelity to his employers required the prosecution of the voyage. So, with a disappointed heart, he endeavored to do the work to which he was committed, though his thoughts were with the brave men who were already marshalled for deadly conflict with our foes.

He writes in his journal as he started on this voyage, " I have been reading the 'Atlantic Monthly.' It is all war. How is this? I am trying to do my duty, and yet a deathly sickness comes o'er me when I think what a feeling of joy it would have given me could I have gone home and given up all for my country." At a later date he adds, " All my hope now is, that having chosen this path I may command myself and give my thoughts to the present, trusting that through some great good luck I may yet find myself among the New England heroes." Who of us imagined that on the far Pacific main there was a heart beating with such lofty patriotism ; reckoning as its chiefest trial that it could not share in our struggle for national existence. And yet, like thronging doves to their windows came the patriots of our land, travelling homeward from every quarter of the globe that they might swell the hosts who battled for truth and freedom.

He speaks at this time of the change in his views of life, — " It is so real, so earnest, and can be so noble." Then reverting to his country, he remarks, "I begin to think the war is the best thing which could have happened to us. I know it must stir up our young men to action and fill their veins with new life. I honor the brave fellows and am proud of dear old Connecticut. The spirit of our Puritan Fathers is not yet dead."

While at Mauritius, hearing of his father's sudden death, young Goddard hastened back with the utmost expedition that he might visit his bereaved mother and mingle with the afflicted family. Taking the East India route through the Red Sea and Europe, he arrived at his home in the fall of 1862. He hoped then to enter the army and gratify thus the deepest longing of his heart. But his business engagements compelled him to go back once more to the Sandwich Islands, and with great reluctance he turned his face toward the Pacific. He seemed at this time keenly sensitive lest his absence from the country while in so critical a condition should not be understood. Many are the journal entries which betray this fear. " If my choice could be recalled," he writes in one place, " I would go through anything to get upon the battle field." He speaks also of the moral issues of the conflict, demonstrating his ardent love of liberty for all classes — " It seems strange the country should have been ruled so long by this small party. (Slaveholders.) But the time for a change has come, and I think the curse of slavery will now be removed from our beautiful land."

Dispatching with promptness his business at the Islands, and closing his connection with the firm he had served so long and well, he was enabled to return home in May, 1863. Then the cherished purpose of his soul seemed at length possible to be carried out.

On the following July, he received a commission as First Lieutenant in Company B of the Eighth Connecticut Regiment, but was at once detached for duty on the Staff of General Harland, the former Colonel of the Eighth Regiment. In this capacity he rendered faithful service until March, 1864, when, at the request of officers and men, he rejoined his regiment. " It is a hard thing to do," says his diary, " but I am sure it is right." His associates on the Staff parted with him, not without the greatest reluctance and the most genuine regret. To General Harland he was strongly attached, and by him in turn was esteemed as an able officer and a personal friend. The heart which had chafed so when business prevented his connection with the army, was still dissatisfied with the less arduous duties of staff officer, so he took his place in the ranks, and the long yearning of his soul seemed about to be appeased when the hardships and dangers of the field were to be his.

March 13, 1864, the regiment, under command of Col. J. E. Ward, left its old camp at Portsmouth, Va., and marched to Deep Creek, where it performed outpost and picket duty until April 13. Thence it was ordered to Yorktown, and was assigned to the Second Brigade of the Eighteenth Corps. Forming part of General Butler's command, it was engaged in a reconnoisance of the enemy's lines before Petersburg. On the morning of May 8, the regiment led the advance in an attempt to press back the enemy. Forming in battle line, it repeatedly charged the foe, driving him before them, and continued fighting till the ammunition was exhausted and the regiment was relieved by order, receiving, as it returned from the bloody field, the cheers of the whole brigade. It was in this action that the fatal bullet struck Lieutenant Goddard. While bravely fighting and cheering on his men in this his first battle, he fell, mortally wounded.

The day before, his entry in his diary, when it was apparent an engagement was imminent, was both touching and significant, — "And the children of Israel prevailed, because they trusted in the Lord God of their Fathers." The day of the battle, Saturday, May 7, he wrote : ' 7 A. M. we go to the front with only arms and ammunition." Before sundown he was borne from the field, and ere another day had gone, the knightly youth of high hopes and unflinching courage passed away. Of his carriage on the day of battle, his Captain writes : " He was so thoughtful and considerate, not rash or impetuous, but cool and collected, ready for any emergency, willing for every duty. While most bravely fighting and cheering on our men, the fatal bullet struck him, and he was taken from the field. As he was carried past me, he said that he was wounded, but that he had done his duty. Most truly can I echo those last words." He had won in no common degree the esteem of officers and men, and his loss was felt by all.

Upon the examination of his wound, he asked the regimental surgeon whether it was likely to prove fatal, adding, at once, that he thought it must ; in which opinion the surgeon was obliged to concur. Immediately he added : " Tell my mother that I die in the front, that I die happy." Removed to the Chesapeake Hospital at Fortress Monroe, he lingered for little more than a day, suffering intensely but patiently.

Writes one who knew him well : " He was one of the few men whom I have known in my life whose steadfast honesty was proof against all temptations, and his varied life exposed him to not a few." Another friend, intimately associated with him while in the army, wrote when the news of his death was received : " May God rest the soul of our martyr-hero. He is no more. But the memories which the thought of him suggests, are of the most tender and pleasing character. How kind and unselfish he was. What a sturdy champion for everything just, noble, and right. How he loathed oppression and injustice. How he loved his country."

Few excelled him in the earnestness and unselfish devotion which so eminently characterized him. A whole-hearted consecration to others' good, made his career beautiful and his death glorious. While in the strength of his young manhood, God permitted him to die, and his death adds another to the list of heroes whose memory and example are the nation's heritage.

Who dares tell us that such lives are brief, for

>"We live in deeds, not years ; in thought, not breaths ;
>In feelings, not in figures on a dial,
>We should count time by heart throbs. He most lives
>Who thinks most, feels the noblest, acts the best."

JOHN McCALL, Captain Company K, Eighth Regiment. In the summer of 1861, when the government called for three hundred thousand men to array themselves under the national flag to crush the rebellion, among those who nobly responded to the summons was John McCall, of Yantic.

He enlisted as a private in Company D, of the Eighth Regiment. At the election of non-commissioned officers for the company, he was chosen a Sergeant, and acted as such during the first few months after the regiment had been mustered into service. The death of Lieutenant Charles A. Breed, and the promotion of Captain Ward to be Major, opened the door for the advancement of young McCall, and he was first appointed Second, then First Lieutenant of his company.

Skillful as an officer, faithful in the discharge of his duties, and intrepid on the battle-field, he won the confidence of his superior officers, and was subsequently promoted to the Captaincy of Company K, in which position he remained until his decease.

He served under General Burnside during his North Carolina campaign, and participated in the battles of Roanoke Island, Fort Macon, and Newbern; and when the troops who had so nobly sustained the Stars and Stripes on the soil of North Carolina were called North to aid in driving the rebels from Pennsylvania and Maryland, the Eighth Connecticut came with them, and Captain McCall, ever ready to endure the privations, and share the perils of the battle-field, was again distinguished for his coolness and courage, in the sanguinary conflicts of South Mountain and Antietam.

At the last-named battle, he was severely wounded by a minie-ball in the thigh, and being unable to leave the field with the regiment in its retreat, was taken prisoner, but immediately paroled. He was soon after exchanged, and, as soon as recovery permitted, again took command of his company.

He was at Fredericksburg under General Burnside,— cool, cheerful, ready for any duty. At the siege of Suffolk, he was one of the band of two hundred who crossed the

Nansemond in broad day-light, stormed Fort Huger, and held it in the face of ten thousand rebels, — one of the neatest little achievements of the war. Captain McCall was ordered, with Company K of the Eighth, to take and hold the rifle pits commanding the approach to the fort. He was the first man to reach the land, and his part was strictly and gallantly performed.

He was under General Butler in his expedition up the James River for the capture of Richmond. In the bloody conflicts that took place between the Union and the rebel troops on the banks of that stream, the Eighth Regiment was placed in the front of the battle, and the family of Captain McCall received a letter from him, dated but a day or two before he was shot, saying, that though many of his comrades had been wounded or killed in the successive struggles, that he had escaped all injury. The next intelligence received by his father, was a telegram, stating that his gallant boy was dead.

At five o'clock on Saturday morning, May 14, the enemy had broken the flank of Brooks' division. There was a severe fire along the whole line, the men lying down and firing, Captain McCall in a sitting position. The fatal bullet passed through his heart. He rose to his feet, saying, "I shall be dead in a minute," and fell backwards dead.

The loss of this gallant comrade and able officer was severely felt by the brave old regiment. He was a general favorite with the officers and men, "a prompt, bold, enterprising officer — a soldier by nature. He was stern and harsh when he believed it to be his duty, but in his usual conduct he was generous, just, and noble. As a companion he was frank, genial, and lively, as a friend, manly and true-hearted." Few of our young men who have offered their lives on the altar of their country, leave a more unsullied reputation for honor, bravery, and patriotism than

John McCall. Brought home for burial, his grave lies near those of his lamented comrades-in-arms, Lieutenants Wait, Goddard, and Breed, in our beautiful cemetery along the banks of the Yantic. The Mayor and Board of Common Council attended in a body at his funeral service, and put on record this public testimonial to his character and patriotic devotion:—

"*Resolved*, That in the death of this gallant and truly meritorious officer, this community has lost one of its brightest ornaments, the regiment to which he belonged, an able, skillful, and courageous officer, ready at all times to share the dangers and privations of the battle-field, and to offer up his life on his country's altar." I. T. W.

JOHN W. BENTLEY, Acting Master U. S. N., died at his residence in Norwich, May 27, 1864, after an illness of little more than a week. He received his appointment as Acting Master in the Navy soon after the war broke out, and continued in active service till his death. He was one of the officers of the "Wabash," Admiral Dupont's flag-ship, at the capture of Port Royal. Appointed to the command of the "Banshee," a captured blockade runner, just placed in commission, he was preparing to put to sea, when his fatal illness came upon him. He was a brave and skillful officer, and in whatever duty he was engaged, always secured the approval and commendation of his superiors. He was a genial, kind hearted man, and made friends wherever he was; indeed few men had so extensive a circle of acquaintance, and among them all, so many warm, earnest friends.

E. BENJAMIN CULVER, Adjutant Eighteenth Regiment, was the only son of Benjamin and Adelaide Culver; born in the city of New York, October 27, 1840.

During his school and business life he became well known here, and by those most intimately acquainted with him, he was esteemed as a young man of more than ordinary excellence and promise. One of his early instructors speaks of him as "the peacemaker," while his teacher in Norwich, with whom he spent nearly a year and a half, mentions his marked truthfulness of character.

His personal appearance gave all the impression of youthful manliness. Generous in his feelings, self-possessed in his manners, young Culver was the favorite of a large circle of friends. .

As a clerk in the store of Lee & Osgood, he has left the reputation of rare fidelity and skill. Energetic and quick to learn, he mastered the business, and gave promise of great success. Between himself and his employers a warm attachment existed, broken only by his early death. His admirable business qualities, as well as personal worth, had attained for him a position not often reached by those as young as he.

When the Eighteenth Regiment was forming, the duty of entering his country's service came to him with new force. Seeking the advice of friends and parents, he finally registered his conviction of what was duty, by enlisting. The purest of motives prompted him in this act, for it was when his earthly prospects were brightest that he entered the army, and his parents knew that at pecuniary sacrifice he remained in the service. He was moreover an only son, tenderly beloved, and relinquished more than many in leaving father and mother at his country's call.

In August, 1862, he left Norwich with the Eighteenth Regiment, commanded by Col. William G. Ely. While stationed at Baltimore, Culver was detailed to act as clerk at the headquarters of General Schenck, Commandant of the *Middle Department*. His executive ability secured him the appointment, and so valuable were his services considered by the General, that he was retained some time after his promotion to the Adjutancy of the regiment. While in this position, in one of his letters he speaks of his dissatisfaction with such labor. Though it was safer and more lucrative than a soldier's service, still he said it was not for this kind of work he enlisted. He was eager to engage in active campaigning — to meet the hardships and brave the perils of the field.

He rejoined his regiment just after the unfortunate battle of Winchester, June 14-15, 1863, when the Colonel and a large proportion of the officers and men were taken prisoners. His first letter, dated at Maryland Heights, spoke of "a disconsolate band" he had succeeded in gathering together, — the remnants of the splendid regiment which had left Norwich less than a year previous. He furnished to anxious friends the first reliable account of the casualties of that action. Entering upon the duties of Adjutant, he proved himself at once a most efficient officer.

In April, 1864, he returned home on a furlough, and many remember with deep interest that last visit. The campaign of the spring was about to open, and the indications were that there would be hard fighting. The earnestness with which Culver spoke of the increased perils showed his full appreciation of his own exposure, when he returned. Coming events appeared to have wrought an unusual thoughtfulness. And though he spoke calmly and with hope, it was with a half betrayed impression that this would prove his final visit with Norwich friends.

At the last interview with his parents, his mother remarked: "You look care-worn, but I do not ask you to resign." He replied: "I could not be induced so to do; for, dear mother, calmly and deliberately I give my service and my life if necessary, for my country."

When he returned to his regiment, the army of the Shenandoah, of which it formed a part, had started upon its long and tedious campaign. At New Market, Va., occurred the first engagement with the rebels. In this the Eighteenth Regiment participated, losing fifty-six in killed, wounded, and missing. The report of this battle was the last Adjutant Culver lived to make. Retreating to Cedar Creek, Va., the army rested several days, and was reorganized under General Hunter, who relieved General Sigel.

On May 27, equipped for rapid marching, the regiment, with the army, advanced with little opposition until arriving in the vicinity of Piedmont, June 5, 1864. A battle here ensued, resulting after severe and protracted fighting, in the total rout of the enemy, and the capture of 1500 prisoners. Among the first mortally wounded on our side was Adjutant Culver. While engaged with the regiment in one of the earliest charges made that day, he was struck by a piece of shell, and fell from his horse.

Removed at once to the hospital, he died the following day, June 6, 1864. He had fought his last fight, and received his death-wound while joining in the charge which brought victory to our arms. What he had said he was willing to do, he was by the providence of God permitted to do, in thus cheerfully laying down his life for his country.

So the youth whom fond parents had watched as he developed into all that was noble and pure, fell bravely fighting for our liberties and our land. One more name his death adds to the roll of heroes, whose generous self-sacrifice sanctifies the cause. An earnest Christian, a faithful clerk, a devoted patriot, he has left behind the record of a noble life.

His firmly outlined integrity, united with his quiet enthusiasm, had won him a high position in the esteem of many here, and long will his memory be cherished by friends and citizens in Norwich. In an epoch of great events he acted a noble part, and sincerely and bravely performed his every duty.

Recalling his faithfulness in all things committed to him here, I think of the promise which is the inheritance of such servants, made by —

"That monarch whose 'well done' confers a more than mortal fame."

WILLIAM A. BERRY, Captain Company , Second Artillery, New York. He was an Englishman, who had recently settled in Greeneville, and who, sharing with our citizens in the patriotic enthusiasm awakened by the war, was among the first to enlist in Captain Chester's company, in which he was commissioned Second Lieutenant. He served with credit through the three months' campaign. He again offered his service to the government, by enlisting in a company that was raised by Thomas Maguire, for the regiment of Colonel Colt (the Fifth). When the latter threw up his interest in it, owing to some misunderstanding, Maguire carried most of his command, including Berry, with him, and was accepted in the Second Regiment Artillery, Maguire receiving the commission of Captain, and Berry that of Lieutenant. The regiment was a long time confined to garrison duty at Washington, where Berry was promoted to Captain, his friend Maguire having been made Major. He was a brave soldier, rather noted for his coolness, and was regarded with no ordinary esteem by those who knew him best.

In the early part of the summer of 1864, the regiment was called to the front, and participated in one of the battles near Petersburg, June 18, 1864, where Captain Berry was killed. He was interred on the battle-field, but subsequently, in November, 1864, his remains were brought to Norwich by his friend and comrade-in-arms, Lieutenant Thomas Scott, and buried in Yantic Cemetery. Berry made an excellent soldier, having previously served several years in the British army; and though a comparative stranger here, left behind him the record of a true devotion to his adopted country. There were not a few who, coming to us from other lands, were among the foremost to offer their services in behalf of a country they had learned to love with all that affection which we sometimes think can be cherished by only those to the manor born.

Young Berry's history is one which has for us a peculiar interest, for it is the record of one who stood for our defense ; and with a patriotism, which made him seem as if always of us, he went forth to battle for our own and his chosen country, and in thus doing, fell in the cause that was materially aided by just such generous devotion as he evinced.

JAMES R. NICKELS, Captain Company I, Fourteenth Regiment, was born in the town of Cherryfield, Maine, July 14th, 1843. Left an orphan at an early age, he removed to Norwich, to reside with an aunt, and that most picturesque and beautiful of New England cities was thenceforward his home. Here he made hosts of friends among the young lads of his age, and here was laid the foundation of a friendship toward young Nickels by the writer, that grew with his growth, and which makes him feel this brief memorial to be a most paltry tribute to one of the most generous and noble hearts that ever beat. Completing his school studies, Nickels entered the crockery store of R. M. Haven, and became a member of his family. At the outbreak of the war he enlisted in Captain Harland's Company of the Third Connecticut Regiment, with which he passed creditably through the three months' campaign, being particularly remarked for his coolness at the first Bull Run, where his company was one of the few from Connecticut which suffered any casualties.

Returning home at the close of the campaign, he resumed his former avocation, devoting his spare time to the study of military tactics. His patriotism and adaptation to a military career were such, however, that he could not remain quietly at home, but on the President's call for 50,000 men, in May, 1862, he again enlisted as a private in Company E of the Fourteenth. He was speedily made First Sergeant, and left the State as such, August 23d, 1862. In less than four weeks he passed with his regiment through the bloody fight of Antietam.

At Fredericksburg, where fourteen out of eighteen officers were killed or wounded, Nickels escaped with his clothes riddled with bullets. December 20th, 1862, he was commissioned Second Lieutenant of Company I, and in less than a month, January 19th, 1863, promoted to be First Lieutenant of Company K. That year he passed unscathed through the engagements of Chancellorsville, Antietam, and Bristoe Station. On the 5th of November he was commissioned Captain of Company I. In the campaign of 1864 he was with the regiment in the terrible carnage of the Wilderness, and Spottsylvania, the numerous minor engagements on the North and South Anna River, and at Cold Harbor. In the latter battle he commanded the regiment and led it in a brilliant charge, for which he was highly complimented by his brigade commander — the fearless Colonel Smyth.

Through the constant fighting and perilous picket duty of that summer, in front of Petersburg, Nickels was ever at the post of duty, but never was scratched. But his hitherto uninterrupted career of success was terminated August 27th, 1864, in the struggle for the possession of the Weldon Railroad, known as the battle of Ream's Station. Here he was severely wounded in the leg, and left on the field, where he was stripped by the rebels, who left him, not dreaming that he would survive the night. During the night his casualty was reported to the regiment, when Adjutant Hincks, and Privates Goff and Rigney, sought him out on the abandoned field, and bore him through the darkness *eight miles* into our lines. Such was the love he inspired, and such the devotion of the brave boys who risked their lives for him. Taken to City Point, he was removed to Armory Square Hospital, at Washington, where, after lingering six months, he died, February 20th, 1865. Many times his prospects of recovery were deemed very fair, but the long confinement at last broke down his constitution — and with his faithful aunt and brother by his bedside, he quietly pined away, saying to his aunt, who told him of his situation, and pointed him to Christ, "It is all right with me."

Connecticut lost no nobler son in the war, — a genial companion, a thorough officer, always remarkable for his knowledge of and attention to his duties; loved and respected by his brother officers and men. He had won high encomiums from his superiors of all grades, and bid fair in time to have acquired more than a local reputation. His perfect coolness under fire, and his cheerfulness and freedom from despondency or irritability during his long and weary confinement to a hospital bed, show the prominent traits in his character, — intrepidity, trustfulness, and amiability.

Into twenty-one short years Captain Nickels crowded a life-time of noble deeds, and dying he left no enemy but mourning friends among his soldier comrades, his schoolmates, and his townsmen. It was granted to him to live long enough to see the impending triumph of his country's cause, and to leave an untarnished name—

"And so he laid his laurels down at his great Captain's feet."

THE LOST IN OTHER THAN CONNECTICUT REGIMENTS.

DOUGLAS R. BUSHNELL, Major Thirteenth Regiment, Ill. Vols. Killed in action at Chattanooga.

PETER L. HYDE, Lieutenant Twenty-sixth Regiment, Ohio Vols. Killed at Arkansas Post.

NON-COMMISSIONED OFFICERS AND PRIVATES.

"THE LEAST IN RANK, BUT NOT IN HONOR."

DAVID C. CASE, Third Regiment C. V. Killed by a cannon ball at Bull-Run, July 21, 1861. Age 26. He was the son of Dea. Samuel Case of Norwich Town, and the first soldier from Norwich killed in the War of the Rebellion.

JOSEPH STOKES, Second Regiment C. V. Died in hospital, July 25, 1861.

THOMAS D. HUNTINGTON, Eighth Regiment C. V. Son of Benjamin Huntington, Norwich Town. He enlisted September 21, 1861, and went into camp at Hartford, where he was taken sick. He returned home, and died eight days after being mustered into service, September 29, 1861.

ERASTUS D. VERGASON, Tenth Regiment C. V. Killed in the battle of Roanoke Island, February 8, 1862. He was a farmer. Age 27.

PATRICK MARO, Tenth Regiment C. V. Killed in the capture of Newbern, N. C., March 14, 1862. He was a mechanic. Age 18.

DANIEL H. BROWN, Ninth Regiment C. V. Died of disease at New Orleans, May 14, 1862. Age 43. By trade a mechanic.

WILLIAM HUTCHINS, Eleventh Regiment C. V. Died of disease, June 14, 1862. Age 20.

JAMES MONINGHAM, Ninth Regiment C. V. Died of disease at Vicksburg, Miss., July 21, 1862. He was a laborer. Age 33.

JOHN KERLEY, Ninth Regiment C. V. Died on the transport, July 24, 1862. Age 18.

JOHN P. KEHR, U. S. N. Died of disease at Vicksburg, July 30, 1862.

ALEXANDER S. AVERY, Sergeant, Fifth Regiment C. V.

Killed in the battle of Cedar Mountain, Va., August 9, 1862.

CHARLES H. POTTER, Ninth Regiment C. V. Died of disease at Baton Rouge, La., August 10, 1862. He was a machinist by trade. Age 24.

PATRICK WELDON, Sergeant, Ninth Regiment C. V. Died at New Orleans, August 14, 1862. Age 34.

JAMES MURPHY, Ninth Regiment C. V. Died August 16, 1862, at New Orleans. Age 19.

JAMES MCVAY, Fourteenth Regiment C. V. Fell out of the ranks on the march to Antietam and died of exhaustion at Rockville, Md., September 9, 1862. Age 42.

DAVID M. FORD, Eleventh Regiment C. V. Killed in the battle at Antietam, September 17, 1862. Age 20.

JOHN C. HOLWELL, Eleventh Regiment C. V. Killed at Antietam, September 17, 1862. Age 40.

EZRA M. LOOMIS, Eleventh Regiment C. V. Died of wounds received at Antietam, September 19, 1862.

HENRY P. YERRINGTON, Fourteenth Regiment C. V. Died of wounds received at Antietam, September 21, 1872. Age 25.

HENRY M. SCHOFIELD, Eleventh Regiment C. V. He was a young man of much promise, enlisted in the First Regiment, April 22, 1861. Died of wounds received at Antietam, September 28, 1862.

JOHN W. WOOD, Eleventh Regiment C. V. Died of wounds received at Antietam, September 1862. Age 23.

EDWARD DORCEY, Corporal, Fourteenth Regiment C. V. Died of wounds received at Antietam, October 8, 1862.

JOHN SIMPSON, Sergeant, Ninth Regiment C. V. Died of disease at New Orleans, October 8, 1862. Age 27.

HORATIO BURDICK, Eighteenth Regiment C. V. Died at Fort McHenry, October 19, 1862. Age 30.

THEODORE A. FANNING, Eighth Regiment C. V. Died of wounds received at Antietam, October 19, 1862. Age 24.

FERDINAND VOLKMAN, Sixth Regiment C. V. Died at Beaufort, S. C., October 21, 1862. Age 36.

DAVID BLACK, Thirteenth Regiment C. V. Killed in the battle of Georgia Landing, La., October 27, 1862. Age 38.

HENRY C. FANNING, Eighth Regiment C. V. Died of wounds received at Antietam, October 28, 1862. Age 18.

JOHN MEANY, Ninth Regiment C. V. Died at New Orleans, November 12, 1862.

CHARLES H. BECKWITH, Eighteenth Regiment, C. V. Served in the three months' campaign. Died of disease at Norwich, December 1, 1862. Age 22.

MICHAEL CARVER, Corporal, First Regiment Cavalry C. V. Killed in action at Stafford Court House, Va., January 3, 1863. Age 18.

DANIEL WILBUR, Eighteenth Regiment C. V. Accidentally shot while on guard duty at Fort Howard, Baltimore, Md., January 5, 1863. Age 19.

CHARLES BURDICK, Tenth Regiment C. V. Son of Evan Burdick of Norwich. Died in the hospital at Newbern, N. C., January 16, 1863. Age 19.

JOSIAH L. D. OTIS, Fourteenth Regiment C. V. Wounded at Fredericksburg, and died after extreme suffering in a hospital at Washington, D. C., February 10, 1863. He was a physician by profession, and enlisted in the company of Captain James B. Coit. At his death was 41 years of age.

WILLIAM R. ALLYN, Fourteenth Regiment C. V. Died at Falmouth, March 9, 1863. He was a farmer by occupation. Age 18.

JOHN MCSORLEY, Ninth Regiment C. V. Died at New Orleans, April 18, 1863. Age 35.

JAMES TORRANCE, Sergeant, Thirteenth Regiment C. V.

Killed at Port Hudson, Louisiana, May 24, 1863. He was the youngest son of a widowed mother, born November 29, 1841, near Edinburgh, Scotland. He possessed in a high degree the qualities of self-reliance and integrity which characterize so generally the Scotch. With a bright earnest face, a manly form, those who observed him in the Sabbath-school class, or in the workshop, were attracted by his appearance. At the first call of the Government for troops, he promptly responded, and went out in Captain Harland's company of the Third Regiment, and was in the battle of Bull Run. Returning with the regiment, he was not contented to remain at home. His heart was in the cause, and he longed once more to enroll himself among the country's defenders. Though his mother sought to retain him by her side, reminding him that she was now dependent upon her boys, he still seemed to think it was her duty to give him up, and his to go.

Meanwhile, his mother noticed the boy's strong desire to enlist once more, and was not wholly unprepared for the decision which brought him again to that step. "Mother," he said, as nearly as his words can now be recalled, "you know we have adopted this as our land, and we ought in this hour of peril to do something for the Government, and I think I ought to enter its service." The time had come, and sorrowfully, yet hopefully, the fond parent replied, "Jamie, if you must go, one condition I have to propose, — that you will read a chapter in this Testament (handing him the copy), when not on duty, every night at nine o'clock, and your mother will do the same ; and so we will remember each other." He assented to this, and in the Thirteenth Regiment, under Colonel Birge, soon took his departure. Young Torrance was regarded in his company as a brave and upright soldier, and his Captain reports him as one of the most reliable in his command.

In the battles of Georgia Landing, October 27, 1862, and of Irish Bend, April 14, 1863, Sergeant Torrance acquitted himself with honor. On Sabbath, May 24, 1863, was the assault on Port Hudson, with the Thirteenth Regiment in the advance, leading the charge. Just previous to the battle, Torrance remarked to a comrade, "The only thing I dislike in the service is the being obliged to fight on the Lord's Day, at least commencing any engagement which could as well be postponed till after the passage of holy time."

It was in this action that young Torrance received his death shot. After little more than a year's service he fell, as the hero should fall, facing the foe and leading in the charge. He had staked all in his country's behalf, and died in her defense. His was a humble career, for it was a modest yet manly youth who lived it, who sought ambitiously for no personal renown, but who was earnestly intent on the Government's deliverance.

His brother, Colonel David Torrance of the Twenty-ninth Regiment, who served with great faithfulness and honor, wrote to his mourning mother, when the sad intelligence reached him, "Our starry flag where'er it floats, will be dearer now to me, hallowed and consecrated by a brother's blood. Let us give thanks that God has accepted our sacrifice, and that we are permitted to do and to suffer in the cause of liberty, right, and truth."

MICHAEL CORBETT, Thirteenth Regiment C. V. Died of wounds at Baton Rouge, La., May 25, 1863. Age 25.

MYRON W. STARRETT, Twenty-sixth Regiment. Missing in action, and was supposed to have died at Port Hudson, May 27, 1863.

JAMES PARKERSON, Twenty-sixth Regiment C. V. Mortally wounded at Port Hudson, May 27th, and died June 1, 1863. Age 27.

ALBERT BURNETT, Eighteenth Regiment C. V. Killed in the battle of Winchester, Va., June 15, 1863. Age 24.

JAMES MCCRACKEN, Eighteenth Regiment C. V. Killed at Winchester, Va., June 15, 1863. Age 28.

CHARLES C. NOYES, Eighteenth Regiment C. V. Mortally wounded in the battle of Winchester, and died June 15, 1863. He was a young man of promising talents, exemplary in his life, and the only child of his parents.

COURTLAND C. AVERY, Twenty-sixth Regiment C. V. Died of fever near Port Hudson, La., June 23, 1863. He was a son of Courtland Avery of Scotland, Conn., but for many years a resident in Norwich.

WILLIAM M. SHERMAN, Sergeant, Twenty-sixth Regiment C. V. Died June 28, 1863, in the hospital at New Orleans, from wounds received at Port Hudson. Age 25.

NELSON C. THOMPSON, Eighteenth Regiment C. V. Died of wounds received in the battle of Winchester, Va., June 30, 1863. Age 21.

JOHN CRAWFORD, Eighteenth Regiment C. V. Died of wounds received in the battle of Winchester, July 2, 1863. He was a young man of estimable character, and resided in Greeneville. Age 25.

ISLAY B. MARTIN, Eighteenth Regiment C. V. Died of wounds received at Winchester, Va., July 2, 1863. He was a well educated and promising youth. Age 18.

HENRY BROOKS, twenty-sixth Regiment C. V. Died of wounds received in the first charge on Port Hudson, La., July 3, 1863. He was a native of Canada, but for a number of years a resident in Norwich. Age 44.

FRANK WHITE, Sixth Regiment C. V. Killed in the assault of Fort Wagner, S. C., July 18, 1863. A carpenter by occupation. Age 28.

CHARLES MEISSER, Sixth Regiment C. V. Killed at Morris Island, July 18, 1863. Age 24.

John Shea, Thirteenth Regiment C. V. Died of disease at Baton Rouge, La., July 18, 1863.

George F. Edgerton, Twenty-sixth Regiment C. V. Died at Port Hudson, La., July 23, 1863. Age 35.

James Dugan, Twenty-sixth Regiment C. V. Wounded in the hand at Port Hudson, and died of disease on board the steamer while returning home, July 28, 1863.

Stephen T. Johnson, Twenty-sixth Regiment C. V. Died in the hospital at Mound City, Ill., August 3, 1863. Age 39.

Joseph Forestner, Corporal, Eighteenth Regiment C. V. Died at Camp Parole, Md., August 9, 1863. Age 37.

William McKnight, Twelfth Regiment C. V. Died at Brashear City, La., August 18, 1863.

Lemuel Bolman, Twelfth Regiment C. V. Died at Brashear City, La., August 22, 1863. Age 44.

William T. B. Osborne, unassigned recruit. Died at New Haven, September 2, 1863.

Alfred S. Chappell, Eighteenth Regiment C. V. Died in Philadelphia, September 17, 1863. Age 37.

Henry M. Beckwith, First Artillery C. V. Died at Fort Ward, Va., October 10, 1863.

Abner T. Potter, unassigned recruit. Died at Norwich, December 24, 1863.

Frederick W. Baker, First Regiment Cavalry C. V. Died at Baltimore, Md., January 27, 1864.

Stephen H. Smith, Thirty-first Regiment U. S. C. T. Died at Philadelphia, Pa., February 23, 1864.

E. C. Buckingham, Fourteenth Regiment C. V. Died at Brandy Station, Va., March 3, 1864.

Dennis Murphy, Twenty-first Regiment C. V. Died at Newbern, N. C., March 12, 1864.

Henry A. Bottomly, Corporal, Seventh Regiment C. V. He had reënlisted as a veteran, and died during his veteran furlough, while on a visit to his family near Boston, March 13, 1864. Age 34. His death was occasioned by disease contracted while in the service.

JOHN CULLIN, Twenty-first Regiment C. V. Died in the hospital at Newbern, March 22, 1864.

WILLIAM H. TOWN, Eighteenth Regiment C. V. Died in hospital at Sandy Hook, Md., March 28, 1864. Age 29.

JOSEPH H. WINSHIP, Eighteenth Regiment C. V. He was left at Winchester, after the battle of June 15, 1863, to look after the sick and wounded ; was taken prisoner, sent to Richmond, thence transferred to Andersonville, Ga., and there died April 5, 1864. Age 23. He was an only child, leaving behind him sad parents and a desolate home.

JOHN MELDRUM, Ninth Regiment C. V. Died at New Orleans, April 8, 1864.

JAMES W. HICKS, Eighteenth Regiment C. V. Died at Martinsburg, Va., April 13, 1864.

MOSES TYLER, Fourteenth Regiment C. V. Captured at Morton's Ford, Va., and died in prison at Andersonville, Ga., April 14, 1864. Age 19.

ALONZO S. CUSHMAN, Corporal, Eleventh Regiment C. V. Mortally wounded at Swift's Creek, Va., and died May 9, 1864. He had reënlisted as a veteran.

PATRICK LLOYD, Fourteenth Regiment C. V. Killed at Spottsylvania, Va., May 11, 1864. Age 25.

DAVID H. BROWN, Thirteenth Regiment C. V. Died May 15, 1864. A reënlisted veteran. Age 23.

DAVID LACEY, Second Artillery C. V. Killed at Cold Harbor, Va., June 1, 1864.

RONALD MCALLISTER, JR., Eleventh Regiment C. V. Killed at Cold Harbor, June 3, 1864. (His father, of the same name, served 14 months in the same regiment.)

JAMES SOUTER, Sergeant, Eleventh Regiment C. V. Killed at Cold Harbor, June 3, 1864. He was born in

Dundee, Scotland, December 8, 1841, and came to this country with his parents in 1851, who have resided in Greeneville since 1855. When the rebels began hostilities by firing upon Fort Sumter, James, who was a clerk in the house of C. D. Browning & Co., comprehended the nature and magnitude of the impending struggle, as few then did, and after mature deliberation, enlisted in Company F, Eleventh Regiment C. V. He was soon chosen Sergeant; afterwards upon the illness of the First Lieutenant of the Ambulance Corps, he was detailed to fill his place. He returned to his regiment in season to participate in the battle of Cold Harbor, June 3, 1864, where he fell, and was buried on the field with about one hundred others in the darkness of the night, without lights.

He is remembered as a dutiful son, a diligent scholar, a faithful clerk, and conscientious Christian. His Captain, in a letter of condolence to his parents, says: " The Sergeant is very much missed in the Regiment. Cool, courageous, never faltering, and always ready for every duty, and every inch a model soldier, and by none can the loss be felt more deeply than by myself, for I had almost learned to look upon him as a brother." COMMUNICATED.

THOMAS DUGAN, Twenty-first Regiment C. V. Died in prison at Andersonville, Ga., June 4, 1864.

JOHN T. BRADLEY, Corporal, Eighteenth Regiment C. V. Killed in the battle of Piedmont, Va., June 5, 1864. Age 19.

CHARLES T. FANNING, Eighteenth Regiment C. V. Mortally wounded at Piedmont, Va., June 5, 1864.

WILLIAM H. HAMILTON, Eighteenth Regiment C. V. Killed in the battle of Piedmont, Va., June 5, 1864. Age 18.

THOMAS MCMAHON, Eighteenth Regiment C. V. Killed at Piedmont, Va., June 5, 1864.

DANIEL EMMONS, Twenty-ninth Regiment, Colored C. V. Died at Beaufort, S. C., June 13, 1864.

WALTER M. FOX, Second Artillery C. V. Killed at Petersburg, June 22, 1864.

AUGUST EHLERS, Twenty-first Regiment C. V. Died from wounds at Point of Rocks, Va., July 2, 1864.

THOMAS M. BALDWIN, First Regiment Cavalry C. V. Died in prison at Andersonville, Ga., July 3, 1864.

HENRY STEWART, Thirty-first U. S. C. T. Killed at Petersburg, July 7, 1864.

BYRON CROCKER, Thirteenth Regiment C. V. Died of wounds received at Georgia Landing at New Orleans, July 16, 1864. He was the son of the late Thomas Crocker, and one of the party that volunteered to storm the works at Port Hudson under the lead of General Birge.

JOHN DELANEY, Eighteenth Regiment C. V. Killed in the engagement at Snicker's Ford, Va., July 18, 1864. Age 18.

KARL REDER, First Conn. Cavalry. Died of wounds at David's Island, N. Y., July 29, 1864.

PATRICK CONKLIN, Twenty-first Regiment C. V. Died of disease at Fortress Monroe, Va., August 2, 1864.

JOHN F TREADWAY, Corporal, First Conn. Cavalry. Died in prison at Andersonville, August 3, 1864. He was the son of F. W. Treadway, of Norwich, and enlisted at New Haven.

JOSEPH A. TRACY, Eighteenth Regiment C. V. Wounded at Snicker's Ford, July 18, 1864, and died in hospital at Sandy Hook, Md., August 7, 1864. Age 18.

HENRY F. CHAMPLIN, Tenth Regiment C. V. Died at Andersonville, Ga., August 11, 1864.

JOSEPH A. BAILEY, First Conn. Cavalry. Died in prison at Andersonville, August 13, 1864.

JOHN BARNEY, Twenty-first Regiment C. V. Died of wounds at Fortress Monroe, Va., August 14, 1864.

JAMES S. McDAVID, First Conn. Cavalry. Captured at Ashland Station, June 1, 1864, died at Andersonville, Aug. 21, 1864. Age 17.

HENRY N. LOOMIS, Twenty-first Regiment. Mortally wounded at Petersburg, and died August 21, 1864. Age 18.

WILLIAM DAVIS, First Conn. Cavalry. Captured at Craig's Church, Va., May 3, 1864, died at Andersonville, August 30, 1864. Age 42.

WILLIAM G. HAYWARD, Eighteenth Regiment C. V. Captured at Winchester, was exchanged, and rejoined his regiment; captured again at New Market, Va., May 15, 1864, and died in prison at Andersonville, September 11, 1864. Age 34.

AUGUSTUS BERG, Second Artillery C. V. Killed in action at Winchester, Va., September 19, 1864.

ALBERT MOFFETT, First Conn. Cavalry. Killed at Winchester, Va., September 19, 1864.

DANIEL LAIRD, Thirteenth Regiment C. V. Killed at Winchester, Va., September 19, 1864. Age 18.

MARTIN CARL, Eighteenth Regiment C. V. Died of disease at Sandy Hook, Md., September 25, 1864.

EDWARD F. TISDALE, First Conn. Cavalry. Was captured after his horse had been shot under him, and died at Andersonville, September 29, 1864. Age 18.

ADAM ACKSLER, Eighteenth Regiment C. V. Died in prison at Madisonville, Ga., October 5, 1864.

EDWARD BLUMLEY, Eighth Regiment, C. V. Captured in an engagement upon the Petersburg Railroad, May 7, 1864, and died at Andersonville, Ga., October 6, 1864. Age 39.

GIDEON McCALL, Thirty-first Regiment U. S. C. T. Died of wounds at Alexandria, Va., October 8, 1864.

EDWARD ROE, Ninth Regiment. Killed in action at Cedar Creek, Va., October 19, 1864.

THOMAS FILLBURN, Seventh Regiment C. V. Died in prison in Millen, Ga., October 21, 1864.

MOSES STEPHENSON, Twenty-ninth Regiment C. V. Died of wounds, October 27, 1864.

HENRY W. GREENOUGH, First Conn. Cavalry. Died in prison in Salisbury, N. C., October 29, 1864.

HENRY LYNCH, Second Artillery C. V. Died of wounds at Baltimore, Md., October 31, 1864.

WILLIAM B. CARROL, Corporal, Seventh Regiment, C. V. Died of disease, November 5, 1864.

SYLVANUS DOWNER, Eighteenth Regiment C. V. Died in prison at Andersonville, November 5, 1864. He had been chief engineer of the fire department in Norwich, was captured at Winchester, exchanged, rejoined his regiment, and was promoted Color-sergeant. Afterwards wounded in the battle of Piedmont, he was taken prisoner a second time, and carried to the prison-pen at Andersonville, where he died. Age 44.

PATRICK GLYNN, Ninth Regiment C. V. Died of disease, November 25, 1864.

HORACE B. WOOD, Second Artillery C. V. Died in prison at Richmond, Va., December 27, 1864.

HERBERT E. BECKWITH, Corporal, Second Artillery, Mass. Captured at Plymouth, N. C., and taken to Andersonville, Ga., from which he returned, but in so exhausted a condition that he lived but six days, dying December 30, 1864. He was the son of Elisha W. Beckwith, of Norwich, and was born June 23, 1845. Early in the war he manifested a strong desire to enlist, but his youthful age and the wishes of his parents for a while deterred him. Many thought him too young to endure the hardships of a soldier's life, but the excitement and novelty of such a career had a fascination for him, and, boy as he was, he too felt the stirrings of that mighty passion which can make of even youth, patriots and heroes. Not that he at this time thoroughly defined his motives, but it was more than idle curiosity that had made him wish to do what he instinctively felt was noble. To have part in the mighty conflict, was his strongest desire. He was a lad of noble impulses, and not unintelligently did he choose that his place should be among the brave defenders of his country.

After some debate as to the wisdom of such a course, he enlisted, October 1, 1861, in the Tenth Regiment, under Colonel Russell. For nearly two years he shared the fortunes of that noble regiment. He passed safely through the battles of Roanoke Island, Newbern, and Kingston. Through all this period till June, 1863, he acquitted himself well as a soldier. His fragile form, and boyish countenance frequently excited the wonder as to how he should have come into the rough scenes and stern experiences of military life.

At his father's request he was honorably discharged, June, 1863. His soldierly conduct had gained him the esteem of both officers and men, and at the time of leaving he was to have been promoted Sergeant-major.

In November, 1863, he enlisted for the second time in the Second Massachusetts Heavy Artillery. With this regiment he left for Norfolk, Va., the following month, and was stationed at Camp O'Rourke, near the city. On the 10th of January, 1864, he was made Corporal, and was detailed soon after as Orderly to the Adjutant. In February, the regiment was ordered to Plymouth, N. C., where it performed garrison duty at Fort Wessels, one of the defenses of that place. On the 20th of April, Plymouth was attacked by the enemy in force, and after a determined resistance was captured. Young Beckwith, with his regiment, was among the prisoners taken. They were immediately marched off, and taken under strong guard first to Tarboro, and thence to Wilmington, Charleston, and finally to Andersonville.

Here five weary months were passed. Beckwith's journal gives his experience in that terrible prison-pen. It is substantially a history of suffering, cruelty, and of every inhumanity possible to a desperate and unprincipled foe. "This is a miserable place," he writes in one place, "so little care is taken of it, especially of the sick, who die in large numbers." Exposure to the summer's scorching sun, and then to the night-dews, made its impress soon on the youthful soldier. It is painful to read of the struggle he and others had to make to live on the scanty and unwholesome rations dealt out there. On the 4th of July, he writes: "This most glorious day has passed almost in misery, in the most miserable place almost on earth." Sometimes he speaks of rations of rotten bacon, and again of the non-issue of the usual rations. The tale of suffering is affecting to read, and yet no word of complaint escapes him. Of his personal sufferings and patient hopeful spirit, friends at home knew comparatively little, till companions of his escaped from that pen of death, and told what they witnessed. Their account of his hopeful courage and resolute endurance, was most full and touching. Unable to digest the only food furnished them, Beckwith was among the first to experience the pangs of unsatisfied hunger. His calm relation in his diary of some terrible fact, such as the failure of water, or the appearance of disease, shows how the fearful schooling of these months had familiarized him with the most excruciating suffering. Singularly reticent as to his own interior life, he notes usually whatever he sees of interest. The recurrence of the holy Sabbath appeared to make him long most of all for his Christian home. "At times," he says, "I fancy I hear the church bells in Norwich."

September 12th, 1864, came the welcome news of deliverance through exchange, and he left the prison, though with the signs of a not far distant death. Taken to Charleston, he with the rest was transferred to one of our transports, and brought North. December 24th, he reached Camp Parole, Annapolis, Md., and on the 28th was removed to the hospital. Pale and weak, with his lungs almost gone, after the exposures incident to his prison-life, he went directly to his bed in the hospital, and died two days after, December 30, 1864.

JAMES MASSEY, Eighteenth Regiment C. V. Died in prison at Florence, S. C., January 7, 1865.

CHARLES H. MONROE, Twenty-ninth Regiment C. V. Died at Fortress Monroe, Va., January 11, 1865.

EDWARD CAMPBELL, Fourteenth Regiment C. V. Died of disease at Washington, D. C., January 18, 1865.

PATRICK MCNAMARA, Eighteenth Regiment C. V. Died of disease, January 18, 1865.

SILAS BROWN, Twenty-ninth Regiment C. V. Died at Santiago, Texas, January 25, 1865.

GEORGE BROWN, Tenth Regiment C. V. Died at the Point of Rocks, Va., January 27, 1865.

WALTER BURGOYNE, Twelfth Regiment C. V. Died February 5, 1865.

GEORGE W. WARD, Eighteenth Regiment C. V. Died in prison at Andersonville, Ga., February 6, 1865. He was taken prisoner at Winchester, and confined successively at Belle Isle, Danville, and Andersonville. His manly fortitude and genial temperament long sustained him, but continued hunger, confinement, and ill-usage at length brought him to the grave, after he had been twenty-one months a

260   THE NORWICH MEMORIAL.

prisoner. He had fine musical talents, was a steadfast patriot, and had many warm personal friends. Age 26.

ISRAEL VARNEY, Eighteenth Regiment C. V. Captured at New Market, Va., May 15, 1864. Died in prison at Florence, S. C., February 10, 1865.

HENRY C. GASKILL, Eighteenth Regiment C. V. Died while en route to be exchanged, at Danville, Va., February 20, 1865. He was the son of Benjamin Gaskill, of Greeneville, was wounded at Piedmont, taken prisoner at Winchester, and kept in long and barbarous captivity. When at length released he was so reduced by starvation and exposure that he died on his way home. Age 33.

RICHARD H. BOGUE, Sixth Regiment C. V. Died of disease, February 23, 1865.

ALEXANDER DRISCOLL, First Conn. Cavalry. Died of disease at Annapolis, Md., March 7, 1865.

JOSEPH DAVIS, Eighth Regiment C. V. Died at the Point of Rocks, Va., March 10, 1865.

JOHN BEST, Second Artillery C. V. Killed near Petersburg, Va., March 25, 1865.

DAVID CRAMER, Second Artillery C. V. Killed in action at Petersburg, March 25, 1865.

THOMAS KEELER, Second Artillery C. V. Killed at Fort Fisher, N. C., March 26, 1865.

FRANCIS W. TAYLOR, Eighteenth Regiment C. V. Died at Annapolis, Md., March 28, 1865.

JAMES KENELEY, Tenth Regiment C. V. Killed at Petersburg, April 2, 1865.

ANTON BURGMAYER, First Conn. Cavalry. Died at Annapolis, Md., April 11, 1865.

GEORGE W. FOX, Eighteenth Regiment C. V. Died at Martinsburg, Va., April 17, 1865.

CHARLES E. BREED, U. S. N. Engineer. Died of disease contracted in the service, April 1, 1865. He entered

the navy in April, 1864, and though not able at that time to endure a soldier's hardship, he hoped to be of some service to the Government on one of its vessels. With a generous feeling that what he could he ought to do, he took his place on the ship, and by faithful unpretentious duty did his part in crushing out the rebellion. The exposures and labors of his position, however, proved too much for his strength, and reluctantly, though after persistent trial, he was obliged to seek discharge from duty. He came home in February, 1865, with the symptoms of fatal disease, and lingered till the following April, when he died. Age 19.

JOHN McDONALD, Ninth Regiment C. V. Died May 2, 1865.

ABBOTT HOWELL, Thirty-first U. S. C. T. Died at Brownsville, Texas, July 16, 1865.

EDWARD FRANCIS, Twenty-ninth Regiment C. V. Died at Brownsville, Texas, September 17, 1865.

THE LOST IN OTHER THAN CONNECTICUT REGIMENTS.

JAMES WILLIAMS, Second N. Y. Artillery. Died of disease, at Alexandria, February, 1862.

WILLIAM D. LATHROP, Fifteenth Regiment Ill. V. Died at Paducah of wounds received at battle of Shiloh, April 22, 1862.

EDWARD R. MOORE, Fifty-seventh Regiment N. Y. V. Died of disease at Newport News, Va., September 16, 1862.

JACOB W. MILLER, Fifty-first Artillery. Son of J. W. Miller, Norwich Town. He was with his regiment, which he joined soon after the war broke out, in the North Carolina campaign, under General Burnside; in the Army of the Potomac at South Mountain and Antietam; in Grant's army at Vicksburg; and in the battles of the Wilderness. In the conflict near Spottsylvania, May 18, 1864, he was shot through the heart. Age 16. He had never been absent an hour from his post during his connection with the army, and was buried on the battle-field. His commanding officer, writing to his friends, bore grateful testimony to his soldierly faithfulness and courage.

JOHN W. PETERS, Fourteenth Regiment R. I. V. Died of disease, at Fort Jackson, La., August 24, 1864.

CHARLES J. TOSSETT, Fourteenth Regiment R. I. V. Died of disease, at Fort Jackson, La., November 20, 1864.

CHESTER H. HALLAM, Fourteenth Regiment R. I. V. Died of disease, at Fort Jackson, La., March 1, 1865.

XIII.

IN REBEL PRISONS.

"For I was an hungered, and ye gave me no meat ; I was thirsty, and ye gave me no drink ; I was a stranger, and ye took me not in ; Naked, and ye clothed me not ; Sick and in prison, and ye visited me not.

"Lord, when saw we thee an hungered, or athirst, or a stranger, or naked, or sick, or in prison, and did not minister unto thee ?

"Verily I say unto you, inasmuch as ye did it not to one of the least of these, ye did it not to me."

THE saddest memories of all the war are awakened by the names,— Andersonville, Libby, Belle Isle, Florence, Salisbury, Charleston. They are the names of prison pens, so hideous and foul, where the treatment was one of such systematized and unrelenting cruelty, that before them the cheek still blanches, and the heart of every patriot is stirred with emotions he cannot trust to utterance. The story of the inhumanity with which they were managed, of the brutality, sickness, disease, starvation, and death that were inseparable from life in them, makes one shudder who is obliged to look even now into their history.

The public were slow in coming to any realizing sense of the barbarity of the rebel authorities as displayed in the arrangement and conduct of these fearful prisons, but every returned prisoner brought back his tale of suffering, and soon Congress itself instituted an official inquiry, which though failing to reach the public ear, substantiated, in the facts developed, the worst reports that had become current.

The thorough rousing of the nation, however, to all the

unutterable barbarities to which our prisoners were subjected, was due to the report of the "Committee of Investigation," appointed by the United States Sanitary Commission. This committee was carefully selected, and embraced those in whom the public could place entire confidence. The names of those composing it were as follows: Ellerslie Wallace, M. D., Hon. J. I. Clark Hare, and Rev. Treadwell Walden, of Philadelphia; Valentine Mott, M. D., LL. D., Edward Delafield, M. D., and Gouverneur M. Wilkins, Esq., of New York. The narrative of the report was written by a former Norwich resident, still held in loving and honored remembrance, — Rev. Treadwell Walden, Rector of Christ Church, from 1857 to 1863. It was admirably arranged; the history, based on the irrefutable testimony taken, was calmly and dispassionately related, and as might have been anticipated, the impression produced was most profound and wide-reaching. On its publication, it had an immense circulation in this country, and was extensively read in Europe, startling the whole civilized world by the facts it established, and the appalling details it made public. Oliver Wendell Holmes wrote to Mr. Walden concerning the facts embodied in the report, "Their interest is terrible; the world will shudder and sicken as it reads them. .... I shall read in it at times, and when I can read without cursing and swearing. . . . To palliate these infernal savagisms, to call them barbarisms, is a compliment at the expense of barbarism, to which they are not entitled."

Many other equally earnest and strongly worded testimonies were received from prominent men throughout the country, which together with the unprecedented demand for the report, and its vast circulation in various forms, showed that its purpose was attained, and that the public heart was deeply touched, and the mind of the nation convinced. The preparation of this report cost the writer much time and labor, and to the admirable and wise accomplishment of his work, was due the lasting and needed good of which it was unquestionably productive.

Among those who contributed testimony, based on personal experience and observation, was Lieutenant-colonel Charles Farnsworth, of this city. His letters were of great interest; his evidence on points of fact emphatic, exposing clearly the sufferings and horrors incident to life in Libby and Belle Isle.

Indeed, when the true state of things in these southern prisons became publicly known, the marvel was that so many of those incarcerated survived the fearful ordeal.

When the subject was brought before Congress, by the report of "the Committee on the Conduct of the War," which confirmed the fact that the most unparalleled atrocities had been inflicted upon Union prisoners, some advocated a system of strict retaliation. This was, however, decidedly negatived. In reference to the facts, which some even at this time (1865, Jan.) affected to gloss over, Senator Foster, in his place in the Senate, thus emphatically, and yet with characteristic carefulness, spoke: "I am astonished that any intelligent man should express a doubt, whether our prisoners in the hands of the rebels, *from the first day of the war,* have been treated barbarously, inhumanly, and that this treatment continues to the present time. Who are our opponents? They are a band of insurgents, robbers, traitors, malefactors on land, and pirates on the deep, and because such men descend to what would disgrace savages in the treatment of prisoners, not disgracing any National name, for they have no National name to disgrace, shall we who are citizens of the United States of America, each man feeling that he has a part of the National honor to sustain, do that which disgraces them? No, Mr. President, no, no."

Mr. Lincoln, when the report of these rebel barbarities

came to him, authenticated beyond a doubt, nobly said, when urged to retaliate, "I never can, I never can starve men like that."

The facts are such as are too painful to be dwelt upon, but they cannot be forgotten or overlooked. They stand rather to point the moral of that system of human bondage, which so largely debauched the consciences of those who had aught to do with it, and made millions of our fellow countrymen willing to embroil a peaceful and happy country in civil war, for the purpose of establishing a separate confederacy, whose "corner stone should be slavery." This prison treatment is the last hideous monument of unrelieved terror and shame, that will memorialize with eternal infamy the slaveholders' rebellion. No picture of torture or misery was ever presented by a civilized people to the world, comparable to this, — the treatment of our defenseless prisoners by the rebels. And now that enough years have passed to abate the immediate enmities and bitternesses occasioned by this unprecedented strife, the impartial historian reluctantly touching upon this dark chapter, cannot make of it other than an unrelieved tale of needless and wicked barbarism, of cruelty so inhuman and persistent, of deliberate and systematized inhumanity, which in savages would not have been palliated.

The number of Union prisoners held in the South during the rebellion, was one hundred and twenty-six thousand nine hundred and forty (126,940). Of this number twenty-two thousand five hundred and seventy-six died or were starved to death. For the only complete roll of the prisoners who perished at Andersonville, the nation is indebted to Private Dorance Atwater, of Plymouth, in this State. Two hundred and ninety Connecticut soldiers are known to have lost their lives in this worst of the prisons of the South.

In some or all of these accursed prison-pens Norwich

soldiers were confined, some falling victims to the treatment which was to such vast numbers fatal; others, surviving their imprisonment, returned to friends and kindred, rejoicing over their escape from death in its most dreaded and distressing form. The exact number of our soldiers that were captured, and for longer or shorter periods confined, cannot now be actually determined.

Much was done by citizens at home to mitigate the sufferings of those known to be imprisoned, by sending boxes of provisions and clothing, and delicacies for the sick. Not all of these were allowed by the Confederate authorities to be delivered, some were misappropriated, and some reached their destination, bringing untold cheer and comfort to those whose needs were by them supplied. The investigation conducted by the committee of the Sanitary Commission, showed that at one time in Richmond, three thousand boxes had accumulated, sent to the prisoners in Libby and Belle Isle, by their anxious and devoted friends in the North, and these were maliciously kept back, though piled in warehouses in full sight of many of the hungry captives. The contents of not a few of them were thus entirely spoiled, while those containing clothing were in some known instances appropriated by the rebels. In this way not only were the sufferings of the imprisoned aggravated, but those who begged the poor boon of ministering to their actual necessities, were insulted and deceived.

The Libby — which was the chief prison in Richmond, and the one best known — consisted of a row of brick buildings three stories high, situated on the canal and overlooking the James River, which were formerly tobacco warehouses. The partitions between the buildings were pierced with door-ways on each story, and the entire range of rooms on each floor thus connected, and utilized for prison purposes. The rooms were one hundred feet long by forty feet broad, and in six of them were twelve hundred officers at one time confined, including all grades from a brigadier-general to a second lieutenant. Here, crowded together amid vermin and filth, with no furniture but what the prisoners made, with no sanitary regulations, in the power of a brutal guard, and with rations insufficient to appease the cravings of hunger, were those who, under the instigation of a lofty patriotism, left homes of comfort and affluence at the North to enter the service of the Government, put in peril by the Rebellion.

Norwich had, during the course of the war, a number of representatives in this prison. On the surrender in part of the Eighteenth Regiment, after the disastrous battle of Winchester, officers and privates were taken to Richmond and confined, the former in Libby, the latter in Belle Isle. From this town there were: Colonel W. G. Ely, Captains H. C. Davis, Joseph P. Rockwell, S. T. C. Merwin, M. V. B. Tiffany, John E. Woodward, and Quartermaster Dwight W. Hakes; also, Lieutenants Adam H. Lindsley, James D. Higgins, Henry F. Cowles, John Francis, and Francis McKeag. Nearly all of the privates were soon paroled, but the officers were held in durance vile, some for almost a year, and six for twenty-one months. The latter, during their captivity made the acquaintance of eight different prisons, being removed from one to another for no well-defined reason. The monotony of prison life was broken up by these repeated changes, and by their diversified experience they acquired a reliable knowledge as to the condition of these various places of confinement.

Major (afterwards Lieutenant-colonel) Farnsworth, of the First Regiment Cavalry, was also an inmate of Libby, and while there did what he could to see that those of his own command, captured with him, as well as others whom he knew, shared in the good things sent to him from his own home. His thoughtfulness and zeal in this particular was remembered with devout gratitude by some who returned to speak of it, and who felt that their own preservation from death by starvation was due to him. When he was exchanged, and returned home, he not only had words of testimony concerning the inhuman prison treatment which prevailed in Richmond, but he forwarded, as early as possible, to those he had left behind him in weary confinement, a box containing such things as, from experience, he knew would comfort and cheer them.

After the battle of Gettysburg, the fare in Libby improved somewhat, owing to the wholesome fear of retaliation, the balance of prisoners being in our favor. The monotonous prison life was varied in every possible way. Classes in the modern languages were formed, a literary society was organized and maintained with great spirit, a journal called the "Libby Chronicle" was edited with interest and marked ability. Music classes, theatrical entertainments, and other diversions were resorted to, by which the depressing imprisonment was made somewhat endurable. All this was possible in Libby to an extent never allowed in other prisons, because those confined in the former were officers, and were within reach of those ever-helpful and life-cheering boxes sent them from the North. The Sabbath-school of the Second Church, which had a large representation among the prisoners in Libby, was specially forward and generous in this work of providing boxes for those of their number there confined. On Thanksgiving Day, 1863, it sent twenty-two packages of sundries, fruit, meat, and vegetables to the "boys in Libby," for the purchase of which two hundred and forty-one dollars were raised by the school. At the same time, in the Broadway Church, at the union Thanksgiving service, one hundred and sixty dollars were raised for the same purpose. This money, subsequently increased by a few additional contributions, was turned over to Mr. Charles Johnson, who inclosed the whole amount to Mr. C. C. Fulton, of Baltimore, who made the following report : —

BALTIMORE, *December* 28, 1863.

CHARLES JOHNSON, Esq., —

Dear Sir: Your draft for $174.20 was duly received, and I will to-day ship to Colonel William G. Ely the following articles : —

Two barrels of flour.
One barrel Bologna sausages.
One barrel smoked beef.
One barrel hams.
One barrel chewing and smoking tobacco, pipes, matches, scissors, thread, needles, combs, etc.
One box of articles of luxury and necessity, to make palatable the substantial food that accompanies it.

I inclose your letter to me, with the box, with a list of articles forwarded. I have direct information from Richmond that all the articles I forward are promptly delivered.

Yours for the Union,   CHARLES C. FULTON.

In acknowledging this timely and most considerate gift of Norwich friends, Colonel Ely wrote back from Libby, January 28, 1864 : —

"I have this day visited Belle Isle, by permission of the Confederate authorities, and was also permitted to carry many things for the comfort of the soldiers of the Eighteenth and Sixth Regiments. I can almost say that it has been the happiest day of my life."

Mr. Johnson made, about this time, another attempt to forward supplies to those who were confined in and about Richmond, but it was found impossible to communicate with them, and not till some months later were any boxes or packages allowed to be sent for the relief of those in Libby or Belle Isle.

In February, 1864, Colonel Ely and one hundred and eighty officers made their escape from Libby, through the famous tunnel, on which some fifty-five days of hard work were spent.

The Richmond "Inquirer" thus describes this ingenious undertaking to escape from a prison life, which never was comfortable enough to make contented and patient, those who were waiting to be released in the ordinary and only legitimate way : —

"It appears that the tunnel under Twentieth Street was dug entirely with an old hinge, and the loosened earth — a brittle marl and sand — removed with an old sugar scoop, stolen from the hospital quarters. As the tunnel progressed, the miner took with him, besides his tools, an old-fashioned knapsack made upon a wooden frame, to which a cord was attached. When he filled this with earth it was drawn out by an accomplice who remained in the cellar. The contents safely deposited out of the way, it was then shoved back to the digger with a pole. The basement in which this work was carried on was kept constantly locked, never used, and the windows being tightly nailed, it was dark as pitch."

About fifty of those who escaped, including Colonel Ely, were recaptured, and had to pay for this inordinate love of liberty — this daring to work a passage out towards friends and freedom — by close confinement in the underground cells of the Libby, which were infested with rats, and foul with a dampness that dripped from the walls. Still our boys kept up a brave heart during their long and exhausting imprisonment. Captain Davis of the Eighteenth, represented the pluck and noble spirit that dwelt in his comrades, when he wrote from Libby, October, 1863 : —

"On the walls of the Conciergerie, in the days of the French Revolution, was written the sentiment, ' He who retains his patriotism can never be wholly miserable.' So here in these days, having their parallel with those, in fraternal bloodshed, this is the sentiment of many a prisoner enduring incarceration to which the fortunes of war have consigned him. Deprived of personal liberty, of the comforts of even camp life, subsisting on a scanty diet, yet we are not of all men most miserable, when we remember for what we are here."

It was not an easy thing to escape from these rebel prisons, and those who tried to, paid pretty dear for their liberty if they gained it, while if they failed, it subjected them to all the more rigorous treatment when taken back. We give the following experience of one of our Norwich men, who got out of Libby by means of the tunnel just referred to, as illustrative of what risks those venturing an escape encountered : —

NARRATIVE OF ESCAPE FROM LIBBY.

"Just as the rebel guard appeared to see that all was right we had started on our slide, feet foremost, through a hole in the brick chimney into the cellar below. Dropping on the cellar bottom, we crept across it in the dark, found the opening to the tunnel occupied by the retiring boots of another aspirant for liberty. As we were rather stalwart in size, hitching along three inches at a hitch, was the best we could do. It was all elbow work, the limited area of the tunnel not admitting any use of the legs. Hitching and perseverance brought us to the exit of the tunnel. Here we waited with head out of the hole (marmot style), took a survey of the empty boxes under the shed that once had been filled by the United States Sanitary Commission supplies, waited for our comrade from Willimantic, with whom we had sworn to make a strike for liberty. We waited about ten minutes, when we felt a pull at our leg, and speedily emerging from the tunnel made room for Lieutenant Clifford, of Ohio. Next came Quartermaster ———, from New York. Through the cracks of the shed which separated us from the street the rebel guard could be plainly seen patrolling in front of the prison, and watching it closely. It was not a good place to wait even for sworn friends, and the ten minutes seemed like ten hours.

"Here we quietly took off our shoes and walked on tip-toe to the corner of the shed. It was evident that we must pass the width of the shed on the beat of the guard. The only time to do it was when he was walking towards the prison. It was done; and safely around the corner, we three agreed to stand by each other till we reached the Union lines. If ragged uniforms could have disguised us we were well disguised, but not knowing the city we ran plump on to a rebel guard around the City Hospital. 'Halt! who goes there?' rang like a death knell to our hopes of freedom, but the prompt reply, 'None of your business; can't a fellow see his girl without being halted?' proved a pass-word, and the striking up of 'Dixie' in a half drunken songster style by Clifford, disarmed any suspicion that the sentinel may have had.

"We crossed the street in front of the sentinel, and threaded our way to the outskirts of the city on the east side. Every house was dark, and the streets were deserted. When fairly outside of the city we proceeded with great caution, but found ourselves close upon the fortifications before we were aware of it. These appeared to be unoccupied, and further observation showed us that this was even the case. A single man with a handful of files might have spiked forty or fifty pieces of artillery. Peering over the parapet, the faint glow of camp-fires revealed long lines of stacked muskets and rows of tents. Dusky forms could be seen grouped around fires farther distant, that were supposed to be reserved picket fires. Several spots were tried before we succeeded in finding a gap in the picket lines. We soon found one that promised to be a good outlet, and pushed through without disturbing the sentinels, who could be plainly seen counteracting the chill of a frosty night by the warmth of a few embers.

"We were hardly outside of the picket lines, well under way putting as much distance between us and the City of Richmond as possible before dawn, when the sudden neighing of a horse brought us to a stand, and not a second too soon, for careful examination showed that a large cavalry picket was dead ahead. The cavalry picket proved more easily evaded than the pickets just passed, so on we pushed, through woods, and over brooks, sometimes floundering in the cold water up to our arm-pits. The night was cold, but exercise and excitement kept us warm. The increasing light of early dawn warned us that it was time to seek a hiding-place for the day. The spot selected was a bushy hill-side covered with scrub oaks. Here we sat down to rest and wait for the next night.

"Our Norwich representative now found to his astonishment that he was the only one of the party who had any provisions. A boiled tongue, shriveled and mouldy, three months' old, kept in anticipation of this emergency, with eighteen soda crackers, comprised the entire stock of provisions, which was divided into three equal lots. A light breakfast was eaten, and by turns two slept, while the third kept watch. Our hiding-place proved well selected, overlooking a road a half-mile distant. Twice during the day a company of rebel cavalry passed by, also several foot soldiers. Unable to light a fire from fear of attracting attention, we suffered greatly with the cold. At night the march was resumed.

"Keeping the North Star in view as a point for reference, we aimed in the direction of Charles City Court House. The second night was much like the first, with fewer indications of the enemy. The next morning's breakfast finished all that was left of the tongue and soda crackers, but failed to satisfy the cravings of our hunger. Our refuge the second day was a large swamp. Want of sleep, want of food, as well as suffering from the cold began to tell on systems already debilitated by long imprisonment. A search was made for acorns to eat ; but it was evident that the acorn crop had been disposed of earlier in the winter by the squirrels and turkies. The latter were frequently seen, but showed great lack of confidence in us refugees, who looked at them with longing eyes, and wished in vain for a shot-gun or rifle. The swamp seemed sufficiently unfrequented, dark, and dense to give a feeling of security from cavalry and infantry. At night the march was resumed, and as we knew that we had already left Bottom's Bridge in the rear we confidently anticipated being within the lines of General Butler's corps the next morning.

"The third night's march was one of great suffering and faintness from hunger. The New York Quartermaster showed signs of extreme weakness, and retarded the march of the other two greatly. The last two hours of the night was over mostly open country, and the gray of dawn found us wearily struggling through a thinly wooded tract of timber. We much disliked the appearance of a lonely house about three quarters of a mile distant, — there was no shelter where we were, and we pushed on as rapidly as possible, hoping to reach what seemed to be a dense swamp about a mile ahead, and expecting there to find a secure hiding-place, from which we could watch for the blue coats of Uncle Sam's cavalry.

"Just now the sound of cavalry was heard in our rear, but it came from the wrong direction. Only a half a mile to the swamp, and no place to hide even a man's head till it was reached. So on we pushed, the Quartermaster falling behind from exhaustion. The sound of horsemen came nearer and a triumphant yell announced that the Quartermaster was again in the hands of the rebels. We had succeeded in getting out of the timber, and were going down the hill-side for the swamp, going at a lively pace, too. Soon we heard shouts of, 'Halt!' but heeded them not. Crack! crack! crack! crack! went the carbines till there was a rattling fire, nearer and nearer sounded the horses' feet, till these seemed more fearful than the fusilade and whistling of bullets. Only one hundred yards, and horses would not have been able to follow! Another yell, and Clifford was taken. A horseman dashed by us, sprang from his saddle, and intercepted us with a Colt's navy pistol leveled at our head.

"Libby Prison loomed up again! The captured were gathered together, three in number, in company with our pursuers, who were Major Robertson's cavalry, forty in number.

"'I say, Yank, ain't you hit?' was a frequent inquiry. And 'No; wish I had been,' the sullen reply. And some laughing was done at the expense of the crack shots of the company by their comrades. A proposition was made to us by the sergeant of the company: 'Say! You tell the Major that I did the right smart thing in overhauling you, and you shall have a good breakfast.' The proposition was accepted, and we breakfasted with Major Robertson, and received handsome treatment that day. We now learned, much to our chagrin, that we were captured on ground held by General Butler's command forty-eight hours previously, and were several miles above Charles City Court House.

"The next morning we were turned over to the home cavalry guard, a mean, cruel set of devils, who marched us till noon, and then turned us over to a relief, who marched us to the doors of Libby Prison, forty miles, in one day!

"Dick Turner, jailor, smiled grimly upon us, and ordered us to the cells below, and put us on a diet of corn bread and water. Below, we found companions, — forty men, stowed away in four cells, seven feet by twelve feet each, — many of whom, like our trio, had the entire soles of their feet blistered in the attempt to escape. Ten men were confined for three weeks in a cell seven feet by twelve, with not room for them all to lie down at once, and when they did lie down wharf rats and vermin were too plenty to permit rest."

Belle-Isle — a small island in the James River, opposite the Tredegar Iron Works of Richmond — was in part used for prison purposes. The upper portion, being broken and rocky, was ill-adapted to use of this sort; so the lower end, which was flat and sandy, comprising from three to six acres, was made into a pen. It was inclosed by an embankment of earth, with a ditch inside, in which from ten to twelve thousand prisoners were herded like cattle, with no shelter but worn-out tents, and these sufficient to accommodate only a meagre number of the suffering and exposed. On this low, unhealthy island, enduring all that results from overcrowding, from inadequate rations, from uncleanliness, from exposure to rain and night dews, were the captured privates of the Eighteenth, and representatives of Norwich in other regiments, confined.

Lieutenant-colonel Nichols, of the Eighteenth Regiment, who was nine months a prisoner in Libby, in a letter to General Schenck, Chairman of the Congressional Military Committee, dated March, 1864, thus describes the state of things on Belle Isle: —

"On the island, where at times there were as many as nine or ten thousand, the tents for the men were poor. No straw was furnished as bedding, and at no time was there enough to accommodate all. Vitality was so reduced by starvation, that many were absolutely frozen to death, and numerous amputations of frozen toes and feet were made necessary. But it seems to be a standing regulation to prevent the men from dying on the island, hence they are borne off when in a dying condition, that the officials may be able always to show but comparatively few graves in the island burial place, and yet have it to say that all who have died upon the island have been buried there. It would be well, if all who even died there were decently buried. . . . . The first demand of the poor creatures on the island was always for food, and we have seen them die clutching the half-eaten crust."

The patient courage and inflexible loyalty of these suffering Union prisoners were hardly appreciated by the country, and it was only as facts and incidents from their prison experience became known, that the public began to realize their heroism. Colonel Farnsworth stated, that while he was in Richmond, some three hundred shoemakers were confined at one time on Belle Island, and although men were there dying from starvation, and all were on rations so meagre, that their hunger was never appeased, yet they indignantly refused the offer of extra rations and other privileges, if they would work for the Confederacy. Such was the honor that even the most barbarous treatment could not tempt or break down.

Andersonville, — the name which starts echoes fraught only with horror, — was an open space of twenty-five acres, resembling in shape a parallelogram, bisected by a little brook which flowed through it, with barely a perceptible ripple. The fence or stockade was made of upright trunks of trees about twenty feet high, near the top of which, at regular intervals, were small platforms, where the butcher-like guards were stationed. Twenty feet inside of this fence ran a light railing parallel to it, which formed " the dead line." Visiting it in 1868, there were still to be seen the remains of the caves in which the prisoners sought shelter from the torrid heat of summer, or the cold dews and frosts of winter, or the drenching rains which pitilessly descended upon them, as they were crowded in this otherwise uncovered camp. The soil was of red clay, and could be cut or moulded into any shape, so that caves, and sleeping holes, and fire-places could be fashioned by the industrious prisoner. Relics of the sheds which they were allowed to build could still be seen, and remains of the rude self-made implements constructed for their use, were found scattered through this fearful place. Here were confined at one time as many as twenty-seven thousand prisoners, with the death-rate in the summer of 1864, because of its unutterably horrible condition, over one hundred and thirty a day. The history of this prison-pen is too frightful to be read; it has no parallel for fiendish cruelties and barbarities. Like Dante's " Inferno, " it soon came to be understood —

" Who enters here, leaves hope behind."

In this accursed place were some of our soldiers confined, and here met their sad torturing death.

HERBERT BECKWITH, Private in the Tenth Regiment Infantry, afterwards Corporal in the Second Heavy Artillery of Massachusetts, was captured at Plymouth, April, 1864, and taken to Andersonville. Here he spent five weary months, leaving in his journal the record of sufferings and patient waiting for release, affecting to read. Boy that he was, he was spared none of the rigors and inhumanities, under which he gradually gave way. He lived to reach Camp Parole, Annapolis, Md., to behold once more the flag for which he had periled his young life, and there, in the hospital, kindly cared for by a Christian woman, he died in peace.

GEORGE W. WARD, of the Eighteenth Regiment, taken prisoner at the battle of Winchester, June 15, 1863, after being confined successively at Belle Isle and Danville, was brought to Andersonville. Here he, too, fell a victim to treatment it was given to but few so long imprisoned, to survive. Twenty-one months of dreary, wasting, heart-breaking captivity he endured, hoping for that which to so many never came — release from the sufferings that made each prison one of deeper despair. He found his liberation through death, February 6, 1865. An earnest patriot, loved for qualities and gifts which made life full of promise and happiness, he is numbered with our martyred dead.

JOSEPH H. WINSHIP, of the Eighteenth Regiment, had a prison experience, in nearly all of its features, like that of his comrade and townsman, Ward. Unable to bear up under his long confinement, attended as it was with increased suffering and lessening strength, he died at Andersonville, April 5, 1864.

JOSEPH A. BAILEY, First Regiment Cavalry. Captured June 1, 1864. Died at Andersonville, August 13, 1864.

THOMAS M. BALDWIN, First Regiment Cavalry. Captured May 5, 1864. Died at Andersonville, July 3, 1864.

EDWARD BLUMLEY, Eighth Regiment. Was taken prisoner in an engagement on the Petersburgh R. R., May 7, 1864, and died at Andersonville, October 6, 1864.

HENRY F. CHAMPLIN, Tenth Regiment. Captured near St. Augustine, Fla., while on picket duty, December 30, 1863, and died at Andersonville, August 11, 1864.

WILLIAM DAVIS, First Regiment Cavalry. Captured at Craig's Church, Va., May 5, 1864. Died at Andersonville, August 30, 1864.

THOMAS DUGAN, Twenty-first Regiment. Died at Andersonville, June 4, 1864.

SYLVANUS DOWNER, Eighteenth Regiment. Captured at Winchester, Va. Was paroled June 15, 1863; returned to the ranks, and was a second time taken prisoner, at New Market, Va., June 5, 1864. Died at Andersonville, November 5, 1864.

WILLIAM G. HAYWARD, Eighteenth Regiment. Captured at Winchester, June 15, 1863. Was paroled and rejoined his comrades, and again taken prisoner at New Market, Va., May 15, 1864. Died at Andersonville, September 11, 1864.

JAMES S. MCDAVID, First Regiment Cavalry. Captured at Ashland Station, June 1, 1864. Died at Andersonville, August 21, 1864.

EDWARD F. TISDALE, First Regiment Cavalry. Captured May 14, 1864. Died at Andersonville, September 29, 1864.

JOHN F. TREADWAY, First Regiment Cavalry. Died at Andersonville, August 3, 1864.

MOSES TYLER, Fourteenth Regiment. Died at Andersonville, April 14, 1864.

On the third of January, 1866, Mr. G. W. Smith of this city was dispatched to Andersonville, to recover the bodies of those Norwich soldiers, known to be interred there, and whose graves could be identified. The expense of his journey, and the removal of the bodies was provided for out of the patriotic fund. Mr. Smith succeeded in bringing away the remains of nine of our Norwich boys. The city authorities awarded them a public funeral and a burial lot in Yantic Cemetery. Commemorative services were held in Breed Hall, and the coffins placed on a funeral car, covered by the American flag, were borne in solemn procession by friends and citizens, societies and soldiery, to the place prepared for their reception. Their graves are now with us, and this last tribute, of providing them a burial amid kindred dust, and in the precincts of the town their patriotism and sufferings honored, has been paid their memory.

In addition to these martyrs to the terrible prison treatment of Andersonville, two of our soldiers are known to have perished at Florence, S. C.

JAMES MASSEY, Eighteenth Regiment. Captured May 15, 1864, and died January 7, 1865.

ISRAEL VARNEY, Eighteenth Regiment. Died February 10, 1865.

Besides these, and completing the list of our prison-dead, are

ADAM ACKSLER, Eighteenth Regiment. Captured June 5, 1864, and died at Madisonville, October 5, 1864.

THOMAS FILLBURN, Seventh Regiment. Captured May 16, 1864, and died at Millen, Ga., October 21, 1864.

HENRY W. GREENOUGH, First Regiment Cavalry. Died at Salisbury, N. C., October 9, 1864.

HORACE B. WOOD, Second Regiment Artillery. Died at Richmond, December 27, 1864.

HENRY C. GASKILL, Eighteenth Regiment. Wounded and captured at battle of Piedmont, June 5, 1864. Died at Danville, Va., on his way to be exchanged, February 20, 1865, after a long and barbarous captivity.

This by no means exhausts the number of those who for a longer or shorter period were confined in some of the numerous prison-pens, with which the South abounded, but the rest survived, living to reach home and die among their friends, or to recover the health their imprisonment had in many instances seriously impaired.

What *a fearful* commentary, however, on the prisons of the Confederacy, is this list of our dead. Among the latter were men fully up to the average of human strength and endurance, and brave soldiers animated by patriotic impulses; yet such was the deliberately planned treatment and fare, that they perished, victims of rebel inhumanity. Some discrimination was made in dealing with commissioned officers, but on the private soldier fell the unrelieved brutality that made confinement in prison so largely fatal.

CAPT. JOHN B. DENNIS, of the Seventh Regiment, was captured with part of his command, while guarding the picket line in front of Bermuda Hundreds. He was taken from one prison to another, being a temporary tenant in six different pens, but made a bold and successful escape from Richland jail, Columbus, S. C., the last one in which confined. He, with six of the longest imprisoned officers of the Eighteenth Regiment, was among the six hundred Union prisoners exposed to the fire of our batteries by General Gillmore, in retaliation for the bombardment of the nursery-city of the rebellion, — Charleston, S. C. The jail of the latter, in which at one time eighteen hundred prisoners were confined, suffering from lack of clothes and food, was in keeping with the other prisons already described. It was so crowded as to render the condition of the inmates one of extreme wretchedness. Lieutenant James D. Higgins of the Eighteenth Regiment escaped from this prison, by a bold stratagem, making out to reach Hilton Head, S. C., in safety.

From Camp Sorghun, Columbia, S. C., Captain H. C. Davis of the same Regiment, made his escape, but after a tramp of one hundred and fifty miles, through wood and swamp, was tracked and run down by a pack of hounds, and taken back to the fearful prison, after an absence of twenty-three days.

The following is the narrative of Lieutenant H. F. Cowles' escape from captivity:—

"We left the prison in Columbia, S. C., February 14, 1865, and were marched to the Railroad, where a special train, going north, awaited us. We were packed into box cars, the same as are used here for carrying freight, with a sliding door on each side. One of these doors was locked, and the other generously left open that we might breathe. The guards were placed on top of the car, the Rebels having once before detected an attempt to overpower them when stationed inside.

"As the night came on and we got under way, rain began to fall, which turned into hail, and the storm became so furious that we had to push the door nearly together, leaving only a small aperture for breathing purposes. I had determined to effect my escape, for I did not feel, knowing how poor the Confederacy was, that I could any longer trespass upon its hospitality. I had talked over the matter with Captain Hawkins, of the Seventy-eighth Illinois and Lieutenant Sears, of the Ninety-sixth New York, when we watched in turn at the door for a favorable chance to escape. As the train stopped for wood and water about thirty miles out of Columbia, it was found that seven out of the nine cars of our train had been lost on the road. After a council was held, it was determined to back down and find the missing cars. I told my comrades that now was our time; so after making them both promise to follow me, I jumped out. The ground was covered with sleet, and as soon as I struck, my feet went from under me, and I rolled down the side of the track against the fence. For an instant I expected to have a volley of musket balls poured into me, but as they did not come, I gathered myself up and tried to vault over the fence.

I got half way over and there stuck, doubting not at this time I should be riddled; but giving another desperate lurch, I tumbled head first into the field on the opposite side. I drew myself along for a few lengths, and then ran on all fours, until I had placed a few rods between me and the train. I then lay perfectly still, not daring to rise for fear of being seen, and awaited the coming of my companions. I was scarcely over the fence myself before I heard Hawkins come crashing out, and it seemed to me as though he was making noise enough to wake the dead; then Lieutenant Sears came, and as I thought two others, and then all was quiet. Not a shot had been fired, which astonished me more than anything else. I immediately gave the signal which we had agreed upon, a quail call, and out they came, one, two, three, four. They seemed to rise out of the very ground, and upon getting together, we found not only our original party of three, but two more, who seeing how safely we escaped, followed us on the spur of the moment.

"Our first care was to place as great a distance between us and the guard as possible, so we took up a line of march across the country at a right angle with the Railroad.

"Our cramped prison life for twenty months previous, and the food we had received, had not particularly fitted us for such work as this, but we were on the road to freedom. Pluck and nerve kept us going, and we got over the ground in a style that did us all credit under the circumstances. After repeated attempts, we got a fire started, and bringing forth our corn bread and hard tack, we all sat around the fire and warmed ourselves and ate our breakfast as free men once more.

"We then went as far into the forest as we could, and still keep the fire in view, where we waited for something to turn up. We remained here, I suppose, about two hours, all too thoroughly drenched and too excited by our novel position to sleep, when to our great joy we saw our picket approaching the fire, accompanied by a negro. He listened very quietly to all we said, and then assured us in the first place that we ran no risk in staying near our fire, as there would probably be no white persons along

that way. We told him that, as our provisions were nearly exhausted, he could best serve us if he would go back to his cabin and get from the other negroes, or any one else, such eatables as we could most readily carry.

"At nightfall our faithful guide came back, bringing with him corn-meal, corn-bread, and cooked and raw bacon, upon which we all fell like wolves, and ate a good substantial supper. Gathering from him all possible information as to our route, and being led by him for some little way, we pushed on our exciting course, meeting with a variety of adventures, and finding our way to freedom about as 'hard a road as Jordan' to travel. Two days and nights passed in this sort of weary wandering, when I was startled while on watch by the distant booming of artillery. At once it occurred to us, 'this is old Tecumseh giving them a little serenade at Columbia!' Inspirited by this music, we started on again, heading for Wilmington, N. C. Through swamps and roads, weary, hungry, and ragged, we still held on our route, until we came across another negro. He also proved a friend in need, and from him we learned that we were near one of the principal roads, and that his master said that probably some of General Sherman's army would pass that way, and advised us, instead of trying to pass the rebel lines to reach our own, to let him secrete us in one of those almost impenetrable swamps, and there wait for the rebels to pass and our army to come up. At midnight his son came to guide us to his father's cabin. We were introduced to his wife, who had prepared a substantial supper for us. I can't remember all the courses, but the principal feature was an immense roasted goose, with appropriate fixtures, thinking of which even now makes my mouth water. The way that we went for that fowl, and the other things on the table, would have astonished any member of a civilized community, I think. After concluding our supper, we all sat around the fire-place and had a good smoke, and then, having expressed our thanks to our hostess, we started for the swamp. Here we were secreted for nearly a week, visited nightly by our colored friend, who brought us provisions, and cheered our hearts by his own hopeful assurances. Near the close of this week of confinement he brought the glad news that Sherman's troops had come up, and led us to one of the cabins near his own, where we found the orderly of General Howard. By him we were taken to headquarters, and there met such a reception as only the blue-coats could give us. We were fitted out with clothing contributed by our fellow-officers, and in due season were forwarded to Wilmington, and thence to New York. Thus ended our life of captivity, and our long and exciting escape from the prison-pen of Columbia and the land of Dixie. H. F. COWLES."

The fittest conclusion we can make to this chapter on the sufferings of our heroes in these wretched spots, is in the words taken from a letter in the "American Missionary," dated Atlanta, Ga., May 13, 1867.

"Did they ever imagine, those rebel officers, who used our poor boys to erect those buildings, — buildings put up to enable them to hold thirty thousand prisoners in unheard of tortures, — did they imagine to what use these buildings were to be put so soon? Did they dream that the wail of the captive would scarcely be hushed, and the last victim laid to sleep his last sleep in those awful witness-bearing trenches, before two angels of mercy should take up their abode there, transforming that hell upon earth into a little earthly heaven? Yes, 'Andersonville' has been cleansed and sanctified, and, thank God, by the purity, the presence, the labor and the love of woman. Where the rebel soldiers' jeer and oath used to be heard, now daily ascends the sweet sound of prayer and praise. For the howl of the hungry hound, eager to chase the perishing Union fugitive, you may now hear the sweet voices of the children blending in song. The jailor has fled, haunted by the memory of his crimes (for Wirtz was not alone in the charge), and two gentle women have taken possession of his dwelling. The persecuted slave has found a shelter in the huts erected by his persecutors, and the freedman's corn is now growing in the empty stockade."

In 1868 we were permitted to attend a school meeting in

what was part of the barracks of the rebel garrison. Here in this place of saddest memories, a school had been opened, through Northern benevolence, in which was gathered from near and far, those who were hungry for knowledge. We listened to their weird songs, learned in the dark days of their bondage, and then speaking words of cheer to them, reminded them of their new responsibilities, resulting from their lately gained liberty, which had at last lifted them to the dignity of freemen and citizens. From the schoolhouse, where we watched with a pathetic sort of interest the bright eyed boys and girls recite, we crossed the yard, passing what was formerly the rebel officers' quarters, and took our course to the stockade. Within the inclosure we stood awhile, its suffering memories coming back to us, and thought of the change that had come over this once populous and dreary spot. Thence we went to the cemetery, hard by, where rest the twelve thousand that were borne from out the awful prison to grateful sepulture. The trees were just coming out in their new spring foliage, the air was resonant with singing birds, the mellow light of the setting sun irradiated the simple white head-boards, which had been erected by our Government to mark the close and neatly arranged graves of our martyred dead, while over their sleeping dust the southern pines cast their benignant shade, and swept by the evening breeze, made a low dirge-like music.

There, standing in the silence of that beautiful cemetery, where the unnamed thousands of our patriotic dead lie buried, over whose graves the National Government watches, I thought of the change that even here had taken place. What was but a little while before a rude burial spot, in which the lifeless forms of once brave and fondly loved men were hurriedly laid in the long and fast filling trenches, was now a tastefully arranged cemetery. Each grave was designated and carefully turfed, while ramifying paths led every whither through this sacred inclosure ; and over the principal gate of the cemetery were the following appropriate lines : —

"The muffled drum's sad roll has beat
　　The soldiers' last tattoo,
No more on life's parade shall meet
　　The brave and daring few.
On Fame's eternal camping ground
　　Their silent tents are spread,
And glory guards with solemn round,
　　The bivouac of the dead."

This was the altered and redeemed Andersonville. Prison days were ended, the rude cheap sepulture of lamented dead, had ceased, and on every side appeared the signs of, "the good time coming," in which these sleeping heroes believed, and for the hastening on of which they devoted life itself. We thanked God for the change, and breathed a prayer of thanksgiving for what the sacrificial sufferings of those all about us in their quiet graves, had accomplished, and took hope for that better future, whose dawn we even here beheld.

"New England ! on thy spotless shield, inscribe thine honored dead,
　Oh ! keep their memory fresh and green, when turf blooms o'er their head ;
　And coming nations yet unborn, will read, with glowing pride,
　Of those who bore thy conquering arms, and suffering, fought and died ;
　Who, foremost in the gallant van, laid life and honor down —
　Oh ! *deck with fadeless bays their names who've won the martyr's crown.*"

XIV.

1865.

CLOSE OF THE WAR.—FALL OF RICHMOND.

"Thank God! the bloody days are past,
Our patient hopes are crowned at last;
And sounds of bugle, drum, and fife,
But lead our heroes home from strife!

"Thank God! there beams o'er land and sea
Our blazing Star of Victory;
And everywhere, from main to main,
The old flag flies and rules again!"
                                GEORGE H. BOKER.

THE quiet of the grand army under Grant, during the eventful winter of 1864-5, was part of that General's strategy. Instead of wishing to drive the Rebel Government and army from the banks of the James, he was only apprehensive that they would voluntarily abandon Virginia for a time, and that Lee would attempt to attack Sherman, as he was making his splendid though hazardous march to the sea. This expedient, however, seems not to have occurred to the Confederate leaders. Prior to the opening of the Spring Campaign, General Lee had been appointed to the command of all the armies of the Confederacy, and as indicative of the desperate condition in which the rebels found themselves, the Legislature of Virginia on the Sixteenth of February, 1865, passed resolutions, "authorizing, and consenting that such number of able bodied slaves might be enlisted into the military service as might be deemed necessary." The Confederate Congress subsequently passed a bill to the same effect, but too late to be of any practical avail.

Mr. Hunter, of Virginia, in connection with this strange measure, said he voted for the bill to arm and emancipate negroes, under instructions from the Virginia Legislature, but entered a protest against it, as an abandonment of the contest, and a surrender of the ground upon which the South seceded.

"When we left the old Government, we thought we had got rid forever of the slavery agitation; but, to my surprise, I find that this (Confederate) government assumes the power to arm the slaves, which involves also the power of emancipation. This proposition would be regarded as a confession of despair. If we are right in passing this measure, we were wrong in denying to the old Government the right to interfere with slavery and to emancipate slaves. If we offer the slaves their freedom as a boon, we confess that we are insincere and hypocritical in saying slavery was the best state for the negroes themselves. I believe that the arming and emancipating the slaves will be an abandonment of the contest."

Time, and stern necessity had at last made unwilling converts of the Confederate authorities, and the "black cornerstone" of their government was reluctantly removed, and those who had heaped unmeasured abuse on Mr. Lincoln for his edict of emancipation, and had ridiculed the suggestion that negro slaves could ever be transformed into effective soldiers, now turned in the hour of their direst need to these same despised menials, and sought to replenish the thinned ranks of their armies with blacks.

It was time now that the Confederacy came to its deserved downfall. It had hauled in the flag it gave to the breeze with such defiance of all the best thought and civilization of the world, in the Spring of 1861. The Providence of the Almighty had made the fated chiefs of this wicked rebellion take back their infamous proclamation, and brought them to where they were glad to seek aid of the 'inferior race,' and proffer freedom to them if they would help save their crumbling government.

The Richmond "Examiner," proclaiming with its characteristic boldness, what were "Southern Principles," thus spoke forth in no equivocal language in May, 1863 : —

"The establishment of the Confederacy is verily a distinct reaction against the whole course of the mistaken civilization of the age. For *Liberty, Equality, Fraternity*, we have deliberately substituted *Slavery, Subordination, and Government*. These social and political problems which rack and torture modern society, we have undertaken to solve for ourselves, in our own way, upon our own principles. There are slave races born to serve; master races born to govern. Such are the fundamental principles which we inherit from the ancient world, which we lifted up in the face of a perverse generation that has forgotten the wisdom of its Fathers. By these principles we live, and in their defense we have shown ourselves ready to die."

Behold the sequel! Two years of terrible war, and their boasted principles neither save them, nor for them are they ready to die. Now they will concede liberty and military service, if their former bondsmen will only die for them. Here indeed is the pitiable spectacle of the Confederacy, whose corner-stone gave way, whose new doctrine of human rights was to correct and enlighten the "mistaken civilization of the age." The "lost cause," may it disappear among the vanished barbarisms, which in earlier centuries, and before the mild teachings of the Gospel appeared, had some apology for seeking to exist. Yea! may it be so lost, that none will be found to acknowledge they struck a blow, or shed a drop of blood in behalf of what brought back on man the gloom and shame and servitude, from which it had taken long ages of suffering and struggle to escape. Heaven pity the deluded men, who periled life for their anomalous, their ever infamous cause.

We cannot feel otherwise than indignant, that at this late period, a prominent English Review (The Edinburgh), should attempt to hold up for the admiration of the world one of the leaders of the Rebellion. For the men who fought in the ranks, much can be said in their behalf. They had no choice in the main, as to whether they would espouse the cause or not. They were conscripted, overborne by the governments that soon left them but one alternative, — either to fight or else suffer such persecutions as the desperateness of the usurping rulers could invent.

Englishmen, it is but reasonable to suppose, might by this time show some intelligent appreciation of the peculiar criminality of those who inaugurated the rebellion, who committed the meanest and extremest crime of which army honor is cognizant, — that is, treason. Yet that was the unblushing deed of the chieftain of the Confederate armies. He broke his oath of fealty to the Government that educated and honored him, and with politic equivocalness, delayed the doing of it, till he might add to the role of traitor the part of spy.

And yet Lee is held up to us even at this day by this reviewer as a man who was a victim of fate, an "innocent expiator of the truth he told, of wrongs done in ages past to helpless Africans." He died, we are informed, "without the sign of ailment outwardly, without a word of pain; that great heart that repined not for his own loss of dignity or of ancestral fortune, giving way at last, under the continued pressure of the ruin and degradation of the beloved State to the freedom of which the prospects of his whole life had been sacrificed." Lee was fighting for Virginia, which the

Federal Government was trying to enslave. To that point has the once liberal " Edinburgh Review " arrived, eight years after the final defeat of the great struggle of the South in behalf of the peculiar institution.

During the winter there were unauthorized attempts to make terms with the Confederates, by some of the irrepressible peace-men, under the lead of Mr. Blair. The latter made out a rather melancholy view of our situation and prospects, and approached Mr. Lincoln with the query, " Assuming that Grant is baffled and delayed in his efforts to take Richmond, will it not be better to accept peace on favorable terms than to prolong the war ? " etc. To which the President replied with that imperturbed calmness that made him long-suffering towards these annoying " go-betweens," who were eager for a peace they knew would practically destroy the integrity of the Union, " There are, first, two indispensable conditions to peace, — *national unity and national liberty*. The national authority must be restored through all the States, and I will never recede from the position I have taken on the slavery question." The steadfast purpose of Mr. Lincoln to secure the reestablishment of the federal authority, made him a safe leader ; no wiles of politicians could turn him aside from this supreme object. And when a dispatch came to him from General Grant, on the third of March, saying General Lee desired an interview with him to arrange terms of peace, the Secretary of War promptly telegraphed back Mr. Lincoln's reply : " The President directs me to say to you, that he wishes you to have no conference with General Lee, unless it be for the capitulation of General Lee's army. He instructs me to say that you are not to decide, discuss, or confer upon any political question. . . . . Meantime you are to press to the utmost your military advantages."

The sublime devotion of the man to his one grand purpose, the courage and hopefulness with which he adhered to it, shows of what stuff he was made. Less firmness, less faith, less consecrated effort to effect one great end, might have lost for us the cause, for which four years of battling was not too much to pay.

And now, as the fourth of March dawned, this man, tried as few men in his position before him had been, and trusted by the people with a new lease of office, was to pronounce his second inaugural. It was delivered not as the first had been, to a nation on the eve of civil war, but to one about to come forth victoriously from it. It was spoken, not in a city filled with traitors, seeking to betray it, but in the Capital, which had been preserved from its foes, and was now more than ever the seat of a great and free government. It was short, but full of the grandest sentiment, the profoundest wisdom, and characterized by a deeply Christian spirit. No state paper, in American annals, ever made such an impression upon those who heard or read it. A distinguished jurist of New York said, "A century from to-day that inaugural will be read as one of the most sublime utterances ever spoken by man." How often has the following magnificent passage in it been quoted: "Fondly do we hope, fervently do we pray, that this mighty scourge of war may pass away. Yet if God wills that it continue until all the wealth piled by the bondman's two hundred and fifty years of unrequited toil shall be sunk, and until every drop of blood drawn with the lash, shall be paid by another drawn with the sword, as was said three thousand years ago, so still it must be said, that the judgments of the Lord are true and righteous altogether;" while with equal frequency has that other golden sentence, the best epitome of his own moral nature, been repeated, passing into a proverb among our people: "With malice toward none, with charity for all."

The English people were slow in coming to appreciate

Mr. Lincoln; but by this time his rare merit as a man, and the head of a Great Republic, was by the best part of the British press recognized. The London "Spectator" paid this discriminating tribute to him: —

"There is something in that steady borne persistence, that resolve so iron, that it cannot even bend to make phrases, which is indefinitely impressive to the spectator, which, in the South must, more even than defeat on the field, produce a sense of the hopelessness of the contest. The President does not boast, shows no hate, indulges in no cries of triumph over the steady advance of his armies, threatens no foreign powers, makes no promises of speedy success, comforts the people with no assurance of a Utopian future, but, as if compelled by a force other than his own will, slides quietly but irresistibly along the rails."

Meanwhile the armies of the Republic had not been idle. General Sherman, after a victorious though hazardous march through the very heart of the Confederacy, exposing its exhausted condition, had presented himself, and his bronzed veterans, as a Christmas gift to the city of Savannah, and left it no option as to whether it would accept. The most brilliant exploit of the war, the capture of Fort Fisher by the combined forces of the army and navy, marked the opening of the campaign for 1865. General Sherman, in February, resumed his march from Savannah northward, capturing Columbus, S. C., Goldsboro, N. C., and forcing the enemy to evacuate Charleston, S. C., and effected a junction with Generals Terry and Schofield. The romance of war has nothing comparable to this triumphant march of Sherman through the rebel territory, gleaning the belt of country he covered with his columns of all that could be used or destroyed. The Union flag now floated over Sumter, and the once rebellious city, where treason always had its most fiery advocates, while the rebel territory was decidedly narrowed. The admirable strategy of the Commander-in-chief now began to be recognized by all; for, differ as we may as to the fighting and manœuvering of the last campaign, it was the splendid conclusion of the war, the successful combinations, which bore witness to the far-sighted plans and skillful and resistless execution of the same on the part of him who controlled the armies of the government. The verdict of history will attest the military sagacity and superior generalship of the conqueror of the rebellion. The whole country waited, amid the suppressed excitement, the denouement of the movements known to be in progress. Sheridan had started on his daring raid from Winchester, aiming at Lynchburg and the westward communications of the Confederacy, and now came the anxiously planned for moment for the grand advance of the columns under Grant. It began on the twenty-ninth of March, and ten days' marching and fighting finished the campaign. The fate of the rebel Capital and its defending army was sealed, as the iron grip of the investing forces tightened. Petersburg fell first, yielding to the assault along our whole line, April second. On the day following, the rebel army was in full retreat, and before noon the same day, Monday, April third, General Weitzel, commanding a detachment of the army of the James, entered Richmond, General Draper's Black Brigade in the advance, all the regiments displaying the National colors, and the band playing "Rally round the Flag." Among the first to enter the rebel capital were the First Connecticut Battery, and the Twenty-first, Twenty-Ninth (colored), and the Eighth Regiment, the Twelfth Regiment of Maine supplying the flag that was speedily elevated over the dome of the Capitol of Virginia.

So promptly had our forces entered the city, that the rear guard of the enemy passed up Main Street just ahead of our advance. One of the Connecticut Chaplains (De Forrest of the Eleventh Regiment), wrote: —

"Our reception was grander and more exultant than even Roman Emperor leading back his victorious legions with the spoils of conquest could ever know. The slaves seemed to think that the day of Jubilee had fully come. How they danced, shouted, waved their rag-banners, shook our hands, bowed, scraped, laughed all over, and thanked God for our coming."

In nondescript ways they sought to tell to the entering troops their joy. "I was jus' so happy wen I knowed it," said one, "dat I couldn't do nuffin', but jus' lay right down and larf. I could jus' roll up an' larf. I declare I felt jus' as happy as a man's got religion in his soul." "Some folks says a man carn't 'tote a bar'l flour," added with quaint humor another; "but I could 'tote a bar'l flour *dat day*, — or a bar'l sugar." "I seed a rebel gwine down de street dat mawnin'" said another with a chuckling laugh, and swelling with a sort of prideful appreciation of his freedom, "wid a big haam; an' I just took dat haam from him, an' run right down de street, an' he holler to me to stop; but I jus' keep dat haam."

Already the news of the fall of Richmond had been flashed across the loyal States, and confirmatory telegrams from President Lincoln, then at City Point, and from Mr. Stanton, Secretary of War, at Washington, D. C., gave to the rejoicing people the assurance that the Rebellion was finally crushed.

The stronghold of the Confederates was at last taken by the army that, often defeated, had with rare patience and heroism held on to its purpose, until triumphant. The defense of Richmond required four years of fighting, and in all seven hundred thousand men before it was captured.

"Up-hoist the Union pennon — uplift the Union Jack, —
Up-raise the Union standard, — keep not a banner back!
Fling out in silk or bunting, the Ensign of the Stars!
God grant it never more may know accursed intestine jars!

> "Hurrah for skill! Hurrah for will! Hurrah for dauntless hearts!
> Mourn those who bled, praise those who led against insidious arts!
> A cheer for those who lived it out; a tear for those who died;
> Richmond is ours! we thank the Lord with heartfelt chastening pride!"

At once all public offices were closed and business suspended by the excited populace, who hailed with the most enthusiastic demonstrations of joy and thankfulness the glad tidings of the hour. The national triumph, so patiently waited for, so unselfishly fought for by brave men, thousands of whom had died without the sight, so intensely longed for by the millions who had endured the wearying heart-sickness of hope deferred, had at last come. In all the large towns impromptu gatherings of the citizens filled the streets and largest halls, and listened with straining eyes, and with praising hearts to dispatches and addresses. Chiming bells, and saluting cannon, were made to join in the popular expression of gratitude and exultation, accompanying with their wild music the " Te Deum " of the nation.

In New York the citizens hardly knew how to express their joy at the great news. Staid merchants were seen embracing each other, the national flag was universally displayed, and salutes were heard reverberating through the city and its outskirts. In front of the Custom House some ten thousand people assembled, where congratulations were exchanged, speeches by prominent men were made, and the proceedings closed, amidst the intensest enthusiasm, by singing " Old Hundred." Everywhere throughout the land did the fever of excitement run, and the mass-meetings and celebrations were of the most impressive character.

In Norwich the news created as profound a sensation as in other places. It was the day of the State election, and the returns, as they came in, seemed to indicate that the people were rolling up Union majorities, as one way of celebrating the grandest event of these years of war. The Stars and Stripes were once more given to the breeze from every staff, and store, and dwelling, and a salute of one hundred guns was fired from a six-pounder drawn up from Trolan's boiler works by a four-horse team, which was driven by a freedman, bearing the American flag.

Breed Hall was crowded in the evening by the citizens, Mr. Amos W. Prentice presiding, where patriotic addresses were made by Hon. J. T. Wait, Senator Foster, and Connecticut's honored "War Governor," on that day for the eighth time elected to the position he had filled with such noble fidelity; by Hon. H. H. Starkweather, and others. The meeting, with much fervor, joined in singing " Praise God from whom all blessings flow," and for a parting song, " America," and then with reverent hearts the great assembly hushed into quietude while a prayer of thanksgiving was offered to the Almighty Father, who, after long years of discipline, had disappointed not the expectation of the people.

In the evening the city was encinctured with blazing bonfires, around which gathered exultant boys and youth, by whom the joy of this signal day was shared.

The Common Council, at its special meeting Tuesday night, unanimously adopted a series of resolutions " on the late great victories to our arms," introduced by Mr. Devotion, city clerk, and member with his Honor, Mayor Greene, and Mr. Whittemore, of the committee appointed to prepare them : —

Resolved, That we regard the great events of the past few days, resulting in the capture of Richmond and Petersburg, as the crowning success and virtual closing of the war.

Resolved, That in this hour of triumph our first chief duty is reverently, humbly, and with overflowing hearts to thank the great God, who has guided us through this struggle, who has given us the victory, and saved our country.

Resolved, That we sincerely pray God, in this hour of success, that our hearts may be free from malice and revenge; that we may be imbued with the principles of justice and charity, and act for the advancement and glory of His name, and the happiness, peace and good will of ourselves and mankind.

Resolved, That our heartfelt thanks are due to the great leaders and brave men, who by sea and land have taken their lives in their hands, and through four weary years defended our country against the assaults of her foes, and trodden them down. May the lives they have given prove the bond of undying peace and union.

Resolved, That we recognize with pride the great debt we owe those who have been maimed and crippled in defense of our country, and will joyfully do what we may to assuage their suffering and show our gratitude.

Resolved, That we truly sympathize with those who are mourning for their dead, and tenderly remind them that their loved ones, though dead, shall always live in the cherished remembrance of a grateful country.

Resolved, That we fervently pray that the eyes of the South may be opened to the utter hopelessness for her in further contest; that her entire submission to the laws and government of the United States may soon close the war; and that those who are wearily waiting for the war to cease, hoping with trembling hearts for the return of their friends, may soon be permitted to welcome their dear ones home, and lay aside their care.

Resolved, That we do recognize this war as a blessing to us, to our children and to mankind, inasmuch as it has forever removed the curse of slavery, which, like the upas tree was spreading its poison in every direction, demoralizing all classes of society, hardening our hearts, blunting our sense of justice, degrading our manhood, and which bid fair to extinguish the light of our free institutions, and make us a nation of oppressors and oppressed, and though we have paid much blood, and wounds, and

tears, and suffering, yet we have gained a boon far exceeding its cost, whose value cannot be estimated, and we do fervently thank God that the curse is removed and that we can be a free people.

Resolved, That the splendid tenacity of the people, their courage under defeat and disaster, their valor in the field and on the sea, their unflinching endurance under suffering, their freehearted and generous care of their army and navy, their illimitable resources and their intelligent use of them, their humanity to their prisoners, their unwavering confidence of success, and their sublime trust in God and their cause, have shed a lustre upon our land which shall glow through the ages, and make us proudly rejoice in our country and our birthright.

This great and universal joy reached its culmination six days later, April ninth, when the news of General Lee's surrender to General Grant, at "Appomattox Court House," was received. The tidings of the final ending of the rebellion in the defeat and capture of its last army, reached Norwich late Sunday night, April ninth.

As Monday morning dawned, the bells of all the city churches pealed for an hour, and gave, doubtless, the first intimation to most of the citizens of the glorious news. The long yearned for time had come when "They shall beat their swords into ploughshares, and their spears into pruning hooks." Again the city broke forth into every expression of joy, and in all directions the national colors were seen, while the stores tastefully decorated their show windows, and the holiday attire of the town but mirrored forth the gladness of all hearts.

At Breed Hall, an immense gathering was convened at noon. The hall had been appropriately draped with flags; one at the rear of the stage bore the inscription which was the watchword of the day, and the occasion of the celebration, — "VICTORY!"

The meeting was called to order by Mr. Ebenezer Learned, who named for chairman "the man whom all knew," Governor Buckingham. The latter, on coming forward, spoke briefly, "adverting to the fact, that almost exactly four years ago to-day, a company of men assembled at Apollo Hall, on the reception of the thrilling news that the power of the United States had been overborne at Fort Sumter." He spoke "of the clinched fist, the compressed lip, that then indicated the purpose of a free people to right the wrong thus suffered. From that day onward a like feeling has been manifested throughout the country; and now, after many a brother, and many a son, had been laid in his blood on Southern soil, that army which was the chief power of the rebellion has been taken captive. Surely, then, to-day we are assembled on a far different occasion. The army of Northern Virginia has given its parole of honor to be obedient to the laws of the United States. But this is an hour not so much for speech, as for the manifestation of feeling in songs of joy. This is an hour to sing praises to Him who hath given and is giving to us the victory."

Rev. John V. Lewis then read the Psalm, "O sing unto the Lord a new song," after which Rev. Samuel Graves led in prayer, when the vast audience united in singing "All hail the power of Jesus' name," to the tune of "Coronation."

The Chairman then introduced Rev. J. P. Gulliver, who spoke as follows: —

"Last Sunday, a week ago, the evacuation of Richmond; yesterday the surrender of Lee's army; next Sabbath the anniversary of the memorable Sumter Sunday. Then, all was indignation and consternation; to-day, all is confidence, exultation, victory. There are some events whose greatness we are unable to compass in thought, or express in words. This is one of them. We hardly know what to say, because we know not how to feel.

As at the first view of the Falls of Niagara our conception is at fault, so with the great event we celebrate to-day, — the future alone can discern its full significance. These three Sundays of April will be connected in history. They reach far onward into the future, and far back into the past. We must gradually rise to the conception of the mighty events that have just transpired. Our first thought on hearing the news was of the feelings of our brave boys in the Army of the Potomac, those who followed McClellan, Burnside, Hooker ; our second, of the joy of the fathers and mothers of those soldiers ; then the joy of the emancipated race looking forward to the liberty of doing the best they know how, of standing up as men ; then, of the feelings of the aristocrats of Europe. Rather even than look upon our soldiers in the Army of the Potomac in the flush of victory, we would be in the English House of Parliament when the news of the surrender of Lee's army first reaches there. There was a lesson to be learned from this struggle by men in politics and of business. From this hour let us be a God-fearing nation, in our Senate houses and in our Executive mansions. Then will the Republic rise and grow, magnificent in outline, and beautiful in proportions."

"Victory at last," was then sung, the solo by H. V. Edmond, the choir and audience joining in the chorus.

Hon. L. F. S. Foster was next introduced. He commenced by saying : —

"It is difficult to give utterance to feelings on such an occasion. The natural language of the heart at such a time was — Thank God! Thank God! What a sublime spectacle. From the Atlantic to the Pacific there is the ringing of bells and the glad shouts of the people. The Nation is delivered, and never before in the history of the world was there such manifestation of joy. The shore of the Pacific at this hour joins in celebration with the States along the Lakes, upon the Gulf, and in the valley of the Mississippi. Not a single individual lives throughout our whole land who does not hear to-day the roar of cannon. When before was there an event so mighty? The lessons, moral, political, and religious to be learned from it are too vast for our comprehension. We are overpowered by the magnitude of the occurrence. The human mind is not great enough to compass it.

"As one practical lesson to be learned, we should see to it that the soldiers who have gone forth be remembered. In no way can we better show our gratitude to God than by opening our hands liberally to them, or to their widows, or to their orphans. Let us not flatter ourselves that this is charity. It is not. It is paying a debt. We are to pay it as we would a debt too vast to be discharged at once."

The speaker briefly alluded to our triumph as a triumph of the rights of man, and said that its effect in Europe would be immediate and great.

Governor Buckingham then spoke of John Brown's invasion of Virginia, the excitement that ensued throughout that Commonwealth on its occurrence, and the resulting decree that his name should not be even uttered in that State, on penalty of expulsion from it. He then mentioned the fact that only a few days since the Twenty-ninth Regiment (colored) marched into its capital to the music of the drum and fife, singing "John Brown's soul goes marching on."

The John Brown song was then sung by Mr. Edmond, the choir and audience joining in the chorus with an unction that the regiment might doubtless have profitably emulated.

Rev. Mr. Dana spoke next, and was followed by Hon John T. Wait, Rev. B. F. Clark, Ebenezer Learned, and Colonel H. B. Crosby, of the Twenty-first Regiment. Amid these addresses were interspersed the following songs : "Johnny comes marching home," solo by J. N. Crandall. "The Battle-cry of Freedom," solo by Geo. H. Martin. The audience then united with Rev. Mr. Lewis in the Lord's Prayer, who also pronounced the benediction.

CLOSE OF THE WAR. — FALL OF RICHMOND. 305

Thus ended Norwich's Jubilee meeting. Thanksgiving and praise, rather than loud exultation, characterized this last grand rally of the citizens for purposes connected with the now gloriously ended war.

In the afternoon there was a procession, under the marshalship of Colonel David Young, consisting of the Infantry Company of State Militia, under Captain Parlin; the Free Academy Cadets, Captain Gilbert; and the Fire Department, under Chief Engineer Andrews. The engines were gaily decorated with flags, and along the route repeated salutes were fired.

In the evening the general illumination of stores and private dwellings gave to the city a brilliant appearance. It was a memorable day, fittingly honored for the great event with which, in our country's annals, it will ever be associated.

> "O beautiful! my country! ours once more!
>   Smoothing thy gold of war-disheveled hair
>   O'er such sweet brows as never other wore,
>   And letting thy set lips
>   Freed from wrath's pale eclipse,
>   The rosy edges of their smile lay bare.
> What words divine of lover or of poet
> Could tell our love and make thee know it,
>   Among the nations bright beyond compare?
>   What were our lives without thee?
>   What all our lives to save thee?
>   We reck not what we gave thee;
>   We will not dare to doubt thee,
>   But ask whatever else, and we will dare!"

The General Assembly, a little later, put on record this public acknowledgment of the glorious issue of the long struggle, and the Commonwealth's indebtedness to the heroes, living and dead, whose valor contributed to the grand result: —

"*Resolved*, That the heartfelt thanks and lasting gratitude of the people of this State are due and are hereby tendered to all Connecticut officers and soldiers, of every rank and grade, who in the war of the Rebellion have gallantly borne the flag, and nobly sustained the honor of our State ; and who, by long years of faithful service, and on many a hard fought field, have aided in preserving to us our institutions, and in demonstrating to the world that no government is so strong as that which rests in the will of a free and enlightened people, and that no armies are so invincible as citizen-soldiers battling for their own liberties and the rights of man.

" That this State will ever gratefully cherish and honor the memories of those victims of the war and rebel barbarities, who went forth from us for our defense, but who come not back to participate in the blessings of that peace which, through their efforts and sacrifices a just God has vouchsafed to us."

His Excellency the Governor gave publicity to these, in the following proclamation : —

" Therefore I, William A. Buckingham, Governor of the State of Connecticut, in order to effect the object designed by the General Assembly, hereby issue this proclamation, and call upon the citizens of this Commonwealth to manifest by expressions of gratitude, and by acts of kindness, both to the living and to the families of the honored dead, their high appreciation of the sacrifices made by each of the fifty-three thousand three hundred and thirty men, who from this State have entered the military service of the Nation during our recent struggle with rebellion, and to impress upon their children and their children's children the duty of holding such patriotic services in honor and perpetual remembrance, and thus prove the enduring gratitude of the Republic."

This great gladness was soon tinged with an unexpected and universal sorrow. Hardly had the pean of the people died away, and the sounds of rejoicing with which the land were filled quieted down, ere the mournful news came of the death of President Lincoln by the hand of an

CLOSE OF THE WAR. — FALL OF RICHMOND.   307

assassin. He had returned from City Point to Washington on the evening of April ninth. From this time until the fourteenth were memorable days, filled up with a succession of events, which marked the complete overthrow of the rebellion. The joy of the people continued to manifest itself, as the magnitude of the late occurrences came to be more fully appreciated   Before Mr. Lincoln the sable clouds of war were rolling away, and as he entered, amid such glorious successes, upon his second term in office, were rising four years of sunny peace, with their rich harvest of results, flowing from the laborious and faithful service he had, amidst unprecedented trials, rendered. At a cabinet meeting, between the hours of eleven and twelve o'clock, where he met General Grant and heard his final report, he bore himself with a hopeful, joyous spirit. In the afternoon, when driving out with Mrs. Lincoln, he had remarked, "We have had a hard time together since we came to Washington, but now the war is over, and with God's blessing upon us, we may hope for four years of happiness, and then we will go back to Illinois, and pass the remainder of our lives in peace." The shadow of the swift approaching tragedy had not fallen upon him, and all unsuspicious, "with malice towards none, with charity for all," he went in the evening, as had previously been announced, to Ford's Theatre. The assassin deftly entering the box in which the President and his party were seated, accomplished his fatal purpose, and by a single shot murdered the Nation's honored Magistrate. Mr. Lincoln lingered through the night, though without returning consciousness, and died on the morning of April 15, 1865.

The terrible tidings of his death was at once borne by telegraph to every part of the Republic. From joy and exultation the Nation was in an instant turned to weeping and lamentation. Business was suspended, gloom and sadness sat upon every face. Strong men wept, and the waving flags, which were still floating in triumph from every spire and masthead, were lowered, and the people commenced to drape their dwellings, and put on the garb of mourning.

"He lived to see the Republic's success, and to feel his veins swelling with that rich joy which swept like a current of quickening life throughout the land, and then died a martyr to the cause he had championed, sealing his service with his life, leaving the Nation which he had rescued in the wildest grief; throwing the shadow of a strange sorrow over lands which he had never seen, and seeking the rest denied him here in the presence of Him who had raised him up."

Our citizens were appalled by the dread intelligence, and speechless and sad, mused upon the event that had no parallel in our history. All cherished feelings of honor and affection for the martyred President, and but one sentiment pervaded the hearts of the loyal masses. The city itself was filled with gloom, and the long, grief-ful day will not soon be forgotten. Hon. L. F. S. Foster, who was now President of the Senate, Governor Buckingham, and others of our leading men, started for Washington, to be of such service as might be possible in this unlooked-for emergency, and also to represent the State at the funeral solemnities in the Capital.

On Sunday, April sixteenth, all the churches in town were dressed in mourning, and discourses appropriate to the sad occurrence were preached. It was Easter Sabbath, and the white festal flowers with which the pulpits and altars in many of the sanctuaries were adorned, stood out in their sweet symbolism against the draperies which memorialized the Nation's departed chief. Large congregations and the marked solemnity of the usually joyous services of this festival Sabbath, showed how profoundly the hearts of our citizens shared in the universal grief.

As indicating what the voice of the Norwich pulpit on the grievous event was, we give here the following very brief abstracts of the sermons preached:—

At Trinity Church Rev. John V. Lewis took for his text Psalm lviii. 10: "The righteous shall rejoice when he seeth the vengeance; he shall wash his feet in the blood of the wicked." The preacher began with an acknowledgment that he had an unusual text for an Easter sermon. It was not the text he had chosen, but God himself had chosen it and preached a sermon to the nation. And when he heard that text announced yesterday morning, he thanked God that the Gospel had a strong side, a sternly retributive side; that it was a Gospel of vengeance upon the evil-doer, no less than of peace to the righteous. He thanked God that the risen Lord rose a conqueror as well as a saviour, to put all enemies under his feet. He thanked God for the Psalms of David, with their religious intolerance of the workers of iniquity, and for the Revelation of St. John, which truly shows us there is such a thing as "the wrath of the Lamb." The resurrection of Christ proclaimed undying war upon every form of evil. The risen Lord is irresistible. He will make no unholy compromise with sin: offering pardon to the misguided and repentant, he offers only vengeance to the obstinate rebel. The remainder of the discourse was an exposition of the necessity of executing vengeance legally and by lawfully constituted authority. The great Easter of the Resurrection will redress all grievances.

Rev. Mr. Graves, in the Central Baptist Church, spoke as follows:—

"I cannot proceed further with these services without alluding to the event which crowds all other thoughts from our minds, which has draped our sanctuaries, and filled the hearts of the nation with sadness. Abraham Lincoln is dead. The people's President. The man whom God had raised up to guide this nation through its great life struggle. Dead by the hand of an assassin. Murdered in the Capital by the spirit of secession, which for four years has been deluging our land in blood. It is a tragedy without parallel in the world's history, since the assassination of Julius Cæsar in the Roman Forum, and a crime surpassed only by the crucifixion. God, 'who maketh the wrath of man to praise him,' has suffered this for some end, wise in his inscrutable providence. Perhaps it is to teach us in this most critical juncture of national affairs the utter folly of trusting in man, however tried and trusty that man may be, and to make God our refuge, who is a very present help in time of trouble. Perhaps because he saw that the executive administration, in the hands of this kind, this tender-hearted man, would not mete out to treason the justice which is its due, and which He, as the God of justice means it shall have at the hands of a sterner man. His work is done, and well done. He lived to see the spirit of rebellion broken, and the glad dawn of peace. Abraham Lincoln is saved to history, and to-day he takes his place among the great and good of all times. Let us bow with reverence and submission, even in the depth of our grief, to the will of God."

In the Universalist Church, Rev. Mr. Ambler announced as his text Job v. 8 : " Affliction cometh not forth of the dust."

"Our hearts are all clothed with the drapery of sadness. The circumstances attending the death of our President were such as to render the shock to us more than ordinarily terrible. If his frame had been wasted by disease, if he had been taken from us by some gradual and invisible process, we might have bowed more easily to the Providential decree. But that he, a leader of the people, the President, not of a party but of a nation, a friend no less to the South than to the North, whose sole desire was to promote the common good, and whose official labors have been honestly and wisely designed to secure the best interests of this Republic — that he should have been coolly assassinated in the very Capital of the nation, with no provocation except that which may be supposed to be in the venom of rebellion — is a circumstance which has no precedent in history, and which may call forth not only the lamentations of the American people, but the universal execration of mankind. It is not now a proper time to say much about the punishment which ought to follow an act like this, though some punishment, severe and signal will, in the course of justice, be visited not only on the actual perpetrators of the deed, but on the no less guilty instigators of it. At present we can think of little else save our loss. The hand which guided the Ship of State in its peril, till we could see the haven of peace, is powerless; the wise counsels, tempered always by humane feeling, will no more shed their light upon us, but as records of the past; the cheerful spirit which kept up the courage of the people, and which for their sake never allowed itself to be entirely overcome, even in the darkest period, will now smile upon us only from the heavens, where we shall turn for consolation in our bereavement. Let us find it in the providential care and government of God. The proclamation of liberty has been sealed with blood. Henceforth let it be sacred in the eyes of the American people, and may He who inspired the martyr's soul on earth help us to guard aright those principles of justice and freedom which have been left to us as our legacy."

In the Broadway Church, Rev. Mr. Gulliver took for his text Psalms xlvi. 10: "Be still and know that I am God. I will be exalted among the heathen; I will be exalted in the earth." The preacher remarked: —

"That he would be glad to obey the first injunction of the text literally. It was a task any man might well shrink from, to give expression to the feelings of horror, indignation, and grief, that fire all our hearts. But the second injunction, contained in the latter part of the text, is one that can be more easily complied with. We may be still, so far as any attempt to give an adequate utterance to our emotions is concerned, but we are bound to see God in what has occurred, and to know what He is designing to teach us. The first point of instruction is, that God is an absolute sovereign. He asks counsel of no man! He doeth all his own will. No man can say unto Him, 'What doest thou?' Men would not have selected Abraham Lincoln to be President of the United States, if it could have been known that he would be called to pass through such an ordeal. But the history of the past four years shows that he was precisely the man to do a great work of philanthrophy, and to lead a nation divided in sentiment and interest, wild with alarm and doubtful of the future, to unanimity of opinion and action. But the same sovereign God who put Abraham Lincoln into the seat of power has taken him out of it. He has not consulted us. We mourn and we wonder. But God has done it. Perhaps there was a radical defect in Mr. Lincoln's character, which unfitted him for the closing up of the war. He lacked the early religious instruction which would have given him very different views of law and penalty, and the relation of mercy and justice, and the necessity for the general good of individual retributive suffering.

"Just at this point a new man is brought forward, certainly not the man we should have selected. This too, is God's work. And at the end of four years we may rejoice as much in the elevation of Andrew Johnson, as we now do in that of Abraham Lincoln. He certainly has had a peculiar experience of the rebels; and of his own frailties. Let him have a generous support, and be received as the Lord's anointed, appointed by Him to this high position.

"These events also teach us that God purposes all, even the most minute events, and even the wicked acts of wicked men. They show also why God hates, and so severely punishes slavery, whose spirit and character reached a culmination and fit expression in this assassination. Finally, they show each one of us the plague of our own hearts. The selfishness of slavery is essentially the same as all other selfishness. Every rebel against God is lifting his hand against the Government of the universe, as did John Wilkes Booth against the President of the United States. The horror we feel to-day at that crime is but a reflection of the horror which angels feel at the assaults we are making upon God's Government. And let us remember we are dealing with one who never confounds mercy and justice, and "will by no means clear the guilty."

Wednesday, April nineteenth, the day of the funeral, was one of general mourning throughout the land. The services at the White House, held in the East Room, were simple and impressive, and attended by a large concourse of the dignitaries in the Capital, Foreign Ministers, Judges, Congressmen and Citizens. The remains of the President were then conveyed to the Capitol and placed in the rotunda, beneath the statue of Liberty, and guarded by sad and weeping soldiers.

In Norwich the bells were tolled during the day, guns fired every half-hour, while the National colors were displayed at half-mast, and trimmed with black. Business was suspended, while in the windows and doorways of almost every building were the trappings of woe to be seen. Tasteful devices, expressive of the popular sorrow, lent variety and impressiveness to the city's unaffected grief.

In many of the churches public religious services were held, attended by large and serious congregations. His Honor, Mayor Greene, issued through the morning papers the following deep feeling appeal to the citizens of Norwich : —

"FELLOW CITIZENS: To-day the Nation stands with sad heart and uncovered head around the grave of one it dearly loved. To-day noon, our beloved friend and President is buried. His death is the most dastardly murder that ever occurred in the

tide of time. Let all places of business be closed from eleven A.
M. to three o'clock P. M. Let every one attend his respective place
of worship, and participate in the solemn duties of the hour, and
while bowing submissive to the hand of God, let every one swear
in his heart, eternal, undying hate of slavery, — the damned institution that has sowed the South with treason, — has drenched
our land with blood, — has maimed and crippled thousands of
heroes, — has extinguished the light of joy in thousands of hearts,
and has now consummated its wickedness by murdering one of
the noblest, wisest, and best of men, ABRAHAM LINCOLN, our
cherished Friend and President.
"JAS. LLOYD GREENE, *Mayor.*"

The funeral procession which on Friday, the twenty-first,
started from the Executive Mansion, was one never before
paralleled. Moving solemnly through city and country, the
cortege swelling in numbers, held on its sorrow-traced
course, till the martyred dead was borne back to a quiet
resting-place amid the scenes and friends of earlier days.
Halting in the great cities, the grief-smitten citizens crowded
round the bier, and looked for the last time on the sad
weary face of him who had held and guarded the people's
imperial trust.

> "So he grew up, a destined work to do,
>   And lived to do it; four long suffering years
> Ill-fate, ill-feeling, ill-report, lived through,
>   And then he heard the hisses change to cheers.
>
> "The taunts to tributes, the abuse to praise,
>   And took both with the same unwavering mood,
> Till as he came on light, from darkling days,
>   And seemed to touch the goal from where he stood."

The funeral train reached the Capital of Illinois, May
third, and the body was placed under the rotunda of the
Court House. The latter was decorated with flowers. Over

its north door was the motto, "*The altar of freedom has borne no nobler sacrifice;*" over the south door, "*Illinois clasps to her bosom her slain, but glorified son.*"

The last words of the funeral oration, by Bishop Simpson, were as follows: —

"Chieftain! farewell! The Nation mourns thee. Mothers shall teach thy name to their lisping children. The youth of our land shall emulate thy virtues. Statesmen shall study thy record and learn lessons of wisdom. Mute though thy lips be, yet they still speak. Hushed is thy voice, but its echoes of liberty are ringing through the world, and the sons of bondage listen to it with joy. Prisoned thou art in death, and yet thou art marching abroad, and chains and manacles are bursting at thy touch. Thou didst fall not for thyself. The assassin had no hate for thee. Our hearts were aimed at, our National life was sought. We crown thee as our martyr, and humanity enthrones thee as her triumphant son. Hero, martyr, friend, farewell!"

Thus with joy shaded down with profoundest sorrow, the Nation accepted its costly, but sacred triumph, rejoicing over the rebellion crushed; sorrowing over the grave of him who consecrated himself to so grand a work, and sealed it when finished, with his own life's blood.

XV.

MISCELLANEOUS.

TOWN ACTION — COST OF THE WAR.

The amount of indebtedness of the town of Norwich September 1, 1861, was one hundred and seven thousand three hundred and seventy dollars ($107,370). On the first of September, 1865, the debt had risen to one hundred and eighty thousand three hundred and three dollars ($180,303), showing an increase in the four years of seventy-two thousand nine hundred and thirty-three dollars ($72,933). During the war the town disbursed for directly war purposes one hundred and sixty-four thousand one hundred and seventy-eight dollars and sixty-eight cents ($164,178.68), and at its close its distinctive war debt was in the form of loans amounting to eighty four thousand and ninety-six dollars ($84,096.00).

The town action in the frequent meetings held during the progress of our civil conflict, to devise means for promoting enlistments and filling up the quotas, under the various calls of the President for volunteers, was remarkably unanimous. Very little, if any, opposition was made to the liberal appropriations voted for war purposes. There was not only great unanimity of spirit, but the utmost energy and promptitude of action, so that the town was kept in advance of the calls made upon it for men. Its contributions to the national armies were of its most worthy and promising citizens, and nobly did the latter maintain the

MISCELLANEOUS.   317

reputation of Norwich for patriotic devotion to the country's weal.

The first action of the town in reference to war matters was on July 16, 1862, when, after a spirited meeting, the following votes were passed:—

Voted, That a bounty of thirteen dollars be paid from the town's treasury of the town of Norwich to every man who shall, on or before the twentieth of August, 1862, enlist into any company enlisted in the town of Norwich. The same to be paid when he is mustered into the service of the United States.

Voted, That the same bounty of thirteen dollars be paid to those who have already enlisted into companies now enlisting in the town of Norwich.

Voted, That the sum of eight thousand dollars be, and the same is, hereby appropriated from the town treasury for the purpose of paying said bounty, and such necessary expenses of recruiting, as are not provided for by the General and State Government, and for the purpose of aiding and encouraging, in any proper way, the enlistment of volunteers.

Voted, That the Selectmen of the town of Norwich be and are hereby instructed to raise, by loan or otherwise, and to place at the disposal of the Committee, consisting of James Lloyd Greene, Amos W. Prentice, William M. Converse, Lorenzo Blackstone, N. C. Brackenridge, and F. M. Hale, from time to time, such sums of money as said Committee shall desire, not exceeding the sum of eight thousand dollars, to be by said Committee expended according to their judgment in carrying into effect the preceding vote, and said Committee are authorized to pay said bounty of thirteen dollars for enlistments after said twentieth day of August, if, in their discretion, it is deemed desirable to do so.

These measures were carried by a unanimous vote. On the fourth of August, 1862, in accordance with the warning of the Selectmen, a town meeting was held in the Town Hall. The attendance was very large, and the proceedings of the meeting were marked with great enthusiasm. Amos W. Prentice was called to preside, when it was —

Voted, That a bounty of thirty-seven dollars, in addition to the bounty heretofore voted by the town of Norwich, be paid from the town treasury to every resident of the town who has enlisted, or who shall, on or before the twentieth day of August, enlist into any company raised in the town of Norwich, under the recent call of the Government, and said bounty shall be payable when he is mustered into the service of the United States. And the same shall also be paid to every resident of the town of Norwich who has been enlisted by Captain William H. Tubbs and James B. Coit, for the Fourteenth Regiment.

Voted, That the Selectmen be authorized and directed to raise, by loan or otherwise, a sum not exceeding twenty thousand dollars, or so much of the same as may be necessary to pay the bounties provided for in the previous vote, and to pay such expenses of recruiting as are not provided for by the State or General Government.

On the thirtieth of the same month (August, 1862), when the call for three hundred thousand nine months' troops was made, the town, in regular meeting convened —

Voted, That a bounty of one hundred dollars be paid to any resident of the town who has volunteered, or who shall volunteer, in any regiment of militia of this State, and who shall be accepted into the service of the United States, under the recent call of the President for three hundred thousand nine months' men.

The Selectmen were further instructed to raise a sum not exceeding twenty-two thousand dollars, to be placed at the disposal of the "War Committee" for the purpose of paying the first voted bounty, and defraying the general expenses incident to recruiting. This meeting was one of the most spirited held during the war, and after it resolved itself into a Committee of the Whole to obtain volunteers, as elsewhere described, rose to the very highest pitch of enthusiasm.

In January, 1863, the debt of the town, incurred for "war expenses" was reported to be over forty thousand dollars, and it was voted to provide for this by the issue of town bonds, authorized by the action of the Legislature, at the December session, in 1862. These bonds bore interest at the rate of six per cent., the attached coupons being payable semi-annually.

On May 29, 1863, and by virtue of more recent legislative provision, the town voted to repeat this action, funding in the same way its increasing debt. The issue was limited, by vote, to sixty thousand dollars, and the bonds were made payable at the expiration of twenty years' time. It should, however, be stated that this new issue of town bonds was to provide for the general indebtedness of town, and not for exclusively war expenditures.

On Wednesday, August 5, 1863, a town meeting was regularly warned, "to take action on the bounty question." There was a very large attendance, and the discussion showed a general interest to have those who were called into service under "the enrollment act" impartially provided for. The action taken was intended to meet any cases of distress that might occur in connection with the drafting of those who would leave their families in a dependent condition. The benevolence of the citizens, however, never permitted this to occur, and the town and State appropriations were always liberal enough to meet any exigency of this kind. Still, as showing the public interest in this matter, Judge Hovey presented the following resolution, which, after some debate, was passed with but one dissenting voice : —

"*Whereas*, Four hundred and thirty-five persons residing in this town, have been recently drafted for military service in the army of the United States, pursuant of the act of Congress, entitled 'An act for enrolling and calling out the national forces, and for other purposes,' approved March 3, 1863 ;

"*And whereas*, Nearly all the persons so drafted have been found to be exempt from military duty under said act, or have furnished substitutes to take their places in the draft, or paid the sum of money required by said act for the procuration of said substitutes ;

"*And whereas*, Fears are entertained that a further draft may be ordered, pursuant to the provisions of said act, and that thereby individuals and families may become chargeable to the town, and otherwise greatly distressed, unless adequate measures of relief are adopted by the town ;

"*And whereas*, Under the warning for this meeting, it is believed that such measures cannot be legally adopted ; therefore,

"*Resolved*, That in case a further draft from this town shall be ordered, pursuant to the said act of Congress, the Selectmen be and are hereby directed to convene, as soon as possible, a meeting of the town, for the purpose of adopting such measures for the relief of those who may be drafted, as the town shall deem adequate and proper."

At a town meeting held January 26, 1864, Mr. George Pratt, stated that the quota of the town, numbering two hundred and six, had been filled by the Selectmen, at a cost to the town of twenty thousand nine hundred and fifty dollars and seventy-six cents ($20,950.76). After the quota was full, the Selectmen enlisted forty-three additional recruits, at a cost of two thousand one hundred and fifty dollars, with the assurance on the part of the "War Committee" that if the town did not pay this additional sum they would. A few men enlisted at Fort Trumbull would swell the number of recruits from the town on the present quota to two hundred and sixty. The following vote was then passed : —

"*Voted*, That the Selectmen be authorized to draw on the

town treasurer for a sufficient sum to reimburse the "War Committee" for actual expenses incurred by them in enlisting recruits over and above the number required to fill the quota of the town, such expenses being audited and approved by the Selectmen, the amount not to exceed two thousand one hundred and fifty dollars."

After some discussion as to how this money had been used, and whether it was paid to brokers or the men enlisting, it was shown that the latter in every instance received it, and that the cost of securing these extra recruits had not averaged over fifty dollars per man. Mr. Starkweather then offered the following vote: —

"That the Selectmen of the town of Norwich be authorized to pay to each veteran who is a resident of this town, and who has reënlisted into the service of the United States, and shall count on the quota required of this town, the sum of one hundred dollars, and the Selectmen are authorized to draw orders on the treasurer."

This developed some discussion, and sticklers for the legality of such a forehanded measure, which in after months proved of great relief to the town, when new calls for men were made, ventilated their views at some length, and then, with but one dissenting voice, the vote was passed. The wisdom of thus securing in advance recruits to count on future apportionments, under other calls likely to be issued, led to the passage of the next vote: —

"That the Selectmen of the town of Norwich be authorized to obtain recruits to apply on the present or any other quota of the town of Norwich, provided the expenses to the town shall not exceed twenty-five dollars per man, and the Selectmen are hereby authorized to draw orders on the treasurer for that purpose."

Again, under date of July 15, 1864, after the President's call for five hundred thousand troops made the town feel the need of prompt action to fill up its quota, it was now voted, with no dissenting voices —

"That the Selectmen of the town of Norwich be and they hereby are authorized to pay to each resident of this town, who enlists or procures a substitute or recruit, who shall count on the quota of this town, under the recent call of the President, the sum of one hundred dollars, and to draw orders on the town treasurer to pay the same. The Selectmen were also authorized to employ persons to aid them in filling up the quota of the town."

The bounty of one hundred dollars to veterans reënlisting and counting on this quota, was continued. At this period of the war the business of raising the men apportioned to the town devolved upon the Selectmen, and they, together with the most active and interested of our citizens, labored earnestly to secure recruits, and to keep the quota of the town full. And yet this was no easy task, for volunteering on the part of our citizens had perforce largely ceased, and good recruits were difficult to be procured. Still, their efforts were successful, and the town never failed to raise promptly its assignment of men.

On December 1, 1864, at a regularly convened town meeting, a new committee, consisting of Messrs. Samuel B. Case, Charles Crawley, John T. Brown, Henry B. Tracy, and William Peckham, was appointed to have in charge the moneys appropriated for bounties, and by vote, this committee was authorized —

"To pay to any person of this town liable to a draft, who hereafter may furnish an acceptable and lawful military substitute, under the laws of the United States, to be credited to the town, such sums of money, as to such shall seem necessary and proper, provided the number of such substitutes does not exceed the number required, in the judgment of the Committee, to fill the next quota.

"*Voted*, That the Selectmen are authorized to borrow, from

time to time, on the credit of the town, such sums of money as shall be approved by the Committee, not to exceed, in the whole, the sum of seventy-five thousand dollars."

Under this liberal provision the quota of the town was again raised, and a surplus secured to apply on any future calls. At the close of the war Norwich was found to be in advance of the number regularly assigned to her to be raised, and this highly creditable fact was due to the energetic action of the town officers, supported as they always were by the loyal coöperation of all the citizens. These town meetings were always well attended by our leading citizens, and though there were occasionally some sharp discussions, yet there were no war measures adopted by the town that did not receive a practically unanimous vote. It should be recorded to the honor of our citizens that, differing as they did in political views, yet, in the town assemblages to which they so often were summoned, they acted with great cordiality, debated measures with earnestness, but uniform courtesy, and maintained the reputation of the town for loyalty to the Government, and liberality in providing for all war expenses.

TABLE OF DEBT.

United States Debt.		Connecticut Debt.		Norwich Town Debt.	
July 1, 1860	$64,769,703 08	Mar. 31, 1860	$34,142 04*	Sept. 1, 1860	$113,582 28
" 1861	90,867,828 68	" 1861	7,709 30*	" 1861	107,370 05
" 1862	514,211,371 92	" 1862	2,030,000 00	" 1862	124,270 52
" 1863	1,098,793,181 37	" 1863	3,392,300 00	" 1863	135,387 75
" 1864	1,740,690,489 49	" 1864	7,249,660 00	Sept. 15, 1864	169,918 95
" 1865	2,783,425,879 21	" 1865	10,523,113 74	" 1865	180,303 71

* After deducting the amount in the Treasury.

TOWN EXPENSES FOR WAR PURPOSES.

Amount paid to Volunteers or Substitutes	$139,149 68
Amount paid families of Volunteers, additional to State allowance	15,000 00
All other War Expenses	9,021 00
Total expenses for War purposes	163,170 68
Estimated amount paid for Bounties to Volunteers and Substitutes	19,600 00
Estimated amount paid by individuals for Commutation	5,700 00
Present indebtedness of Town for War purposes	84,096 00
Grand List of the Town	$10,494,035 00

STATE EXPENSES FOR WAR PURPOSES.

Expended for Bounties	$5,195,877 80
Estimated amounts paid by individuals for Bounties, Volunteers, or Substitutes	1,134,762 80
Estimated amount paid by individuals for Commutation	292,940 00
Amount paid families of Volunteers	2,413,338 48
Grand list for 1864	276,086,457 00

ESTIMATE *of the number of men to whom the United States Bounty has been paid, the amount paid each man, and the total amount paid from May 3, 1861, to the end of the War. Taken from final report of the Provost-marshal General of U. S., James B. Fry.*

Period embraced.	Class of Men.	Term of Service.	Number of men.	Amount per man.	Total Amount p'd.	Aggregate for each Period.
May 3, 1861, to Oct. 17, 1863	Volunteers	3 yrs.	905,867	$100	$90,586,900	$90,586,900
Oct. 17, 1863, to July 18, 1864	Veteran Vols.	"	158,507	400	63,402,800	
	Recruits	"	257,021	300	77,108,400	
	"	"	11,025	100	1,102,500	146,417,500
July 18, 1864, to close of War	Drafted Men and Substitutes	3 yrs.	48,038	100	4,803,800	
	Volunteers	1 yr.	191,936	100	19,193,600	
	"	2 yrs.	10,606	200	2,121,200	
	"	3 yrs.	138,681	300	41,604,300	63,219,100
Total			1,722,670		$300,223,500	$300,223,500

CHARITIES OF THE WAR.

The data necessary for making out a tabular statement of these, are not of equal value in point of precision, in all departments of the inquiry. Only the charitable giving, which was public and in organized methods, can even be approximately estimated. The reports of Colonel Lockwood L. Doty, Chief of the Bureau of Military Statistics for the State of New York, have been made the basis of estimating what was given in the form of benevolent contributions, while in other cases, such as the receipts of charitable agencies, their own returns afford the necessary information.

Contributions of the Eastern and Atlantic States for the promotion of enlistments, and the relief of drafted men	$15,000,000	
Contributions of the Western and Central States for the same purpose	13,000,000	
		$28,000,000
Total amount given in aid of the families of Volunteers, including what was contributed by societies, individuals, etc.		$4,500,000
United States Sanitary Commission, organized, June, 1861, President, Rev. H. W. Bellows, D. D., of New York, cash received up to January 1, 1865		3,471,000
Cash received from January 1, 1865, to close of war		500,000
Value of supplies received		9,000,000
Total		$12,971,000
Received by branches of this Commission, which had an independent treasury, and expended in part their own income		1,000,000
Estimated amount, in money and supplies, sent to the Army before the Commission was organized, and thereafter through independent Aid Societies		5,000,000
Collections of the Western Sanitary Commission, in money and stores, including proceeds of Mississippi Valley Fair		2,800,000
Receipts of the Illinois Commissioner-general, appointed to collect money and stores from the people of the State		500,000
Receipts of Iowa Sanitary Commission, up to the period of its incorporation with Sanitary, and Western Sanitary Commissions		175,000

THE NORWICH MEMORIAL.

Collections of Indiana Sanitary Commission, in money and supplies, from 1861 to 1865	$534,000
Collections of the Philadelphia Ladies' Aid, money and stores	320,000
Collections of the Ladies' Union Aid Society of St. Louis, money and stores	150,000
Collections of Ladies' Union Relief Association of Baltimore, money and stores	60,000
Collections of four similar Societies in Baltimore	30,000
Receipts of the New England Soldiers' Relief Association of New York — Money	40,000
Supplies	200,000
Receipts of Soldiers' Rest, New York, and such portion of the State Soldiers' Depot, due to private bounty	25,000
Receipts of the Pennsylvania Relief Association of Philadelphia, Cash, $12,000 ; Supplies, $37,000 ; total	49,000
Receipts of the Rose Hill Ladies' Soldiers' Relief Association of New York, money and stores	25,000
Value of contributions, in money and stores, made casually by visitors to the 233 Government Hospitals established in different parts of the country (estimate)	2,225,000
United States Christian Commission, organized in November, 1861, George H. Stuart, of Philadelphia, President, received in cash and supplies	4,530,000
Value of Tracts, Testaments, and general Religious Publications distributed in Army and Navy, by the Tract, and Bible, and other kindred Societies	300,000
Value of Railroad, Express, and Telegraph facilities given to Commissions, Societies, etc., exclusive of those reported by latter	1,500,000
Collections of New England Freedmen's Aid Society, money and stores	126,000
Collections of National Freedmen's Relief Association, New York, money and stores	400,000
Receipts of the Pennsylvania Freedmen's Relief Association	61,000
Receipts of the Orthodox Friend Association of Philadelphia, (Freedmen's Relief), exclusive of Foreign contributions	100,000
Receipts of the Hicksite Friends' Association of Philadelphia	12,000
Receipts of the North Western Freedmen's Aid Society of Chicago	140,000
Amounts raised in New York and Philadelphia for recruiting colored regiments	50,000
Amount raised in New York for relief of colored victims of riots of July, 1863	41,000

MISCELLANEOUS.

Amount raised for benefit of members of Fire Department, Police Force, and National Guard, injured in the riot	$55,000
Collections of various International Relief Committees in behalf of distressed operatives of Great Britain	347,000
Collections made in New England in behalf of East Tennesseeans, Edward Everett, Chairman of Committee	102,000
Collections of Pennsylvania Relief Association for East Tennessee	30,000
Collections of American Union Commission, cash and clothing	70,000
Collections of New England Refugees' Aid Society	25,000
Fund collected in Boston, New York, and Philadelphia, for relief of people of Savannah, in January and February, 1865	100,000
Fund collected in Philadelphia for relief of people in Chambersburg in 1864	35,000
Fund collected in Baltimore for the same	3,000
Volunteer Refreshment Saloon in Philadelphia, cash and supplies	117,000
Cooper-shop Refreshment Saloon in Philadelphia, cash and supplies	78,000
Citizen's Union Volunteer Hospital Association of Philadelphia, cash and supplies	185,000
Union Relief Association, Baltimore, cash and supplies	180,000
Pittsburg Subsistence Committee	45,000
Amount spent by Fire Companies of Philadelphia, and by the Ladies' Transit Aid Association in conveyance of wounded from the boats to the hospitals	28,000
Amount spent, or received in provisions for the Army and Navy Thanksgiving Dinner of 1864	300,000
Spent in previous Festival Dinners for Army and Navy	100,000
Proceeds of National Sailors' Fair in Boston, November, 1864	247,000
Receipts of Patriot's Orphans' Home at Flushing, N. Y.	65,000
Donation of Pennsylvania R. R. Co., for maintenance of Education of Soldiers' Orphans	50,000
Other donations to same	20,000
Received by "Northern Home for Friendless Children," Philadelphia, for support to Soldiers' Orphans	10,000
Receipts of other Orphan Homes	20,000
Receipts of Milwaukee Fair, June and July, 1865, for Asylum for disabled Wisconsin Soldiers	110,000
Roosevelt Estate Endowment for Soldiers' Home	1,000,000
Scholarships for Soldiers and their Children in Colleges and Academies	75,000
Value of Steamship presented Government by Cornelius Vanderbilt	800,000

Commissions returned Government by W. H. Aspinwall	$25,000	
Salary of Solicitor-general Whitney, not drawn	20,000	
		45,000
Amount spent by Miss Clara Barton in aiding soldiers, and in keeping a list of missing men		10,000
Amount spent in entertaining soldiers in 1865, on their way home (exclusive of Sanitary Commission Disbursements)		20,000
Amount presented to General Anderson, Meade, Captain Worden, and others, $70,000; raised for family of General Birney, $50,000; presented to Admiral Farragut, $50,000; General Grant, $50,000; raised for officers and men of "Kearsarge," $25,000; for General Sedgwick's statue, $20,000; and other monuments, etc., $35,000		300,000
Grand Total		$69,696,000

These almost seventy millions represent the free-will offerings of the American people during the war, and grand as this sum is, does not include what was raised by taxation for bounties, and for relief of soldiers' families. This splendid exhibit stands as a memorial of the self-sacrifice, devotion, and intelligent patriotism of the people.

MILITARY POPULATION OF THE UNITED STATES.

Loyal States (excepting California and Oregon)		4,785,105
Western Virginia		66,000
Colorado, Dakotah and Nebraska Territories		30,065
District of Columbia		12,797
Total military population furnishing Volunteers		4,393,967
California and Oregon	185,756	
Nevada, New Mexico, and Washington Territories	46,149	
Loyal military population of the Pacific and vicinity		231,905
Military population of the insurgent States		998,193
Total military population of the United States		5,624,055

This estimate, of course, includes the very large number exempt from enrollment.

The total white male population between 20 and 45 years, neither exempt from military duty, nor serving May 1, 1865, was by enrollment about 2,254,000, which would seem to indicate that rather more than one half of that number was exempt, although of military age.

INCREASE OF MILITARY POPULATION.[1]

	1860-1.	1861-2.	1862-3.	1863-4.	1864-5.
Number attaining age of 18	215,020	212,630	217,600	226,740	237,710
Number attaining age of 45	98,928	95,600	95,560	94,930	95,170
Deaths in military population not in the army	37,676	35,518	33,712	32,955	33,230
Natural increase during the year	78,416	81,512	88,328	98,855	109,310
Increase by immigration during the year	46,092	31,819	32,380	56,518	62,663
Total increase of military population	124,508	113,391	120,708	155,373	171,973

This estimate takes account only of those arriving in the country by regular immigration. There is abundant proof that many volunteers from the Continent of Europe and the British Provinces, animated by the loftiest sympathies with us in our struggle to maintain our government and Republican institutions against those who were aiming to destroy them, came to our support. They served in the Union armies as privates and officers, though to what extent there are no statistics to show.

[1] Compiled from the elaborate volume of "Statistics," published by the U. S. Sanitary Commission.

TABLE SHOWING NUMBER OF MEN CALLED FOR.

Date of Call.	Number called for.	Periods of Service.	Numbers obtained.
April 15, 1861	75,000	3 months.	93,000
May and July, 1861	582,748	3 years.	714,231
May and June, 1862	—	3 months.	15,007
July 2, 1862	300,000	3 years.	431,958
August 4, 1862	300,000	9 months.	87,588
June 15, 1863	100,000	6 months.	16,361
October 17, 1863	300,000	3 years. }	374,807
February 1, 1864	200,000	3 years. }	
March 14, 1864	200,000	3 years.	284,821
April 23, 1864	85,000	100 days.	83,652
July 18, 1864	500,000	1, 2, & 3 yrs.	384,882
December 19, 1864	300,000	1, 2, & 3 yrs.	204,568
Total	2,942,748		2,690,401

The population of the twenty-three loyal States, which during the war constituted the United States, was 22,046,472. This includes Missouri, Kentucky, and Maryland, which furnished soldiers for the armies on both sides, and which had a population of 3,025,745 ; and also California and Oregon, on the Pacific, which, because of their distance from the scene of conflict, contributed comparatively but few men, leaving the population from which the soldiers were mainly taken at 18,588,268. This makes the number of men obtained for the service of the government equal to fourteen and a half per cent. of the whole population.

TOTAL NUMBER OF ENLISTMENTS IN THE UNITED STATES.

Enlistments of white soldiers, exclusive of Veteran Volunteers	2,268,743
Enlistments of Veteran Volunteers	148,376
Enlistments in Navy and Marine Corps	104,674
Enlistments of Colored Troops	46,594
Enlistments of unknown and uncertain character	63,322

Credits allowed by adjustments 35,290
Number of drafted men who paid commutation . 86,724

Grand total of enlistment table 2,753,723

ENLISTMENTS AND DISCHARGES DURING EACH YEAR OF THE WAR.

	ENLISTMENTS.		DISCHARGES.	
	Total.	From States named above.	Returned Home.	Died in Service.
Before July, 1862 . .	822,500	810,000	207,000	35,000
1862–3	527,500	517,000	271,000	74,000
1863–4	637,000	639,000	432,000	68,000
After July 1st, 1864 .	430,000	430,000	358,000	62,000
	2,417,000	2,396,000	1,268,000	239,000

For the end of the war, May 1, 1865, the Secretary of War reported : —

Serving in the Volunteer Army . 1,034,000
Serving in the Regular Army 22,000

Total number in service, about 1,056,000
Number of Colored Troops not far from . 120,000

Total number of White Troops serving 936,000

AGES OF THOSE IN MILITARY SERVICE.

There were of the age of 18 . . 13.27 per cent.
There were under the age of 21 . . . 29.52 "
"   "   "   25 . . 58.34 "
"   "   "   30 . 76.57 "

NUMBER DISCHARGED FOR DISABILITY,

According to Surgeon-general's Rolls.

Enlisted men of Regular Army	6,541
Enlisted men of Volunteer Army	269,197
Enlisted men of Colored Troops	9,807
Total	285,545

STRENGTH OF THE ARMY AT DIFFERENT DATES.

REGULARS, including Officers and Men.

	Present.	Absent.	Aggregate.
January 1, 1861	14,663	1,704	16,367
January 1, 1862	19,871	2,554	22,425
January 1, 1863 .	19,169	6,294	25,463
January 1, 1864	17,237	7,399	24,636
January 1, 1865	14,661	7,358	32,019
Average mean strength . .	17,735	5,194	22,929

The total number of deaths in the Regular Army being 5,724, between the 15th of April, 1861, and the 30th of June, 1865, a period of four years, two months and a half, would give an annual average of 1,360 deaths, or an annual death-rate of 59 per 1,000 of strength, which, divided between violent deaths, and those from disease, would give an annual ratio of 27 violent deaths, and 32 deaths from disease, per 1,000 of strength.

VOLUNTEERS, OFFICERS AND MEN, EXCLUSIVE OF COLORED TROOPS.

	Present.	Absent.	Aggregate.
July 1, 1861	169,480	849	170,329
January 1, 1862	507,333	46,159	553,492
" 1, 1863	676,175	212,859	889,034
" 1, 1864	540,643	237,650	778,293
" 1, 1865	523,536	309,395	832,931
March 31, 1865	554,720	294,351	849,071
Average mean strength	544,704	196,803	741,507

The total number of deaths of this class was 265,265, deducting 4,553 who died subsequent to June 30, 1865, and it leaves a total of 260,712 deaths from the outbreak of the war to that time, a ratio of 65,178 deaths annually, or 88 per 1,000 of average mean strength. Subdividing this ratio between violent deaths, and deaths from disease, in accordance to the proportion of these classes already indicated, and we shall have an annual ratio of 33 violent deaths, and 55 deaths from disease per 1,000 of average mean strength.

COLORED TROOPS.

Total number of colored enlistments 178,895
Total number of deaths 33,380

This makes an annual death rate of 148 per 1,000 of average mean strength, or subdivided in accordance with the ratio of violent to other deaths already indicated for this class, we shall have an annual ratio of 15 violent deaths and 133 deaths from disease per 1,000 of strength.

TOTAL NUMBER OF DEATHS IN MILITARY SERVICE,

According to the Surgeon-general's Returns.

	Regulars.	White Volunteers.	Colored Volunteers.	Total.
Killed in battle	1,335	41,369	1,514	44,238
Died of wounds and injuries	1,174	46,271	1,760	49,205
Suicide, homicide and execution	27	442	57	526
Died of disease	3,009	153,995	29,212	186,216
Unknown causes	159	23,188	837	24,184
Total	5,724	265,265	33,380	304,369

Disease thus carried off twice as many victims as violence; or in other words, of every three deaths from known causes, but one was due to violence. This ratio, however, is a very favorable one in a sanitary historical point of view. The black troops lost almost three times as heavily by disease as the whites; the white regulars somewhat less so than the white volunteers.

According to the elaborate tables of the Surgeon-general, among the leading causes of mortality is placed, first, the several forms of dysentery, etc., next come the various types of camp-fever, reported under such heads as typhoid, typhus, remittent, common continued, and typho-malarial fevers. The next most important cause of death was pneumonia, following which are ranged small-pox, varioloid, measles, and consumption.

The largest number of discharges for disability was among the white troops, in consequence of consumption; among the colored troops, in consequence of rheumatism.

MISCELLANEOUS.   335

The number of rebel troops finally surrendered, was in round numbers 175,000. The number of prisoners in the hands of the National authorities during the last year of the war was 98,802. These were all sent to their homes by the United States. The theatre of the war was in the rebellious States. Their cities were besieged and captured, their territory desolated, and their people suffered all the evils of war at their own homes.

These appalling statistics, so far as we can really appreciate them, show us at what cost of human life the rebellion was put down. It seems sad enough to contemplate this vast number taken from the ranks of the strong, the young, those whose life was most valuable, and to the industries of the country most essential. Yet this is but the unchanged tale of woe that every war brings to the ears of mankind.

Grouping with these figures which represent our losses during our great struggle those that show the expense in men and money of other prominent wars, we can better realize what warfare has cost the world.

Estimated.	Killed.	Cost.
The Crimean War	785,000	$1,700,000,000
The Italian War	45,000	300,000,000
The Danish War	3,000	36,000,000
The American War, North	281,000	3,700,000,000
" " South	519,000	3,750,000,000
The Austro-Prussian War	45,000	350,000,000
Various other Wars	65,000	200,000,000
Total for 14 years	1,743,000	$10,036,000,000

XVI.

"OUR ROLL OF HONOR."

Major-generals.

JOSEPH LANMAN, U. S. N. Appointed Midshipman from the State, January 1, 1825; Passed Midshipman June 4, 1831; commissioned Lieutenant March 3, 1835; Commander September 14, 1855; Captain July 16, 1862; Commodore August 29, 1862; commissioned *Rear-admiral* December 8, 1867.

Brigadier-generals.

DANIEL TYLER, First Regiment Infantry, Colonel April 13, 1861. Promoted Brigadier-general March 13, 1862. Resigned.

EDWARD HARLAND, Third Regiment Infantry, Captain May 11, 1861. Sixth Regiment Infantry, Lieutenant-colonel August 30, 1861; Eighth Regiment Infantry, Colonel October 5, 1861; promoted Brigadier-general November 29, 1862. Resigned June 20, 1865.

HENRY W. BIRGE (by brevet Major-general), Fourth Regiment Infantry (changed to First Heavy Artillery); Major May 23, 1861; Thirteenth Regiment Infantry, Colonel November 2, 1861; promoted Brigadier-general September 19, 1863; appointed while in the service, *Brevet Major-general* February 26, 1865; Resigned October 18, 1865.

Colonels.

WILLIAM G. ELY (by brevet Brigadier-general), Brigade Commissary (rank of Captain) May 28, 1861, and Vol. A. D. C. Staff Colonel E. D. Keyes, Battle Bull Run ; Sixth Regiment Infantry, Lieutenant-colonel September 4, 1861 ; Eighteenth Regiment Infantry, Colonel July 24, 1862 ; *Brevet Brigadier-general* March 12, 1865. Resigned September 18, 1864.

JOHN E. WARD, Third Regiment Infantry. First Lieutenant May, 1861 ; Eighth Regiment Infantry, Captain, September 21, 1861 ; Major, March 28, 1862 ; Lieutenant-colonel, December 23, 1862 ; Colonel, April 2, 1863. Mustered out March 14, 1865.

ALFRED P. ROCKWELL (by brevet Brigadier-general), First Light Battery, Captain January 21, 1862 ; Sixth Regiment Infantry, Colonel June 11, 1864 ; appointed *Brevet Brigadier-general* March 13, 1865. Honorably discharged February 9, 1865.

HIRAM B. CROSBY, Twenty-first Regiment Infantry, Adjutant August 22, 1862 ; Major September 3, 1862 ; Lieutenant-colonel June 8, 1864 ; Colonel June 27, 1864. Honorably discharged September 14, 1864.

HENRY CASE (by brevet Brigadier-general). Fourteenth Regiment Infantry, Illinois, First Lieutenant May 3. 1861 ; promoted Captain November 25, 1861 ; Seventh Regiment Cavalry, Major February 1, 1862. Resigned April 24, 1862. One Hundred and Twenty-ninth Regiment Infantry, Lieutenant-colonel September 8, 1862 ; promoted Colonel May 8, 1863 ; appointed *Brevet Brigadier-general* (while in service) March 16, 1865. Mustered out June 8, 1865.

Lieutenant-colonels.

DAVID YOUNG, Second Regiment Infantry, Lieutenant-colonel May 7, 1861. Honorably discharged August 7, 1861.

JOSEPH SELDEN, Twenty-sixth Regiment Infantry, Captain September 6, 1862 ; Lieutenant-colonel September 22, 1862. Honorably discharged August 17, 1863.

CHARLES FARNSWORTH, First Regiment Cavalry, Adjutant October 19, 1861 ; Captain November 26, 1861 ; Major March

21, 1863; Lieutenant-colonel January 18, 1864. Resigned May 17, 1864.

HENRY PEALE, Second Regiment Infantry, Captain May 7, 1861; Eighteenth Regiment Infantry, Captain August 8, 1862; Major May 20, 1863; Lieutenant-colonel September 24, 1864. Mustered out June 27, 1865.

DAVID TORRANCE, Twenty-ninth Regiment Infantry, Captain January 6, 1864; Major July 21, 1864; Lieutenant-colonel November 24, 1864. Mustered out October 24, 1865.

CALVIN GODDARD, Twelfth Regiment Infantry, Ohio, commissioned First Lieutenant and A. D. C. staff of General Rosecrans January 9, 1862; appointed A. D. C. by President Lincoln on staff of Major-general Rosecrans (with rank of Major) November 14, 1862; appointed A. A. G. (with rank of Lieutenant-colonel) January 23, 1863. Resigned October, 1863.

Majors.

THOMAS MAGUIRE, Second Regiment Heavy Artillery, N. Y., Captain November 1, 1861; Major June 14, 1862. Discharged August 24, 1863. Re-commissioned.

JAMES H. COIT (by brevet Brigadier-general), Fourteenth Regiment, First Lieutenant August 8, 1862; Captain December 20, 1862; Major October 3, 1862; appointed Brevet Lieutenant-colonel, Brevet Colonel, *Brevet Brigadier-general* March 13, 1865. Resigned September 6, 1864.

FRANK S. BOND, Tenth Regiment Infantry, First Lieutenant March 29, 1862. Resigned February 25, 1863; Major and A. D. C. staff General Rosecrans, March 11, 1863. Resigned December 3, 1864.

JOHN B. DENNIS (by brevet Brigadier-general), Seventh Regiment Infantry, Captain August 26, 1861; Major and Paymaster, U. S. V. January 15, 1865; appointed *Brevet Brigadier-general* March 13, 1865. Mustered out July 31, 1866.

WILLIAM J. ROSS, Twenty-ninth Regiment Infantry, Captain February 3, 1864; Major May 12, 1865. Mustered out October 25, 1865.

"OUR ROLL OF HONOR." 339

D. R. BUSHNELL, Thirteenth Regiment Infantry, Ill. Killed at Chattanooga, Tenn.

FRANK H. ARMS, commissioned Acting Assistant Paymaster, U. S. N., April 14, 1864, U. S. Steamer Memphis; promoted Paymaster (with rank of Major) October 6, 1871. Still in service.

Quartermasters.

JOSEPH B. BROMLEY, Thirteenth Regiment Infantry, Quartermaster November 12, 1861. Honorably discharged December 29, 1863.

DE LAROO WILSON, Thirtieth Regiment Infantry, Quartermaster April 14, 1864. Mustered out November 7, 1865.

BENJAMIN F. TRACY, Twenty-sixth Regiment Infantry, Quartermaster September 1, 1862. Honorably discharged August 17, 1863.

I. V. B. WILLIAMS, Sixth Regiment Infantry, Quartermaster September 2, 1861. Resigned May 11, 1863.

Adjutants.

GEORGE W. WHITTLESEY, Thirteenth Regiment Infantry, First Lieutenant July 17, 1862; promoted Adjutant December 31, 1862. Honorably discharged October 9, 1863.

ENOCH B. CULVER, Eighteenth Regiment Infantry, Adjutant May 20, 1863. Mortally wounded in battle of Piedmont, June 5, 1864. Died June 6, 1864.

STEPHEN B. MEECH, Twenty-sixth Regiment Infantry, Adjutant August 30, 1862. Honorably discharged August 17, 1863.

JAMES L. RICHARDSON, First Regiment Cavalry, Adjutant December 31, 1864. Mustered out August 2, 1865.

JOSEPH H. JEWETT, Eighth Regiment Infantry, First Lieutenant April 1, 1865; appointed Acting Assistant Adjutant-general on staff of Brigadier-general J. C. Briscoe, July 1, 1865. Mustered out as Adjutant December 12, 1865.

GEORGE W. BRADY, Eighteenth Regiment Infantry, Adjutant October 17, 1864. Mustered out June 26, 1865.

AMOS R. LADD, Seventy-third Regiment U. S. C. T., First

Lieutenant December 14. 1863 ; promoted Adjutant 1863. Mustered out June, 1866.

Surgeons.

CHARLES M. CARLETON, Eighteenth Regiment Infantry, August 6, 1862. Honorably discharged April 17, 1863.

NATHAN A. FISHER, Thirteenth Regiment Infantry, March 7, 863. Declined commission.

DEWITT C. LATHROP, Eighth Regiment Infantry, Assistant Surgeon September 21, 1861. Died April 13, 1862.

J. HAMILTON LEE, Twenty-first Regiment Infantry April 21, 1863. Honorably discharged October 31, 1864.

ELISHA PHINNEY, Twenty-sixth Regiment Infantry, Assistant Surgeon November 1, 1862. Honorably discharged August 17, 1863.

EDWARD BENTLEY, First Regiment Artillery, Assistant Surgeon June 5, 1861 ; promoted Brigade Surgeon October 4, 1861.

C. B. WEBSTER, Acting Assistant Surgeon U. S. A. December, 1862 ; resigned April, 1864 ; recommissioned A. A. Surgeon U. S. A. June, 1864. Resigned September, 1865.

JOHN O. BRONSON (by brevet Lieutenant-colonel), Surgeon of Volunteers November 7, 1862, District of California, subsequently Chief Medical Officer of Northern District of the South. Mustered out November 27, 1865.

Captains.

FRANK S. CHESTER, Second Regiment Infantry, Captain May 7, 1861. Honorably discharged August 7, 1861.

BELA P. LEARNED (by brevet Major), First Regiment Artillery ; Second Lieutenant February 21, 1862 ; promoted First Lieutenant May 26, 1862 ; promoted Captain December 29, 1864 ; appointed *Brevet Major* while in service April 9. 1865. Mustered out September 25, 1865.

OSCAR A. DENNIS, First Regiment Artillery, Captain May 11, 1861. Resigned December 11, 1861.

JOAB B. ROGERS, First Regiment Cavalry, Second Lieutenant

December 1, 1862; promoted First Lieutenant March 25, 1863; promoted Captain October 12, 1863. Honorably discharged February 2, 1865.

HENRY T. PHILLIPS, First Regiment Cavalry, Second Lieutenant January 18, 1863; First Lieutenant May 5, 1864; promoted Captain September 24, 1864. Mustered out August 2, 1865.

JOHN H. PIATT (by brevet Major), First Regiment Cavalry, Ohio, Adjutant October 2, 1861; appointed Captain U. S. V. and A. D. C. staff General Pope July, 1862; Captain Thirty-first Regiment Infantry, U. S. A., September, 1866; appointed *Brevet Major* July, 1866. Resigned May, 1869.

THEODORE BURDICK, Seventh Regiment Infantry, First Lieutenant September 2, 1861; promoted Captain July 1, 1862. Killed in action at Fort Wagner July 11. 1863.

JOHN MCCALL, Eighth Regiment Infantry, Second Lieutenant March 28, 1862; promoted First Lieutenant August 1, 1862; promoted Captain December 23, 1862. Killed in action at Fort Darling May 16, 1864.

JAMES R. MOORE, Eighth Regiment Infantry, First Lieutenant September 21, 1861; promoted Captain March 28, 1862. Honorably discharged May 30, 1865.

CHARLES M. COIT (by brevet Lieutenant-colonel), Eighth Regiment Infantry, Adjutant September 18. 1861; promoted Captain March 27, 1862; declined commission as Major October 12, 1864; appointed *Brevet Lieutenant-colonel* March 13, 1865. Honorably discharged May 30, 1865.

HORACE P. GATES, Eighth Regiment Infantry, Adjutant March 27, 1862; appointed Assistant Adjutant-general U. S. Vols. May 26, 1863. Resigned December 19. 1865.

ADDIS E. PAYNE, Ninth Regiment Infantry, Second Lieutenant September 15, 1861; promoted First Lieutenant September 15, 1862; promoted Captain November 21, 1863. Mustered out October 26. 1864.

SILAS W. SAWYER, Ninth Regiment Infantry, Captain September 10, 1861. Resigned February 16, 1864.

JOSEPH H. NICKERSON, Eleventh Regiment Infantry, Second Lieutenant October 27, 1862 ; promoted First Lieutenant October 30, 1862 ; promoted Captain August 6, 1863. Discharged October 12, 1864.

ALBERT E. DANIELS, Eleventh Regiment Infantry, Captain October 1, 1861. Resigned July 27, 1862.

JAMES E. FULLER, Eleventh Regiment Infantry, Second Lieutenant October 27, 1862 ; promoted First Lieutenant April 1, 1864. Mustered out November 11, 1864. Appointed Assistant Quartermaster (rank of Captain) December 8, 1864. Resigned July 6, 1865.

EDWARD K. ABBOTT, Twelfth Regiment Infantry, Captain November 20, 1861. Resigned August 25, 1862.

ALFRED MITCHELL, Thirteenth Regiment Infantry, Captain February 14, 1862 ; promoted Major May 12, 1863 (declined appointment). Resigned March 11, 1864.

ROBERT A. RIPLEY, Thirteenth Regiment Infantry, First Lieutenant December 31, 1862 ; promoted Captain October 15, 1864 ; Mustered out January 6, 1865. Term expired.

JAMES J. MCCORD, Second Regiment Infantry. Second Lieutenant May 7, 1861 ; Thirteenth Regiment Infantry, C. V. ; commissioned Captain January 29, 1862 ; mustered out January 6, 1865. Term expired.

WILLIAM H. TUBBS (by brevet Major), Fourteenth Regiment Infantry, Captain June 15, 1862 ; resigned February 20, 1863 ; appointed Captain of C. S. U. V., January 28, 1865, A. D. C. staff of General Stagg ; appointed *Brevet Major* April 17, 1865. Mustered out July 10, 1866.

JAMES R. NICKELS, Fourteenth Regiment Infantry, Second Lieutenant December 20, 1862 ; promoted First Lieutenant January 19, 1863 ; promoted Captain November 5, 1863. Died of wounds February 20, 1865.

MORTON F. HALE, Fourteenth Regiment Infantry, First Lieutenant June 15, 1862. Discharged for promotion December 28, 1862. Captain and C. S. U. S. V.

HENRY P. GODDARD, Second Regiment Cavalry N. Y.,

Second Lieutenant May 7, 1862. Discharged May 26, 1862; Fourteenth Regiment Infantry, Second Lieutenant September 17, 1863; promoted First Lieutenant December 20, 1862; promoted Captain March 19, 1864. Resigned April 26, 1864.

FREDERICK A. PALMER, Eighteenth Regiment Infantry, First Lieutenant August 8, 1862; promoted Captain December 26, 1862. Discharged May 28, 1864.

SAMUEL R. KNAPP, Eighteenth Regiment Infantry, Captain August 8, 1862. Resigned June 6, 1863.

ISAAC W. HAKES, Jr., Eighteenth Regiment Infantry, Captain August 8, 1862. Resigned December 26, 1862.

ISAAC H. BROMLEY, Eighteenth Regiment Infantry, commissioned Captain August 8, 1862. Honorably discharged March 31, 1863.

HENRY C. DAVIS, Eighteenth Regiment Infantry, commissioned Captain August 8, 1862. Honorably discharged April 25, 1865.

JOHN E. WOODWARD, Eighteenth Regiment Infantry, First Lieutenant August 8, 1862; promoted Captain October 10, 1863. Mustered out June 27. 1865.

DWIGHT W. HAKES (by brevet Major), Eighteenth Regiment Infantry, Quartermaster August 4, 1862; promoted Captain and C. S. U. S. V. April 13, 1865; appointed Brevet Major June 20, 1865. Honorably discharged June 20, 1865.

SAMUEL T. C. MERWIN, Eighteenth Regiment Infantry, First Lieutenant August 8, 1862; promoted Captain June 22, 1865. Mustered out June 27, 1865.

JOSEPH P. ROCKWELL, Eighteenth Regiment Infantry, Second Lieutenant December 22, 1862; promoted Adjutant June 5, 1864; appointed Captain October 17, 1864. Mustered out June 27, 1865.

JOHN LILLEY, Eighteenth Regiment Infantry, First Lieutenant June 5, 1864; promoted Captain October 17, 1864. Mustered out June 27, 1865.

MARTIN V. B. TIFFANY, Eighteenth Regiment Infantry, First

Lieutenant October 19, 1863; promoted Captain August 12, 1864. Mustered out June 27, 1865.

JOHN H. MORRISON, Eighteenth Regiment Infantry, First Lieutenant August 8, 1862; promoted Captain October 19, 1863. Dismissed September 1, 1864.

CHARLES J. ARMS, Twentieth Regiment Infantry. Adjutant August 20, 1862; promoted Captain November 18, 1862. Resigned May 15, 1863, to take staff appointment Sixteenth Regiment Infantry; First Lieutenant May 30, 1863, A. D. C. to General Harland. Mustered out June 24, 1865.

CLARKE HARRINGTON, Twenty-sixth Regiment Infantry, commissioned Captain September 6, 1862. Honorably discharged August 17, 1863.

JOHN L. STANTON, Twenty-sixth Regiment Infantry, commissioned Captain September 6, 1862. Killed in action May 27, 1863, at Port Hudson.

LOREN A. GALLUP, Twenty-sixth Regiment Infantry, First Lieutenant September 6, 1862; promoted Captain September 22, 1862. Honorably discharged August 17, 1863.

SAMUEL P. HUNTOON, Twenty-sixth Regiment Infantry, Captain September 6, 1862. Honorably discharged August 17, 1863.

J. LEWIS SPALDING, Eighteenth Regiment Infantry, Massachusetts, Captain August 20, 1861; resigned October 20, 1862; appointed Adjutant Twenty-ninth Regiment Infantry C. V. January 24, 1864; mustered out October 24, 1865; commissioned Second Lieutenant First Regiment U. S. A. April 6, 1866; promoted First Lieutenant August 9, 1866. Resigned January 1, 1871.

GEORGE GREENMAN, Thirtieth Regiment Infantry, First Lieutenant April 7, 1864; appointed Adjutant April 7, 1864; promoted Captain Thirty-first Regiment U. S. C. T. January 31, 1864. Mustered out November 7, 1865.

B. B. BLACKMAN, Forty-third Regiment Infantry U. S. Colored Troops, Captain March 8, 1864. Honorably discharged (term expired) November 30, 1865.

JESSE D. WILKINSON, Forty-third Regiment U. S. Colored Troops, commissioned Captain March 8, 1864. Honorably discharged (term expired) November 30, 1865.

GEORGE R. CASE, First Regiment Infantry Corps d'Afrique, Louisiana. First Lieutenant September 27, 1862; promoted Captain March 5, 1863. Honorably discharged February 11, 1864.

WILLIAM T. LUSK, Seventy-ninth Regiment Infantry, New York. Second Lieutenant August 3, 1861; promoted Captain January 19, 1862; resigned February 28, 1863; appointed A. A. G. staff General Daniel Tyler (rank of Captain) June 26, 1863. Resigned October, 1863.

CHARLES H. ROCKWELL, Assistant Quartermaster U. S. V. (rank of Captain). Mustered out.

WILLIAM A. BERRY, Second Regiment Infantry. Second Lieutenant May 7, 1861. Honorably discharged August 7, 1861. Second Regiment New York Artillery, First Lieutenant November 1, 1861; promoted Captain June 14, 1862. Killed in action near Petersburg, Va., June 18, 1864.

WARRINGTON D. ROATH, commissioned Acting-Master U. S. N. May, 1861; promoted Volunteer Lieutenant July 11, 1863. Resigned March 7, 1865.

ROBERT B. SMITH, commissioned Volunteer Lieutenant U. S. N. December 3, 1863. Honorably discharged November, 1865.

FRANCIS S. WELLS, commissioned Acting Volunteer Lieutenant U. S. N. May 7, 1863. Honorably discharged —— 1865.

First Lieutenants.

THOMAS SCOTT, Second Regiment Infantry, May 7, 1861. Honorably discharged August 7, 1861. Second Regiment Artillery, N. Y., Second Lieutenant November 1, 1861; promoted First Lieutenant June 14, 1862. Mustered out (term expired) October 7, 1864.

CHARLES W. SPALDING, Third Regiment Infantry, May 11, 1861. Resigned May 20, 1861.

FRANK J. JONES, First Regiment Artillery, Second Lieutenant February 28, 1862 ; promoted First Lieutenant January 1, 1863. Resigned July 27, 1863.

GEORGE W. ROGERS, Second Regiment Infantry, May 7, 1861. Honorably discharged August 7, 1861.

MARVIN WAIT, Eighth Regiment Infantry, Second Lieutenant December 25, 1861 ; promoted First Lieutenant March 28, 1862. Killed in action September 17, 1862.

CHARLES H. CARPENTER, Twenty-ninth Regiment Infantry, First Lieutenant March 10, 1864. Mustered out October 24, 1865.

CHARLES A. BREED, Eighth Regiment Infantry, Second Lieutenant September 21, 1861 ; promoted First Lieutenant March 28, 1862. Died July 30, 1862.

SAMUEL S. FOSS, Eighth Regiment Infantry, First Lieutenant August 2, 1864. Mustered out January 27, 1865.

WILLIAM H. PECK, Eighth Regiment Infantry, First Lieutenant April 1, 1865. Mustered out December 12, 1865.

ALFRED M. GODDARD, Eighth Regiment Infantry, First Lieutenant July 24, 1863, Aid-de-camp, staff of Brigadier-general Harland. Died of wounds May 9, 1864.

GEORGE C. RIPLEY, Tenth Regiment Infantry. First Lieutenant Fourteenth Regiment December 22, 1863 ; transferred to Tenth Regiment, First Lieutenant January 19, 1863.

JOSEPH H. LAWLER, Ninth Regiment Infantry, Second Lieutenant January 26, 1863 ; promoted First Lieutenant December 5, 1864. Mustered out August 3, 1865.

GEORGE H. KEABLES, Eleventh Regiment Infantry, Second Lieutenant November 30, 1864 ; promoted First Lieutenant January 3, 1865. Honorably discharged May 4, 1865.

JOHN H. NORRIS, Eleventh Regiment Infantry. First Lieutenant October 1, 1861. Resigned April 5, 1862.

HENRY A. WHITE, Twelfth Regiment Infantry, First Lieutenant December 2, 1864. Commission revoked January 10, 1865.

JOHN C. ABBOTT, Thirteenth Regiment Infantry, Second Lieutenant January 29, 1862 ; promoted First Lieutenant September 1, 1863. Transferred to Signal Corps September 19, 1864.

JAMES S. MAPLES, Twenty-sixth Regiment Infantry, Second Lieutenant September 6. 1862 ; resigned to accept promotion August 11, 1863 ; First Lieutenant July 27, 1863. Commission revoked August 11, 1863.

EDWARD W. EELLS, Twenty-sixth Regiment Infantry, First Lieutenant September 22, 1862. Honorably discharged August 17, 1863.

EDWARD P. ROGERS, Twenty-ninth Regiment Infantry, First Lieutenant January 26, 1864. Resigned August 3, 1865.

ALBERT LATHAM, Thirtieth Regiment Infantry. Second Lieutenant April 20, 1864 ; promoted First Lieutenant January 31, 1865. Mustered out November 7, 1865.

JAMES H. KANE, First Regiment Cavalry, First Lieutenant January 2, 1864. Mustered out August 2, 1865.

TIMOTHY W. TRACY, Twenty-sixth Regiment Infantry, First Lieutenant September 6, 1862. Honorably discharged August 17, 1863.

CHESTER W. CONVERSE, Third Regiment Louisiana Native Guard, Second Lieutenant April 3, 1863 ; promoted First Lieutenant December 23, 1863. Resigned and honorably discharged May 28, 1864.

PETER L. HYDE, Twenty-sixth Infantry, Iowa, First Lieutenant September 30, 1862. Killed at Arkansas Post, Arkansas, January 11, 1863.

EDWIN T. LEACH, Thirtieth Regiment Infantry. First Lieutenant March 12, 1864. Dismissed May 9, 1864.

A. DWIGHT MCCALL, Twelfth Regiment Infantry, First Lieutenant November 20, 1861. Mustered out (term expired) November 21, 1864.

WILLIAM P. MINER, Thirteenth Regiment Infantry, Second Lieutenant January 30, 1862 ; promoted First Lieutenant February 20, 1863. Discharged July 16, 1864.

FREDERICK E. SCHALK, Fourteenth Regiment Infantry, Second Lieutenant May 16, 1863 ; promoted First Lieutenant November 5, 1863. Died of wounds May 4, 1864.

WILLIAM CARRUTHERS, Eighteenth Regiment Infantry. Second

Lieutenant October 17, 1864; promoted First Lieutenant January 7, 1865. Mustered out June 27, 1865.

ROBERT KERR, Eighteenth Regiment Infantry, Second Lieutenant June 5, 1864; promoted First Lieutenant June 22, 1865. Mustered out June 27, 1862.

JOHN A. FRANCIS. Eighteenth Regiment Infantry, Second Lieutenant August 8. 1862; promoted First Lieutenant January 30, 1865. Mustered out June 27, 1865.

HENRY F. COWLES. Eighteenth Regiment Infantry, Second Lieutenant August 8, 1862; promoted First Lieutenant October 10, 1863. Honorably discharged May 15, 1865.

ADAM H. LINDSLEY. Eighteenth Regiment Infantry, First Lieutenant August 8, 1862. Honorably discharged April 17, 1865.

CHRISTOPHER A. BRAND. Twenty-first Regiment Infantry, Second Lieutenant October 12. 1862; promoted First Lieutenant November 8. 1862. Resigned February 23, 1863.

JAMES STANLEY, Twenty-first Regiment Infantry, Second Lieutenant August 3, 1862; promoted First Lieutenant February 23, 1863. Honorably discharged September 20, 1864.

PLINY BREWER. Twenty-sixth Regiment Infantry, Second Lieutenant September 6, 1862; promoted First Lieutenant May 27, 1863. Honorably discharged August 17, 1863.

THOMAS C. LAWLER. Ninth Regiment Infantry, First Lieutenant October 29, 1861. Resigned February 25, 1862.

LUTHER M. LEONARD. Twenty-ninth Regiment Infantry, First Lieutenant March 15, 1864. Mustered out October 25, 1865.

WILLIAM A. AIKEN, commissioned Acting Assistant Paymaster U. S. A. August 10, 1861. Honorably discharged to receive appointment as Quartermaster-general State Militia, July 10, 1862.

GEORGE W. HUNTINGTON, commissioned Acting Assistant Paymaster U. S. N. October, 1863. Honorably discharged November, 1865.

JOHN W. BENTLEY, commissioned Acting Master U. S. N. May 24, 1861. Died May 24, 1864.

"OUR ROLL OF HONOR." 349

CHARLES C. ADAMS, commissioned Acting Assistant Paymaster U. S. N. May 6, 1861. Resigned October 1, 1865.

LEWIS G. COOK, commissioned Acting Master U. S. N. December 19, 1861. Honorably discharged, 1865.

AMOS D. ALLEN, appointed Paymaster's Clerk U. S. N. November 9, 1863; commissioned Acting Assistant Paymaster October 21, 1864. Honorably discharged September 5, 1865.

GEORGE E. MARTIN, appointed Paymaster's Clerk U. S. N. December 30, 1861; commissioned Acting Assistant Paymaster November, 1864. Honorably discharged August, 1865. Reappointed, and died August 16, 1867.

Second Lieutenants.

WILLIAM W. BARNES, Third Regiment Infantry, May 11, 1861. Honorably discharged August 12, 1861.

WILLIAM P. FORD, First Regiment Cavalry, Second Lieutenant November 30, 1864. Mustered out August 2, 1865.

JAMES BRADLEY, First Regiment Cavalry, Second Lieutenant November 30, 1864. Mustered out August 2, 1865.

EDWARD L. TYLER, First Regiment Artillery, Second Lieutenant March 29, 1862. Resigned for disability April 9, 1864.

JOHN H. TINGLEY, First Regiment Artillery, Second Lieutenant March 1, 1862, and A. D. C. on Staff General Dan Tyler. Resigned December 31, 1862.

CHARLES A. MURRAY, Eighteenth Regiment Infantry, Second Lieutenant January 30, 1865. Mustered out June 27, 1865.

FRANCIS MCKEAG, Eighteenth Regiment Infantry, Second Lieutenant December 22, 1862. Mustered out June 27, 1865.

JAMES D. HIGGINS, Eighteenth Regiment Infantry, Second Lieutenant August 8, 1862. Honorably discharged October 27, 1864.

JOSEPH D. PLUNKETT, Twenty-first Regiment Infantry, Second Lieutenant October 11, 1862. Discharged December 20, 1862.

ISAAC N. LEONARD, Twenty-sixth Regiment, Second Lieutenant August 11, 1863. Honorably discharged August 17, 1863.

HERVEY F. JACOBS, Twenty-sixth Regiment Infantry, Second Lieutenant September 6, 1862. Died July 5, 1863.

EDWARD P. MANNING, Twenty-sixth Regiment, Second Lieutenant July 27, 1863. Died August 17, 1863.

GORHAM DENNIS, Seventh Regiment Infantry, Second Lieutenant August 30, 1861. Resigned January 3, 1862.

AMOS L. KEABLES, Eighth Regiment Infantry, Second Lieutenant August 1, 1862. Honorably discharged May 15, 1865.

CHARLES SHEPARD, Eighth Regiment Infantry, Second Lieutenant February 1, 1862. Resigned February 14, 1863.

EDMUND DOWNING, Ninth Regiment Infantry, Second Lieutenant December 5, 1864. Mustered out August 3, 1865.

T. BRENNAN, Second Regiment Heavy Artillery, New York, Second Lieutenant.

JAMES H. NASH, commissioned Acting Ensign U. S. N. January 20, 1863. Honorably discharged, 1865.

GENERAL MUSTER ROLL OF ALL NORWICH SOLDIERS.

Showing Rank, Regiment, Date of Enlistment, Period of Service, and Date of Muster Out.

Those whose names are marked with an asterisk re-enlisted as veterans in 1864.

Name and Rank.	Regiment.	Enlistment.	Remarks
Abbott, E. Kempton.....	1	April 22, '61	Capt. 12. Res. Aug. 25, '62.
Abbott, John C., 2 Lt....	13	Feb. 20, '62	Lt. Transf. to Signal Corps.
Acksler, Adam.........	18	July 15, '62	Died Madisonville, Oct. 5, '64.
Adams, Anthony........	18	July 17, '62	M. O. June 27, '65.
Adams, George.........	8	Mch. 19, '64	M. O. Dec. 12, '65.
Adams, Lewis	30	Jan. 15, '64	Deserted, March 27, '64.
Adams, William	12	Dec. 3, '61	Deserted, Feb. 22, '62.
Adams, William N......	18	Aug. 11, '62	Transf. V. R. C.
Alford, George.........	2 Art.	Jan. 27, '64	Deserted May 9, '64.
Alger, Silas J..........	18	Aug. 4, '62	M. O. June 2, '65.
Alldrich, Albert C......	18	Aug. 15, '62	M. O. July 18, '65.
Allen, Charles.........	18	Dec. 28, 64	M. O. July 27, '65.
Allen, Daniel B........	1 Art.	Jan. 17, '64	M. O. Sept. 25, '65.
Allen, James A........	3	May 11, '61	Sgt. 18. M. O. June 27, '65.
Allen, Nelson R........	18	July 16, '62	M. O. June 27, '65.
Allen, Raymond........	11	Nov. 14, '61	Hon. discharged, Nov. 13, '64.
Allyn, William R.......	14	July 11, '62	Died March 9, '63.

THE NORWICH MEMORIAL.

Name and Rank.	Regiment.	Enlistment.	Remarks.
Amesbury, Marvin H.*	1 Art.	Feb. 26, '62	M. O. Sept. 25, '65.
Anderson, Charles W.	18	Aug. 7, '62	M. O. June 27, '65.
Anderson, James S.*	1 Art.	Mch. 20, '62	M. O. Sept. 25, '65.
Appleton, Henry	18	July 17, '62	M. O. June 27, '65.
Arms, Charles J., *Adj.*	20	Aug. 20, '62	Lt. 16. M. O. June 24, '65.
Armstrong, Harvey S.	3	May 11, '61	M. O. Aug. 12, '61.
Armstrong, Joseph C.	26	Aug. 30, '62	M. O. Aug. 17, '62.
Arnold, Ludwig	3	May 11, '61	M. O. Aug. 12, '61.
Ashley, Charles	1 Art.	Jan. 3, '65	Deserted July 6, '65.
Atchison, Robert	Cav.	Dec. 8, '64	M. O. Aug. 2, '65.
Avery, Alexander S., *Sgt.*	5	July 22, '61	Killed, Cedar Mt., Va., Aug. 9, '62.
Avery, Courtland C.,*Corp.*	26	Aug. 27, '62	Died June 23, '63.
Babcock, George W.	14	June 10, '62	Discharged dis. Oct. 20, '62.
Bacon, Harrison E.	18	Aug. 1, '62	M. O. May 23, '65.
Bacon, Isaac B.	21	Aug. 31, '64	M. O. June 16, '65.
Bacon, James M.	8	Oct. 1, '61	Discharged dis. Jan. 19, '63.
Bailey, Amos E.	11	Aug. 8, '64	M. O. Dec. 21, '65.
Bailey, Joseph A.	Cav.	Dec. 15, '63	Died And'sonville, Aug. 13,'64.
Bailey, Levi H.	8	Sept. 21, '61	Discharged dis. Dec. 19, '62.
Baird, Thomas W.,* *Corp.*	5	July 22, '61	V. R. C. April 21, '65.
Baker, Frederick W.	Cav.	Jan. 12, '64	Died Jan. 27, '64.
Baldwin, Thomas M.	Cav.	Jan. 5, '64	Died Andersonville July 3, '64.
Barber, Ezra N.	2	May 7, '61	Sgt. 11. Hon. dis. Oct. 26, '64.
Barlow, James G.	2	May 7, '61	M. O. Aug. 7, 61.
Barlow, Otis W.	2	May 7, '61	1 Art. Deserted July 31, '65.
Barnes, Owen	6	Dec. 9, '64	Deserted April 10, '65.
Barnes, Wm. W., 2 *Lt.*	3	May 11, '61	M. O. Aug. 12, '61.
Barney, John	21	Aug. 12, '62	Died of wounds Aug. 14, '64.
Barrett, Joseph*	1 Art.	Mch. 1, '62	M. O. Sept. 25, '65.
Barry, James*	13	Dec. 22, '61	Deserted Aug 30, '64.
Barstow, Charles S.	Cav.	Jan. 5, '64	M. O. June 1, '65.
Bassett, Reuel H.*	9	Oct. 30, '61	M. O. Aug. 3, '65.
Beckwith, Charles H.	2	May 7, '61	18. Died Dec. 1, '62.
Beckwith, Henry M.	1 Art.	Mch. 10, '62	Died Oct. 10, '63.
Beckwith, Herbert E.	10	Oct. 1, '61	Corp. Mass. Art. Died Annapolis Dec. 30, '64.
Beckwith, John A.	8	Oct. 5, '61	Hon. discharged Sept. 20, '64.
Beckwith, William	Cav.	Dec. 22, '63	M. O. July 15, '65.
Beebe, Daniel E.	2	May 7, '61	Corp. 18. M. O. May 30, '65.
Bemont, Nelson J.	14	Aug. 6, '62	M. O. May 31, '65.
Bennett, Elisha	26	Aug. 30, '62	M. O. Aug. 17, '63.
Bennett, John A.	18	July 18, '62	Discharged dis. May 3, '63.
Bennett, Steward C.	26	Aug. 30, '62	M. O Aug. 17, '63.
Benson, Olaph.	2 Art.	Jan. 20, '64	M. O. Aug. 18, '65.
Benticy, Edwin, *A. Surg.*	1 Art.	May 23, '61	Still in service U. S. A.
Bentley, John W.	30	Jan. 11, '64	M. O. Nov. 7, '65.
Bentley, Samuel	21	Aug. 21, '62	M. O. June 16, '65.
Berg, August	2 Art.	Feb. 2, '64	Killed in action Sept. 19, '64.
Berry, William A., 2 *Lt.*	2	May 7, ,61	Capt. 2 N.Y. Art. Killed June 5, '64

GENERAL MUSTER ROLL OF ALL NORWICH SOLDIERS. 353

Name and Rank.	Regiment.	Enlistment.	Remarks.
Best, John............	2 Art.	Dec. 30, '63	Killed Petersb'g. Mar. 25, '65.
Bexner, John..........	Cav.	Jan. 31, '64	M. O. Aug. 2, 65.
Billings, Samuel D......	18	Aug. 4, '62	M. O. June 27, '65.
Birge, Henry W., *Maj.*, *M. G. V.* by brevet....	1 Art.	May 23, '61	Col. 13. M. O. Oct. '65.
Black, David............	13	Dec. 30, '61	Killed Geo. Lan. Oct. 27, '62.
Blackman, Burril B......	18	July 26, '62	Capt. 43 U. S. C. T. M. O. Nov. 30, '65.
Blackman, John F.......	Cav.	Aug. 12, '61	
Blake, Charles S........	18	July 21, '62	Deserted May 25, '63
Blake, George W........	13	Jan. 7, '62	Corp. 18. M. O. June 27, '65.
Blake, John G..........	5	July 22, '61	Hon. discharged July 22, '64.
Blau, Anthony.........	6	Sept. 6, '61	Hon. discharged Sept. 11, '64.
Blumley, Edward *.....	8	Oct. 1, '61	Died Andersonville Oct. 6, '64.
Bogue, Richard H......	6	July 13, '63	Died Feb. 23, '65.
Bolles, Orin S..........	Cav.	Dec. 15, '63	Captured Oct. 17, '64.
Bolman, Lemuel........	12	Dec. 27, '61	Died Aug. 22, '63.
Bond, Frank S., *Lt.*.....	10	Mch. 29, '62	Maj. U. S. V. Res. Jan. '65.
Bond, John T.*.........	9	May 24, '62	M. O. Aug. 3, '65.
Booth, John............	18	July 22, '62	M. O. June 27, '65.
Bottom, William H.*....	11	Dec. 2, '61	Discharged July 15, '65.
Bottomly, Hen. A.,* *Corp.*	7	Sept. 5, '61	Died March 13, '64.
Bowen, Ezra P.........	18	July 12, '62	M. O. May 29, '65.
Boyle, James...........	1 Art.	Dec. 22, '63	M. O. Sept. 25, '65.
Bradley, Jno. T........	18	Aug. 8, '62	Killed Piedmont, June 5. '64.
Bradley, William.......	2 Art.	Jan. 10, '64	U. S. N. April 4, '64.
Brady, George W......	18	Aug. 8, '64	Pro Adj. M. O. June 27, '65
Brady, Patrick.........	18	July 26, '62	M. O. June 27, '65.
Brady, Terence........	14	July 15, '62	M. O. May 31, '65.
Braman, Edwin W.....	26	Sept. 1, '62	M. O. Aug. 17, '63.
Braman, Henry T.,*.....	3	May 11, '61	M. O. July 20, '65.
Braman, Lucius R......	18	July 30, '62	Discharged dis. Nov. 16, '64.
Brand, Christ. A.......	18	July 26, '62	Lt. 21. Resigned Feb. 23, '63.
Brandon, Ben.*.........	9	May 24, '62	M. O. Aug. 3, '65.
Brash, Hen. J..........	6	Dec. 9, '64	Deserted March 5, '65.
Bray, John.............	2 Art.	Jan. 30, '64	Deserted April 2, '64.
Breed, Chas. A.........	3	May 11, '61	Lt. 8. Died July 30, '62.
Breed, John...........	3	May 11, '61	Hon. discharged Aug. 12, '61.
Brennan, Cornelius	14	June 21, '62	V. R. C. M. O. July 5. '65.
Bresnahen, John	26	Sept. 10, '62	M. O. Aug. 17, '63.
Brewer, Pliny, *2 Lt.*....	26	Aug. 23, '62	Pro. Lt. M. O. Aug. 17, '63
Brewster, William H....	21	Jan. 21, '64	Transf. 10. M. O. Aug. 25, '65.
Brierly, John J.	14	June 10, '62	M. O. May 31, 65.
Briggs, Abram........	18	Aug. 4, '62	Deserted Nov. 11, '64.
Broadhead, John P......	29	Nov. 14, '64	M. O. Oct. 24, '65.
Brogan, John..........	2	May 7, '61	M. O. Aug. 7, '61.
Bromley, Edwin F......	26	Aug. 30, '62	M. O. Aug. 17, '63.
Bromley, Isaac H., *Capt.*	18	July 26, '62	Hon. discharged March 31, '63.
Bromley, Joseph B.,*Qr. M.*	13	Feb. 19, '61	Resigned Dec. 20, '63.
Brooks, Albert O.......	11	Feb. 15, '64	M. O. Dec. 21, '65.
Brooks, Henry.........	26	Aug. 30, '62	Died July 3, '63.

THE NORWICH MEMORIAL.

Name and Rank.	Regiment.	Enlistment.	Remarks.
Brown, Asher P., Corp...	26	Sept. 11, '62	M. O. Aug. 17, '63.
Brown, Charles H.	14	July 18, '63	Transf. 2 Art. May 31, '65.
Brown, Daniel H.	9	Oct. 30, '61	Died May 14, '62.
Brown, David H.*	13	Jan. 11, '62	Died May 15, '64.
Brown, Edward	21	Aug. 16, '62	M. O. May 20, '65.
Brown, George	2	May 7, '61	Corp. 13. Drop'd Oct. 31. '64
Brown, George	10	Dec. 20, '64	Died Jan. 27, '65.
Brown, George E.	17	Jan. 15, '64	M. O. July 19, '65
Brown, James	2 Art.	Jan. 29, '64	Deserted Feb. 24, '64.
Brown, John	1 Art.	Dec. 22, '64	Deserted Jan. 27, '65.
Brown, Leander	3	May 11, '61	M. O. Aug. 12, '61.
Brown, Reuben B., Sgt.	18	Aug. 5, '62	M. O. June 23, '65.
Brown, Silas	29	Jan. 5, '64	Died Jan. 25, '65.
Brown, William	2 Art.	Feb. 2, '64	Deserted Feb. '64.
Brown, William H.	2	May 7, '61	M O. Aug. 7, '61.
Brown, William, Sgt.	30	Jan. 22, '64	M. O. Nov. 7, '65.
Buchanan, Howard R.	Cav.	Jan. 11, '64	Deserted June 30, '65.
Buck, Charles B.	29	Sept. 2, '64	M. O. Oct. 24, '65.
Buckingham, E. C.	14	July 25, '63	Died March 3, '64.
Buckley, Daniel C.	13	Jan. 19, '64	Deserted July 25, '64.
Bump, Henry G., Jr.	1 Art	May 23, '61	Hon. discharged May 22, '64
Burdick, Charles	10	Oct. 29, '61	Died Jan. 16, '63.
Burdick, Horatio	18	July, 23, '62	Died Oct. 19, '62.
Burdick, Joel	18	July 25, '62	Discharged Aug. 25, '62.
Burdick, Samuel	18	July 25, '62	Discharged dis. Jan. 4, '64.
Burdick, Theodore, 2 Lt.	7	Sept. 5, '61	Capt. Killed Ft. Wagner July 11, '63.
Burdick, William H.	18	July 26, '62	M. O. June 19, '65.
Burghmayer, Anton	Cav.	Jan. 2, '64	Died April 11, '65.
Burgoyne, Walter*	12	Dec. 27, '61	Died Feb. 5, '65
Burke, Charles F.	3	May 11, '61	M. O. Aug. 12, '61.
Burke, Horace E.	3	May 11, '61	M. O. Aug. 12, '61.
Burke, John*	9	May 24, '62	Deserted July 17, '64.
Burke, Patrick	2 Art.	Jan. 23, '64	Deserted Feb. 3, '64.
Burnett, Albert	18	Aug. 9, '62	Killed Winchester June 15, '63
Burns, George	1 Art.	Jan. 14, '64	Deserted Feb 12, '64.
Burns, John	2 Art.	Jan. 20, '64	Deserted Feb. 19, '65.
Burns, Peter	1 Art.	Dec. 22, '64	Deserted Aug. 2, '65.
Butler, Francis	Cav.	Jan. 19, '64	Deserted Feb. 5, '64.
Butler, John	2	May 7, '61	M. O. Aug. 7, '61.
Butler, John B.	11	Oct. 25, '61	Hon. discharged Oct. 24, '64.
Butler, Roswell	18	July 14, '62	M. O. June 27, '65.
Butler, Rufus	11	Oct. 25, '61	Discharged dis. June 14, '62.
Buttery, Ira	17	Jan. 15, '64	M. O. July 19, '65.
Button, Guy D.	18	Aug. 2, '62	Discharged dis. June 18, '65.
Button, Samuel A.	8	Oct. 5, '61	Discharged dis. March 16, '62.
Byford, John	2 Art.	Jan. 21, '64	Deserted Feb. 13, '65.
Byrnes, James	9	Nov. 25, '61	Discharged dis. Oct. 16, '62.
Byron, James	18	Aug. 6, '62	M. O. June 27, '65.
Calhoun, Martin	3	May 11, '61	1 Art. M. O. Sept 25, '65.
Callahan, Jeremiah	14	May 23, '62	M. O. May 31, '65.

GENERAL MUSTER ROLL OF ALL NORWICH SOLDIERS.

Name and Rank.	Regiment.	Enlistment.	Remarks.
Cameron, Daniel	14	Aug. 5, '64	Transf. 2 Art. May 31, '65.
Campbell, Edward	14	July 18, '63	Died Jan. 18, '65.
Campbell, Thomas *	9	Oct. 12, '61	Discharged dis. Jan. '65.
Canfield, Lawrence	2 Art.	Jan. 19, '64	Deserted Feb. 13, '65.
Cantwell, William	21	Aug. 20, '62	M. O. June 16, '65.
Carey, Andrew E.*	11	Dec. 3, '61	M. O. Dec. 21, '65.
Carey, Charles W.	18	July 24, '62	M. O. July 1, '65.
Carey, Joel	18	Aug. 2, '62	M. O. May 22, '65.
Carkins, Amos B.	2	May 7, '61	M. O. Aug. 7, '61.
Carl, Martin	18	Aug. 8, '62	Died Sept. 25, '64.
Carleton, Charles M. *Surg.*	18	Aug. 6, '62	Resigned April 17, '63.
Carlton, George	Cav.	Jan. 22, '64	Deserted Feb. 4, '64.
Carney, Daniel	18	July 22, '62	M. O. May 28, '65.
Carney, John *	13	Jan. 11, '62	M. O. April 25, '66.
Carpenter, Chas. H., *Corp.*	3	May 11, '61	Lt. 29, March 10, '64. M. O. Oct. 24, '65.
Carpenter Charles H., *Sgt.*	18	Aug. 6, '62	M. O. June 27, '65.
Carpenter, Daniel D.	8	April 2, '64	M. O. Dec. 19, '65.
Carpenter, Delano N.*	5	July 22, '61	M. O. July 19, '65.
Carpenter, Franklin L.	11	Jan. 25, '64	M. O. Dec. 21, '65
Carroll, Charles H., *Sgt.*	18	July 12, '62	M. O. June 27, '65.
Carroll, George	18	Aug. 4, '62	M. O. June 27, '65.
Carroll, Joseph W	18	July 14, '62	M. O. Aug. 17, '65.
Carroll, Mortimer	1 Art.	Aug. 25, '64	Deserted Aug. 8, '65.
Carroll, Theodore R.*	12	Dec. 27, '61	M. O. Aug. 12, '65.
Carroll, Timothy	Cav.	Nov. 2, '61	M. O. Aug. 2, '65.
Carroll, William B.*	2	May 7, '61	Corp. 7. Died Nov. 5, '64.
Carruthers, William	3	May 11, '61	Pro. Lt. 18. M. O. June 27, '65.
Carter, Thomas S.	2 Art.	Jan. 27, '64	Deserted May 9, '64.
Carver, James	18	July 28, '62	M. O. June 27, '65.
Carver, Michael	Cav.	Oct. 26, '61	Killed (Stafford C. H. Va.) Jan. 3, '63.
Carver, Thomas	Cav.	Aug. 15, '62	M. O. June 3, '65.
Carver, William	18	Apr. 21, '64	Dishon. disch. May 8, '65.
Case, Charles E.	18	July 29, '62	M. O. June 27, '65.
Case, Benjamin	2 Art.	Jan. 19, '64	Deserted Feb. 14, '64.
Case, David C.	3	May 11, '61	Killed Bull Run July 21, '61.
Case, George R.	1	Apr. 22, '61	Capt. La. N. G.
Case, James *	13	Dec. 30, '61	Disch. dis. July 3, '65.
Case, John P.	2	May 7, '61	M. O. Aug. 11, '61.
Case, Joseph	5	July 22, '61	Disch. dis. July 20, '62.
Cassidy, Patrick	5	July 22, '61	Disch. dis. Sept. 19, '61.
Chalmers, John	18	July 22, '62	M. O. June 27, '65.
Champlin, H. F.	10	Oct. 1, '61	Died And'sonville Aug. 11, 64.
Chandler, Nelson	Cav.	Jan. 5, '64	Captured May 5, '64.
Chantley, William H.	1 Bat.	Aug. 8, '64	M. O. June 11, '65.
Chapman, C. E.	1 Art.	Jan. 6, '64	M. O. Sept. 25, '65.
Chapman, Giles D.	26	Aug. 30, '62	M. O. Aug. 17, '63.
Chappell, Alfred S.	18	July 22, '62	Died Sept. 17, '63.
Chappell, Charles L.	26	Aug. 27, '62	M. O. Aug. 17, '63.
Chappell, Samuel H.	18	July 19, '62	Deserted May 22, '63.

Name and Rank.	Regiment.	Enlistment.	Remarks.
Charlton, John	26	Aug. 27, '62	M. O. Aug. 17, '63.
Cheschri, James F.	8	Sept. 21, '61	Disch. dis. May 14, '62.
Chester, Frank S., *Capt.*	2	May 7, '61	M. O. Aug. 7, '61.
Chism, Samuel	30	Jan. 23, '64	M. O. Nov. 7, '65.
Church, Daniel B.	18	July 25, '62	M. O. June 27, '65.
Clancey, William	14	July 23, '63	Tr. 2 Art. M. O. May 31, '65.
Clark, Edward S.	18	July 29, '62	M. O. June 27, '65.
Clark, Henry T.	18	Aug. 4, '62	M. O. June 27, '65.
Clark, James	18	July 23, '62	Tr. V. R. C. M. O. June 27, '65.
Clark, James N., *Sgt.*	26	Aug. 25, '62	M. O. Aug. 17, '63.
Clark, John	18	Dec. 24, '64	M. O. June 27, '65.
Clark, John S.	18	Aug. 2, '62	M. O. June 27, '65.
Clark, Patrick	18	Feb. 29, '64	M. O. June 27, '65.
Clark, Vinson H.	2 Art.	Feb. 2, '64	Deserted Apr. 29, '64.
Clayton, John	2 Art.	Jan. 27, '64	Deserted Feb. 11, '64.
Cobb, Charles H., Jr.	26	Aug. 30, '62	M. O. Aug. 17, '63.
Cobb, James L., *Sgt.*	2	May 7, '61	M. O. Aug. 7, '61.
Cochran, Alexander R.	18	Aug. 7, '62	Deserted May 22, '63.
Coggswell, George	18	Aug. 6, '62	M. O. June 27, '65.
Coit, John	18	July 9, '62	M. O. June 27, '65.
Coit, Charles M., *Adj.*, *Lt. Col.* by brevet	8	Oct. 5, '61	Pro. Capt. M. O. May 30, '65.
Coit, James B.	2	May 7, '61	Pro. Maj. 14 (B. G. V. by bvt). Resigned Sept. 6, '64.
Cole, Henry B.	26	Aug. 30, '62	M. O. Aug. 17, '63.
Colegrove, Chas. H., *Corp.*	13	Dec. 22, '61	Discharged dis. May 13, '63.
Collins, Andrew	13	Jan. 7, '62	Discharged dis. May 20, '62.
Collins, James	2 Art.	Jan. 22, '64	U. S. N. April 4, '64.
Colton, James S.,* *Corp.*	8	Sept. 21, '61	M. O. Dec. 12, '65.
Comins, George E., *Corp.*	18	Aug. 24, '62	M. O. June 27, '65.
Conant, Oscar	14	Sept. 2, '64	Transf. 2 Art. May 31, '65.
Congdon, John C., *Corp.*	26	Aug. 28, '62	M. O. Aug. 17, '63.
Conger, Thomas B., *Corp.*	26	Aug. 30, '62	M. O. Aug. 17, '63.
Conklin, Patrick	21	Mch. 11, '64	Died Aug. 2, '64.
Connell, Daniel O.	26	Sept. 5, '62	M. O. Aug. 17, '63.
Connell, Joseph	18	Jan. 25, '64	Discharged dis. June 21, '65.
Connell, Michael O.	26	Aug. 30, '62	M. O. Aug. 17, '63.
Converse, Chester W., *Corp.*	2	May 7, '61	Lt. La. N. G. Resigned.
Conway, Thomas	Cav.	Sept. 5, '64	M. O. July 14, '65.
Conway, Thomas	1 Art.	Feb. 26, '62	Discharged dis. Jan. 27, '63.
Cook, Frederick N., *Sgt.*	26	Aug. 27, '62	M. O. Aug. 17, '63.
Cooley, Charles B.	26	Aug. 30, '62	M. O. Aug. 17, '63.
Cooper, George	Cav.	Nov. 28, '63	M. O. July 17, '65.
Corbet, Michael	13	Dec. 22, '61	Died Baton Rouge May 25, '63.
Corcoran, Michael	26	Aug. 30, '62	M. O. Aug. 17, '63.
Corcoran, Stephen *	5	July 22, '61	Discharged dis. June 5, '65.
Corey, Caleb R., *Corp.*	18	July 21, '62	M. O. May 10, '65.
Corey, Charles W., *Corp.*	26	Aug. 26, '62	M. O. Aug. 17, '63.
Corey, John F.	18	Aug. 7, '62	M. O. June 27, '65.
Corney, Patrick	13	Jan. 22, '62	Capt'd dr. fr. Rolls Dec. 31, '64.

GENERAL MUSTER ROLL OF ALL NORWICH SOLDIERS. 357

Name and Rank.	Regiment.	Enlistment.	Remarks.
Cotter, William.........	Cav.	Dec. 15, '64	M. O. Aug. 2, '65
Cowles, H. F., *Sgt. Maj.*...	2	May 7, '61	Pro. Lt. 18. M. O. May 15, '65.
Cox, Charles H.*.........	12	Nov. 20, '61	M. O. Aug. 12, '65.
Cox, John.............	8	July 27, '64	M. O. Dec. 12, '65.
Cragg, George G........	2	May 7, '61	M. O. Aug. 7, '61.
Cramer, David.........	2 Art.	Jan. 27, '64	Killed Petersburg Mch. 25, '65.
Crandall, John.........	14	July 17, '62	M. O. May 31, '65.
Cranston, Joseph J. S....	26	Aug. 28, '62	M. O. Aug. 17, '63.
Crawford, John.........	18	July 22, '62	Died Winchester July 2, '63.
Crary, John T., *Corp*.....	26	Aug. 26, '62	M. O. Aug. 17, '63.
Crocker, Byron.........	13	Feb. 5, '62	Died July 15, '64.
Crosby, Hiram B........	18	July, 26, '62	Pro. Lt. Col. H. d. Sept. 14, '64.
Cross, George W.......	18	Aug. 6, '62	M. O. June 27, '65.
Crowther, James A......	8	Sept. 21, '61	Tr. V. R. C. M. O. July 1, '63.
Crowthers, John........	2 Art.	Jan. 19, '64	M. O. Aug. 18, '65.
Culver, Enoch B., *Corp*..	18	July 26, '62	Pro. Adj. Died (of wds.) June 6, '64.
Cullin, John............	21	Aug. 9, '62	Died March 22, '64.
Cummings, William.....	13	Jan. 11, '62	Deserted March 17. '62.
Cunningham, Michael ...	14	July 16, '62	Hon. discharged May 19, '63.
Curtis, William R.......	1 Art.	Jan. 15, '64	Hon. discharged Sept. 25, '65.
Curtis, William R.......	2 Art.	Jan. 22, '64	Deserted Feb. 7, '64.
Cushman, Alonzo S.*....	11	Dec. 3, '61	Killed Swift's Creek, Virginia, May 9, '64.
Cushman, David F......	18	July 21, '62	M. O. June 27, '65.
Cutler, Charles.........	7	Sept. 5, '61	Hon. discharged Sept. 12, '64.
Cutler, Leonard.........	26	Aug. 30, '62	Hon. discharged Aug. 17, '63.
Daffett, Lewis..........	6	Sept. 6, '61	Hon. discharged Sept. 5, '64.
Dailey, John............	1 Art.	Aug. 27, '64	M. O. Sept. 25, '65.
Daily, Charles H........	18	July 24, '62	Discharged Feb. '64.
Davidson, Oscar........	2 Art.	Feb. 2, '64	Deserted June 22. '64.
Davis, George P.........	29	Jan. 2, '64	M. O. Oct. 24, '65.
Davis, Henry C., *Capt*...	18	Aug. 8, '62	M. O. Apr. 25, '65.
Davis, Isaac...........	29	Dec. 9, '63	M. O. Oct. 24, '65.
Davis, Joseph..........	8	Nov. 18, '64	Died March 10, '65.
Davis, Job A...........	29	Jan. 2, '64	M. O. Oct. 24, '65.
Davis, Marcus..........	11	Jan. 4, '64	M. O. Dec. 21, '65.
Davis, William	Cav.	Jan. 5, '64	Died And'sonville Aug. 30, '64.
Davis, William	2 Art.	Jan. 27, '64	M. O. July 8, '65.
Davis, William L.	18	Aug. 15, '62	M. O. June 27, '64.
Davis, William F.......	30	Jan. 19, '64	M. O. Nov. 7, '65.
Dayton, Nathaniel F.....	Cav.	Jan. 22, '64	M. O. Aug. 2, '65.
Dean, Jerry B..........	17	Jan. 18, '64	M. O. July 19. '65
Degnan, John..........	14	June 5, '62	Tr. V. R. C. M O. June 20, '65.
Delaney, John.........	9	Nov. 25, '61	Discharged dis. Oct. 16, '62.
Delany, John..........	18	July 17, '62	K'd Snicker's Ferry Jul. 18, '64.
Deming, Alfred H......	18	Aug. 9, '62	M. O. June 27, '64.
Deming, Henry R......	1 Art.	Jan. 14, '64	Deserted Aug. 1, '65.
Dennis, Gorham, *Corp*...	2	May 7, '61	2 Lt. 7. Resigned Jan. 3, '62.
Dennis, J. B., *Capt*......	7	Sept. 5, '61	M. O. Feb. 17, '65. (B. G. V. by bvt.)

358   THE NORWICH MEMORIAL.

Name and Rank	Regiment	Enlistment	Remarks
Dennis, Oscar A., *Capt*..	1 Art.	May 23, '61	Resigned Dec. 11, '61.
Dennison, Andrew J......	7	Sept. 5, '61	Hon. discharged Sept. 12, '64.
Dennison, John J........	2	May 7, '61	Hon. discharged Aug. 7, '61.
Derby, Charles, *Corp*....	18	Aug. 4, '62	M. O. June 27, '65.
Dexhinair, William......	2	May 7, '61	M. O. Aug. 7, '61.
Diamond, John *.........	9	May 22, '61	Deserted July 23, '64.
Dillaby, Asa, *Corp*.......	18	July 18, '62	M. O. June 27, '65.
Dittmus, Edward A. *Corp*.	29	Jan. 2, '64	M. O. Oct. 24, '65.
Dixon, Lawrence........	26	Oct. 17, '62	M. O. Aug. 17, '63.
Dole, Abe..............	30	Jan. 22, '64	Deserted July 3, '65.
Donahue, John *.........	9	May 21, '61	Deserted Aug. 6, '64.
Donahue, William.......	20	Sept. 1, '64	5. Deserted on way to Regt.
Dorrigan, Hugh.........	14	July 16, '62	Discharged dis. Feb. 8, '63.
Donnivan, Tim	26	Aug. 30, '62	M. O. Aug. 17, '63.
Donovan, John..........	11	Oct. 25, '61	Discharged dis. Feb. 1, '63.
Dorcey, Edward, *Corp*...	14	June 23, '62	Died of w'ds An'tam Oct. 8, '62.
Dorkins, William........	30	Jan. 20, '64	M. O. Nov. 7, '65.
Dorrance, George E.....	18	Aug. 4, '62	Tr. Inv'd Corps Mch. 15, '64.
Douglass, William P.....	Cav.	Jan. 22, '64	M. O. Aug. 2, '65.
Dowling, Michael W.....	26	Aug. 29, '62	Transferred Sig. Corps.
Downer, Sylvanus, *Corp*..	18	Aug. 11, '62	Died Andersonville Nov. 5, '64.
Downing, Edmund *.....	9	May 31, '62	2 Lt. M. O. Aug. 3, '65.
Doyle, James...........	9	Oct. 4, '61	Hon. discharged Oct. 26, '64.
Doyle, Timothy O.......	18	Aug. 11, '62	M. O. July 14, '65.
Draper, Albion..........	18	Aug. 11, '62	M. O. June 27, '65.
Draper, George.........	18	Aug. 18, '62	Discharged dis. Oct. 22, '63.
Drew, William..........	2 Art.	Dec. 23, '64	Deserted March 3, '65.
Driscoll, Alexander.....	26	Sept. 10, '62	Cav. Died March 7, '65.
Dryer, Henry...........	2 Art.	Jan. 21, '64	Deserted July 26, '64.
Dubois, George S.......	30	Jan. 6, '64	Deserted Feb. 11, '65.
Duff, John..............	29	Jan. 5, '64	M. O. Oct. 24, '65.
Dugan, James..........	26	Sept. 9, '62	Died July 28, '63.
Dugan, Thomas.........	2	May 7, '61	21. Died And'ville June 4, '64.
Dunbar, Edmund, *Corp*..	26	Aug. 28, '62	M. O. Aug. 17, '63.
Dunton, William W.....	2	May 7, '61	9. Veteran, des. May 20, '64.
Dunn, John*............	9	Dec. 1, '62	M. O. Aug. 3, '65.
Durfey, Henry M.......	18	Aug. 9, '62	M. O. June 27, '65.
Dutton, Rodman........	30	Jan. 6, '64	M. O. Nov. 7, '65.
Dwyer, Edward.........	21	Aug. 20, '62	Discharged dis. Oct. 11, '62.
Eagan, James...........	26	Sept. 11, '62	M. O. Aug. 17, '63.
Eastman, Shirland L....	8	Sept. 21, '61	Discharged dis. Nov. 2, '61.
Edgerton, George F.....	26	Aug. 23, '62	Died July 23, '63.
Edwards, Alfred........	8	Oct. 7, '61	Discharged dis. May 14, '62.
Edwards, George L.....	Cav.	Jan. 13, '64	Deserted Jan. 21, '64.
Edwards, Henry........	14	May 31, '62	Discharged dis. Nov. 23, '62.
Edwards, Thomas F....	8	Sept. 21, '61	Discharged dis. Feb. 12, '63.
Edwards, William......	8	Sept. 21, '61	Discharged dis. March 28, '63.
Eells, Edward W., *Lt*...	26	Aug. 30, '62	M. O. Aug. 17, '63.
Ehlers, August.........	21	Aug. 19, '62	Died of wounds July 2, '64.
Ehmer, Ferdinand......	6	Sept. 6, '61	Hon. discharged Sept. 11, '64.
Eldridge, Daniel D.....	18	Aug. 12, '62	M. O. June 27, '65.

GENERAL MUSTER ROLL OF ALL NORWICH SOLDIERS.

Name and Rank.	Regiment.	Enlistment.	Remarks.
Elliott, William	10	Dec. 17, '64	Deserted Aug. 4, '65.
Ellis, William H. H.	18	Aug. 6, '62	M. O. June 27, '65.
Ely, W. G.	1	April 24, '61	Col. 18. B. G. V. by bvt. Res'd
Emmons, Daniel	29	Jan. 7, '64	Died June 13, '64. [Sept. 18, '64.
Enwright, John	26	Aug. 30, '62	M. O. Aug. 17, '63.
Erskine, Edward	26	Aug. 29, '62	M. O. Aug. 17, '63.
Erwin, Edward	9	Nov. 25, '61	Discharged dis. March 9, '64.
Fanning, Charles T.	18	July 31, '62	Killed Piedmont June 5, '64.
Fanning, George W.	18	July 29, '62	Discharged dis. March 25, '64.
Fanning, Henry C.	8	Sept. 21, '61	Died wd's Ant'tam Oct. 28, '62.
Fanning, John T., *Corp.*	3	May 11, '61	M. O. Aug. 12, '61.
Fanning, Theo. A.	8	Sept. 21, '61	Died wd's Ant'tam Oct. 19, '62.
Fanning, William D.	2	May 7, '61	M. O. Aug. 7, '61.
Farnsworth, Chas., *Capt.* Cav.		Nov. 26, '61	M. O. May 17, '64.
Farrell, James	9	Nov. 25, '61	Hon. discharged Oct. 26, '64.
Farrell, Laurence P.*	12	Dec. 28, '61	Deserted April 7. '64.
Farrell, Thomas	21	Aug. 18, '62	V. R. C. M. O. June 29, '65.
Farris, John W.	11	Jan. 26, '64	Deserted June 18, '64.
Fellowes, Joshua, *Corp.*	26	Aug. 30, '62	M. O. Aug. 17, '63.
Fenner, Frank A.	8	Jan. 13, '64	M. O. Dec. 12, '65.
Fenton, James E.	18	Aug. 9, '62	M. O. June 27 '65.
Ferguson, Orrin	2 Art.	Jan. 30, '64	Deserted Feb. 23, '64.
Field, Stephen O.	11	Oct. 24, '61	Discharged Nov. 14. '62.
Fillburn, Thomas.*	7	Sept. 9, '61	Died Millen Ga. Oct. 21, '64.
Finken, William, *Corp.*	18	Aug. 6, '62	M. O. June 27, '65.
Fisher, George W.	30	Jan. 11, '64	M. O. Nov. 7, '65.
Fisher, Nathan A. *A.Surg.*	13	Feb. 4, '61	Resigned June 16, '63
Fitch, Edwin S.	18	Aug. 8, '62	M. O. June 27, '65.
Fitch, James E.	Cav.	Oct. 26, '61	Deserted Oct. 30, '63.
Fitzgerald, Edward	14	July 25, '63	Deserted July 24, '64.
Fitzgerald, Michael	1 Art.	Jan. 11, '64	M. O. Sept. 25, '65.
Flannagan, Edward	2	May 7, '61	M. O. Aug. 7, '61.
Flannagan, James	Cav.	Jan. 23, '64	Deserted Dec. 15, '64.
Fletcher, Freeborn O.	18	July 28, '62	M. O. June 27, '65.
Fletcher, Joseph E.	2	May 7, '61	Sgt. S. Disch. dis. Jan. 9, '63.
Flynn, John	5	Aug. 6, '63	Deserted.
Ford, David M.	11	Nov. 14, '61	Killed Antietam Sept. 17, '62.
Ford, William P.*	Cav.	Nov. 2, '61	Pro. 2 Lt. M. O. Aug. 2, '65.
Forestner, Joseph, *Corp.*	18	Aug. 7, '62	Died Aug. 9, '63.
Foss, Samuel S.	8	Sept. 21, '61	Pro. Lt. Discharged Jan. 27, '65.
Foster, Charles	18	Jan. 18, '64	M. O. June 27, '65.
Foster, Joel M.	3	May 11, '61	M. O. Aug. 11, '61.
Fowler, Samuel F.*	13	Dec. 30, '61	M. O. April 25, '66.
Fox, David D.	1 Art.	April 1, '62	Hon. discharged April 1, '65.
Fox, George W.	18	July 26, '62	Died Martinsb'g April 17, '65.
Fox, Patrick	21	Aug. 21, '62	M. O. June 16, '65.
Fox, Thomas	2 Art.	Jan. 4, '64	M. O. Aug. 18, '65.
Fox, Walter M.	2 Art.	Jan. 20, '64	Killed Petersb'g June 22, '64.
Francis, Charles	3	May 11, '61	M. O. Aug. 11, '61.
Francis, Ed.	29	Aug. 29, '64	Died Sept. 17, '65.
Francis, Edwin S., *Sgt.*	2	May 7, '61	M. O. Aug. 7, '61.

THE NORWICH MEMORIAL.

Name and Rank.	Regiment.	Enlistment.	Remarks.
Francis Jno. A., 2 Lt.	18	July 14, '62	Pro. Lt. M. O. June 27, '64.
Francis, William	30	Jan. 2, '64	M. O. Nov. 7, '65.
Fraser, Daniel	26	Aug. 30, '62	M. O. Aug. 17, '63.
Frazier, George W.	3	May 11, '61	Sgt. 7. Hon. dis. Sept. 12, '64.
Frazier, Richard	30	Jan. 5, '64	M. O. Nov. 7, '65.
Freeman, S. H., Corp.	18	Aug. 7, '62	M. O. June 27, '65.
Frink, Lewis F.	Cav.	Jan. 22, '64	M. O. Aug. 2, '65.
Frisbie, Lyman, Corp.	18	Aug. 4, '62	M. O. June 27, '65.
Fuller, Geo. H., Corp.	26	Aug. 30, '62	M. O. Aug. 17 '63.
Fuller, James E., Sgt.	11	Oct. 25, '61	Pro. Lt. Nov. 11, '64.
Fuller, Wallace	26	Aug. 29, '62	M. O. Aug. 17, '63.
Gardel, Paul	2 Art.	Dec. 30, '63	M. O. Aug. 18, '65.
Gallagher, Francis	14	July 23, '62	M. O. May 31, '65.
Gallivan, David	26	Aug. 30, '62	M. O. Aug. 17, '63.
Gallivan, Humphrey	26	Sept. 8, '62	M. O. Aug. 17, '63.
Gallup, Loren A., Capt.	26	Aug. 30, '62	M. O. Aug. 17, '73.
Gardner, John	5	Aug. 20, '63	M. O. June 14, '65.
Gaskill, Henry C.	18	Aug. 1, '63	Died Danville, Feb. 20, '65.
Gates, Horace P.	3	May 11, '61	Adj. S. App. A. A. G. U. S. V.
Gates, William H.	Cav.	Jan. 23, '64	Deserted Feb. 2, '64.
Gattel, Peter	8	Sept. 21, '61	Hon. discharged Sept. 20, '64.
Gavitt, Edwin	3	May 11, '61	Hon. discharged Aug. 11, '61.
Gibson, James	30	Jan. 22, '64	Disch. dis. March 18, '65.
Gibson, Savillian F.	18	Aug. 2, '62	M. O. June 27, '65.
Gilchrist, John W.	2	May 7, '61	M. O. Aug. 7, '61.
Giles, William	30	Jan. 18, '64	M. O. June 18, '65.
Gilleran, Owen	26	Sept. 2, '62	M. O. Aug. 17, '65.
Gilligan, Thomas	14	Aug. 3, '64	Deserted Aug. 20, '64.
Gilroy, Charles	18	July 24, '62	Deserted Aug. 21, '66.
Gleason, Henry D., Corp.	18	Aug. 6, '62	Captured June 11, '64.
Gleason, John	9	Nov. 25, '61	Discharged dis. Oct. 16, '62.
Glynn, Patrick *	9	May 26, '62	Died Nov. 25, '64.
Goddard, Alfred M., Lt.	8	July 24, '63	Died Petersburg May 9, '64.
Goddard, Henry P., 2 Lt. Sgd.	Cav.	May 7, '62	Pro. Capt. 14. Res. Apr. 26,'64.
Gorry, John	18	July 22, '62	M. O. June 27, '65.
Gorry, John	26	Aug. 30, '92	M. O. Aug. 17, '63.
Goss, James W.	26	Aug. 30, '62	M. O. Aug. 17, '63.
Gould, Augustus	2	May 7, '61	M. O. Aug. 7, '61.
Gould, John	26	Aug. 29, '62	M. O. Aug. 17, '63.
Gould, Munroe A.	Cav.	Jan. 12, '64	M. O. Aug. 5, '65.
Grady, James *	9	May 24, '62	M. O. Aug. 3, '65.
Graham Thomas H.	Cav.	Dec. 23, '64	Deserted.
Graves, Albert G.	29	Jan. 2, '64	M. O. Oct. 24, '65.
Green, Lafayette M.	5	July 22, '61	Discharged dis. Dec. 20, '62.
Green, R. J., Corp.	26	Aug. 22, '62	M. O. Aug. 17, '63.
Green, William B.	1 Art.	Jan. 4, '64	M. O. Sept. 25, '65.
Greenman, George	18	Aug. 18, '62	Pro. Capt. 31 U. S. C. T. M. O. Nov. 7, '65.
Greenman, Rufus	13	Feb. 1, '62	Discharged dis. May 13, '63.
Greenough, H. W.	Cav.	Jan. 8, '64	Died Salisbury, N.C. Oct. 9, '64.

GENERAL MUSTER ROLL OF ALL NORWICH SOLDIERS. 361

Name and Rank.	Regiment.	Enlistment.	Remarks.
Greenwood, George	30	Jan. 25, '64	Deserted Apr. 9, '64.
Griffin Peter	21	Jan. 13, '64	Discharged dis. Apr. 3, '64.
Griffin, Thomas	3	May 11, '61	M. O. Aug. 11, '61.
Gunn, Augustus W.	30	Jan. 19, '64	M. O. Nov. 7, '65.
Guttman, C. B.	2 Art.	Jan. 20, '64	Trans. to Penn. Regt. as deserter, May 24, '64.
Guyle, John W.	3	May 11, '61	M. O. Aug. 12, '61.
Hakes, Dwight W., *Qr.M.*	18	Aug. 4, '62	Capt. (Com. Sub) U. S. V.
Hakes, Isaac H., *Capt.*	18	July 12, '62	Resigned Dec. 26, '62.
Hale, Morton F., *Qr.M.*	1	May 28, '61	Capt. (Com. Sub.) U. S. V.
Hall, Aaron M., *Corp.*	29	Jan. 7, '64	M. O. Oct. 24, '65.
Hall, George	13	Dec. 22, '61	Discharged dis. May 20, '62.
Hall, William	18	Aug. 11, '62	M. O. June 27, '65.
Hallam, Chester H.	14 R. 1 Art.		Died May 4, '64.
Hallapan, T. A.*	1 Art.	May 23, '61	Sept. 25, '65.
Hamilton, F. T.*	9	May 24, '62	Deserted May 24, '64.
Hamilton, James	8	July 26, '64	Captured Sept. 29, '64.
Hamilton, William H.	18	July 29, '62	Killed Piedmont, June 5, '64
Hancock, Joseph A.	18	July 23, '62	M. O. June 27, '65.
Hanley, Michael	18	July 22, '62	Discharged dis. June 16, '64.
Hanson, H. C.	26	Aug. 30, '62	M. O. Aug. 17, '63.
Hanson, Olet T.	2 Art.	Jan. 20, '64	U. S. N. April 14, '65.
Harland, Edward, *Capt.*	3	May 11, '61	Col. S. B. G. V. Apr. 29, '63. Resigned June 20, '65.
Harper, William	26	Aug. 28, '62	M. O. Aug. 17, '63.
Harrington, Clark, *Capt.*	26	Aug. 25, '62	M. O. Aug. 17, '63.
Harrington, Joseph W.*	7	Sept. 5, '61	M. O. July 20, '65.
Harris, George L.	18	July 19, '62	Transf. V. R. C.
Hartie, Philip C.	14	June 7, '62	Discharged dis. Dec. 9, '62.
Harvey, George F.	21	Aug. 19, '62	Discharged Nov. 7, '62.
Harvey, James	2	May 7, '61	M. O. Aug. 7, '61.
Harvey, St. John	26	Nov. 6, '62	M. O. Aug. 17, '63.
Haslem, Wesley W.	18	July 25, '62	M. O. May 18, '65.
Hathaway, Philip B.	Cav.	Jan. 4, '64	Discharged Sept. 15, '64.
Hawthorne, Andrew	26	Aug. 28, '62	M. O. Aug. 17, '63.
Hayes, Charles	14	July 28, '64	Transf. 2 Art. May 31, '65.
Hayes, William	18	Aug. 2, '62	Deserted Dec. 16, '62.
Hayward, William G.	18	Aug. 1, '62	Died Andersonville Sept. 11, '64.
Hazlehurst, Edwin	13	Jan. 28, '62	Discharged dis. May 20, '62.
Healey, Edward	14	July 16, '62	Discharged dis. Nov. 25, '62.
Heath, Leonard	1 Art.	Jan. 18, '63	M. O. Sept. 25, '65.
Heath, Thomas	1 Art.	Aug. 29, '64	Deserted Aug. 9, '65.
Hempstead, Albert	18	Aug. 8, '62	M. O. June 27, '64.
Hempstead, Henry	2	May 7, '61	M. O. Aug. 7, '61.
Henderson, Andrew	1 Art.	Feb. 26, '62	Deserter from 2d N. Y. Art.
Hennessey, Thomas J.	18	July 31, '62	M. O. June 27, '65.
Henney, George	20	Jan. 21, '64	Deserted April 22, '64.
Hernandez, John	Cav.	Jan. 13, '64	Deserted Jan. 21, '64.
Herrick, James	5	July 22, '61	Discharged dis. Jan. 6, '63.
Hickey, John *	9	May 24, '62	M. O. Aug. 3, '65.

Name and Rank.	Regiment.	Enlistment.	Remarks.
Hickey, Patrick.........	13	Jan. 28, '62	Deserted March 17, '62.
Hicks, James W	18	July 30, '62	Died Martinsburg Apr. 13, '64.
Higgins, James D........	2	May 7, '61	2 Lt. 18. Hon. dis. Oct. 27, '64.
Highey, Patrick.........	21	Aug. 29, '62	M. O. June 16, '65.
Hill, Edwin.............	26	Aug. 30, '62	M. O. Aug. 17, '63.
Hill, Elisha D..........	18	July 21, '62	M. O. June 27, '65.
Hill, Jahleel B..........	27	Sept. 25, '62	2 Art. Deserted Aug. 10, '65.
Hilliard, William C., Sgt.	18	July 14, '62	Discharged Dec. 3, '64.
Hills, Herman..........	18	Aug. 8, '62	Deserted Aug. 30, '62.
Hinckley, Edwin F......	Cav.	Oct. 26, '61	Discharged dis. Nov. 3, '62.
Hislop, James..........	21	Aug. 21, '62	M. O. June 16, '65.
Hoey, John............	Cav.	Jan. 12, '64	M. O. Aug. 2, '65.
Hoey, William.........	Cav.	Jan. 12, '64	M. O. Aug. 2, '65.
Hogan, James..........	20	Aug. 15, '62	5. Deserted on way to Regiment
Holmes, Joseph........	Cav.	Oct. 26, '61	Discharged dis. Nov. 3, '62.
Holmes, Joseph W.....	1 Art.	Feb. 27, '62	Deserted March 14, '62.
Holwell, John C	11	Nov. 23, '61	Killed Antietam Sept. 17, '62.
Hotchkiss, Edwin O,...	26	Aug. 30, '62	M. O. Aug. 17, '63.
Hovey, Henry, C. Sgt...	18	Aug. 4, '62	M. O. June 27, '65.
Howard, Francis........	2 Art.	Jan. 20, '64	M. O. Sept. 18, '65.
Howard, Solomon M., Sgt.	29	Jan. 2, '64	M. O. Oct. 24, '65.
Howard, William H.....	18	Aug. 14, '62	M. O. June 27, '65.
Howell, Abbott.........	30	Jan. 4, '64	Died July 61, 65.
Hughes, Asa L.........	2	May 7, '62	14. Disch'd dis. Dec. 15, '62.
Hull, Henry H..........	14	May 27, '62	Discharged dis. Feb. 15, '65.
Huntington, C. L. F.....	3	May 11, '61	M. O. Aug. 11, '61.
Huntington, Daniel.....	26	Sept. 11, '62	M. O. Aug. 17, '65.
Huntington, George F...	14	July 5, '62	V. R C. Jan. 15, '64.
Huntington, Thomas D..	8	Sept. 21, '61	Died Sept. 29, '61.
Huntoon, Samuel, Capt..	26	Aug. 26, '62	M. O. Aug. 17, '63.
Hutchins, Lyman.......	11	Oct. 25, '61	Discharged dis. May 18, '62.
Hutchins, William......	11	Nov. 14, '61	Died June 14, '62.
Hyatt, Isaac B..........	17	Jan. 15, '64	M. O. July 19, '65.
Hyde, John P..........	18	July 12, '62	M. O. June 27, 65.
Hyland, John *.........	9	Nov. 25, '61	M. O. Aug. 3, '65.
Irons, Thomas.........	14	June 12, '62	M. O. May 31, '65.
Ittell, George, Corp.*...	6	Sept. 6, '61	Deserted Feb. 27, '64.
Jacobs, Hervey F., 2 Lt..	26	Aug. 29, '62	Died Port Hudson July 5, '63.
Jaques, Benjamin F.....	2	May 7, '61	Corp. 18. M. O. June 27, '65.
Jaques, David D.*.....	13	Jan. 28, '62	M. O. Apr. 25, '66.
Jaques, William *.......	9	Nov. 18, '61	M. O. Aug. 3, '65.
Jennings, John B., Corp..	2	Apr. 22, '61	Captured July 21, '61.
Jewell, William C	18	Aug. 1, '62	Discharged dis. March 28, '63.
Jewett, Eleazar	26	Aug. 30, '62	M. O. Aug. 12, '63.
Jewett, Joseph H.......	2	May 7, '61	Adj. 8. M. O. Dec. 12, '65.
Jewett, Lee L..........	26	Aug. 25, '62	Discharged dis, May 8, '63.
Jillson, George W... ...	3	May 11, '61	M. O. Aug. 11, '61.
Johnson, Abel *........	13	Dec. 22, '61	M. O. Apr. 25, '66.
Johnson, Charles H.....	29	Jan. 2, '64	M. O. Oct. 24, '65.
Johnson, D. H.........	18	July 29, '62	M. O. June 27, '65.
Johnson, Irvin *........	1 Art.	Feb. 26, '62	M. O. Sept. 25, '65.

GENERAL MUSTER ROLL OF ALL NORWICH SOLDIERS. 363

Name and Rank.	Regiment.	Enlistment.	Remarks.
Johnson, John W	9	Oct. 21, '61	Deserted Nov. 18, '61.
Johnson, Lovell	11	Jan. 25, '64	M. O. June 19, '65.
Johnson, Marquis L	13	Jan. 28, '62	Discharged dis. July 29, '62.
Johnson, Robert *	2	May 7, '61	Sgt. 9. M. O. Aug. 3, '65.
Johnson, Samuel *	9	Oct. 17, '61	M. O. Aug. 3, '65.
Johnson, Stephen T.	26	Aug. 28, '62	Died Aug. 3, '63.
Johnson, William	9	Jan. 12, '64	M. O. Aug. 3, '65.
Jones, Frank J., 2 *Lt.*	1 Art.	Mar. 13, '62	Pro. Lt., resigned July 27, '63.
Kampf, George	1 Art.	Apr. 8, '62	Hon. discharged April 8, '65.
Kampf, Herman	26	Aug. 30, '62	M. O. Aug. 17, '63.
Kane, J. Hammond	1 Cav.	Jan. 4, '64	M. O. Aug. 2, '65.
Keables, Amos L., *Sgt.*	8	Sept. 21, '61	Pro. 2 Lt. Disch. May 15, '65.
Keables, Charles F.	18	Aug. 6, '62	Tr. V. R. C. M. O. Aug. 17,'65.
Keables, N. Armand	3	May 11, '61	26. M. O. Aug. 17, '65.
Keane, Michael *	9	May 22, '62	Deserted May 20, '64.
Keech, Charles	2 Art.	Jan. 21, '64	M. O. Jan. 13, '65.
Keeler, George W	18	Aug. 8, '62	M. O. June 29, '65.
Keeler, John M	3	May 11, '61	M. O. Aug. 11, '61.
Keeler, Thomas	2 Art.	Jan. 4, '64	Killed Ft. Fisher Mar. 26, '65.
Kehr, Jacob *	13	Jan. 28, '62	M. O. April 25, '66.
Keigwin, Daniel	18	Dec. 19, '63	M. O. June 27, '65.
Kelly, Andrew J	18	Aug. 2, '62	M. O. June 27, '65.
Kelly, Henry	8	Sept. 21, '61	Discharged Feb. 26, '64.
Kelly, James A	13	Feb. 1, '62	Hon. discharged Jan. 6, '65.
Kelly, John	21	July 31, '62	Deserted Sept. 19, '62.
Kelly, Michael	8	July 15, '64	Deserted Aug. 20, '65.
Kelly, Thomas	2 Art.	Jan. 22, '64	Deserted Feb. 3, '64.
Keneley, James	10	Jan. 19, '64	Killed Petersburg April 2, '65.
Kenney, Charles L	26	Sept. 1, '62	M. O. Aug. 17, '63.
Kenney, Ralph	26	Sept. 1, '62	M. O. Aug. 17, '63.
Kepler, Sebast. B., *Corp.*	18	Aug. 12, '62	M. O. June 27, '65.
Kerley, John	9	Nov. 25, '61	Died on transport July 24, '62.
Kerr, Francis	13	Jan. 22, '62	Discharged dis. Nov. 23, '63.
Kerr, John	18	July 23, '62	V. R. C. M. O. May 1, '64.
Kerr, Robert	2	May 7, '61	Pro. 2 Lt. 18. M.O. June 27,'65.
Kerr, Robert *	9	Oct. 22, '62	Q. M. Sgt. M. O. Aug. 3, '65.
Kerrigan, Thomas	26	Aug. 29, '62	M. O. Aug. 17, '63.
Kies, David B	11	Jan. 25, '64	M. O. Dec. 21, '65.
Kimball, James	26	Aug. 29, '62	M. O. Aug. 17, '63.
Kimball, John	26	Aug. 30, '62	M. O. Aug. 17, '63.
King, David	14	July 13, '63	Transf. 2 Art. May 31, '65.
Kingsley, Jared L	18	Aug. 4, '62	M. O. June 27, '65.
Kingsley, Willet W.*	8	Oct. 5, '61	M. O. Dec. 12, '65.
Kingston, Elias, Jr	2	May 7, '61	M. O. Aug. 7, '61.
Kinney, Albert B.*	7	Sept. 5, '61	M. O. July 20, '65.
Kinney, William H	18	Aug. 12, '62	M. O. June 27, '65.
Kirby, John	26	Sept. 1, '62	M. O. Aug. 17, '63.
Klein, John	Cav.	Jan. 13, '64	M. O. Oct. 10, '65.
Knapp, Samuel R., *Capt.*	18	Aug. 21, '62	Resigned June 6, '63.
Knox, Joseph W	Cav.	Jan. 12, '64	M. O. Aug. 2, '65.
Kohler, William S	2 Art.	Jan. 29, '64	Deserted Feb. 10, '64.

Name and Rank.	Regiment.	Enlistment.	Remarks.
Kraus, Adam	18	Aug. 6, '62	M. O. June 27, '65.
Krepps, James	15	Dec. 20, '64	7. M. O. Aug. 14, '65.
Lacy, David	2 Art.	Jan. 23, '64	Killed Cold Harbor June 1, '64.
Ladd, Albert W	1 Art.	Jan. 4, '64	Disch. dis, April 6, '64.
Ladd, Amos R	2	May 7, '61	Adj. 73 U. S. C. T.
Ladd, Daniel	18	July 24, '62	M. O. June 27, '65.
Laferty, James	18	Aug. 11, '62	M. O. June 23, '65.
Laird, Daniel	13	Feb. 11, '62	Killed in action Sept. 19, '64.
Laird, John	18	Aug. 8, '62	M. O. June 27, '65.
Lamb, George W., *Corp.*	26	Aug. 26, '62	M. O. Aug. 17, '63.
Lampheare, Charles H.	8	Oct. 7, '61	Deserted Oct. 31, 61.
Lampheare, Chauncey G.	26	Aug. 30, '62	M. O. Aug. 17, '63.
Lampheare, James M.*	10	Oct. 5, '61	Deserted Aug. 16, '65.
Lamphere, Calvin J	14	July 20, '63	Transf. 2 Art. May 31, '65.
Lampson, Charles E	2 Art.	Jan. 20, '64	M. O. Aug. 18, '65.
Lane, Joseph M	26	Sept. 5, '62	M. O. Aug. 17, '63.
Lapierre, H. H	26	Aug. 28, '62	Transf Sig. Corps.
Lasthins, August	26	Oct. 13, '62	Discharged dis. Feb. 18, '63.
Latham, Albert	18	July 25 '62	Lt. 30. M. O. Nov. 7, 65.
Latham, Ira C	21	Jan. 13, '64	Tr. 10. M. O. Aug. 25, '65.
Lathrop, Dewitt C., *Surg.*	8	Oct. 5, '61	Died, April 18, '62.
Lathrop, Erastus D	2	May 7, '61	1 Art. Dis. dis. Dec. 24, '62
Lathrop, Joseph O	18	Aug. 6, '62	M. O. June 27, '65.
Laughlin, Patrick	14	July 25, '63	Deserted Feb. 5, '64.
Lawler, Joseph H., *Corp.*	9	Oct. 30, '61	Pro. Lt. M. O. Aug. 3, '65.
Lawler, Thomas C., *Corp.*	2	May 7, '61	Lt. 9. Resigned Feb. 25, '62.
Leach, Edwin T	18	Aug. 7, '62	Lt. 31 U. S. C. T. Dis. May 9,
Leahy, Edward *	9	May 5, '62	Deserted June 5, '64. ['64.
Learned, Bela P., 2 *Lt.*	1 Art.	Mar. 12, '62	Maj. by bvt. Pro. Capt. Sept.
Leary, James*	9	Nov. 25, '61	M. O. Aug. 3, 65. [25, '65.
Lee, Charles C	18	Dec. 24, '63	M O. June 27, '65.
Lee, J. Hamilton, *A. Surg.*	21	Aug. 22, '62	Surg. Discharged Oct. 31, '64.
Lee, Samuel J., *Sgt.*	18	Aug. 2, '62	M. O. June 27, '65.
Leman, Theodore	6	Sept. 6, '61	Hon. discharged Sept. 11, '64.
Leonard, Isaac N	3	May 11, '61	Sgt. 26. Hon. dis, Aug. 17, '63.
Leonard, M. L	18	July 25, '62	2 Lt. 29. M. O. Oct. 24, '65.
Leruscher, William	6	Sept. 6, '61	Hon. discharged Sept. 12, '64.
Lester, Henry W., *Corp.*	2	May 7, '61	Discharged dis. June 26, '61.
Lewis, Charles	8	Feb. 20, '64	Deserted March 15, '64.
Lewis, James S	26	Aug. 30, '62	Deserted Nov. 24, '62
Levison, Moritz*	1 Art.	Mar. 1, '62	Deserted April 16, '64.
Lilley, John, *Sgt.*	18	Aug. 14, '62	Pro. Capt. M. O. June 27, '65.
Lillibridge, Clark	2	May 7, '61	M. O. Aug. 7, '61.
Lillibridge, M. M	2 Art.	Dec. 30, '63	Discharged dis. June 13, '65.
Lindsley, Adam H., *Lt.*	18	Aug. 8, '62	Hon. discharged, April 17, '65.
Livingston, F. D., *Corp.*	6	July 22, '61	Discharged dis. Jan. 10, '62.
Lloyd, Patrick	14	July 15, '62	Died of wounds May 11, '64.
Loomis, Charles A.*	2	May 7, '61	Sgt. 13. Deserted Aug. 30, '62.
Loomis, Ezra M	11	Dec. 3, '61	Died of wounds (Antietam) Sept. 19, 62.
Loomis, George W. *Corp.*	18	July 26, '62	M. O. June 27, '65.

GENERAL MUSTER ROLL OF ALL NORWICH SOLDIERS. 365

Name and Rank.	Regiment.	Enlistment.	Remarks.
Loomis, Henry N.	21	Aug. 20, '62	Died Aug. 21, '64.
Loomis, James W.	18	Aug. 14, '62	Discharged Nov. 1, '64.
Loomis, John W.	2	May 7, '61	M. O. Aug. 7, '61.
Long, John	18	July 15, '62	M. O. June 27, '65.
Lovering, Fred. E.	Cav.	Jan. 5, '64	M. O. Aug. 2, '65.
Lowrey, Joshua	8	Oct. 7, '61	Rejected Nov. 2, '61.
Lumis, T. J.	18	Aug. 5, '62	M. O. June 27, '65.
Lydon, James	9	Oct. 17, '61	Discharged Oct. 26, '64.
Lynch, Charles	18	Aug. 6, '62	M. O. June 27, '65.
Lynch, Henry	2 Art.	Jan. 13, '64	Died of wounds Oct. 31, '64.
Lynch, James	2 Art.	Jan. 30, '64	Deserted March 8, '64.
Lyon, George N.	1 Art.	Jan. 4, '64	M. O. Sept. 25, '65.
Lyon, Nelson A.	21	Aug. 22, '62	M. O. June 16, '65.
Maguire, Patrick*	9	Nov. 26, '62	M. O. Aug. 3, '65.
Mahony, William	1 Art.	Mar. 5, '62	Deserted March 15, 62.
Manion, Thomas	Cav.	Dec. 30, '63	M. O. Aug. 2, '65.
Manning, David W.	2 Art.	Jan. 27, '64	Discharged dis. July 15, '65.
Manning, Ed. P., C. Sgt.	26	Aug. 30, '62	2 Lt. Died Aug. 17, '63.
Manning, Lem. A.	18	July 29, '62	M. O. June 27, '65.
Maples, C. H., Qr. M. Sgt.	26	Aug. 27, '62	M. O. Aug. 17, '63.
Maples, James S.	2	May 7, '61	U. S. C. T.
Maples, Wm. L.	3	May 11, '61	M. O. Aug. 11, '61.
Marks, Michael	9	Nov. 25, '61	Hon. discharged Oct. 26, '64.
Maro, Patrick	10	Oct. 1, '61	Killed Newbern March 14, '62.
Marrarty, John	8	Sept. 21, '61	V. R. C.
Marsh, F. B.	7	Sept. 5, '61	Discharged dis. Jan. 3, '62.
Marshall, Geo. B.	3	May 11, '61	Corp. 1S, M. O. June 27, '65.
Marshall, Hamlet J.	26	Sept. 2, '62	Disch. July 24, '63.
Marshall, John	18	Aug. 12, '62	M. O. June 23, '65.
Marshall, William S.	Cav.	Dec. 22, '63	M. O. June 3, '65.
Marshall, Wilson C.	18	July 23, '62	M. O. June 27, '65.
Martin, Islay B.	18	Aug. 5, '62	Died w'ds W'chester July 2, '63.
Martin, Jno. W.	18	July 17, '62	M. O. June 27, '65.
Martin, Patrick	13	Jan. 22, '62	Hon. discharged Jan. 6, '65.
Mason, John	Cav.	Nov. 19, '64	M. O. Aug. 2.
Massey, James	18	July 15, '62	Died Florence S. C. Jan. 7, '65
Matson, George	29	Dec. 4, '64	M. O. Oct. 24, '65.
Maurer, Richard	1 Art.	Jan. 15, '64	M. O. Sept. 25, '65.
Maynard, Roswell E.	26	Aug. 29, '62	M. O. Aug. 17, '63.
McAllister, Ronald	11	Nov. 12, '61	Discharged dis. Jan. 10, '63.
McAllister, Ronald, Jr.	11	Oct. 25, '61	Killed Cold H'bor June 3, '64.
McCall, A. Dwight, Lt.	12	Jan. 1, '62	M. O. Nov. 21, '64.
McCall, John, S.t.	8	Sept. 21, '61	Capt. K'd F't Darl'g May 16, '64.
McCall, Gideon, Corp.	30	Jan. 25, '64	Died of wounds Oct. 8, '64.
McCarty Michael	14	Aug. 5, '63	Discharged Dec. 6, '63.
McCarty, Thomas	2 Art.	Feb. 1, '64	Deserted April 14, '64.
McCaulay, Thomas	2 Art.	Jan. 21, '64	Deserted July 14, '64.
McClure, George	26	Aug. 30, '62	M. O. Aug. 17, '63.
McClure, John	18	July 19, '62	M. O. June 27, '65.
McCool, John	2 Art.	Jan. 21, '64	Deserted Aug. 28, '64.
McCora, James J., 2 Lt.	2	May 7, '61	Capt. 13, M. O. Jan. 6, '65.

24

Name and Rank.	Regiment.	Enlistment.	Remarks.
McCoy, George	2 Art.	Jan. 23, '64	V. R. C. M. O. Sept. 22, '65.
McCracken, Henry	Cav.	Dec. 16, '63	M. O. Aug. 2, '65.
McCracken, James	18	Aug. 8, '62	Killed Winchester June 15, '63.
McCusker, Hugh	18	Aug. 4, '62	M. O. June 27, '65.
McCusker, John*	18	July 25, '62	M. O. June 26, '65.
McDavid, George	18	July 19, '62	Discharged dis. March 1, '63.
McDavid, James S.	Cav.	Jan. 4, '64	Died Andsonville, Aug. 21, '64.
McDonald, John*	9	May 27, '62	Died May 2, '65.
McDonald, John	14	June 3, '62	M. O. June 29, '65.
McDonnell, Thomas	9	Jan. 17, '64	Deserted Jan. 10, '65.
McGarry, Andrew	2	May 7, '61	Corp. 9. Disch. dis. Oct. 16, '62.
McGlone, James	1 Art.	Feb. 26, '62	Deserted March 15, '62.
McGovern, Michael	14	July 15, '62	Deserted Aug. 25, '62.
McGovern, Thomas*	9	Nov. 25, '61	Deserted June 10, '64.
McGrath, John	18	Jan. 6, '64	Deserted Nov. 13, '64.
McGuigan, Frank	9	Sept. 27, '61	Hon. discharged Oct. 26, '64.
McKay, James*	5	July 22, '61	M. O. July 19, '65.
McKeag, Francis, Sgt.	2	May 7, '61	2 Lt. 18. M. O. June 27, '65.
McKee, James	2	May 7, '61	Corp. 18. M. O. June 27, '65.
McKenna, John,* Corp.	9	Oct. 30, '61	M. O. Aug. 3, '65.
McKenna, John	21	Aug. 1, '62	Deserted March 17, '63.
McKenna, Peter	21	Aug. 11, '62	Discharged dis. Feb. 18, '63.
McKnight, William	12	Dec. 3, '61	Died Aug. 18, '63.
McLaughlin, Thomas	5	July 22, '61	Deserted July 1, '63.
McLeland, George	10	Oct. 1, '61	Discharged dis. Oct. 16, '62.
McMahon, Gilbert	2 Art.	Dec. 30, '63	Discharged dis. June 4, '65.
McMahon, Thomas	18	Nov. 16, '63	Killed Piedmont June 5, '64.
McNamara, John*	9	May 20, '62	M. O. Aug. 3, '65.
McNamara, Patrick	18	Jan. 1, '64	Died Jan. 19, '65.
McNeil, John	26	Aug. 30, '62	M. O. Aug. 17, '63.
McSorly, John	9	Oct. 12, '61	Died April 18, '63.
McVay, Francis	14	Aug. 13, '62	M. O. May 31, '65.
McVay, James	14	July 14, '62	Died Sept. 9, '62.
McVay, Michael	14	July 5, '62	M. O. May 31, '65.
McWhirr, John F.	18	Aug. 4, '62	M. O. June 27, '65.
Meany, John	9	Sept. 27, '61	Died Nov. 12, '62.
Meech, Stephen B., Adj.	26	Aug. 30, '62	M. O. Aug. 17, '63.
Meehan, Peter*	9	Oct. 12, '61	Deserted May 20, '65.
Meehan, William*	9	May 10, '62	M. O. Aug. 3, '65.
Meisser, Charles	6	Sept. 6, '61	Killed Morris Isl'd July 18, '63.
Meldrum, John*	9	May 28, '62	Died April 8, '64.
Meledy, Michael, Sgt.	26	Aug. 29, '62	M. O. Aug. 17, '63.
Mell, Augustus*	5	July 22, '61	M. O. June 14, '65.
Merwin, S. T. C.	1	April 22, '61	Capt. 18. M. O. June 27, '65.
Metcalf, John G.	3	May 11, '61	M. O. Aug. 11, '61.
Meyer, Adolph L.	6	Sept. 6, '61	11. M. O. Dec. 21, '65.
Miller, Henry C.	2	May 7, '61	Sgt. 14. Disch. dis. Nov. 17, '62.
Miller, Jacob W.			Killed Spotsylva'a May 18, '64.
Minard, Enos G.	2	May 7, '61	M. O. Aug. 7, '61.
Miner, Charles H., jr.	18	Aug. 5, '62	M. O. June 27, '65.
Miner, William P., 2 Lt.	13	Feb. 18, '62	Lt. M. O. July 16, '64.

GENERAL MUSTER ROLL OF ALL NORWICH SOLDIERS. 367

Name and Rank.	Regiment.	Enlistment.	Remarks.
Mitchell, Alfred, *Capt.*	13	Feb. 18, '62	Resigned March 11, '64.
Moan, Owen*	1 Art.	March 1, '62	M. O. Sept. 25, '65.
Moffett, Albert	Cav.	Jan. 4, '64	Killed Winch'ter, Sept. 19, '64.
Moore, Allen L., *Sgt.*	18	Aug. 13, '62	M. O. June 27, '65.
Moore, James R., *Sgt.*	3	May 11, '61	Capt. S. Discharged May 30,'65.
Moore, John	2 Art.	Jan. 20, '64	Transf. U. S. N.
Moore, Michael	26	Sept. 9, '62	M. O. Aug. 17, '63.
Moningham, James	9	Sept. 27, '61	Died July 21, '61.
Monroe, Austin G., *Sgt.*	2	May 7, '61	Sgt. 18. M. O. June 27, '65.
Monroe, Charles H.	29	Jan. 2, '64	Died Jan. 11, '63.
Morgan, Charles D., *Corp.*	26	Aug. 26, '62	M. O. Aug. 17, 63.
Morris, John	Cav.	Jan. 23, '64	Deserted Feb. 2, '64.
Morris, Patrick	20	Aug. 30, '64	Deserted while on way to Regt.
Morris, Thomas	2 Art.	Jan. 16, '64	M. O. Aug. 18, '65.
Morris, William C.	2 Art.	Jan. 20, '64	M. O. Sept. 18, '65.
Morrison, John H.	2	May 7, '61	Capt. 18. Dismissed Sept. 1,'64.
Morrow, George	1 Art.	Jan. 15, '64	M. O. Sept. 25, '65.
Morrow, Joseph, *Sgt.*	9	Oct. 30, '61	Hon. discharged Oct. 26, '64.
Mossman, Alexander	18	July 19, '62	M. O. June 27, '65.
Mott, Oramel M.*	11	Oct. 25, '61	M. O. Dec. 21, '65.
Mott, Willard L.	7	Sept. 5, '61	Transf. Sig. Corps Feb. 29,'63.
Mowry, Bernard R. O.	18	Aug. 7, '62	Deserted Aug. 1, '63.
Mouch, Peter	26	Oct. 24, '62	M O. Aug. 17, '63.
Moush, Adolph*	5	July 22, '61	M. O. July 19, '65.
Mulcaley, Michael	26	Sept. 1, '62	M. O. Aug. 17, '63.
Mulcaley, Thomas	26	Sept. 1, '62	M. O. Aug. 17, '63.
Mulligan, Peter	26	Oct. 30, '62	M. O. Aug. 17, '63.
Mumford, Henry	29	Dec. 4, '63	M. O. Oct. 24, '65.
Munroe, John C.*	5	July 22, '61	M. O. July 19, '65.
Murphy, Dennis	21	Aug. 13, '62	Died March 12, '64.
Murphy, Frank E.	18	July 16, '62	M. O. June 27, '65.
Murphy, James	21	Aug. 13, '62	M O. June 16, '65.
Murphy, James	9	Oct. 4, '61	Died Aug. 16, '62.
Murphy, Jeremiah*	9	Sept. 2, '61	M. O. Sept. 7, '65.
Murphy, John	5	Aug. 27, '63	Deserted Oct. 2, '63.
Murphy, Orlando C.	26	Aug. 27, '62	M. O. Aug. 17, '63.
Murphy, Patrick	2 Art.	Jan. 23, '64	M. O. Aug. 7, '65.
Murphy, Wm. M., *Corp.*	8	Sept. 21, '61	Discharged dis. May 5, '63.
Murray, Charles A.	2	May 7, '61	2 Lt. 18. M. O. June 27, '65.
Murthagh, Patrick	21	July 31, '62	M. O. June 16, '65.
Musharue, Henry	29	Aug. 26, '64	M. O. Oct. 24, '65.
Mussel, Christian	Cav.	Jan. 4, '64	M. O. Aug. 2, '65.
Muzzy, Ben. H.	18	July 31, '62	M. O. May 20, '65.
Muzzy, Harvey L.	18	July 30, '62	M. O. June 10, '65.
Muzzy, Walter H.	18	Aug. 12, '62	M. O. June 27, '65.
Nash, Eugene S.*	2	May 7, '61	Corp. 13. Des. Aug. 30, '64.
Neff, A. Martin	26	Aug. 27, '62	M. O. Aug. 17, '63.
Neill, Henry P.	18	July 28, '62	M. O. June 27, '65.
Nelson, Sam.	2 Art.	Jan. 21, '64	Transf. U. S. N., April 14, '64.
Nelson, William F.	14	July 25, '63	Deserted Aug. 17, '63.
Newman, Thomas	26	Sept. 8, '62	M. O. Aug. 17, '63.

Name and Rank.	Regiment.	Enlistment.	Remarks.
Newton, Charles J.	14	July 23, '63	Transf. U. S. N. April 23, '64.
Nichols, Robert*	13	Dec. 30, '61	Deserted Aug. 30, '64.
Nicholson, Michael*	9	May 22, '62	Deserted May 20, '64.
Nickels, James R., Sgt.	14	May 29, '62	Capt. Died of w'ds Feb. 20,'65.
Nickerson, Jos. H. Sgt.	11	Oct. 25, '61	Capt. Disch. dis. Oct. 12, '64.
Nickerson, Paris R., Corp.	3	May 11, '61	M. O. Aug. 11, '61.
Nickle, Arthur	8	Oct. 2, '61.	Discharged dis. Feb. 28, '63.
Norris, John H., Lt.	11	Nov. 27, '61	Resigned April 5, '62.
Northrop, George	8	Sept. 25, '61	Discharged dis. May 10, '62.
Norton, George B.	26	Aug. 29, '62	M. O. Aug. 17, '63.
Noyes, Caleb H.	26	Aug. 30, '62	M. O. Aug. 17, '63.
Noyes, Charles C.	18	Aug. 11, '62	Killed Winch'ster June 15, '64.
Noyes, John D.	10	Oct. 1, '61	Hon. discharged Oct. 7, '64.
O'Brien, Edward	2 Art.	Jan. 30, '64	M. O. Aug. 18, '65.
O'Conner, Cornelius	8	Sept. 23, '61	Hon. discharged Sept. 20, '64.
O'Donnell, George	2	May 7, '61	M. O. Aug. 7, '61.
O'Donnell, Matthew	21	Aug. 9, '62	M. O. June 16, '65.
O'Donnell, Olney	14	July 7, '62	Discharged dis. Jan. 12, '63.
O'Neil, David	26	Aug. 30, '62	Cav. M. O. Aug. 2, '65.
O'Neil, James*	9	May 21, '61	M. O. Aug. 3, '65.
O'Neil, John	14	July 7, '62	M. O. May 31, '65.
Osborne, Charles*	7	Sept. 5, '61	M. O. July 20, '65.
Osborne, James	7	Sept. 5, '61	Hon. discharged Sept. 12, '65.
Otis, Josiah L. D.	14	July 25, '62	Died w'ds F'burg, Feb. 10, '63.
Page, James F.	Cav.	Jan. 5, '64	M. O. Aug. 2, '65.
Palmer, Almon B.	18	Aug. 18, '62	M. O. June 27, '65.
Palmer, Andrew	18	July 25, '62	M. O. June 27, '65.
Palmer, Fred. A., Lt.	18	July 12, '62	Capt. Discharged May 28, '64.
Palmer, Julius	18	Aug. 4, '62	M. O. June 27, '65.
Palmer, Lewis O.	7	Sept. 5, '61	Transf. Inv. Corps.
Palmer, Orin V.	18	Jan. 14, '64	M. O. June 27, '65.
Palmer, Roswell	18	Aug. 6, '62	M. O. June 27, '65.
Parker, Henry W.	2 Art.	Jan. 21, '64	U. S. N. April 14, '64.
Parker, Joseph M.	2	May 7, '61	Capt. 32 U. S. C.
Parker, Timothy	18	July 23, '62	M. O. June 27, '65.
Parkerson, James	26	Aug. 28, '62	Died w'ds Pt. Hud. June 1, '63.
Parkinson, George	18	July 17, '62	M. O. June 27, '65.
Parkus, Simon, Sgt.	30	Jan. 18, '64	M. O. Nov. 7, '65.
Parrish, William W.	1 Art.	May 22, '61	Hon. discharged May 26, '64.
Patten, Charles*	13	Jan. 11, '62	M. O. April 25, '66.
Payne, Burton H.	Cav.	Jan. 22, '64	M. O. Jan. 10, 65.
Payne, Ichabod S.	8	Sept. 27, '61	M. O. April 25, '66.
Peale, Henry, Capt.	2	May 7, '61	Lt. Col. 18. M. O. June 27, '65.
Pearce, Martin	18	July 16, '62	M. O. June 27, '65.
Peck, Seth L.	26	Aug. 27, '62	M. O. Aug. 17, '63.
Peck, William H.,* Corp.	8	Sept. 21, '61	Lt. M. O. Dec. 12, '65.
Pendergrast, James*	9	Jan. 10, '63	Deserted May 20, '64.
Perkins, Chas. W.,* Corp.	9	Oct. 30, '61	M. O. Aug. 3, '65.
Perry, Hylon N.	18	Aug. 4, '62	M. O. June 27, '65.
Peter, William	18	July 28, '62	Deserted Aug. 30, '62.
Peters, Charles	29	Jan. 2, '64	Deserted March 7, '64.

GENERAL MUSTER ROLL OF ALL NORWICH SOLDIERS.

Name and Rank.	Regiment.	Enlistment.	Remarks.
Peters, William	6	Sept. 4, '61	Discharged dis. July 5, '63.
Peterson, John	2 Art.	Jan. 20, '64	U. S. N. April 14, '64.
Phillips, Benjamin F.	Cav.	Oct. 5, '63	Deserted Dec. 8, '63.
Phillips, Henry T.	Cav.	Nov. 18, '62	Capt. M. O. Aug. 2, '65.
Phillips, Thomas D.	Cav.	Jan. 5, '64	M. O. Aug. 2, '65.
Phinney, Elisha, A., Surg.	26	Nov. 1, '62	M. O. Aug. 17, '63.
Phinney, Henry E.	13	Jan. 7, '62	Hon. discharged June 6, '65.
Pierce, Thomas H.	1 Art.	Jan. 4, '64	M. O. Sept. 25, '65.
Pitcher, Abner D.	7	Sept. 5, '61	Discharged dis. May 8, '64.
Pitcher, Albert H.	14	July 23, '62	M. O. June 27, '65.
Pitcher, Frank W.	7	Sept. 5, '61	Hon. discharged Sept. 12, '64.
Pitcher, George	1 Art.	Aug. 1, '64	M. O. Sept. 25, '65.
Pitcher, George	18	Aug. 4, '62	M. O. June 27, '65.
Plunkett, Jos. D., C. Sgt.	21	July 31, '62	2 Lt. Discharged Dec. 20, '62.
Porter, Edgar	11	Jan. 14, '64	M. O. Dec. 21, '65.
Porter, Sabart M.	26	Aug. 30, '62	M. O. Aug. 17, '63.
Potter, Charles H.	9	Nov. 1, '61	Died August 10, '62.
Potter, Elisha R.	18	Aug. 8, '62	M. O. June 9, '65.
Potter, James	2	May 7, '61	M. O. Aug. 7, '61.
Potter, Mandeville A.	26	Aug. 30, '62	M. O. Aug. 17, '63.
Powers, Richard*	9	May 21, '61	M. O. Aug. 3, '65.
Price, Joseph H.	30	Jan. 15, '64	Deserted June 30, '64.
Price, Orrin M.*	13	Jan. 11, '62	M. O. April 25, '66.
Primus, Daniel	30	Feb. 15, '64	Deserted April 3, '64.
Purdy, William H.	1 Art.	Jan. 6, '64	M. O. Sept. 25, '65.
Ragan, James	2 Art.	Jan. 29, '64	M. O. Aug. 18, '65.
Ranger, Richard*	8	Sept. 21, '61	M. O. Dec. 12, '65.
Ransom, Henry A.	8	Sept. 21, '61	Discharged dis. Dec. 3, '62.
Rathbone, Oramel W.	Cav.	Dec. 8, '63	M. O. July 28, '65.
Reardon, Patrick	9	Oct. 12, '61	Discharged dis. Oct. 16, '62.
Reder, Karl	Cav.	Dec. 3, '63	Died of wounds July 29, '64.
Reed, Albert O.	26	Aug. 30, '62	M. O. Aug. 17, '63.
Reynolds, John T., *Corp.	13	Feb. 1, '62	M. O. Aug. 5, '65.
Reynolds, Samuel W.	18	July 14, '62	M. O. June 27, '65.
Reynolds, William	13	Jan. 30, '62	Hon. discharged Jan. 6, '65.
Richards, Charles J.	18	Aug. 2, '62	M. O. June 27, '65.
Richardson, James L.	Cav.	Jan. 19, '64	Adj. M. O. Aug. 2, '65.
Rider, James H.	30	Jan. 11, '64	Deserted October 8, '64.
Riely, Bernard*	9	May 31, '62	M. O. Aug. 3, '65.
Riley, John	2 Art.	Jan. 20, '64	M. O. Sept. 15, '65.
Ringroas, Michael	18	July 28, '62	Discharged Nov. 23, '63.
Ripley, George C., Lt.	14	Dec. 22, '62	A. D. C. M. O. Aug. 25, '65.
Ripley, James D.	18	July 17, '62	M. O. June 27, '65.
Ripley, Robert A., Lt.	13	Dec. 31, '62	Capt. M. O. Jan. 6, '65.
Roach, David	5	July 22, '61	Deserted June 7, '62.
Roath, Henry G.	26	Sept. 11, '62	Transf. Sig. Corps.
Roberts, George	2 Art.	Jan. 21, '64	U. S. N.
Robinson, Francis	14	July 23, '61	Discharged dis. March 2, '63.
Robinson, James A.	11	Oct. 24, '61	M. O. Dec. 21, '65.
Rockwell, Alfred P., Capt.	1 Bat.	Jan. 21, '61	Col. 6. M. O. Feb. 9, '65. B. G. V. Bvt.

Name and Rank.	Regiment.	Enlistment.	Remarks.
Rockwell, Jos. P., *Sgt. M.*	14	July 26, '62	Capt. June 27, '65.
Roden, James	26	Sept. 2, '62	M. O. Aug. 17, '63.
Roe, Edward*	9	May 24, '62	Killed Oct. 19, '64.
Rogers, Charles L.*	11	Oct. 25, '61	M. O. Dec. 21, '65.
Rogers, Eben H.	2	May 7, '61	M. O. Aug. 7, '61.
Rogers, E. P.	2	May 7, '61	Lt. 29. Resigned Aug. 3, '65.
Rogers, George W., *Lt.*	2	May 7, '61	Corp. 26. M. O. Aug. 17, '63.
Rogers, Horace E.	3	May 11, '61	7. Disch. dis. March 10, '63.
Rogers, Joab R., *Sgt.*	3	May 11, '61	Capt. Cav. M. O. Feb. 2, '65.
Ross, Daniel V.	21	Aug. 18, '62	M. O. June 2, '65.
Ross, Enos C.	26	Aug. 30, '62	M. O. Aug. 17, '63.
Ross, John	2 Art.	Jan. 20, '64	Deserted Feb. 7, '64.
Ross, William J., *Corp.*	14	July 23, '62	Maj. 29. M. O. Oct. 24, '65.
Rouse, Charles W., *Corp.*	11	Oct. 25, '61	Hon. discharged, Oct. 24, '64.
Rouse, James E.*	7	Sept. 5, '61	Hon. discharged, July 20, '65.
Rozenblatt, David	2	May 7, '61	Miss'g Bull Run July 21, '61.
Ruhl, August*	9	May 24, '62	M. O. Aug. 3, '65.
Ryan, James*	9	May 22, '62	M. O. Aug. 3, '65.
Ryan John O.	Cav.	Jan. 12, '64	Deserted Jan. 21, '64.
Ryan, Michael*	9	May 22, '62	M. O. Aug. 3, '65.
Ryder, Arthur F., *Corp.*	2	May 7, '61	Discharged dis. July 3, '61.
Sanders, David*	7	Sept. 5, '61	Discharged dis. Aug. 7, '65.
Sanders, Julius*	9	June 2, '62	Discharged dis. Aug. 1, '65.
Sanders, Ralph G.	18	Aug 2, '62	V. R. C. Jan. 15, '64.
Sandford, John	20	Sept. 1, '64	Deserted on way to Regiment.
Sawyer, Silas W., *Capt.*	9	Oct. 30, '61	Resigned Feb. 16, '64.
Schneider, Jacob	14	July 24, '62	Discharged dis. Aug. 31, '64.
Schneider, John	3	May 11, '61	M. O. Aug. 11, '61.
Schultz, Peter	2 Art.	Jan. 20, '64	
Scholfield, Henry M.	1	April 22, '61	11. D.w'ds Ant'm Sept.28, '62.
Scholfield, Le Grand.	18	July 17, '62	M. O. June 27, '65.
Scott, John	26	Aug. 30, '62	M. O. Aug. 17, '63.
Scott, Thomas, *Lt.*	2	May 7, '61	Capt. N. Y. Bat.
Selden, Joseph, *Lt. Col.*	26	Aug. 28, '62	M. O. Aug. 17, '63.
Semples, James W.	18	July 26, '62	M. O. June 27, '65.
Service, John	18	July 17, '62	M. O. June 27, '65.
Service, Thomas	18	Aug. 5, '62	M. O. June 27, '65.
Setchel, Charles F.*	18	Aug. 11, '62	M. O. June 27, '65.
Setchel, George C.	18	Aug. 2, '62	M. O. June 27, '65.
Sevin, Nathan D.	26	Aug. 25, '62	M. O. Aug. 17, '63.
Shaik, Frederick E.	3	May 11, '61	Lt. 14. Died w'ds May 6, '64.
Shaw, Bently, *Sgt.*	18	Aug. 4, '62	M. O. June 27, '65.
Shaw, Daniel	18	July 25, '62	M. O. June 27, '65.
Shaw, Jasper A. H., *Sgt.*	3	May 11, '61	M. O. Aug. 11, '61.
Shay, John	14	July 25, '63	Deserted Aug. 12, '63.
Shay, Michael	26	Sept. 18, '62	M. O. Aug. 17, '63.
Shea, James	26	Oct. 17, '62	M. O. Aug. 17, '63.
Shea, John	13	Jan. 22, '62	Died July 18, '63.
Shea, Michael	26	Aug. 28, '62	M. O. Aug. 17, '63.
Sheehan, David D.	9	Sept. 27, '61	Dropped fr. rolls Oct. 3, '64.
Shelden, George W.	1 Art.	May 22, '61	Hon. discharged, May 26, '64.

GENERAL MUSTER ROLL OF ALL NORWICH SOLDIERS. 371

Name and Rank.	Regiment.	Enlistment.	Remarks.
Sheppard, Charles, *Sgt*...	8	Sept 21, '61	2 Lt. Resigned Feb. 14, '63.
Sheppard, Willis D.....	5	Aug. 18, '63	Deserted July 1, '63.
Sherman, Horace W....	18	July 23, '62	M. O. June 27, '65.
Sherman, William M....	2	May 7, '61	Sgt. 26. Died w'ds Pt. H. June
Sherwood, Stephen	Cav.	Jan. 23, '64	M. O. June 10, '65. [2S, '63.
Shugrean, Charles.......	26	Aug. 28, '62	Deserted Dec. 11, '62.
Shumway, Millen.......	18	Aug. 9, '62	M. O. June 27, '65.
Simmons, John H.......	18	July 22, '62	M. O. June 27, '65.
Simons, Leonard........	14	June 9, '62	M. O. May 31, '65.
Simpson, James.........	Cav.	Jan. 23, '64	Deserted.
Simpson, John..........	9	Oct. 30, '61	Died Oct. 8, '62.
Sizer, Charles O........	26	Aug. 30, '62	M. O. Aug. 17, '63.
Smiley, John S.........	2	May 7, '61	M. O. Aug. 7, '61.
Smiley, Lyman.........	12	Dec. 19, '61	Discharged dis. Dec. 11, '62.
Smith, Augustus F.....	13	Jan. 11, '62	26. M. O. Aug. 17, '63.
Smith, Bradford W.....	7	Sept. 5, '61	Discharged dis. March 3, '63.
Smith, Daniel..........	30	Jan. 6, '64	M. O. Nov. 7, '65.
Smith, Edward	2	May 7, '61	M. O. Aug. 7, '61.
Smith, Edward	30	Jan. 20,'64	M. O. Nov. 7, '65.
Smith, George..........	Cav.	Jan. 22, '64	M. O. Aug. 2, '65.
Smith, George E........	2	May, 7, '61	M. O. Aug. 7, '61.
Smith, George S........	Cav.	June 27, '63	M. O. Aug. 2, '65.
Smith, George W.......	7	Sept. 5, '61	Discharged dis. Jan. 3, '62.
Smith, James...........	18	Aug. 6, '62	M. O. June 27, '65.
Smith, John............	2 Art.	Jan. 22, '64	Deserted Feb. 19, '64.
Smith, John, *Corp*......	8	Sept. 21, '61	Discharged Sept. 20. '64.
Smith, John............	20	Sept. 1, '64	Deserted on way to Regiment.
Smith, John A..........	30	Jan. 6, '64	M. O. Nov. 7, '65.
Smith, Joseph	14	July 29, '64	Transf. 2 Art.
Smith, Obed G.........	26	Sept. 1, '62	M. O. Aug. 17, '63.
Smith, Stephen A.......	30	Jan. 25, '64	Died Feb. 23, '64.
Smith, Theodore E......	Cav.	Dec. 15, '63	M. O. Aug. 2, '65.
Smith, Thomas H.......	2	May 7, '61	M. O. Aug. 7, '61.
Smith, William	2 Art.	Jan. 19, '64	Discharged dis. June 19, '65.
Smith, William R.......	2	May 7, '61	M. O. Aug. 7, '61.
Snow, Edward A.......	2 Art.	Feb. 3, '64	M. O. Aug. 18, '65.
Snow, Edwin E.........	21	Aug. 5, '62	Discharged Jan. 29, '63.
Snow, Henry I.........	2	May 7, '61	Discharged.
Snyder, Leander........	2 Art.	Jan. 27, '64	M. O. Nov. 25, '65.
Somerlott, Henry, *Sgt*...	29	Jan. 7, '64	M. O. Oct. 24. '65.
Souter, James	11	Oct. 25, '61	Killed Cold Har. June 3. '64.
Spafford, L. E. Forrest..	8	Sept. 21, '61	Sgt. M. Hon. dis. Sept. 20, '64.
Spalding, Charles W., *Lt.*	3	May 11, '61	Resigned May 20. '61.
Spalding, J. L., *Sgt. Maj.*	1	April 23 '61	Adj. 29, Resigned Aug. 21, '65.
Spalding, William H....	Cav.	Jan. 5, '64	Discharged dis. June 30, '65.
Spencer, Charles C.....	21	Aug. 7, '62	V. R. C. M. O. Sept. 4, '65.
Spencer, Cyrus R.......	21	Aug. 20, '62	Discharged dis. April 8, '64.
Spencer, Orin N........	18	July 30, '62	M. O. June 27, '65.
Spencer, Robert R......	2	May 7, '61	M. O. Aug. 7, '61.
Spencer, Stephen H.....	18	July 26, '62	M. O. June 27, '65.
Standt, George	6	Sept. 6, '61	Deserted June 12, '63.

Name and Rank.	Regiment.	Enlistment.	Remarks.
Stanley, James, 2 Lt.....	21	July 31, '62	Discharged dis. Sept. 20, '64.
Stanton, George H., Corp.	8	Sept. 21, '61	Discharged dis. Jan. 8, '63.
Stanton, John L., Capt...	26	Aug. 23, '62	Killed P't Hudson May 27, '63.
Stark, Henry...........	2	May 7, '61	M. O. Aug. 7, '64.
Starret, Myron W.......	22	Aug. 27, '62	Missing at Port Hudson, May, 27, '63.
Staubly, Anthony, Sgt....	2	May 7, '61	Sgt. 18. M. O. June 27, '65.
Staubly, Michael........	18	Aug. 1, '62	Deserted Aug. 26, '62.
Stearns, Charles J.......	2	May 7, '61	M. O. Aug. 7, '64.
Steers, Thomas A.......	18	Aug. 21, '62	M. O. June 27, '65.
Stephenson, Moses......	29	Dec. 21, '63	Died of wounds Oct. 27, '64.
Sterry, Tully W.........	3	May 11, '61	M. O. Aug. 11, '61.
Stetson, Vine S.........	2	May 7, '61	Sgt. 26. M. O. Aug. 17, '63.
Stetson, William D.*.....	1 Art.	Mch. 15, '62	M. O. Sept. 25, '65.
Stevens, Henry M.*......	13	Jan. 17, '62	M. O. Apr. 25, '66.
Stewart, Henry.........	30	Jan. 2, '64	Killed Petersburg July 7, '64.
Stocket, George.........	29	Jan. 2, '64	M. O. May 29, '65.
Stocking, Theodore B....	18	Aug. 11, '62	M. O. June 27, '65.
Stokes, Joseph..........	2	May 7, '61	Died July 25, '61.
Strange, William*.......	13	Jan. 28, '62	Discharged Nov. 20, '65.
Strauss, Jacob..........	3	May 11, '61	M. O. Aug. 12, '61.
Studley, George H.*.....	10	Oct. 1, '61	M. O. Aug. 25, '65.
Sullivan, Daniel.........	9	Sept. 27, '61	Discharged Oct. 26, '64.
Sullivan, Daniel B.......	18	July 25, '62	M. O. May 18, '65.
Sullivan, James.........	1 Art.	Aug. 25, '64	Deserted May 15, '65.
Sullivan, Jeremiah.......	11	Nov. 17, '64	Deserted Sept. 17, '65.
Sullivan, John O.......	26	Aug. 30, '62	M. O. Aug. 17, '63.
Sullivan, Michael........	21	Aug. 20, '62	Deserted.
Sullivan, Michael........	20	Sept. 1, '64	Deserted on way to Regiment.
Sullivan, Patrick........	26	Aug. 28, '62	M. O. Aug. 17, '63.
Summers, F. B.........	2	May 7, '61	M. O. Aug. 7, '64.
Swain, George W., Sgt...	2	May 7, '61	M. O. Aug. 7, '64.
Swan, Henry W........	3	May 11, '61	13. Discharged dis, June 5, '63.
Sweet, James H.........	3	May 11, '61	Trans. Sig. Corps Nov. 26, '63.
Sweet, James L........	18	Jan. 8, '64	Discharged dis. Mch. 25, '65.
Tanner, J. Frank........	26	Aug. 28, '62	M. O. Aug. 17, '63.
Taylor, Charles W.*.....	12	Dec. 28, '61	M. O. Aug. 12, '65.
Taylor, Francis W......	18	Aug. 7, '62	Died Mch. 28, '65.
Taylor, Henry H., Corp..	7	Sept. 5, '61	Hon. discharged Sept. 12, '64.
Taylor, Samuel.........	18	July 22, '62	M. O. June 27, '65.
Taylor, William H......	18	July 14, '62	Discharged June 1, '64.
Teft, William H........	18	July 25, '62	M. O. May 30, '65.
Tenney, Edward*........	9	May 21, '62	Deserted July 17, '64.
Terhune, Henry.........	26	Aug. 30, '62	Discharged dis. Feb. 18, '63.
Thecklenburg, Henry....	2 Art.	Jan. 29, '64	M. O. Aug. 18, '65.
Thompson, Michael.....	14	Aug. 3, '64	Deserted Aug. 20, '64.
Thompson, Nelson C....	18	Aug. 4, '62	Died of wounds (Winchester) June 30, '63.
Thompson, William.....	2 Art.	Jan. 19, '64	Transf. U. S. N.
Thurber, Charles F......	18	July 28, '62	M. O. June 27, '65
Tiffany, M. V. B........	2	May 7, '61	Capt. 18. M. O. June 27, '65.

GENERAL MUSTER ROLL OF ALL NORWICH SOLDIERS. 373

Name and Rank.	Regiment.	Enlistment.	Remarks.
Tift, John H............	18	Aug. 4, '62	M. O. June 27, '65.
Tilden, Eugene S........	1 Art.	Mch. 20, '62	Discharged dis. Jan. 29, '63.
Tingley, John H........	2	May 7, '61	2 Lt. 1 Art. Res. Dec. 31, '62.
Tisdale, Edward F......	9	Nov. 25, '61	Cav. Died Andersonville, Sept. 29, '65.
Tisdale, James W.......	18	July 29, '62	M. O. June 27, '65.
Toft, Luther............	1 Art.	May 21, '61	Deserted Aug. 26, '62.
Tomlinson, Benjamin L...	29	Jan. 2, '64	M. O. Oct. 24, '65.
Tomlinson, Richard.....	26	Nov. 1, '62	M. O. Aug. 17, '63.
Toomey, Patrick........	21	Aug. 20, '62	M. O. June 16, '65. [7, '63.
Toomey, Thomas........	2	May 7, '61	1 Art. Discharged dis. Mch.
Torbush, Joseph H., *Corp.*	26	Aug. 30, '62	M. O. Aug. 17, '63.
Torpy, Thomas..........	1 Art.	Jan. 15, '64	M. O. Sept. 25, '65.
Torrance, David, *Sgt.*...	18	July 17, '62	Lt. Col. 29. M. O. Oct. 24, '65.
Torrance, James........	3	May 11, '61	Sgt. 13. Killed Port Hudson May 24, '63.
Tourtellotte, Marvin.....	18	July 25, '62	Discharged dis. Feb. 15, '64.
Town, George S.........	2	May 7, '61	Sgt. 18. M. O. June 27, '65.
Town, William H.......	18	Aug. 7, '62	Died March 28, '64.
Tracy, Benj. F., *Qr. Mr..*	26	Sept. 1, '62	M. O. Aug. 17, '63.
Tracy, Joseph A........	18	Aug. 7, '62	Died of wounds Aug. 7, '64.
Tracy, Timothy W., *Lt..*	26	Aug. 26, '62	M. O. Aug. 17, '63.
Trainor, Charles*.......	9	May 21, '62	Deserted July 17, '64.
Trainor, Felix..........	26	Aug. 28, '62	M. O. Aug. 17, '63.
Treadway, Russell*.....	12	Nov. 28, '61	M. O. Aug. 12, '65.
Treadway, John F......	Cav.	Jan. 4, '64	Died Andersonville, Aug. 3, '64.
Trenn, Charles K.T.,*Corp.*	18	Aug. 9, '02	M. O. May 30, '65.
Trinnier, Richard.......	3	May 11, '61	1S. M. O. June 27, '65.
Truman, Frank M.......	18	Dec. 16, '63	Deserted Nov. 27, '64.
Tubbs, Charles A.......	14	June 9, '62	M. O. May 31, '65.
Tubbs, William H., *Capt.*	14	June 15, '62	Resigned Feb. 20, '63.
Tucker, John...........	26	Sept. 6, '62	Deserted Nov. 16, '62.
Turner, Samuel.........	2 Art.	Jan. 29, '64	Deserted Feb. 10, '64
Tyler, Daniel, *Col*......	1	Apr. 23, '61	B. G. V. Resigned Apr. '64.
Tyler, Edwin L., *2 Lt..*	1 Art.	Mch. 29, '62	Resigned Aug. 19, '64. ['64.
Tyler, Moses...........	14	July 15, '62	Died Andersonville, Apr. 14,
Underhill, Joseph.......	30	Jan. 4, '64	Disch. dis. Feb. 9, '65.
Upham, Benjamin M....	18	Aug. 6, '62	V. R. C. Jan. 1, '65.
Upham, George R......	18	July 18, '62	M. O. June 27, '65.
Varney, Israel..........	18	July 16, '62	Died Florence S.C. Feb. 10, '65.
Vergason, Erastus......	10	Oct. 1, '61	Killed Roanoake Island, Feb. 8, '62.
Vergason, Isaac D.......	26	Aug. 30, '62	M. O. Aug. 17, '63.
Vergason, James H.....	3	May 11, '61	M. O. Aug. 11, '61.
Volkman, Ferdinand....	6	Sept. 6, '61	Died Beauf't, S. C. Oct. 21, '62.
Wait, Marvin, *Lt.*	8	Oct. 5, '61	Killed Antietam, Sept. 17, '62.
Walden, Oliver.........	8	Sept. 21, '61	Discharged dis. March 18, '62.
Walden, Winthrop	8	Sept. 21, '61	M. O. Dec. 12, '65.
Walden, William Henry.	2	May 7, '61	M. O. Aug. 7, '61.
Walker, Charles H.*....	8	Sept. 21, '61	M. O. Dec. 12, '65.
Wallace, William	18	Aug. 14, '62	Deserted Aug. 22, '62.

Name and Rank.	Regiment.	Enlistment.	Remarks.
Ward, David	7	Nov. 25, '64	M. O. July 20, '65.
Ward, George W.	18	Aug. 6, '62	Died Andersonville, Feb. 6, '65.
Ward, John E., *Lt.*	5	May 11, '61	Col. 8. M. O. March 13, '65.
Ward, James	18	July 16, '62	M. O. June 27, '65.
Warden, Alexander	2	May 7, '61	M. O. Aug. 7, '61.
Warren, George	21	Aug. 14, '62	M. O. June 16, '65.
Warren, Henry	Cav.	Jan. 23, '64	Deserted Feb. 2, '64.
Warren, Walter P.	2	May 7, '61	M. O. Aug. 7, '61.
Washington, George	30	Jan. 18, '64	M. O. Nov. 7, '65.
Watson, Jonathan	11	Oct. 25, '61	Discharged dis. May 5, '62.
Watson, Myron	11	Oct. 25, '61	Discharged dis. May 7, '62.
Webb, Charles	26	Aug. 29, '62	M. O. Aug. 17, '63.
Webb, William H., *Corp.*	18	Aug. 7, '26	M. O. June 27, '65.
Welch, George H.	Cav.	Oct. 26, '61	Discharged dis. Oct. 9, '62.
Welch, John	Cav.	Jan. 19, '64	Deserted Feb. 5, '64.
Welch, Thomas	2 Art.	Jan. 20, '64	M. O. Aug. 18, '65.
Welden, Patrick	9	Oct. 30, '61	Died Aug. 14, '62.
Weller, John	18	Aug. 6, '62	M. O. June 27, '65.
Wells, John W.	12	Dec. 7, '61	Discharged dis. Aug. 11, '62.
Wenlick, Frank	2	May 7, '61	M. O. Aug. 7, '61.
West, George W.,* *S/t.*	12	Nov. 20. 61	Deserted June 1, '65.
Wetherel, Benjamin S.	18	Jan. 3, '65	M. O. June 27, '65.
Whaley, George G.	18	Aug. 11, '62	M. O. June 27, '65.
Wheatley, Charles	2	May 7, '61	M. O. Aug. 7, '61.
Wheelock, William H.*	7	Sept. 5, '61	M. O. July 20, '65.
Whipple, John A.	Cav.	Jan. 4, '64	M. O. Aug. 2, '65.
White, Edwin	18	Aug. 4, '62	M. O. June 27, '65.
White, Frank	6	Sept. 6, '61	Killed Ft. Wagner July 18, '63.
White, Isaac	30	Jan. 6, '64	M. O. Nov. 7, '65.
White, Mortimer	20	Sept. 1, '64	Deserted while on way to Regt.
White, William	Cav.	Jan. 30, '64	Deserted Feb. 5, '64.
Whiteley, Henry A.	8	Sept. 23, '61	Discharged dis. Aug. 2, '62.
Whiting, Andrew F.	18	July 23, '62	Discharged Feb. 18, '64.
Whitmore, Horace W.	2	May 7, '61	26. M. O. Aug. 17, '63.
Whitney, John	1 Art.	Jan. 13, '64	M. O. Sept. 25, '65.
Whittlesey, George W.	3	May 11, '61	Adj. 13. Resigned Oct. 9, '63.
Wight, Edgar, S.	26	Aug. 30, '62	M. O. Aug. 17, '63.
Wilber, Daniel	18	July 23, '62	Accidentally shot Jan. 5, '63.
Wilber, John A.	18	Aug. 17, '62	Discharged dis. May 8, '65.
Wilbur, Edward O.	1 Art.	Jan. 4, '64	M. O. Sept. 25, '65.
Wilcox, Gordon, *Corp.*	18	July 21, '62	M. O. June 27, '65.
Wilcox, Stephen E.*	10	Oct. 9, '61	M. O. Aug. 25, '65.
Wilcox, Sylvanus J.*	8	Oct. 5, '61	M. O. Dec. 12, '65.
Wilkins, George W.	1 Art.	Jan. 14, '64	M. O. Sept. 25, '65. [30, '65.
Wilkinson, Jesse D., *Corp.*	18	July 12, '62	Capt. 43. U.S.C.T. M.O.Nov.
Willard, Robert	11	Jan. 13, '64	Discharged dis. March 19, '65.
Williams, Calvin	26	Aug. 30, '62	M. O. Aug. 17, '63.
Williams, Charles M.*	8	Sept. 21, '61	M. O. Dec. 12, '65.
Williams, Eri	26	Aug. 30, '62	M. O. Aug. 17, '63.
Williams, George E.	2	May 7, '61	M. O. Aug. 7, '61.
Williams, George E.	3	May 11, '61	M. O. Aug. 11, '61.

GENERAL MUSTER ROLL OF ALL NORWICH SOLDIERS. 375

Name and Rank.	Regiment.	Enlistment.	Remarks.
Williams, George S.	30	July 23, '63	M. O. Nov. 7, '65.
Williams, I. V. B., Qr. M.	1	Apr. 22, '61	Qr.M. 6th Reg. Resigned May [11, '63.
Williams, James.	Cav.	Jan. 4, '64	M. O. Aug. 2, '65.
Williams, John.	2 Art.	Jan. 20, '64	M. O. Aug. 18, '65.
Williams, John.	2 Art.	Jan. 29, '64	M. O. Aug. 18, '65.
Williams, John*.	9	May 24, '62	Deserted Jan. 10, '65.
Williams, John.	26	Aug. 30, '62	M. O. Aug. 17, '63.
Williams, John H., Corp.	30	Jan. 22, '64	M. O. Nov. 7, '65.
Williams, John W.	2 Art.	Jan. 21, '64	Deserted Feb. 13, '64.
Williams, Julius.	26	Aug. 30, '62	M. O. Aug. 17, '63.
Williams, William.	2 Art.	Feb. 1, '64	M. O. Aug. 18, '65.
Williams, William E.	1 Art.	Mch. 20, '62	Discharged dis. Dec. 18, '62.
Wilson, De Laron.	18	Aug. 11, '62	Qr. M. 30. M. O. Nov. 7, '65.
Wilson, George.	2 Art.	Jan. 30, '64	Deserted Feb. 14, '64.
Wilson, James.	8	Sept. 1, '63	Deserted Sept. 11, '63.
Wilson, James.	14	July 25, '63	Transf. U. S. N.
Wilson, James*.	12	Jan. 21, '62	Deserted March 17, '64.
Wilson, James, Corp.	30	Jan. 27, '64	M. O. June 27, '65.
Winship, Joseph H.	18	Aug. 11, '62	Died Andersonville Apr. 5, '64.
Wiserth, George.	Cav.	Jan. 22, '64	Deserted Feb. 12, '64.
Wolf, Henry.	18	Aug. 11, '62	M. O. June 27, '65.
Wood, Alfred.	18	July 23, '62	M. O. June 27, '65.
Wood, Asa F.	18	Aug. 6, '62	M. O. June 27, '65.
Wood, George.	2 Art.	Jan. 29, '64	Deserted Feb. 14, '64.
Wood, Henry.	13	Jan. 7, '62	Discharged dis. July 29, '62.
Wood, Horace B.	2 Art.	Feb. 4, '64	Died Richmond, Va., Dec. 27, '64.
Wood, John.	13	Jan. 7, '62	Discharged dis. June 17, '63.
Wood, John W.	11	Dec. 5, '61	Died of wounds (Antietam).
Woodward, William H.	26	Aug. 30, '62	M. O. Aug. 17, '63.
Wright, Franklin S.	18	Aug. 17, '62	Discharged dis. Jan. 26, '65.
Wright, Henry C.	26	Aug. 30, '62	M. O. Aug. 17, '63.
Wright, Sylvanus.	11	Oct. 25, '61	Deserted Nov. 25, '62.
Yale, Russell*.	13	Dec. 22, '61	Deserted Jan. 30, '66.
Yerrington, Henry P.	14	June 9, '62	Died of wounds (Antietam) Sept. 21, '62.
Yerrington, Perry.	7	Sept. 5, '61	Hon. discharged Sept. 15, '64.
York, James E.	18	July 30, '62	M. O. June 27, '65.
York, Nathan.	26	Aug. 30, '62	M. O. Aug. 17, '63.
Young, Adam, Corp.	6	Sept. 6, '61	Hon. discharged Sept. 5, '64.
Young, Charles.	2	May 7, '61	1 Art. M. O. Sept. 25, '65.
Young, David, Lt. Col.	2	May 7, '61	M. O. Aug. 7, 61.
Young, Robert.	18	July 25, '62	M. O. June 27, 65.
Zamphiropolos, Michael.	13	Feb. 1, '64	V. R. C. April 23, '65.

The names of "unassigned recruits" are not given in this "roll"; they were for the most part unworthy substitutes, who enlisted for the sake of the bounty, and, with few exceptions, never served in their regiments.

XVII.

SOLDIERS' MONUMENT. — ACTION OF THE TOWN.

> "Joint saviors of the land, to-day
> What guerdon ask you of the land?
> No boon too great for you to pray —
> What can it give that could repay
> The men we miss from our worn band?
> The men who lie in trench and swamp,
> The dead who rock beneath the wave —
> The brother-souls of march and camp —
> Bright spirits — each a shining lamp,
> Teaching how nobly die the brave."

WHEN the struggle for the Nation's life was over, and the flag of the Union everywhere waved in triumph, then it was that the country began fairly to realize its indebtedness to those whose self-sacrificing courage and heroic battling had achieved the victory. The soldiers had indeed been welcomed home with every sign of popular rejoicing, all had united in extending to the brave men who had survived the conflict the heartiest greeting, but the profound gratitude of the people craved some more enduring expression. The memory of the triumphs of our citizen-soldiery deserved to be perpetuated, and the national gratitude began to incarnate itself in monuments which should tell the story of the war. Art, which had been able to embellish the castles of king and noble, and had erected its memorials in the great cathedrals and cities of the Old World was invoked to do honor to the heroes of our secured liberties.

The most enduring memorial of the service of those

THE SOLDIERS' MONUMENT
*Erected
in Memory of the Brave Men
who lost their lives in defense
of their country.*
1861–65.

who periled their lives to maintain the Government, is in the ennobling institutions they preserved, and in the popular liberties which they perpetuated. Still, there was a beautiful fitness in each city, town, and village honoring its own patriot dead by the monuments that grateful friends and fellow-citizens should erect to their memory. A monument reared for such a purpose is a public benefit. It embodies patriotism, truth, and faith, it gives form and expression to the best feelings of our nature. Thus would each community bear witness to other generations that those commemorated by the monumental shaft were worthy of all honor. The names, too, engraved on stone or bronze, would descend to posterity as those worthy of being preserved, and ever be spoken with increasing veneration.

A monument dedicated to some distinguished military or civic hero, awakens far different emotions than one which commemorates numbers of fallen braves. No single name in the latter case absorbs our attention, no one majestic figure encinctured with an halo of glory and renown, rises before us. We think rather of the many individual soldiers, of their sacrifice and valor, of their humble or splendid service, of their death in camp, in prison, or on the battle-field. The history of their young lives comes up in review, and the anxiety with which they were watched by those from whose sides they went forth, the sadness and heart-breaking the tidings of their deaths produced, all this the "soldiers' monument" serves to recall.

Norwich citizens very early after the war closed began to agitate the question of securing some fitting public memorial for their patriot dead. The list of those who had lost their lives while in the service of their country was a long one, and included on it the names of some very widely known and tenderly loved. How to unite in some public measure, for the commemoration of all, was a question not easily settled. It was felt that what was done publicly, should be on a scale commensurate with the solemn object in view. No one felt that too much could be done in securing some fit and general testimonial of the gratitude of the people to the dead ; rather was it questioned how best can we honor the memory of those to whom we owe so much. After more or less discussion of the subject by the daily papers, a public meeting was called for June fourteenth, 1869, in Breed Hall. His Honor Mayor Blackstone presided, and in his opening remarks stated, "that all would agree that there is a moral obligation resting on this community to erect a suitable monument to the memory of those who fell in the late war, and the object of this meeting was to raise funds for that purpose."

Senator Buckingham then offered the following resolutions : —

"*Resolved*, That a committee of seven be appointed by the chair to solicit and collect funds, for the erection of a monument to the Norwich soldiers and seamen who fell in our late war for the preservation of the National Union.

"*Resolved*, That the said committee be, and they are hereby, directed to deposit any money that they may collect for the above object, with either of the Savings Societies in this city, and whenever the fund shall in their judgment be large enough to justify action, they shall call a meeting of those who contribute, and of those who subscribe, that they may make arrangements to procure a proper plan and to erect such monument."

The following additional resolution was also offered :—

"*Resolved*, That the same committee be requested to procure the preparation and publication of a Soldiers' Memorial volume, containing some brief account of the service rendered in the war by representatives of this town, and a full obituary record of those

SOLDIERS' MONUMENT. — ACTION OF THE TOWN. 379

who died during the progress of the same, and that the expense of publishing the book, over and above the receipts from its sale, be defrayed from the monument fund."

Senator Buckingham then added, " that he would occupy only a few moments, as the resolutions clearly stated the object of the meeting. When the National Government and all our institutions and rights were imperiled, when an organized rebellion broke out in 1861, and when the demands of the rebels had caused the fall of Fort Sumter, on the twelfth of April the President of the United States called for seventy-five thousand troops to protect the capital of the country. The next day the Governor of this State called for volunteers, and the people of Norwich responded with a public meeting at which three companies were organized under Henry Peale, Edward Harland, and F. S. Chester. These companies were mustered into the service of the United States, and met the enemy at the first Bull Run, and David C. Bliss gave his life to the cause of Nationality. More troops were called for, but it was not until after four years that the power of the rebellion was crushed, and the authority of the government vindicated. It was done by the gallant soldiers of the loyal Northern States, and to them we owe all that is valuable of what we possess. Of that army of two millions of men, Connecticut gave fifty-four thousand, than whom no better ever went out, and Norwich sent not less than fifteen hundred. Of the first grand army of two hundred thousand, what number from Norwich found graves on the battle-field, I know not. But it is a duty we owe to them, and to ourselves to inscribe their names on imperishable granite, and the names of the living on a memorial to hand down to our children as a remembrance of what these soldiers have done for the country."

Rev. Mr. Dana being called on by the chairman, advocated in brief remarks the prompt and generous commemoration in some appropriate way of those to whom the town owes in common with the country, such a debt of gratitude.

The Hon. John T. Wait followed, saying, "the resolutions met with his hearty approval. If ever the country owed a debt it was to the young men who gave up their lives for its preservation. Were we to be remiss in discharging the obligations thus imposed upon us, we should be unworthy the blessings of liberty and good government. I look around me, and see men, some of them far advanced in years who sent forth their sons to battle for their country. Some fell in the heat of battle, some were wounded and languished in hospitals, others returned to spend a few days only in the companionship of their friends, and die from disease contracted in the service. Here beside me is one whose son was starved to death at Andersonville. He feels the debt we owe. You, gentlemen, feel it ; I feel it ; and I trust there is not one in the community but is impressed in the same manner. It is desirable that we act promptly. Long speeches are unnecessary."

General Harland spoke next, saying "he thought this matter should be left in the hands of the citizens, and not of those who were in the army. The cause commended itself, and the army-men would take hold, and help it along. The only question now was as to its practicability, of which he had no doubt. The resolutions were eminently proper."

The Hon. H. H. Starkweather, added, " he supposed every one was in full accord with this project. The town that sent fifteen hundred men to the war, which was always ahead of its quota, and which increased its aid to the cause by private contributions, could hardly be behindhand now. The committee, he thought, would easily raise such a sum, as would put it upon a sure basis. Some felt as if our debts would never be paid, — all know there is one which never can be, and that is to the soldiers who stood like a wall of fire to

SOLDIERS' MONUMENT.—ACTION OF THE TOWN. 381

protect us in our liberties. My mind goes back to the fourteenth of April when we met in this hall to help on the work. Young men from the counter and the shop enlisted, we gave them our blessing, and bade them God speed, and with those who lived we rejoiced when they came back, and gave them honor."

Further remarks were made by General James B. Coit, and Colonel Peale. The following letter from General Ely was then read by the Secretary:—

To the Hon. LORENZO BLACKSTONE.

Dear Sir,— I regret exceedingly that illness in my family prevents my being present at your meeting this evening, to raise funds for a memorial monument to the heroes of Norwich. I shall however take pleasure in subscribing to that fund, with full assurance that the pages of history will be searched in vain for names more worthy of lasting glory than those of Goddard, Culver, Downer, Wait, Breed, Maginnis, and scores of others from Norwich — whose hearts ceased to beat with patriotic and heroic throb, only when shattered by cannon shot and minnie ball. Nor are those less worthy who fell by disease, starvation, and imprisonment, suffering tortures of death, with unyielding fortitude. The least that we owe them is a handsome memorial monument; we owe it to their friends and relations; we owe it to ourselves to prove that we are not entirely cold-blooded and devoid of gratitude; and to our country, especially we owe it, that it may show posterity that the patriots who fell fighting for country and liberty, still live in the hearts of the people.

Yours truly, WM. G. ELY.

The Secretary read the resolutions offered, when they were enthusiastically adopted, and the Chairman announced the following committee in accordance with the requirement of the same: The Hon. W. A. Buckingham, Amos W. Prentice, the Hon. John T. Wait, the Rev. M. McG. Dana, Dr. C. B. Webster, James S. Carew, Edwin P. Avery, E. P.

Slocum; and by special motion, Misses Elizabeth Greene and Eliza Perkins were added. The meeting then adjourned.

While this gathering was not as large as those which were held during war times, yet it was spirited, and had not a little of the fervor and earnest purpose which had characterized the popular assemblies often convened in Breed Hall for objects connected with the war. The sentiment of respect and affection for the fallen soldiers, which the community cherished, found expression in this meeting. Some public presentment of the subject, like that secured through this popular assemblage, seemed indispensable, and it was the means of bringing the matter before the people in a way to secure final action.

The delay in starting the enterprise had not been owing to indifference, but rather to the diversity of judgment as to the best method of commemorating the dead. Many had hoped a large memorial hall would be erected, which serving at once as a monument to the patriot heroes of the town, would also be a public utility, meeting a felt need of the community.

But by the action of the citizens at this public gathering, the form of the memorial was decided upon, and arrangements were made to secure the requisite funds.

Before the committee had made much progress in this direction, the project of meeting the expense town-wise began to be discussed, and in every quarter met with favor. It seemed to be the most equable and expeditious method of disposing of a matter that had already been too long delayed.

Accordingly, at the annual town meeting, October third, 1870, the Hon. William A. Buckingham introduced the following resolutions:—

"*Resolved*, That a sum of money, not exceeding fifteen cents on one hundred dollars of the assessment list of the town, be, and the same is hereby appropriated for the erection of a suitable monument to the memory of all soldiers and seamen who were residents of, and belonged to the town at their enlistment, and who have died in the military or naval service of the United States, during the late war against the Government of the United States.

"*Resolved*, That a committee of three persons be appointed by the moderator of this meeting, who shall determine the design of the proposed monument, erect the same upon what is known as the 'Soldiers' lot' in Yantic Cemetery, and supervise and direct the expenditure of the money hereby appropriated."

After considerable debate, in reference to the best site for the monument, resulting in an amendment changing the location to "the north end of the Great Plain,' the resolutions were heartily adopted. The Moderator named as the committee to take charge of the procuring and erection of the monument, the Hon. W. A. Buckingham, the Hon. J. T. Wait, and James A. Hovey.

A contract was soon made with Batterson, Canfield, & Co., of Hartford, to furnish the monument according to a design submitted to the committee, and by the latter approved.

The monument is of white granite, taken from the celebrated quarries of J. G. Batterson, at Westerly, R. I. The design is of a soldier of the Union Army, supported on a massive pedestal. The statue is colossal, having a height of twelve feet, which imparts an air of grandeur, aside from the natural dignity expressed in the artist's conception of his subject.

The soldier stands in an easy attitude; the left foot slightly advanced, the body supported by the right. His musket rests against the arm, and is held by both hands, while the face, turned slightly towards the left, bears an expression of thoughtfulness, as if recalling to memory the scenes of the past struggle for liberty and the Union.

The plinth under the statue bears in bold relief the arms of the Commonwealth, with the shield of the United States and the State motto —

"Qui transtulit, sustinet."

The die, or principal stone of the pedestal is to hold in relief bronze tablets, cut in Germany, and bearing the names of soldiers from Norwich, who gave their lives to their country.

On the front of the monument is the following inscription : —

ERECTED BY THE TOWN OF
NORWICH
IN MEMORY OF HER BRAVE SONS WHO VOLUNTARILY ENTERED
THE MILITARY SERVICE OF THE UNITED STATES
AND LOST THEIR LIVES IN DEFENSE OF THE
NATIONAL GOVERNMENT DURING
THE REBELLION.

The monument measures ten feet square at the base, and the entire height is twenty-seven feet six inches. The base consists of one stone, and weighs over fourteen tons. Above the base the pedestal is octagonal. The moldings of the cap and base are sharply cut, and the whole monument is executed in the most finished manner, and is highly creditable to the artist, and to the committee who have had the matter in charge.

As a work of art, it is its own advocate ; as a memorial of the brave men who sealed their patriotic devotion with their life-blood, it is confessedly a noble one.

The monument is appropriately located at the head of the "Great Plain," along whose sides in stately row stand the splendid elms which give to it its beauty, and seem like hoary sentinels guarding it from desecrating intruders. The incoming travel from the north which enters the city by its two grand thoroughfares, must pass it ; while all the population south of it, have now this spot made sacred for them, to which they can come in thoughtful hours, and on festival days, leaving behind the noise, and dust, and crowded streets of the city, and find here a fit place for communion with the spirits of the heroic dead whose names are inscribed on the monument's base. The symbolic statue, suggestive to every beholder, will speak to all upon whom its shadow falls, of the soldier's work and worth.

May the monument stand, not for a few years, but for many generations, witnessing in its environment of natural beauty, to self-sacrifice and faith. May the westering sun, sending out its rays over the broad plateau this monument consecrates, linger and play upon the motionless figure which here henceforth shall lift its lines to publish the story of those it commemorates. The town has reared it, as it was meet it should, in grateful recognition of services that have shed new lustre upon its history, and been prolific in benefits not only to its denizens but to the nation as well. The town has reared it, as it was just it should, to perpetuate the names it holds in honored remembrance, and would secure from oblivion to the remotest time. Let the snows and rains of heaven fall upon it; let the winds and sunlight play about it; let the city in its outward sweep of growth fold it in more complete embrace — still may it stand, the memorial of patriotism, courage, and heroic achievements.

By this action of the town, the citizen-committee appointed to raise funds for the monument were relieved of further responsibility in the matter, and had left upon their hands the remaining item which the resolutions offered in the first public meeting contemplated, — the preparation of a soldiers' memorial volume.

This was a far more difficult matter to arrange for, involving, as it did, on the part of whoever should undertake it, great labor, and an amount of time that almost no one could command. Moreover, it must necessarily be a work of love, taxing the patience of such a volunteer author, and requiring no little delicacy and tact in the execution of his task.

The committee, however, were exceedingly in earnest as to this part of the unfulfilled vote of the citizens. No resource was left untried to secure some one to assume the work of editing the proposed volume, and after unavoidable delay, such arrangements were made as to the committee seemed finally satisfactory.

The labor of collecting the material and preparing it for the press, was taken in hand, and accomplished as rapidly as was possible. The publication of the book, with all the pecuniary risks incident thereto, was turned over to Messrs. Jewett & Co., and through them the "Memorial Volume" desired by the public has been issued.

This book, containing the military history of the town of Norwich during the exciting years of the war, recording its patriotism and sacrifices ; memorializing the brave men who went forth from this community and yielded up their lives in the service of the country, is now submitted to the kindly notice and considerate judgment of its readers, with the consciousness on the part of the author of its incompleteness, and unsatisfactory character.

In bringing the pleasant though tasking labors of many months to an end, the Author has to regret that the narrative has been necessarily so meagre. So many years have intervened since the scenes and incidents of the war herein described in part, or in brief referred to, that many facts which would have added to the interest of the history, have passed out of mind.

Some persons, who could have recalled what would have been worth recording, or furnished letters and bits of war experience which constitute oftentimes the charm of a memorial work of this kind, have moved away, or have died. In consequence of this, and for other kindred reasons, the writer in preparing this volume, has labored at great disadvantage. Still, it is doubtless better to have preserved, even if imperfect and incomplete, this chapter of civic history and patriotism, than to have allowed it to fade wholly from memory, — to be always a missing passage from out the annals of the town.

In making our story public, we are but telling what part we took in the preservation of our National Union; what sacrifices were made among us for the suppression of a rebellion that threatened destruction to all our dearest rights. This by ourselves and by our children, will ever be a story which will be read with honest pride, and in the hope that it may deepen our love of country, and help us to remember with tender hearts the heroic dead, has this record of the patriotic services of the sons and daughters of Norwich been written.

INDEX TO NORWICH CITIZENS

MENTIONED IN THE TEXT MORE THAN ONCE.

Adams, John T., 22.
Aiken, William A., 145, 174.
Almy, John H., 175, 187.
Andrews, P. St. M., 99.
Arms, Rev. H. P., 210, 217.
Avery, A. S., 41, 245.

Beckwith, Herbert, 256, 278.
Bentley, J. W., 148, 237.
Berry, William A., 40, 241.
Bill, Henry, 19, 49, 83.
Birge, H. W., 40, 52, 55, 56, 77.
Blackstone, L., 59, 83, 317, 378, 381, 382, 383.
Bond, Alvan, 24.
Brakenridge, N. A., 59, 317.
Breed, Charles A., 210, 214, 215.
Breed, Charles E., 151, 260.
Breed, John, 19, 49.
Bromley, I., 97, 114, 164.
Buckingham, W. A., 16, 19, 20, 50, 58, 65, 84, 101, 109, 115, 119, 159, 167, 179, 299, 302, 304, 306.
Burdick, Theodore, 42, 224.

Carew, James S., 21, 59, 381.
Case, George R., 25, 111.
Chester, Frank S., 21, 25, 379.
Clapp, Edward T., 24.
Coit, James B., 25, 60, 62, 318, 381.
Coit, Charles M., 48.
Converse, Charles A., 59.
Converse, William M., 59, 317.
Cowles, H. F., 268, 283.

Crosby, H. B., 59, 71, 73, 213, 304.
Culver, E. B., 68, 237.

Dana, M. McG., 304, 379, 381.
Davis, H. C., 170, 268, 271, 283.
Dennis, J. B., 25, 41, 42, 170, 282.
Downer, Sylvanus, 256, 280.

Edmond, H. V., 303, 304.
Ely, W. G., 41, 65, 70, 268, 270, 271, 381.

Farnsworth, Charles, 79, 80, 265, 268.
Foster, L. F. S., 20, 22, 171, 265, 299, 303, 308.

Gallup, L. A., 118, 165, 221.
Gaskill, H. C., 260, 281.
Goddard, Alfred, 47, 229.
Greene, J. Lloyd, 59, 71, 83, 91, 119, 299, 313, 317.
Greene, Miss Lizzie, 170, 180, 201, 381.
Greene, William P., 20, 83, 169, 170.
Gulliver, J. P., 49, 302, 311.

Hale, F. M., 19, 21, 317.
Halsey, J., 24.
Harland, Edward, 29, 30, 44, 46, 47, 213, 379, 380.
Hovey, J. A., 19, 20, 22, 319.
Hyde, Lewis, 24.

Jacobs, H. F., 87, 219.

INDEX TO NORWICH RESIDENTS.

Johnson, Charles, 59, 153, 270.

Lanman, Joseph, 136, 142.
Lathrop, DeWitt C., 44, 209.
Learned, B. P., 77, 79.
Learned, E., 21, 24, 49, 302, 304.
Lewis, J. V., 304, 309.

Maguire, Thomas, 40, 241.
Manning, E. P., 225.
McCall, John, 47, 234.
Merwin, S. T. C., 24, 25, 268.
Mowry, James D., 170.
Murphy, J. W., 21, 24.

Nickels, J. R., 61, 242.
Norton, H. B., 21, 59, 169, 171.
Norton, Miss Emeline, 181, 186.

Osgood, Charles, 21.
Osgood, H. H., 26, 99.

Peale, Henry, 28, 65, 69, 70, 119, 189, 379, 381.
Perkins, G. L., 137, 160.
Phillips, H. T., 79, 81.
Pratt, George, 21, 23, 217, 320.
Prentice, Amos W., 19, 59, 153, 299, 317, 318, 381.

Ripley, J. Dickinson, 206.

Rockwell, Alfred P., 21, 24, 41, 82.
Rogers, Joab B., 80, 81.

Schalk, F. E., 61, 227.
Scott, Thomas, 40, 241.
Selden, Joseph, 56, 84, 86, 118.
Slater, J F., 19, 49, 59.
Slocum, E. P., 163, 164, 381.
Smith, David, 19, 21.
Stanton, J. L., 218.
Starkweather, H. H., 18, 24, 49, 83, 99, 101, 299, 321, 380.
Stedman, J. W., 19, 25, 59.

Thomas, Miss Carrie L., 180, 195.
Torrance, David, 109, 110, 249.
Torrance, James, 247, 248.
Tyler, Daniel, 25, 29, 73.

Wait, J. T., 21, 22, 59, 83, 101, 299, 304, 380, 381, 383.
Wait, Marvin, 45, 211.
Walden, T. W., 264, 211.
Ward, J E., 42, 46, 47.
Ward, George W., 259, 279.
Webster, C. B., 172, 189, 381.
Webster, Mrs. Dr., 197, 198.

Young, David, 10, 29, 170, 305.
Young, Mrs. J. B., 186.

INDEX TO BATTLES AND ENGAGEMENTS.

Antietam, 44, 51, 69, 216.

Bolivar Heights, 80.
Bull Run, 29.

Cedar Creek, 67.
Cedar Mountain, 41.
Chancellorsville, 61.
Cold Harbor, 51, 243.

Drury's Bluff, 72.

Fredericksburg, 46.
Fort Darling, 47, 82.
Fort Fisher, 139.
Fort Harrison, 48, 92, 110.
Fort Huger, 46.
Fort Macon, 215.
Fort Sumter, 1, 15.
Fort Wagner, 224.

Gettysburg, 61, 94.

Irish Bend, 54.

James Island, 82.

Newbern, 44.
New Market, 67, 239.

Petersburg, 48, 78, 233, 295.
Piedmont, 67, 240.
Port Hudson, 55, 86, 218, 220, 249.
Port Royal, 146.

Ream's Station, 243.
Roanoke Island, 43, 215.

Seven Days' Battles, 78.
Snicker's Ford, 69.
Spottsylvania, 81, 228.

Walthall Junction, 47.
Wilderness, 112.
Winchester, 56, 65.

www.ingramcontent.com/pod-product-compliance
Lightning Source LLC
Chambersburg PA
CBHW051739300426
44115CB00007B/621